DATE DUE

GAYLORD			PRINTED IN U.S.A.

Josephus Daniels

The Small-d Democrat

Josephus Daniels ∽

The Small-d Democrat

∽ *by Joseph L. Morrison*

The University of North Carolina Press
Chapel Hill

The quotation on pages 216-17 is from the THE JOURNALS OF DAVID E. LILIENTHAL, Vol. I: *The TVA Years, 1939-1945.* Copyright © 1964 by David E. Lilienthal. Reprinted by permission of Harper & Row, Publishers.

The photograph of Josephus Daniels that appears on the title page was supplied by the Prints and Photographs Division, Library of Congress.

For Pearl

Preface

In the year that saw him elected President, Franklin D. Roosevelt wrote a North Carolina enthusiast: "Why don't you or some other admirers of Mr. Daniels in North Carolina write a biography of him, for he is really the greatest man your state has produced. . . . If I ever get out of all this trouble you boys are trying to get me into, I have promised myself to write a biography of Daniels if nobody else does."[1]

Roosevelt never got out of "all this trouble" long enough to write a biography of his old chief, and other would-be biographers may have been intimidated by the five bulky volumes of Josephus Daniels' published memoirs. That delightful autobiography, which reveals its author full of the human juices, paints an idiomatic picture of the man that no biographer can hope to surpass. Still, a record needs to be verified, gaps need to be filled, and Daniels must be placed in perspective in that amazing era through which he

1. FDR to E. Randolph Preston of Charlotte, N.C., 1932, undated; quoted in JD, diary-letter, Dec. 5, 1938, Bagley Family Papers, Southern Historical Collection, University of North Carolina. Mrs. Julia J. Preston, widow of the addressee, informed the writer she did not have the original, and an original likewise was not to be found in the papers of either Josephus or Jonathan Daniels. A search of the Franklin D. Roosevelt Papers at Hyde Park, New York, has failed to unearth a carbon copy, although one may eventually be found when the much-handled and chaotic 1932 papers of the Democratic national committee are put in order.

lived. After all, he was born in the Civil War and died in the Atomic Age.

The published memoirs themselves leave two important gaps, for Daniels included nothing about the decade of the twenties or of his last years after Mexico. Moreover, many of the episodes he scanted, like the Veracruz "invasion" of 1914 and the Naval Investigation sparked by Admiral Sims, have had to be fleshed out here. For all the half-million items in the Daniels Papers, in the Library of Congress, there are gaps in the evidence as well: (1) the fire-destroyed bulk of Daniels' pre-1913 correspondence; (2) the extremely sketchy post-Cabinet diaries of Daniels, some of which apparently have been lost (since my studies began, Daniels' Cabinet diaries have been conscientiously edited and published by E. David Cronon); (3) the apparently lost correspondence after May 1, 1947 (the Daniels Papers unaccountably cease abruptly after that date although many later Daniels letters survive in the personal papers of his correspondents). Still another body of apparently lost correspondence survives after a fashion, for in my early chapters I refer to "typescript copies of Daniels-Bagley Papers." These records are in the personal papers of Jonathan Daniels, who has assured me of their authenticity despite the loss, in most cases, of the originals. The explanation appears to lie in the sheer unmanageability in private hands of such a vast collection, which was in frequent use for two decades prior to its transfer to the Library of Congress.

An invaluable aid in writing this biography has been my unsupervised access to—and unrestricted use of—the personal papers of Jonathan Daniels. These contain, first, an illuminating father-son correspondence over a period of some four decades, important data relating to Josephus Daniels, Sr. (1828-1865), and—best of all—Josephus Daniels' own unfinished and unpublished memoir, "Life Begins at Seventy," which he began writing in his eighty-fifth year. Newly published here, therefore, are his recollections of the 1920's and 1940's. I have also had the same generous use of Josephus Daniels' holograph letters to his other surviving sons, Dr. Worth B. Daniels, Washington, D.C., and Frank A. Daniels, Raleigh, North Carolina. These sons of Josephus Daniels, and their late brother Josephus Daniels, Jr., are due the thanks of all scholars for having donated to the public the literary rights in their father's papers in the Library of Congress. I add my own thanks for their unfailing openness, even to their authorizing me to examine their father's financial and insurance records. I am glad to acknowledge that none of the Danielses ever so much as hinted at a directed verdict, biographically speaking.

The massive collection of Daniels Papers, including the diaries, in the Manuscript Division of the Library of Congress, is the all-important starting place for a biographer of Josephus Daniels. The Franklin D. Roosevelt Papers at Hyde Park, New York, are also valuable because, although typewritten carbon copies are available in the Library of Congress, dozens of handwritten and carbon-less letters flowed from Daniels to Roosevelt. The Southern Historical Collection, of The University of North Carolina at Chapel Hill, is invaluable because, aside from the Jonathan Daniels Papers, it holds the Bagley Family Papers (those of Mrs. Josephus Daniels), the personal papers of friends with whom Daniels corresponded over the years (e.g., Henry Groves Connor and Robert W. Winston), and the Collection's staff also administers the University of North Carolina Archives, containing papers of the Presidents and trustees of the institution Daniels loved and which he himself served as a trustee for forty-seven years. The North Carolina Collection at the University contributes much to the student of Daniels' career, not only a complete microfilm run of Daniels' *News and Observer* but a unique newspaper clipping file and a valuable pamphlet collection. I extend my thanks to the staffs of these repositories for their uniform helpfulness and efficiency.

I acknowledge with thanks three successive grants from the University Research Council which made possible (1) an extended stay at the Library of Congress and the microfilming of some two thousand key Daniels documents for more intensive examination; (2) extensive interviewing, in person and by mail, of surviving friends and correspondents of Daniels; (3) secretarial and typing help. Finally, I salute Josephus Daniels himself for the good and amiable company he has borne me these past years.

Joseph L. Morrison

Chapel Hill, N.C.

Contents

Illustrations

Josephus Daniels

The Small-d Democrat

Washington, N.C., to Washington, D.C.

Hundreds of Danielses gather every summer on Roanoke Island, North Carolina, the site of Sir Walter Raleigh's Lost Colony. Their family reunion is the Daniels Day begun by Josephus Daniels in 1941, and it celebrates a set of forebears who were more recent immigrants than those planted so hopefully by Sir Walter.

One Thomas Daniels ventured onto Roanoke Island with his four sons about the close of the American Revolution, and their descendants have multiplied in North Carolina ever since. Thomas and his sons, sturdy English Protestants from the north of Ireland, exploited the bountiful double line of fishing grounds afforded by Croatan Sound's shallow waters and the ocean's deeper ones. Danielses still inhabit Roanoke Island, some still saying "hoi toide" for high tide, and sharing a proud family memory of having helped the Wright brothers launch their improbable crate at Kitty Hawk. Danielses cluster thickly in North Carolina's coastal counties, where many of them still follow the time-tested occupations of fishing, boat building, and farming.[1]

Clifford Daniels, one of Thomas' four sons, left the island to settle on the mainland near present-day Bayboro in the 1820's. He became a farmer and part-time builder of coast-wide schooners that ventured as far as the West Indies. The patriarchal Clifford sired twelve children by two successive wives; the children all bore plain

3

names except Josephus, born January 21, 1828. Why the boy was thus set apart with that resoundingly pretentious name is unknown. It is likely, however, that in a homogeneous Protestant area where the volumes of Josephus' *Antiquities* decorated many a home, parents might seize upon such a name for its "reverential" value. Josephus, who was later to father the editor of the same name, stayed on his father's farm and worked there until early manhood. The young man retained a lifelong nostalgia for the beautiful view overlooking Bay River, where he learned all that father Clifford could teach him. The latter was said to be a great joker, who laughingly teased his second wife for not being as pretty as his first one. Clifford was remembered by his grandson Frank, as of about 1864, as "a very old and venerable man, with long white hair and beard and large and shapely head, who left on me, young as I was, an impression I still retain."[2]

As to Josephus, his short life story (1828-65) is entirely overshadowed by the gossip that he was disloyal to the Confederacy.[3] Such attacks against his memory were always levied by political enemies of his editor-son, and somehow the alleged crimes grew more horrendous as more and more time separated those charges from the Civil War. The elder Daniels was an outspoken Whig in politics, Unionist in sentiment, a tendency probably strengthened in him when he left his Unionist father's house to learn more about shipbuilding in Rhode Island. He worked for several years in New England before returning to Washington, N.C., where he clerked in a store in addition to working part time at shipbuilding. On January 1, 1856, Daniels married the orphaned Mary Cleaves Seabrook, whose piety was such that he had to join the Methodist Church before she would marry him. The young couple had three children before the Civil War, but only one of the three survived. This was Franklin Arthur Daniels, born in 1858, named for Benjamin Franklin but always called Frank, the Arthur in his name being for his father's storekeeper employer.

The younger Josephus Daniels was born during the Civil War while his father was working in the Confederate-operated shipyard of James Cassidy and Sons in Wilmington, N.C. The baby's birth was recorded at Washington, N.C., on May 18, 1862. Although the father's interim movements are obscure, he certainly "refugeed" with his little family from burned-out Washington to Ocracoke Island in the spring of 1864. Toward the end of that year the father, still weak from a bout of typhoid fever, found employment in the store of a Mr. Hume in Federal-occupied New Bern. In the meantime, Mrs. Daniels was on Ocracoke where she was delivered of her third surviving son, Charles Cleaves Daniels, on September 23, 1864. His father never lived to see him.

The death of the elder Daniels came under circumstances that led to the later gossip about his having been a "pilot for the Yankees." Contemporary evidence, which flatly contradicts the later gossip, is set forth in the *North Carolina Times* (New Bern) of January 21 and January 31, 1865. The earlier of these contains a minutely detailed account, uncontradicted by contemporary records in the National Archives, of the fatal trip. Daniels (a passenger and no pilot) was mortally wounded when the steamer *Mystic*, approaching Washington, N.C., under a truce, was unaccountably fired upon by Confederate troops. The commanding general at Union-held New Bern had granted a request of some civilians at Washington, then not held securely by either side, to establish a trade store where local people could exchange their cotton for food and other necessities. So on Monday evening, January 16, 1865, the little expedition set out from New Bern. An eyewitness aboard the *Mystic* reported, in the *North Carolina Times* of January 21:

> At 7 o'clock P.M., the steamer Mystic, Capt. Edwin S. Williams, left for Washington with a small force, and about fifty citizens, composed of men, women and children. We arrived at our destination on Tuesday morning at 9 o'clock, after a most pleasant run during the night, and it seemed to me that we were received by the citizens that remained in the place with a cordial welcome. . . . We dropped down the river three miles for safety during the night, having made arrangements during the day with the prominent men of the town to meet an agent from Kinston, appointed by the rebel government, to make exchanges of food, clothing and farming implements for their cotton and other products. At 8 o'clock A.M., Wednesday, we tripped anchor, started and arrived at the wharf in Washington at 8 1/2. Just as the Mystic touched the wharf, instead of meeting our cordial friends of yesterday, and the government agents they agreed we should, we had a volley from sixty-two Minnie rifles fired upon the women and children on board from a large brick warehouse, only fifty feet distant from the boat. Mr. Joseph [*sic*] Daniels, of New Bern, formerly of Washington, who went up to bring down his furniture was the

first victim, and fell with his left arm badly shattered by a solid ball from a smooth bore musket. . . . The pilot was particularly aimed at, as the pilot house shows some twenty to thirty bullet holes; but the pilot, Mr. Reuben Willis, true to his trust, stood at the wheel and never deserted his post. He is a native of Washington; he steered her past the wharf, by the orders of Capt. Williams, which saved many lives. . . .

The January 31 issue of the *Times* recorded: "Joseph [*sic*] Daniels, a fine specimen of a man, and a loyal Carolinian, who was wounded mortally in the late cowardly attack upon the Mystic at Washington, N.C., died from the effects of his wounds on Saturday morning last [January 28, 1865]. He leaves a wife and three children."

The mother to whom the three fatherless Daniels boys literally owed everything was born Mary Cleaves Seabrook in Hyde County, N.C., September 4, 1835. Her Cleaves and Seabrook forebears stood a little higher in the social scale than the Danielses, but in the main were farmers with a scattering of planters and professionals. A dominant influence behind widow Daniels' mode of child rearing was her own unhappy life as an orphan, the memory of which she always retained.[4] Later in her youth she came to live with good foster parents in Washington, N.C., Captain William Farrow, a shipbuilder, and his wife Elvira. It was as much to carry food supplies to Mrs. Elvira Farrow as to look after his own property in fire-gutted Washington that Josephus Daniels boarded the *Mystic* on its ill-fated trip in January 1865. When the grim news reached Mary Cleaves Daniels that her husband had been shot, she left Ocracoke immediately for New Bern, but arrived there, entirely distraught, after his death. Not only was she widowed, she did not even have the consolation of knowing her husband's burial place. In all probability he had been attended in the Federal Hospital where, his son Josephus always understood, the elder Daniels refused to permit amputation of the arm without which he could not earn his livelihood.[5]

Mary Cleaves Daniels took her brood to Wilson, N.C., in the summer of 1865 on the invitation of her sister Elizabeth, and Elizabeth's husband, George H. Griffin. At Wilson, always "loveliest village of the plain" to Josephus Daniels, the forlorn little band got an affectionate welcome from Aunt Lib and Uncle George. At once the resolute widow Daniels, determined to be self-supporting, set herself up as a milliner and seamstress. She was skillful enough, but her heart was not in it. All her life the pious Mary Cleaves Daniels conscientiously wore the plainest clothes possible, and she could never enter gladly upon the female vanities associated with needlework. A year later, in December, 1866, she was persuaded to accept appointment as postmistress, for which payment was made in terms of a percentage of stamps canceled. By the end of the following March she had earned $35.[6]

The post office at Wilson was the altered front parlor of an old wooden house rented by Mrs. Daniels on North Tarboro Street. Patrons did not enter the house to claim their mail but mounted the porch and inquired at the outside window. "Mamie," as her adult contemporaries called Mrs. Daniels, was widely esteemed for her good sense and her charitable soul. As soon as she was able, she made her home the haven for every waif and stray. She was, at this time, a tall well-built woman with strong features and the same twinkling gray eyes that people later marked in her son Joe. In her complete devotion to "good works" and her three boys, it was perfectly obvious that the thought of remarrying had simply never entered her mind.[7]

In the days when the Daniels boys were called Big Bud, Little Bud (Josephus), and Babe, young Joe and his brothers moved easily in the equalitarian poverty that was the rural North Carolina of their youth. In those days of haphazard public education (Wilson got its first graded school in 1883), young Joe attended the one-room school of his mother's friend, Miss Annie Bowers, "a fine buxom maiden lady." Later, while the Daniels boys attended the nine-month term of the Wilson Collegiate Institute, they also went to "the free school" conducted during the summer by "Cousin" Edward Morse Nadal, who also taught in the Institute and operated the town's pharmacy.

As soon as he was old enough, young Joe helped out in the front parlor post office. His mother was an accommodating postmistress, quickly volunteering Joe's services in affixing stamps for patrons. The boy then and there conceived a lifelong distaste for licking stamps. In later life he would lick his finger, pass it along the gummed side of the stamp, then sit on the envelope to seal it. One corner of the post office harbored a stand where Joe purveyed newspapers and the requisite balls and bats of baseballing (gloves were for sissies), which was the passion of his school days. As captain of the Swift Foot nine, Joe felt obliged to furnish bats and balls free to his team. By the time he was sixteen his team was playing games in nearby towns, the boys wearing red-flannel-shirt uniforms their mothers made for them. First baseman Daniels had a scatter-shot throwing arm; his reputation was, instead, as a hitter.[8]

Young Joe could not help overhearing his elders talk politics in his mother's post office, where he looked admiringly on Wilson's journalists, first those of the *Plain-Dealer* and later of the *Advance*. At the age of sixteen Josephus and his younger brother Charles were publishing an amateur newspaper, "indifferently printed," called *The Cornucopia*. While at school he was correspondent and subscription agent for two Raleigh papers, the *Observer* and *Hale's Weekly*, at the same time benefiting from the advices of his collegian brother Frank in Chapel Hill. The gentle and serious Frank counseled "Bud" on the contents of the latter's amateur newspaper, advised him to study rhetoric rather than French ("You will have Algebra, Arith., Latin, History, Spelling, and Rhetoric.")[9]

Every decent adult male in Wilson was anxious to help the fatherless Daniels boys, through admiration for their indomitable mother, and the boys had only to show the spark that others would fan. Josephus was always the readiest. He learned to give a warm handshake to everyone he met, and it later became a Josephus Daniels trademark. For many months Josephus taught a Sunday school class four miles out in the country at Barefoot's Mill. He had no horse and buggy, so banker Thomas J. Hadley volunteered his rig and later signed the young man's note in borrowing money for his first newspaper. In his old age Daniels set it down: "It is because of my debts to friends in years when a dollar was as big as a cart wheel to me and harder to get, that I assert that there is no such thing as a self-made man."[10]

Teacher Ed Nadal almost succeeded in making young Joe a pharmacist in the drug store where Joe worked during vacations. He thought briefly about becoming a pharmacist in those days when he was earning thirty-five cents a day. "But," he recalled, "in a day when druggists made their own tinctures, the smell of the drug store made me sick; and I preferred the odor of printer's ink."[11]

In 1880 the eighteen-year-old Daniels left school to become

local editor of the Wilson *Advance,* a connection which was to cost his mother her job. Unfortunately for the Democratic editor, he backed the wrong side both that year and in the mid-term elections of 1882. The result was that despite Josephus' hurrying off to the nation's capital to ask the intercession of Democratic Senator Matt W. Ransom, the demands of Republican patronage made necessary the retirement of the Democratic editor's mother. It was characteristic of Mary Cleaves Daniels that she had already encouraged her son to purchase, on borrowed money, an interest in the Wilson *Advance.* Now she backed him in buying out his partners in the paper, securing the $2,000 purchase with a mortgage on her home, and calmly staking everything she had on his success.

Josephus Daniels preceded his take-over as editor, in his twentieth year, by solemnly inditing a will. He left his business and "good will" to his brothers, his personal property and cash to his mother, provided a $100 tombstone for himself, and bequeathed an additional $100 to Mrs. Elvira Farrow, Mrs. Daniels' foster mother.[12] The young editor was fairly bursting with energy, journeying to court in neighboring counties on Monday and Tuesday and working in Wilson to bring his paper out on time Friday. In the *Advance* shop the old Washington hand press was expertly managed by Stepney Buck, a muscular Negro, and the compositors included Leroy C. Alford, who started with young Daniels on the *Advance,* went to Washington with him to hold office in the Cleveland administration, and returned to the newly purchased *News and Observer,* of which he ultimately became the beloved "Uncle Jimmie" and Daniels "The Old Man." In 1882 the young man and staff stayed up late each Thursday night making up the Friday paper, with a midnight supper of hot food prepared for all hands by Mary Cleaves Daniels.

Brother Frank was now in Goldsboro, the law partner of classmate Charles B. Aycock; Brother Charles was in Kinston editing the *Free Press* bought in partnership with Brother Joe. The latter and the widow Daniels lived alone except for their Negro cook, Dora. "We lived well," Daniels recalled of those days when he was making seventy-five dollars a month on the *Advance* and keeping up with the interest on the house mortgage. "A big turkey cost seventy-five cents and lasted a week. It got better and better until it vanished in soup."[13]

Aside from his Democratic regularity in politics, Daniels had already taken stands strong enough to attract widespread note. In an era when the Louisiana Lottery advertisements were spread thickly through rural America's advertisement-starved journals, Daniels barred the Lottery from the pages of the *Advance*. In an era when statewide prohibition had been overwhelmingly defeated, Daniels fought for prohibition as a progressive reform. In an era when share-cropped cotton was still king in Eastern North Carolina, Daniels avidly followed the first experiments with, and then made wholehearted propaganda for, raising flue-cured tobacco. An eternal optimist in print, Daniels published in his first issue as editor of the *Advance* an editorial endorsing a forward step that was not taken during his entire lifetime—federal aid to education.

In his twenty-third year, Daniels was a rather pleasantly plain young man of medium height. One notices at once the snapping gray eyes, the lower lip that could protrude in stubbornness, but the dominant impression was that of his cheerful energy. As an omnivorous reader, he was influenced most directly by Charles Reade's *Put Yourself in His Place* and George Eliot's *Felix Holt, the Radical*. He made the title of the first his personal creed in life, but both were basic to his sympathy for the underprivileged, his enmity for their exploiters, and his zeal for the equalizing of opportunity. These ideals, along with the ethical loftiness of the King James Version, plus the example of his serenely devout mother, stood him in good stead as he prepared to leave his boyhood home. He was about to interrupt a career in journalism—he was newly established as president of the State Press Association—for additional schooling.

When Josephus Daniels left his mother's home in 1885 to attend the Summer Law School of the University in Chapel Hill, he thought to return home as a practicing lawyer who also, with hired help, could continue to publish the *Advance*. Accordingly, he borrowed a Blackstone from lawyer Frederick A. Woodard for some preliminary "reading" of law, got a friend to edit the *Advance* during the summer, and set out for Chapel Hill where he entered the Law School on May 1. He thus arrived before Commencement and stayed on beyond the opening of the fall session, these months comprising the only term of formal "higher" education of his long life. Daniels quickly fell in love with the University, shortly thereafter becoming secretary of the Alumni Association and later a University trustee for forty-seven years.

He arrived in the pleasant little college town with "privilege" already the lifelong target of his crusading reformer's impulse. His own bent was equalitarian. That equalitarianism was strongly personal in that he was of the yeomanry rather than the aristocracy, and he would refuse membership in any organization not open to all. That attitude would keep him out of fraternities and out of virtually everything else, as he later expressed it, except the Democratic party and the Methodist church. "There are any number of secret societies here," he wrote his mother about fraternities and their clannishness. He belonged to none of them, though invited to join, and instead he associated "with all & hold my own with any of them."[14]

He did admire his aristocratic law professor, John Manning, an antebellum planter and slave-owner, whom he deemed a better man than the coarse "moneyed aristocracy" who had made their fortunes since the Civil War. Yet Daniels still preferred the new day in which careers were open to the talents. Today there was greater opportunity for able young men like his brother Frank and the latter's law partner, Aycock. Josephus' letters home reflected many things: his gratitude to his mother, his light and almost meatless diet ("I prize my health above all the law extant"), his girl acquaintances ("Miss Mangum, my pretty neighbor"), his schoolmates ("Coble . . . so conservative that I like him"), his teaching of Sunday school and resolutely abstaining from his law studies on the Sabbath.

Young Daniels' studies in Chapel Hill that summer were in no way helped by his having to go off to address the State Press Convention at Smithville (now Southport) and having to attend to a multitude of details affecting the Wilson *Advance*. On top of everything else came an opportunity, at the end of that summer of 1885, to edit a paper at the state capital and thus realize an old ambition. Seizing upon the opportunity, he quickly learned what Julian S. Carr, the wealthy banker and tobacco manufacturer of Durham, did not know—that Carr owned stock in two money-losing weekly papers in Raleigh. The editor of the consolidated paper had just died, a Confederate comrade to whom Colonel Carr had advanced money without ever expecting repayment. The energetic young Daniels insisted that he would succeed where the gifted Walter Hines Page had failed (as editor of the Raleigh *State Chronicle*, one of the forlorn and consolidated papers).

Somewhat amused with young Daniels' aplomb, Carr agreed to let him have the stock for whatever a successful paper could later afford to repay him.

Walter Hines Page's experience may help illuminate the extent of Daniels' daring. Page had turned his *State Chronicle* into a daily in hopeless competition with two others for the meager advertising in the state capital (1880 population 9,265). Editor Page had been delighted with a clear news beat fashioned for him by Josephus Daniels, who had sent in a detailed story about a disastrous fire at Wilson. Out of Page's delight with Daniels' enterprise came an invitation to edit, in Page's absence, the *State Chronicle* for the two weeks around Christmas, 1884. In reality Page was using the vacation to shop around for an out-of-state job and, not being able to win appointment as State Printer from the succeeding legislature, Page had to strike his colors. At the time Daniels could not afford to take over the *State Chronicle*, preferring to stay on with his $100 monthly from the Wilson *Advance*. However, it was the *State Chronicle* that he revived the following year and that made him a secure statewide reputation almost at once.

Passing his bar exam in October, 1885, Daniels lost no time in putting down the twenty dollars for the coveted license to practice (he never did). Then he presented a letter of introduction from Judge Connor of Wilson to Judge Walter Clark of Raleigh, later the state's Chief Justice. From the beginning of his *State Chronicle* days, then, Daniels enjoyed the moral and political support of this formidable Confederate veteran and impatient reformer. The new editor's first editorial struck the keynote on October 16, 1885: he was Democratic in politics, "looking to Jefferson as the greatest of Americans." Nationally, Daniels would support civil service reform; locally, the public school system freed of its existing chaos. He would offer his columns free to the state's educators, and would refuse to rehearse old conflicts between private colleges and the State University. Daniels closed with a disclaimer of publishing a "sensational paper" but rather one that was "moral in tone and which no father will hesitate to place in the hands of his children."

On settling in the state capital in 1885, one of young Daniels' first acts was to join the Watauga Club,[15] organized the year before mainly by William J. Peele (later a Populist) and Walter Hines

Page (later a conservative Democrat). The Wataugans were young men in their twenties, who paid only impatient respect to the Confederate veterans who constituted that day's Establishment. The Wataugans agreed with, and went beyond, the vision of an industrialized New South, looking to public education as the lever that would lift North Carolina into the modern age. By the time Daniels joined them, the Wataugans had already pried out of the Bourbons in the 1885 legislature an enabling act for a technical college (though the Bourbons characteristically refused to appropriate any money). While biding their time on the college project, the Wataugans embraced nothing less than federal aid to education. Josephus Daniels showed them the way, that "the education of the Negro was a national responsibility," in a paper he read to his young fellow-members.

One of those ardent young spirits was the inimitable Charles D. McIver, who arrived in Raleigh shortly after Daniels to teach the young ladies at Peace Institute. "The walks and talks we had in those halcyon days when we planned the great things we hoped to do, and rejoiced in youth and strength to overcome obstacles!" Daniels recalled. "I count them as among the happiest of my life, for it was then that our souls were knit together. . . . He was as much interested in my newspaper dream . . . as I was wrapped up in his dream of the great college for women."[16] Young Daniels could also summon up an iconoclastic anger. "Damn society!" he exploded to his mother. "It is hollow, it is silly, it is frivolous, it is selfish, sordid & mean, it is totally irreligious—it is often vulgar."[17]

In those early days Daniels' *State Chronicle* carried a letter each week contributed free of charge from the Wataugan exile, Walter Hines Page. From his newspaper desk in Brooklyn, Page wrote the celebrated Mummy Letters—which Daniels gleefully published—all of which mounted a coherent assault on the backwardness of North Carolina's "mummified" leadership. Instead of allowing every good idea to die of inanition through fear of offending a few Mummies, Page urged that "it would be cheaper to pension them all than longer to listen to them." The Mummy Papers stirred up such a splendid controversy in the *State Chronicle* that public-spirited Tar Heels began reading the paper just to see what "Josephus Daniels says."

He was saying, among other things, that the typically Bourbon operation of the State Agriculture Department was a scandal. Editor Daniels devoted six columns of one front page and three more of his editorial page (the entire paper consisted of only four pages) to a devastating critique. In detail he attacked the basis of the Department's support, a privilege tax on fertilizer manufacturers rather than an appropriation from general revenues, and set down a word picture of the agriculture commissioner who was the very epitome of the Bourbon: "a courtly polished gentleman . . . conservative to a fault . . . [who] rarely leaves his office and has not addressed the farmers on practical topics half a dozen times since he has held his place."[18]

In the *State Chronicle* of early 1886 generally, Daniels made a direct attack on every function of the State Agriculture Department except its immigration agency, and even there he damned it by indirection. The young editor jeered openly at the expensive and self-deceiving expositions that were calculated to attract outside capital and labor, and as a practical editor he bridled at the free advertising that was thus being given to private enterprises. He derided the notion that intelligent would-be immigrants could be fooled by the sight of all those private firms energetically patting themselves on the back. Although Daniels conceded that the immigration agency was managed economically enough, he implied (though one did not say such things openly) that the South was fooling itself in thinking that it could attract yeoman farmers and artisans willing to compete with a mass of economically depressed Negro labor. In championing a state-supported technical college the year before, Daniels and the Wataugans had already attacked the hapless Agriculture Department and the hopeless immigration movement by advocating (1) practical rather than academic agriculture, and (2) training of the home talent that had been wasted in ante-bellum days by the South's having relegated skilled labor almost exclusively to slave-artisans.

The powerful railroads that then dominated so many state legislatures also took their lumps from the vigorous young Daniels. "I do not expect to have a pass many days," he confided to his mother about his war on the railroads, "but I'll stay in Raleigh or tramp before I'll sell myself to these railroad corporations which are eating out the best life of the state and standing in the way of all real progress."[19] From his first day as editor in Raleigh, he fought for the creation of a Railroad Commission. He even became the volunteer spokesman of those who sought a Commission from the 1887 legislature, a body that contained many such railroad attorneys as Jeter C. Pritchard, later a Republican senator and federal judge.

At this juncture Daniels was earning—in his *State Chronicle* partnership with F. B. Arendall, who was not pulling his weight— $30 a month and paying $20 of it for food and lodging. Still, Daniels rejoiced in his work and had great expectations besides— the prize of State Printer that had eluded Walter Page. Despite the censorious tone of his personal letters and some editorials, Daniels continued to show the likable personality that had always commended him to his elders. An active five-month campaign, in which he solidified his position with influential legislators, won him the State Printer appointment from the 1887 legislature. The aspirant for the post had editorialized: "The money, some $1500 a year estimated, will help make a better paper and advance it after awhile to a daily."[20]

No sooner had he won the State Printer appointment, than Daniels boldly proposed to his defeated adversary—Captain Samuel A. Ashe of the rival *News and Observer*—Daniels' buying a majority interest in the other's paper and combining both under Daniels' editorship. "My proposition has this qualification," Daniels wrote in 1887, "that I am to be editor and am to control the policy of the new paper." To be sure Daniels would retain Ashe, whose "counsel would be invaluable," but it was no sale, not even after Daniels raised his offer from $8,000 cash to an offer to take up Ashe's note at its face value of $20,000. Daniels had no such sums, of course, but Julian Carr stood ready to back him in such a venture.[21]

Possessed of the State Printer sinecure, however, Daniels could reasonably think of marriage. Even as Romeo, who admired Rosaline before he met Juliet, Josephus Daniels courted another lady before winning his life partner of fifty-five years of married happiness. Not only did Joe's Rosaline bear the same name—Addie— as the girl he later married, but he and the first Addie were engaged to be married. In May, 1887, he was writing his mother of his desire to marry next winter. The object of his affections, as Mrs. Daniels knew, was Miss Addie Marsh, who taught school in Wilson, N.C. Joe assessed the future somberly enough and wrote rather resignedly to his mother: "We will be brave & poor." In

September the engagement was at an end. "Miss Addie is a true & a sensible young woman, but not the woman for me," he confided. Yes, he planned to marry some day when he found the right girl, but he made it plain: "I am in no big hurry to find her."[22] Perhaps she found him, but in the very next month he began to court Miss Addie Worth Bagley.

Addie Bagley, who was only eighteen years old, had met earlier and casually this older man (he was twenty-five) and had virtually dismissed him from her mind on that account. But when she got back from summer vacation—spent with her Uncle David's family at Wilmington and then in the western mountains—she found Editor Daniels vying with her other admirers, and the *State Chronicle's* little printer's devil coming by with a note every day. The young lady began to watch for the messenger boy's coming, and the editor to spend more and more evenings at the Bagley house. The early notes were tentative, speaking of church: "I was glad to see you taking a high seat in the synagogue last night"; or sending fruit like the James grapes borne by the printer's devil, which were not as delicious, unfortunately, as the Mish grapes from Washington, N.C. On October 19, 1887, Joe made Miss Addie a proposal of marriage. The editor had to wait a month for his answer, but in later years the sentimental couple always observed the anniversary of that proposal.

In January, 1888, the accepted suitor and a committee of Democrats went to Washington to protest to Congress and to President Cleveland against internal revenue taxes. Homeward bound, Joe wrote Addie of his resolve to make his editorials more weighty as a result of his observations in Washington, to which place he might some day return as a Congressman. He then made the requisite formal call upon Mrs. Bagley to ask the hand of her daughter, to whom he had already sent Lowell's lines: "Blessing she is: God made her so." The editor's buoyancy was not to be deflated even by the failure of the bank that held his savings: "My own loss is, for me, very heavy," he wrote his fiancée, "but for my life, I cannot allow it to worry me much. I am so happy and so rich because I possess your love that I would be cheerful if all the banks should break."[23]

The wedding was set for May 2, 1888, the day after Miss Addie's nineteenth birthday. From brother Frank, who would sometimes call his younger brother "son" and who had been married three years, came happy letters that assured Joe: "Your wife will fill the place in my heart that our little sister would have occupied had she been spared to us." Miss Addie's brother, Worth Bagley, recalled "Mr. Daniels' knees shaking with a stage fright at the church wedding." If Daniels' knees shook as he and his bride were married, it was not because of the proximity of "the creme de la creme of Raleigh society" as Ashe's *News and Observer* put it. On being shown the clipping half a century later, the old man wrote playfully to his son Jonathan: "Your mother may have belonged to that set—but not me. . . . You and I may get in on our wives' tickets, but in conviction and in radicalism we belong to the proletariat."[24]

Miss Addie bore the same name as her mother, Adelaide Worth Bagley, who was the daughter of the Quaker pre-Reconstruction Governor Jonathan Worth (1865-68). If Mrs. Bagley was tempted to preen herself on her elevated family connections, she never yielded to it with Josephus Daniels, who as "Brother Joe" became a great favorite with the large Bagley clan. There were daughters Belle and Ethel, sons Worth, Henry, and David, and nearby in Raleigh lived Mrs. Bagley's sister, Elvira Moffitt and her son Herbert Jackson. From a honeymoon in the nation's capital Joe assured Mrs. Bagley: "I never knew how dearly I loved my 'little girl wife' until now, & more than ever can I understand how it was hard for you to give her to me." For her part Mrs. Bagley noted to daughter Belle that Mr. Daniels "looks better and is even more lover than ever. . . . I think he is an unusually good man."[25]

The young couple began their married life as boarders in the home of Miss Addie's aunt, Elvira Moffitt, but since Mrs. Bagley took boarders too, they soon moved in with the bride's mother. They did so on the urging of Mother Daniels, who came up from Wilson and convinced Mrs. Bagley that it was the right thing to do. "All of us thanked my mother for the arrangement," Daniels recalled. It was a happy household, the editor reading to his enlarged family of an evening and basking in their affection. "Ethel & Henry got after him [Daniels] to read in Innocents Abroad, & we all laughed till we were sore," Mrs. Bagley wrote to daughter Belle. When Daniels got the reappointment as State Printer despite Captain Ashe's offer to do the job for 15 per cent less, Mrs. Bagley enthused: "I have never seen a man have such magnetic influence among men. He is honest & that is the reason, & he is fearless to do right."[26]

Unquestionably, Daniels provided the most insistent newspaper voice in the state arguing for progressive measures. He knew he had an uphill fight in contending for civil service reform—opposed by the Establishment and by the adored folk hero, Senator Zebulon B. Vance. Daniels therefore had to oppose discreetly, knowing that to voice open criticism of his state's earthy and revered Civil War governor was strictly taboo. On another front, Daniels put out a special education issue carrying articles by the leading teachers in the State, protesting that the four-month public school term had become a dead letter, and pointing to certain municipalities that were taxing themselves for graded schools. His vividly personal editorials were by way of prodding the penny-pinching old-line Bourbon Democrats, and the editorials carried an undertone of impatience with Bourbon placidity and conservatism. Nevertheless, Daniels acted the part of the young man who knew his time was coming. He carefully kept open his lines of communication with Senator Ransom, protesting in 1888 against an insinuation by "*News-Observer friends* that I am against you." He called attention to his two brothers' services to the senator's cause and added, "I have offended some of my best friends by declining to print articles attacking you."[27]

Ransom's chief opponent for the vote of the Democratic legislators was the president of the State Farmer's Alliance, Sydenham B. Alexander, and it was with his views more than with those of Ransom that Daniels sympathized. Nevertheless, Daniels hewed to the traditional Democratic line instead of embracing the Alliance, not so much because he feared to voice unpopular views as because of his already deep-seated conviction that politics as the art of the possible could succeed only within disciplined organizational lines. At this time, to be sure, the men of the Farmers' Alliance had not yet broken with the Democratic party as many were later to do in the Populist revolt. It was wholly in character for Daniels—and it became the rule of a lifetime—to support the regular candidate by way of cementing party solidarity.

Their joint efforts for reform made Daniels and the Alliancemen close allies within the Democratic party. Their first success came in the chartering in 1887 of the North Carolina College of Agricultural and Mechanic Arts (today North Carolina State University at Raleigh). Daniels and the Wataugans provided the leadership; the newly organized North Carolina Farmers' Association provided the numbers and the political muscle. As leader the farmers had the influential Leonidas L. Polk, editor of the *Progressive Farmer* of Raleigh, and under his guidance they held a mass meeting during the legislative session and hammered out the details of what became a land-grant college. The bill, as co-authored by one of the Wataugans, transferred the land-script certificates of the University of North Carolina to the new college, and the General Assembly compensated the older school by appropriation. In 1889 the A. and M. College opened its doors, and Daniels was off on another educational crusade.

His opportunity came with the providing of teachers' institutes, authorized by the legislature of that year. Two excellent educational leaders, Edwin A. Alderman and Charles D. McIver, were assigned to energize townspeople to give better financial support to their schools, and personally to conduct the institutes by which the untrained teachers of that day could be strengthened and inspired. For two years the two educational missionaries ranged the state with such effect that they converted the politically potent Farmers' Alliance to their program. Daniels' editorials strengthened the educators at every turn.

The scholarly and aristocratic Alderman, later president of the Universities of North Carolina, Tulane, and Virginia, remained always a warm friend of Josephus Daniels. But it was McIver, his fellow Wataugan, for whom he would go through fire and water, and who strengthened in Daniels the resolve that made him a lifelong champion of women's rights. With good humor and persistent faith, McIver repeatedly drove home his guiding principle—of educating women for teaching—to the legislators who loved him for his stories and stayed to listen to his doctrine. People recognized him at once by his trademarks: the white necktie, the massive forehead, the perennial smile that easily transferred itself into a grin. McIver's life slogan, gently insinuated amid the merriment, became a byword in North Carolina: "If you educate a man you educate one citizen; if you educate a woman you educate a family or a community."[28] Nothing pleased Daniels more than having McIver's dream come true and seeing him installed as first president (1891) of the Normal and Industrial School for women (now the University of North Carolina at Greensboro).

That same year brought the Railroad Commission Daniels had fought for, now insistently demanded by the Farmers' Alliance.

Daniels was fairly entitled to regard creation of the Commission as a minor triumph, and he was to win another small victory over the railroads in the matter of the Wilmington and Weldon (since 1889 part of the Seaboard). An expanded portion of this pioneer and therefore tax-exempt railroad was ordered put on the tax books, and the case was now on appeal to the State Supreme Court. What made the issue precarious was the sudden death of Governor Daniel G. Fowle and the accession of the conservative Thomas M. Holt. The latter might appoint a railroad attorney to the Supreme Court in place of a desperately ill justice known to be against the exemption. With Daniels' *State Chronicle* hammering against the tax exemption, the sick judge was brought to court long enough to carry the day against the undertaxed railroad.

That railroad fight was fought by what was now the *Daily State Chronicle*. The advent of that chancy daily was preceded by Daniels' refusal to be tempted by an offer that would have made him a prosperous, if bought, editor. On his reappointment as State Printer in 1889 Daniels was called in by the chief railroad spokesman of the state, Colonel Alexander B. Andrews, a Confederate veteran and one of the few managers of older lines retained when the Southern Railway was later organized by J. Pierpont Morgan. In essence, as Daniels later revealed, Andrews' subsidy scheme would gain Daniels' silence on a Railroad Commission as well as give the colonel a newspaper organ. As compensation Daniels was to preside over the daily *News and Observer,* which Andrews would purchase from the less effective Ashe, at a guaranteed annual salary of $5,000 plus everything the paper earned above that amount. The colonel urged the obstinate young editor not to throw away the opportunity of a lifetime, to consult first with the more practical of his kin. Brother Frank and Daniels' bride agreed in the editor's decision to refuse the offer, while Daniels had to promise Andrews never to reveal the newspaper proposal as long as the colonel lived.[29]

Editing the new *Daily State Chronicle* put Daniels under a heavier burden of work than ever, and Miss Addie took to helping her husband in the office. She introduced a little order where a lackadaisical, and since displaced, business manager had badly mismanaged the accounts. Daniels would snatch at a little lunch on the run, but his health and digestion bore up remarkably with Miss Addie's encouraging devotion. In the midst of his struggles to make the daily paper pay, he had to take time off to help Midshipman Worth Bagley, Miss Addie's younger brother, who was a better football player than scholar at the Naval Academy where he was in academic trouble. He was fated, in 1893, to kick the winning field goal in the Army-Navy game and be carried off on the shoulders of his teammates, and, in 1898, to lose his life to Spanish gunfire off the north coast of Cuba.

The midshipman brother-in-law had expressed to his sister in 1890 his admiration for Daniels: "The people have begun to appreciate his service to them, and though he may not be aided by railroad magnates, etc., the people, in other words, the *votes*, are at his back." The next year Daniels hurried off to Annapolis and there labored to such effect that he got Bagley reappointed to the Academy as member of a new class. Mrs. Bagley thanked Daniels: "My heart goes up in thankfulness every few moments for such a son as you are—and how tender it makes me feel for you, when I know how you were snatched from your business & from your poor dear little sick wife & without a murmur or a questioning word went away on such an unpromising piece of business." Worth Bagley wrote: "Mother, in him you have a son and my sister a husband that we never can appreciate too much. Where could she have gotten a better?"[30]

The young couple were ecstatic at the birth of their firstborn in January, 1892, a daughter Adelaide. The happy father later had the toddler's portrait painted, which was no mark of affluence since a struggling artist was glad to execute this and other portraits in exchange for advertising. Times were hard for all, and Mrs. Bagley wrote: "Never has there been such financial depression—never so little money afloat—never the like of beggars white & colored." In addition to the desperately hard times that cut down on the advertising revenue of the *Daily State Chronicle,* the paper was fighting hopelessly in little Raleigh, where virtually everyone who could pay for a daily paper had been solicited and where most of the country people—in those days before Rural Free Delivery—could not be expected to subscribe. The *Daily State Chronicle* was losing more money than its editor was receiving as State Printer, and Daniels was anxious to stop pouring good money after bad. Thus, when an agent for Governor Thomas M. Holt made an offer to buy the paper as a political organ plumping for the continuance in office of that wealthy cotton mill owner, Daniels agreed to sell—but

not to refrain from re-entering the Raleigh newspaper arena. So
the sale of the *Daily State Chronicle,* the proceeds of which put
Editor Daniels out of debt at last, did not in any way dishearten
him.[31]

Editor-delegates to national conclaves got free railroad passes
in those days, and, as delegate to that year's National Editorial Association, Daniels got two. He used one pass for his mother, got
another from a fellow-editor for Mrs. Bagley, and after the State
Democratic Convention of 1892 the little party spent a month traveling through California and Oregon. To Miss Addie, who had to
stay home with baby Adelaide, Daniels wrote en route: "They [the
two mothers] have both been well, & have entered into all the
pleasures with the zest of young girls." After his return, he wrote
to his mother in Wilson (with whom he had "washed hands in the
Pacific Ocean"), speaking of a short rest and then off to "start a
weekly paper here [Raleigh, *The North Carolinian*], and throw
myself into it with all my soul and make it succeed."[32]

The North Carolinian played an active role in the Democratic
victory of 1892, but not only was the paper losing money but there
was no longer any profit in the post of State Printer. After winning
the post again in the stormy 1893 legislature, Daniels divided the
contract between two Raleigh printing firms (neither his own) and
kept nothing for himself. He worked hard to consolidate his position with Senator Ransom, boosting the old Confederate general
for a Cabinet position and mentioning several federal jobs in which
the editor was interested. He conceded to the senator that some
of the government jobs in Washington were "very big positions
and may be entirely out of my reach," yet "I believe that Mr. Smith
[Hoke Smith, Secretary of the Interior] would do something handsome for me if it should be requested by North Carolina's Senators
and my representative."[33]

Daniels was genuinely reluctant to become a Washington bureaucrat, but North Carolina journalism could not in those hard
times afford him a living. Consequently, he gratefully accepted
from Secretary Hoke Smith a job as Chief of the Appointment Division ($1,600 a year), which led to his quick promotion to Chief
Clerk of the Interior Department at $2,750 a year. He used $100
a month to support himself, his wife, baby, and a nurse, and sent
the balance, along with his editorials, back to the struggling *North
Carolinian* in Raleigh.

"I regard myself here as an exile from home," he wrote a North Carolina friend from Washington, "banished because of the hard times," and he predicted an early return to "the people God made."[34] Unlike Walter Page, who left North Carolina permanently when unable to make his *State Chronicle* pay, Daniels' skill with politics enabled him to hibernate nearly two years in Washington and rebuild his personal resources so as to fight another day. There was no question of his being poised and alert for instant service when recalled to the political wars.

The Road to Wilson's Cabinet

Josephus Daniels went to live in Washington, D.C., in 1893 as a self-described exile; he was to return there in triumph two decades later not as exile but as a member of the President's Cabinet.* In the intervening decades he built up his political strength, like some North Carolina Antaeus, by dint of renewed contact with his native earth. Like all national Democrats he was an "out" politically in those days of Republican-dominated Washington, but like most Southern Democrats he was an "in" at home. Daniels' "door of opportunity" at home was opened once again by his benefactor, "Jule" Carr, the dapper and generous-hearted rich man. It was he who bought the Raleigh *News and Observer* as a distressed property in 1894 and turned it over to the energetic Daniels to operate as the organ of the North Carolina Democrats.

Going home was both challenge and restorative for Daniels and Miss Addie. They had known a great grief when little Adelaide died of an unidentified fever, possibly dysentery, in July 1893. The Interior Department experience involved, besides the memory of the dead child, the complete political disenchantment Daniels shared with his admired chief, Hoke Smith, over President Cleveland's fiscal conservatism in the face of a severe depression. On

* Details of this chapter are systematically elaborated in the author's *Josephus Daniels Says . . . 1894-1913* (Chapel Hill: The University of North Carolina Press, 1962).

24

the other hand, Raleigh beckoned Daniels to make good his long-held ambition to edit the chief daily newspaper at his state's capital. Nobody needed to tell him that the editorship was a great gamble, for his failure with the *Daily State Chronicle* was still fresh. But his avidity for the new opportunity made him brush aside all warnings like the one from Mrs. Bagley's hard-headed merchant brother, David Worth. The latter had been scorched in a newspaper venture in Wilmington, N.C., and now wrote agitatedly of Daniels: "The labor he has to perform now looks to me like suicide almost."[1]

Daniels' installation as editor of a refurbished *News and Observer* was intended to breathe new life into a demoralized Democratic party headed for almost certain defeat. It was really too late for Daniels to affect the outcome; by 1892 it had already become abundantly apparent that a combination of Republicans and Populists could outvote North Carolina's Democrats. Since that time the continued intransigence of Editor Ashe, the Democratic spokesman in the press, and Senator Ransom, the party's do-nothing patronage dispenser, had made assurance of Democratic defeat doubly sure. Nevertheless, from his desk at Washington, Daniels in the summer of 1894 wrote personal letters to one hundred picked Tar Heel Democrats, inviting each to buy one $100 share of stock in the paper. Surprisingly in those hard times seventy of them did so, and the editorship—begun in August while Daniels was still in Washington—gave the paper new life. And Daniels' bright and vivid personal touch quickly enlivened *The News and Observer*, which had languished as a stodgy and ultra-conservative organ under Ashe. That July, a year after little Adelaide's death, Daniels had telegraphed his mother of the birth of "your grandson Josephus." The doughty Mary Cleaves Daniels wrote directly to the new baby: "I hope you may make as good and strong a man as your grandfather."[2]

On returning to Raleigh in early 1895, Editor Daniels had his work cut out for him. The Populists, fed up with Democratic foot-dragging on reform, had fused with the Republicans and won control of that year's legislature. Daniels and the Populists were at one on such matters as anti-trust legislation, free silver, a graduated income tax, direct election of senators, and expansion of public education. The conservative Democrats did not, however, share the young editor's progressive views, and those conservatives ran the Democratic party. Local Populists therefore fused with local

Republicans on a joint program: restoration of county self-govern-
ment (frustrated by Raleigh-appointed Democratic justices of the
peace), nonpartisan election laws, a nonpartisan judiciary, a state
reformatory, and an effective four-month school term. Daniels
thus became a political "out" during Fusion ascendancy, 1894-
1900. Yet at the same time he had to give uneasy support to some
of the enemy's reforms and still try to split the Populists away from
their "unnatural" fusion with the Republicans.

While the three political parties groped uncertainly for fusions
of expediency against one another, Daniels fretted to see the cause
of educational progress suffer. For example, a war on the University broke out during the 1895 legislature. A long history of conflict between the University of North Carolina and the state's private denominational colleges—Wake Forest (Baptist), Davidson
(Presbyterian), and Trinity (Methodist)—now came to a head. The
friends of the denominational colleges, honestly fearful for their
struggling institutions in those hard times, had already tried—and
narrowly failed—to restrict the University to graduate instruction.
Now, with a Fusion legislature in power, a number of anti-Univer-
sity bills were introduced, including one that would have abolished
outright all University appropriations.

The Baptist State Convention secretary, the Reverend Columbus
Durham, found it necessary to inveigh against Editor Daniels, saying to the legislature: "A man who does not vote as he pleases
[against the University appropriation] is no more fit to be a citizen
than Josephus Daniels is to edit a daily newspaper." Daniels' retort was immediate: "If Dr. Taylor [president of Wake Forest]
could be rid of the incubus of Dr. Durham's advocacy of Wake
Forest College, he would have an increase of one hundred more
students there in the next twelve months."[3] Daniels' friend Aycock,
now U.S. District Attorney, was an avid champion of the University,
as was Joseph P. Caldwell, editor of the *Charlotte Observer*, who
had not yet broken politically with his Raleigh contemporary.
But the real vanguard of the pro-University team was composed of
Daniels' nominal foes, the Populists, with whom he was still trying to seek political reconciliation. Populists in the forefront were
Harry Skinner and Senator Marion Butler, whereas an out-and-out
Republican champion of the University was Daniel L. Russell. Also
helping to save the University was a Negro Methodist minister, the
Reverend R. H. W. Leak, who spoke against cutting the appropria-

tion and told of the Negroes' plans to demand a university of their own.

The Negro vote, which was to become the apple of discord tossed between Populists and Republicans, was critical. In fact, the most important political act of the 1895 legislature was a new election law that concentrated power in the boards of county commissioners. This act undid the work of the Democrats, whose Raleigh-appointed J.P.'s had dominated local government and had been the mainstays of Bourbon rule and implicit white supremacy. Editor Daniels, always trying to split the Populists and Republicans, was making effective use of the yellow journalism then being popularized by Hearst and Pulitzer in New York. He could not undo the work of an elected legislature, but he could point a moral. The election law of 1895 meant quite simply that now the Black Belt counties would cast—and count—many more Negro Republican ballots, and indeed the result in 1896 was to be a Republican gain of 59,000 votes and the election of a Republican governor.

Whatever Daniels' political frustrations at home, they were nothing compared to those attendant upon the great Bryan presidential campaign of 1896. Josephus Daniels was one of the earlier partisans of William Jennings Bryan. When Congressman Bryan spoke at the State Normal School commencement in 1894, invited by President McIver for the "advertising," he had come to Greensboro escorted by bureaucrat Josephus Daniels of the Interior Department. The Nebraskan's tumultous reception was such—he had to address an additional crowd gathered outside his hotel—that Daniels recalled being convinced that Bryan "would be the next Democratic candidate for President." The next summer Daniels met in Washington with older and more prestigious Democrats planning pre-Convention strategy, and the editor wrote to Bryan: "I would rather see you head the ticket than anyone else."[4]

In 1896 Daniels attended his first Democratic National Convention, going to Chicago as a reporter and returning in triumph as his state's national committeeman. On Bryan's nomination Daniels exultantly wired his editorial associate in Raleigh: "Write your best editorial, one that will live. North Carolina led the procession."[5] In August the editor and Miss Addie went to New York for Bryan's formal acceptance speech, while in Raleigh Josephus, Jr., prattled of "Bion of Baska." In September Daniels went to Knoxville, Tennessee, to escort candidate Bryan into the Tar Heel state, which the Nebraskan covered thoroughly and to good effect. Daniels recalled: "When the train pulled out of North Carolina for Virginia, I saw, and so informed Bryan, that his trip through the state had cinched it."[6]

Editor Daniels campaigned with Bryan all the way from Virginia to Maine and back. He was by Bryan's side when one of the Yale students threw an egg at the Commoner while the collegians hooted "Ho-ax, Ho-ax," but all New England did not behave like these young sons of privilege. From Hartford Daniels wrote home that "the people here seem more enthusiastic than in the South, if possible," and from Boston, where the Common was jammed with thousands of Bryan idolators, Daniels telegraphed *The News and Observer* that the people of Boston were "wild with enthusiasm." Returned from the trip, he happily predicted a Bryan victory with 292 electoral votes, but he said nothing about the placards he had seen in the mill towns of New England: "This factory will be closed on the morning after the November election if Bryan is elected. If McKinley is elected, employment will go on as usual."[7]

As the voting approached, Daniels' confidence mounted. He editorialized scornfully of Mark Hanna's ruse in trying to discredit Bryan with anti-Catholic voters by issuing circulars showing that Bryan had voted in Congress for Catholic-taught Indian schools. "I do not see how Mr. Bryan can be defeated," Daniels wrote to a friend.[8] The only obstacle at home was the Negro vote, solidly Republican, whereas the Populists and Democrats—white men all— had achieved electoral fusion on Bryan.

Daniels angrily quoted the boastful North Carolina G.O.P. chairman as written up in the New York *World*, happy that the Fusion legislature's election law of 1895 had led to an "enormous registration of unqualified Negro voters." The retort shot back from North Carolina's leading Negro politician, James H. Young, who warned in his Raleigh newspaper that the Democratic party would seek to carry the election by violence, "goaded by the *News and Observer*, its malicious and vindictive negro-baiting organ." The Democrats were, in fact, only several years away from success in persuading the state's white men to oust the Negro bodily from politics and thus to dominate and outvote the Republican party by depriving it of Negro support. For the time, however, Mrs. Bagley reported a Republican-circulated hoax of a doctored ballot designed to trap Raleigh Democrats into voting against their own party. News of this political skullduggery reached Daniels the Sunday before election ("Mr. D came near getting out a paper but could not get all the printers together."). At any rate, North Carolina was one of that minority of states salvaged by Bryan in his defeat for the presidency. Josephus Daniels never swerved from a conviction that Bryan had won the election but had been counted out by "frauds as outrageous as those which kept Tilden out of the White House."[9]

Daniels' admiration for Bryan led him to follow the Commoner in politics, in a moralistic approach to reform, even in dress. Yet the two men differed sufficiently in temperament and in the priorities they assigned various principles to end their careers in vastly different ways. Still, it was Bryan whom Daniels followed in reviving the "old fashioned" liberalism of Jefferson, the equalitarianism of Jackson, and harmonizing these ideals with the new executive reforms of the Progressive Era. Daniels always summed it up by quoting Jefferson's "Equal rights to all, special privilege to none." Starting in 1896 Bryan had awakened politically the sleeping masses, an intolerably vulgar activity in the eyes of his critics. In the ridicule attending his tragic last days, they sought to conceal the fact—but could not from Daniels, who proclaimed it—that Bryan's influence had made possible almost every piece of progressive legislation in the previous quarter-century.[10]

In that first Bryan campaign, the Commoner's compelling figure made possible a Populist-Democratic fusion in North Carolina. But the two parties could agree on nothing and nobody else, so the state campaign of 1896 was characteristic of an era when ignorant armies clashed by night. The three parties began by naming three separate state tickets and three separate candidates for governor. Later, even as Democrats and Populists united on Bryan, Republicans and Populists fused in support of a ticket for congressional and legislative offices. The Populists, in addition, went their separate way in contests for governor, lieutenant governor, and auditor. The outcome was another legislature controlled by a Republican-Populist coalition, the state administration being headed by a Republican governor, Daniel L. Russell.

Daniels' reform ideas kept throwing him into unorthodox company for a Democrat, but never more so than when he fought side by side with Russell. The governor took vigorous action in support of a bill to void the ninety-nine-year lease of the state-owned North

Carolina Railroad to the Southern Railway. This "midnight lease"
(so-called because of its secret negotiation by the outgoing Democratic governor) was a renewal of an earlier lease that still had six
years to run. Colonel Andrews—he who had tried to obtain Daniels' silence by buying him *The News and Observer*—forced the
"midnight lease" by the same threat that had worked before, the
threat of paralleling the state-owned road. Editor Daniels was
forced to hail Governor Russell as his partner in the anti-lease
fight, calling him "the first prominent Republican in high position
who has not been a creature of corporations since 1886."[11]

In fighting for reduction of rail rates, Daniels and Russell were
so much of a mind that hints were thrown out in "some of the railroad papers" that the two of them plus Judge Walter Clark were
forming a new party. Daniels turned the tables on his conservative critics when, in 1897, the Railroad Commission ruled flatly
against any rate reduction. He ran an exposé that charged two
of the three Railroad Commissioners—justly, as it turned out—with
profiting by their positions by operating a hotel which "is the
Southern Railroad's pet and all trains stop there [near Asheville]
to take dinner."[12] His campaign was successful on two counts:
it discomfited the Fusionists who dominated the Commission, and
it embarrassed the railroad lawyers (mostly Democrats) in the
legislature. The Democrats, once returned to power, were thus
virtually shamed by Daniels into transforming the old Railroad
Commission into a Corporation Commission, the first in the United
States.

Daniels did not at first see Colonel Andrews' hand behind the
Raleigh Daily Tribune, which was established as a Republican organ on the opening of the 1897 legislature. When the *Tribune's*
effects were sold at a sheriff's sale some months after the session,
Daniels was alert enough to buy up the defunct paper's letter books
and files. These proved that Andrews, the conservative Democrat,
was a stockholder in the Republican paper as was the openly
Republican Duke family of the American Tobacco Company. The
Daily Tribune was followed the next year by the *Morning Post*,
ably edited by the personally genial Robert M. Furman and Daniels' chief local antagonist for many years. Like the *Tribune*, the
Morning Post was popularly identified with policies friendly to the
Southern Railway. In the free-swinging journalistic language of
those days, Daniels constantly referred to the *Morning Post* as "the

wheezy old railroad organ" and the "Morning Boast." By late
1897 Josephus Daniels had become known as "Mordecai at the
Gate," after the biblical title of one of his editorials warning the
public of the Southern Railway's alleged depredations.

Daniels pounced upon Republican-Populist differences that had
become exacerbated in the McKinley-Bryan campaign and were
destined to weaken the resolve of the Fusion majority in the 1897
legislature. Senator Jeter C. Pritchard (Republican) had been
named by the previous legislature to the late Zeb Vance's unex-
pired term, the understanding being that he would have Fusionist
support in 1897. In the meantime, however, he had deserted free
silver, a symbolic slap in the face of the Populists. Daniels quickly
exploited the breach, for he was a Bryanite ally of the Populists on
free silver and looked upon that issue as an entering wedge in the
fight for comprehensive reform measures. Without making himself an expert in the quantity theory of money, Daniels could justi-
fiably editorialize against some pretty obvious inequities on the
American economic scene: the growing concentration of wealth,
the appreciation of gold, and the grossly outmoded banking and
currency system. He not only hinted editorially at a legislative
alliance, Democratic-Populist, united against sending a Gold Bug
like Pritchard back to the Senate, but Daniels made a direct written overture to Pritchard's Populist colleague, Senator Marion Butler, in hopes they could unite on electing a silver advocate in Pritchard's place.[13] However desirable the reconciliation with the Populists, Daniels found he could not make common cause with them
so long as they refused to agree that the now-dominant local issue
was the Republican Negro in politics.

When Pritchard was re-elected in a legislative fight that at-
tracted nationwide attention, the Republican-Populist rift opened
so wide that it was never to close thereafter. On top of that, the
Fusion legislators further modified the election laws to their advantage. These arrangements plus new town charters meant an
increase in Negro office-holders in counties where Negroes outnum-
bered whites. White resentment began to grow discernibly, fanned
by Editor Daniels who also floodlighted certain Fusionist personnel
scandals of the time. Above all, he hammered away editorially on
the hypocrisy and the cynical expediency by which white Republicans and the generally Negro-hating Populists manipulated and
deceived the Negroes whose votes they courted.

In the same legislature was waged the second stage of the War on the University, in which Daniels again manned the ramparts. The attackers were Josiah W. Bailey, the young editor of the *Biblical Recorder* (Baptist) and President John C. Kilgo of Trinity College, who established his *Christian Educator* (Methodist) in 1896. Together they mounted the Bailey-Kilgo Crusade and made a formidable pair, the lanky, lantern-jawed young Bailey and the fiery and leonine-appearing Kilgo. The Crusaders sought to make it appear that the champions of state-supported higher education were hostile to the common schools, but Daniels and friends Alderman and McIver wisely refused to be put on the defensive. The latter toiled amain in the capitol lobbies and in *The News and Observer* for continued state support for the University and local taxes for public schools. In the end they won from the Fusionist legislature an increase for the University, while they concurred in the general enthusiasm for more public school support.

The educational outlook was, however, only momentarily bright. At the first the men of all political parties got behind the campaign to encourage local communities to levy school taxes and thus earn matching funds from the legislature. Walter Page, now the renowned editor of the *Atlantic Monthly*, spoke in Greensboro where he was invited by McIver and introduced by Josephus Daniels. Page there made his celebrated speech, "The Forgotten Man," in which he again excoriated the Mummies as he had done in Daniels' paper a decade before. But after Page went back North, the issue of "Negro rule" on Fusionist-appointed school boards so agitated racist anxieties that the campaign resulted in flat failure. Negroes as school board members or holders of any other public offices came to be the prime political and emotional issue. Every educational and other reform in which Daniels was interested had to wait its turn while the racist campaign, in which he himself served as Democratic spokesman, ran its bitter course.

Meanwhile, what John Hay called the "splendid little war" with Spain was providing its own tragedy for Danielses and Bagleys. Ensign Worth Bagley became the first American officer to lose his life in the Spanish-American War. He was cut off at age twenty-five, his mother's eldest son. More, as "first fallen" and a Southerner, he was somehow symbolic of a reunited nation.. That was so, certainly, for Mrs. Bagley, widow of a Confederate officer and daughter of a governor who had been removed from office by the Yankees.

Worth Bagley had been transferred from the ill-fated battleship *Maine* in time to lose his life aboard the torpedo boat *Winslow* at Cárdenas Bay, Cuba, on May 11, 1898. His funeral was held in Raleigh's Capitol Square, and at once there arose a spontaneous movement to collect funds for the Worth Bagley statue that stands there today.[14]

The female Bagleys, save Miss Addie alone, now lived in the nation's capital, where the unmarried Belle and Ethel became government clerks. They fairly doted on Brother Joe, who invariably wrote them love letters. There was precious little time for love letters, however, during the furious White Supremacy Campaign of 1898, in which the hapless Populists could never surmount the handicap of their irresolute stand on the Negro issue. That issue overshadowed even the bitter intramural quarrel between Republicans and Populists. Indeed, Daniels worked hard to achieve a Democratic fusion with the Populists and pushed for it as a member of the Democratic state convention's platform committee.

Daniels was being torn from two directions. On the one hand, there was growing certainty that the state Democrats could win unaided and unobligated against the feuding Republicans and Populists. On the other hand, National Committeeman Daniels was bound to exert himself for William Jennings Bryan who, as prospective candidate in 1900, wanted Democrats to align themselves with Populists in a more effective voting bloc. As a member of the state convention's platform committee, Daniels quickly learned that white supremacy brooked no compromise with Populists who had shared power with Republicans and had connived at "Negro rule." Friend Aycock, who scented victory on the Democrats' own terms, warned Daniels: "For God's sake do not bring in a minority report." Josiah Bailey was stating the white supremacy case for the conservatives: "We had as well be frank and declare bluntly that North Carolina can never be assured of making political progress until the millstone of 100,000 Negro votes is loosed from her neck." Daniels later recalled that in that day the Negroes "were as truly slaves and chattels to white and Negro politicians as they had been slaves to their owners in slavery days. They were herded to the polls and voted en masse by political taskmasters."[15]

As the election of November 8, 1898, approached, the Democratic press, Daniels' paper included, stirred up the race issue to fever pitch by reporting conditions of "Negro rule" in the Eastern North

Carolina Black Belt. The white supremacy election swept a Democratic legislature into office, with many Populists re-entering their old party and many Negroes staying away from the polls through intimidation. And the floodlight of fevered journalism which *The News and Observer* cast on conditions in the state's chief seaport, where a sinister "Negro rule" supposedly held sway, did its unworthy part in paving the way for that stepchild of sensationalism, the Wilmington race riot. On the day following the riot, Daniels editorialized his relief that Wilmington's Republican officials had resigned without more violence than had already occurred.

> There is not a good citizen of Wilmington or the State who does not regret that the change from no government by incompetents to good government by competent men was attended by a riot that resulted in the loss of human life. From hundreds of homes in North Carolina to-day prayers will go up that quiet, peace and concord may rest upon the chief seaport of North Carolina, and that never again in North Carolina will the people of any city have to pass through another period like that in Wilmington on yesterday.[16]

Unquestionably, the Negro's removal from politics was in the highest degree arbitrary, but Daniels stood with those who said afterwards that "it had to be."

The restored Democracy caused the progressive Daniels many a pang. F. M. Simmons and other conservative leaders of the White Supremacy Campaign had insured their success by bargaining with the editor's enemies. The Simmons men had promised the corporations a two-year moratorium on any tax increase; they had promised the denominational leaders that the biennium would bring no appropriation increase for the state-supported colleges.[17] So Daniels swallowed his disappointment with the new order and buckled down to help make it work. The first order of business was to pass a Suffrage Amendment to the State Constitution, taking the cue from Mississippi, South Carolina, and Louisiana, all of which had disfranchised their Negroes within the decade.

After the Tar Heel Democrats, in April, 1900, nominated a strong state ticket headed by the magnetic Charles B. Aycock and a platform calling for the ratification of the Suffrage Amendment, Josephus Daniels visited Louisiana to report on the working of the "Grandfather Clause" there. This clause was a device by which to avoid disfranchising the illiterate white voter along with the

Negro. It provided that any applicant could register before December 1, 1908, and enjoy permanent registration thereafter, if he had voted, or was a lineal descendant of one who had voted, on or before January 1, 1867 (before the Fifteenth Amendment gave Negroes the vote). The result was never in doubt for, with many Negroes staying away from the polls as intimidating Red Shirt cavalcades rode by, the Suffrage Amendment carried, and the Democrats could now dominate North Carolina politics through depriving the Republicans of about fifty thousand votes.

Daniels was now ready to take his place in the ranks of those who spoke for what C. Vann Woodward has called "Progressivism—For Whites Only."[18] It is difficult for today's reader to examine the White Supremacy Campaign files of *The News and Observer*, replete with racist talk and cruel cartoons, and avoid judging Editor Daniels by today's rules rather than in terms of the values that he then held most dear. Like other decent white Southerners, Daniels concluded that unless the Negro were removed from politics—for he was deemed a surpassing temptation to corrupt white politicians—there could be no communal peace or progress. Like the other decent white leaders, Daniels wanted economic progress for Negroes as well as for whites, free education for Negroes as well as for whites, and manifested a general paternal concern for Negro well-being. However irresponsible and demagogic, therefore, the North Carolina white supremacy politics of 1898 and 1900 in which Daniels played a role, the editor operated thereafter so effectively as an arbiter of political decency that he helped materially to create that Tar Heel climate of opinion in which a Blease or a Bilbo could not flourish. Daniels knew—and sometimes exploited his knowledge—that civil strife threatened in an area where pre-Civil War racial antipathies were still at work and where Negroes were far less advanced than they were later to become. At the political level, especially, Daniels and his reporters did not have to invent what was a very real incompatibility between the races, for white Southerners of that day deeply resented having to deal with Negro officials. Times did indeed change, and from the vantage point of his serene old age Josephus Daniels could examine his newspaper's files and admit: "The paper was cruel in its flagellations. In the perspective of time, I think it was too cruel."[19]

As a stronger party man than Bryan ever was, Daniels fought his party's battles in season and out, in state and out. As the time approached for Bryan's second try for the presidency, Daniels was ready for battle long beforehand. There was a respite of rejoicing in the birth, in 1899, of the editor's second son, who was without question named Worth Bagley in honor of the family's hero-martyr. Before then, however, *The News and Observer* was already sounding the new Democratic battle cry that was to replace free silver—anti-imperialism, and no U.S. annexation of the Philippines. In fact, every Democrat save Bryan seemed to understand that the return of prosperity plus new gold strikes in South Africa and the Yukon had made free silver a dead letter—that a new issue must be made paramount. During the long Democratic drought between Cleveland's election in 1892 and Wilson's twenty years later, Josephus Daniels took a responsible role in every one of those forlorn campaigns. That of 1900 was one of the most forlorn, but Daniels' loyalty and energy remained fully committed. Only privately, never in an editorial, did he confess that the repeated defeats sometimes got him down. "Never will I get as high on the mountain top," he wrote from the headquarters of Bryan's third campaign, "as to feel the fall as I did in 1896."[20]

The campaign of 1900 was almost wholly overshadowed for Daniels by the double-barreled local effort to elect Aycock and to ratify the Suffrage Amendment. Daniels did fight off local anti-Bryan editors like Josiah Bailey and J. P. Caldwell, the latter of whom persisted in calling the Commoner "O'Bryan." Daniels put in long hours at Washington and Chicago meetings of the Democratic national committee, giving the homefolks such tidbits of comfort as that Adlai Stevenson was the 1900 vice-presidential nominee thanks to the North Carolina delegation, and that the anti-imperialist plank was sure to win the votes of the foreign-born. The high point for Daniels came in prenomination February, when the editor joined Bryan's party as the Commoner spoke in Raleigh. Late in that campaign of 1900 Daniels showed what was afoot in the Anthracite Coal Strike parleys, that Mark Hanna had persuaded the mine owners to raise wages and end the strike lest it hurt McKinley's chances on election day.

Josephus Daniels was thoroughly at home in that period of political and social reform known as the Progressive Era, which covered, generally speaking, the years between the Spanish-American and the First World War. Like other Southern progressives, however, he was fated to toil in a provincial rather than in a na-

tional arena.   The prevalence of Negro lynchings after the turn of
the century—though by no means confined to the South—made
many a Southern progressive defensive and thin-skinned about
Southern race relations.   Further, many of the nation's leading progressives were Republicans in politics, and their hostility toward
Southern Democrats matched their ignorance of Southern conditions.   As late as 1912 Senator Robert M. LaFollette avowed that
he knew of no progressive sentiment or legislation in the South.
Not only had Daniels' *News and Observer* begun serializing La-
Follette's autobiography the year before, but by 1924 LaFollette
was to send an emissary to Raleigh seeking Daniels as his Progressive vice-presidential running mate.[21]

It would be difficult to overemphasize the role of Daniels as an
editor who prodded legislators and governors toward the enactment of progressive legislation and who directed progressive sentiment in North Carolina, where, as historian Arthur Link has pointed
out, there was a far-reaching progressive movement long before
LaFollette proclaimed his ignorance of it.   There was not a legislative session between 1899 and 1913 when Editor Daniels was not
in the forefront of those fighting for an effective antitrust law (always frustrated by ineffective enforcement).   He could be counted
on to urge strong regulatory action against the influential railroads,
generally under-assessed, under-taxed, and over-represented in the
General Assembly.   Daniels never had to defend a libel suit in al-
leging railroad-newspaper ties.   He spoke regularly of "the railroad owners of the Morning Post," and he eventually proved very
nearly the same thing of the evening successor to that newspaper,
the *Raleigh Times,* by showing that its editor was on the Southern
Railway payroll.   Daniels also gave no quarter to American Tobacco Company, the dissolution of which trust gave him momentary
cause for rejoicing, and which he regularly charged with practicing extortion upon the farmers, the consumers, and the independent tobacco manufacturers.   In those days when many progressives wrote prohibition into their catalogue of reforms, Daniels
sounded the tocsin in his newspaper against John Barleycorn. The
editor also crusaded without let-up for an effective child labor law
and, though failing consistently to persuade the legislature to enact
a workable law, he made his mark nationally through support of
the National Child Labor Committee.[22]

Daniels was Governor Aycock's editorial voice when the governor personally canvassed the state on behalf of local school taxes in the Educational Awakening. When McIver, as chairman of the campaign committee of the Southern Education Board, met with other leaders in Aycock's office in 1902 and hammered out the "Declaration Against Illiteracy," Daniels glowed with editorial enthusiasm. He applauded the Declaration in favor of "free public schools open to all, supported by the taxes of all its citizens." Here was unvarnished defiance of the bitter-enders who wanted a racial division of school funds—Negro taxes for Negro schools, white taxes for white schools. The editor also gave unstinted support to the campaigns for local taxes, for consolidation of school districts, for better school buildings, for longer school terms, and for better teacher pay. North Carolina was a poor state, but its school expenditures more than quadrupled between 1900 and 1913, going from $950,000 to $4,067,793 in that time.[23]

Josephus Daniels' quarrels with federal judges, Republicans all, became notorious early in the new century, and those fights nearly always involved railroad matters. After helping in the election of Walter Clark as the state's chief justice, Daniels went back to war with the federal judges in such earnest that he wound up with a $2,000 citation for contempt of court. The trouble stemmed from the "Atlantic and North Carolina Railroad Conspiracy," in which Editor Daniels led the fight against the alleged giveaway of that state-owned line. By 1904 that railroad had become a valuable enough property to become a desirable object in the eyes of private financial interests who tried to get control. The method of securing such control lay in alleging mismanagement and applying to a federal judge (Republican) for a receivership. The receivership, duly and unquestioningly granted, was so raw that Daniels' subsequent contempt of court citation (for too-enthusiastic denunciation of the court order in his paper) made him the most popular man in the state.

Daniels refused to pay the fine, refused the proffered money that friends showered down on the court clerk's table, and repaired to "jail" in Room 28 of the Yarborough House with a federal marshal on guard. Rescue came from Daniels' old Republican adversary, Jeter C. Pritchard, who granted a writ of *habeas corpus* from his post on the U.S. Court of Appeals. While the air still rang with Daniels' "I'll rot in jail first!" Judge Henry Groves Connor, the family friend, wrote to reassure the editor's mother: "I thought that you might feel uneasy about Joe, and write to assure you that he is absolutely tops with all of the *good people* standing by him."[24]

Daniels also led the Democrats in keeping the dissension-torn Republicans at a disadvantage. The "Lily White" Republican party in North Carolina grew out of western sentiment, and now that party would no longer seek or even accept support from Negro Republicans in the east. Editor Daniels' most dramatic campaign succeeded in identifying the Republicans with the widely unpopular "South Dakota Bonds." These were old scaled-down North Carolina railroad bonds that South Dakota was induced to accept so that it could sue the Tar Heel state in the U.S. Supreme Court. North Carolina lost the case, but its Republicans suffered even more because ex-Governor Russell had hatched the scheme against his state, and ex-Senator Marion Butler had worked out the South Dakota subterfuge. Always alert to the opportunity of making political capital editorially, Daniels let no North Carolinian ever forget the "villainy" of Russell and Butler.

As a self-conscious Southerner who had helped to "settle" the Negro question, Daniels was not in his best form during the episode in 1903 when he led the clamor to get Professor John Spencer Bassett removed from the faculty of Trinity College. Although a consistent fighter for academic freedom before and after this time, Daniels was later portrayed as a witch hunter because he interpreted the Bassett issue as political—which, in part, it was—instead of one involving academic freedom. Bassett's "inflammatory" remark that Booker T. Washington was "the greatest man, save General Lee, born in the South in a hundred years" was simply the bull's eye of the target against which Daniels could level his fire. The target itself was composed of Republicans, adversaries of the University (Bassett was Kilgo's lieutenant in the Bailey-Kilgo Crusade against the University), spokesmen for the trusts—every important political foeman against whom Daniels had fought during the political warfare of the nineties.[25]

It was not that he loved the twice-defeated Bryan less but that he loved the Democratic party more that Daniels called for the nomination of conservative Alton B. Parker two years before his nomination in 1904. Daniels was to protest in later party councils that Parker was "a dead one," but for now he was reconciled to giving the Democratic conservatives their turn at the Presidential nomination.[26] He was convinced that progressive principles stood no chance outside a party framework and that he had to fight for them as an insider, as National Committeeman Daniels. His contribution to the campaign was essentially a public relations gesture but an effective one. His letters from campaign headquarters reflected more than his usual anxiety to rejoin his family now that it had been enlarged by two more sons. Jonathan Worth (named after the governor in the family) had been born in 1902, and Frank Arthur (named after the editor's beloved elder brother) was born in 1904. That campaign year he was in New York, from which point he described his publicity scheme to Miss Addie:

> We mapped out a scheme to invite every Democratic editor in the United States to come here to a great conference early in September, to have some speeches by leaders, and then to charter a great streamer and take them all up to Esopus [Parker's home], let one make a speech to Judge Parker, have him reply, and returning to have a great banquet on the steamer. We think this would make a great event, would enthuse the editors and give Parker a chance to make a speech that would help in the campaign. The suggestion developed in a talk between your humble servant and James Creelman [who had covered the Spanish-American and Boer Wars for Hearst].[27]

The resultant news coverage, as Daniels had predicted, was voluminous enough to please any candidate, but the dynamic Theodore Roosevelt, running that year for President in his own right, simply was not to be denied. From New York Daniels wrote his wife in mid-campaign: "It seems to me that I was never so busy and never accomplished so little in my life."[28]

Too often Daniels' political battles have caused observers to slight his considerable ability as a man of business. Daniels became editor of *The News and Observer* while heavily burdened with debt, but two decades later he had not only cleared all debts but also was arranging to buy out the last outside stockholders so he could leave an unencumbered estate to Miss Addie and their four sons. If the philanthropic Julian S. Carr was majority stockholder at first, that fact did not put the paper at his disposal when he ran for the U.S. Senate in 1900. As to control of *The News and Observer*, the agreement gave Carr no power over Daniels except on the editor's failure to continue paying off his debts. Pay off Daniels did, and eventually bought up Carr's majority stock in 1905. The wherewithal came partly from the paper's increased income, partly from the then-profitable almanac that Daniels founded, the *North Carolina Year Book and Business Directory.* He also published, as a money-losing literary supplement (1909-1913), the influential *North Carolina Review.*

As editor, Daniels would never promise to omit or suppress legitimate news items however they might embarrass his friends. As no respecter of persons he boldly printed, as long as permitted by law, the names of local people who listed their income for tax purposes (including his own taxable $1,000 from 1901 through 1904). His editorials contained no scintillating prose, but enough direct language with enough repetition to make his points sink in. And he steadfastly refused to run for elective office, insisting he could do more good where he was. After his death in his eighty-sixth year, part of his last will and testament became a standard heading for *The News and Observer's* editorial page, reading: "I advise and enjoin those who direct the paper in the tomorrows never to advocate any cause for personal profit or preferment. I would wish it always to be 'the tocsin' and devote itself to the policies of equality and justice to the underprivileged. If the paper should at any time be the voice of self-interest or become the spokesman of privilege or selfishness it would be untrue to its history." Long before, it had become a North Carolina truism that Josephus Daniels "can't be bought and can't be scared."[29]

Even physical encounters, common in those days of personal peril to editors, did not deter Daniels, who was by conviction a personal pacifist. Many an antagonist went gunning actively for Daniels, even fellow-editor J. P. Caldwell of the *Charlotte Observer,* whom teetotaler Daniels had criticized for his drinking. There were, among many other encounters, one with Editor R. W. Simpson of the *Raleigh Times,* which Daniels boldly labeled a railroad organ, and with W. B. (Buck) Jones, whose political ring in Raleigh Daniels was crusading against. One Baxter Shemwell, whom Daniels had denounced as a dangerous scofflaw, had killed a man and then almost did the like for Daniels, who was lying helpless in a curtained Pullman berth while a conductor white-lied Shemwell off the train. "I am sure that the angels blotted a tear and blotted out that falsehood told to prevent murder," Daniels recalled of the episode.[30] It is worth noting that Josephus Daniels survived all these encounters with the respect of the people among whom he lived. Above all, there is no evidence that violence, intimidation, or threats ever sufficed to make him change his opinions or change so much as one word in any editorial he ever wrote.

Editor Daniels' family occupied the Bagley house at the once-fashionable corner of East South and Blount Streets. Major Bagley, as Governor Worth's private secretary, had bought it originally because of its proximity to the old Governor's Mansion, but the new one of Victorian gingerbread was built farther away, and the Danielses lived in what was now principally a Negro neighborhood. The old paternal regard for the Negroes was attested by the family's back porch medical dispensary operated by Miss Addie, who once dealt young Jonathan a severe whipping for referring to a Negro hired man as a "nigger." The nearest neighbor was the Negro alderman and merchant Wesley Hoover, who had worked for the Jonathan Worth family. The governor's daughter, later Mrs. Bagley, had taught Hoover to read.[31]

In those years every member of the legislature was invited to the Daniels home for dinner (the guests would have to do their liquor drinking beforehand or not at all). The Daniels home was a regular center for the entertainment of important visitors to Raleigh, especially such notables as William Jennings Bryan, at whose huge appetite the little Daniels boys all goggled. The unveiling of the Worth Bagley statue on Capitol Square was a notable event (May 20, 1907). There were speeches by Spanish-American war heroes, but all took second place to the sight of seven-year-old Worth Bagley Daniels, dressed in a sailor suit and guided by his tall young uncle, Ensign David Worth Bagley, as the lad unveiled the statue of the uncle whose name he bore.[32]

Daniels' own resounding good health seemed to bolster an already alert and confident frame of mind that had made him an ebullient extrovert. Going off to nearby Jackson Springs (to cure an apparently psychogenic sciatica), or to New York or Atlantic City, presented no problems to an editor's family then, for there were always plenty of due bills in the till, exchanges of accommodations for advertising. The same went for circuses and theatricals. In the usual poor-mouth political talk of that day, Daniels always spoke of himself as a poor man. But the cost of living was low and there was little cash outlay (Daniels' annual salary was to rise to $3,000 by 1912), and the busy father would direct his boys to the paper's cashier, with an easy: "Go see Miss Mamie [Horton] and ask her for a nickel."[33]

Every week Daniels taught his Sunday school class of A. and M. college boys, and shared with them his uncomplicated faith that accounted for both his growing serenity and his very real moral courage. Every Sunday afternoon he went walking with the boys, usually letting them clamber all over an old railway locomotive parked near a crossing. The parents had another little girl, in 1911, but it was a "blue baby" and did not survive. "There never was a baby so welcome or so beautiful," the sorrowful father wrote to Miss Addie's spinster sisters. "Addie is brave and brokenhearted. The children are dear in their new grief."[34] Daniels always mourned not having daughters, and he saw to it that there were never daughters-in-law in his family; his son's wives became his daughters.

By this time the editor's mother was living in Goldsboro, N.C., where she had moved in 1906 to help rear the children of son Frank on his wife's death. Mother Daniels was now lame, having broken her hip in stepping off a train a decade before, and she now got about with the help of a silver-headed cane. In Goldsboro, where everybody called her "Granny," she went to church every time the bell rang and sat on the very front row. Not a big talker herself, she had the gift of drawing out people, and her deep interest in others made her a universal favorite. All Goldsboro knew Granny Daniels' Christmas custom, which consisted of buying only one gift, exchanging it for the next one brought to her, and so on finally to a one-gift Christmas with no great mass of wrappings left over. The indomitable ex-postmistress, who read *The News and Observer* every morning, was proud of her three sons, telling Miss Addie about Joe: "Any time you get tired of him, send him back to me."[35] Frank, with his delicate digestion and strict diet, was elected a Superior Court judge in 1910 and remained one all his life. Charles was elected in 1901 as solicitor (prosecutor) of the Fourth District, including his boyhood home of Wilson, N.C., and served there until the Democratic victory of 1912 earned him a federal post.

Josephus Daniels was so wrapped up in his role as political editor that Miss Addie early became accustomed to handing him his tips and spending money. Life moved easily in those innocent days when Editor Daniels regularly appeared at the polls with one of his young sons to deposit the father's ballot as a civics lesson. Everybody recognized Daniels for the almost compulsive neatness of his old-fashioned clothes (a political trademark), and admired the beauty of his family life. The tender-hearted father kissed his sons and expected them to kiss him; he would ride home with one of them from the train and hold his hand all the way. Miss Addie called him Mr. Daniels, in those days of conventional deference to husbands, but in the privacy of the family she called him "Beautiful."[36]

In Bryan's third try for the presidency, Daniels loyally followed his old leader to defeat. The editor's chief contribution to the 1908 campaign turned out to be a difficult piece of diplomacy in getting Governor Charles N. Haskell of Oklahoma to resign in mid-campaign as treasurer of the Democratic national committee. Haskell had been attacked in the Hearst press for allegedly shady railroad dealings in the past as well as for connections with Standard Oil. Haskell had to go, and everyone at Democratic headquarters seemed to agree that Daniels should be the one to bell the cat. The editor hurried to Joliet, Illinois, where he boarded Haskell's Chicago-bound train to perform his unpleasant duty and also keep Haskell away from Republican reporters who might pounce on his angry reaction and make a scandal. "I felt like an executioner," Daniels wrote Miss Addie at the time.[37]

Daniels headed the Press Bureau in Chicago for Bryan's 1908 campaign. This time money was scarce, his letters reported, unlike the well-financed campaign for Parker. He complained to Miss Addie that "there are so many cranks to talk to," apparently referring to the anti-Catholic zealots who were drawn to Bryan because of opponent Taft's alleged over-friendliness to Rome. As he followed Bryan on the campaign trail to New York, Daniels reflected the changing tides: "One day it looks like Bryan is sure to win; the next day it looks like he cannot carry New York. And the conflicts and the problems—how tired I am of it all."[38]

Back in North Carolina, things political were more hopeful. When the still-young ex-Senator Butler, now a Republican, tried for a political comeback in 1910, he ran head-on into Daniels' implacable enmity. The Republican aspirant was not only an ex-Demo-

crat and ex-Populist but, as Daniels inexorably reminded the electorate, a party to the old "South Dakota Bonds" episode. Repeated
almost daily in *The News and Observer* was Daniels' angrily effective slogan: "Butler, Booze, Boodle and Bonds." Predictably, the
electorate refused to listen to the frustrated Butler's explanations
that he was being unjustly attacked for having peddled additional
bonds—fraudulent Reconstruction ones— and the Republican party
was overwhelmed.[39] His fellow Democrats fully recognized Daniels' growth in political influence and his claim on their gratitude.
They took up a state-wide subscription and presented him with a
silver service as a Christmas gift.

After all the lean political years, Daniels scented victory in the
approach to the climactic battles of 1912. There was a pitfall in
North Carolina, where he would have to steer successfully in a three-
way senatorial primary between Chief Justice Walter Clark, Governor W. W. Kitchin, and Senator F. M. Simmons. In the meantime
Daniels was mourning the premature death of Charles B. Aycock,
whom he would have preferred as senator to any of them. After
Aycock's death in April, 1912, National Committeeman Daniels dictated a rigorously neutral course to *The News and Observer* staff.
Because this neutrality seemed to favor the incumbent Simmons, a
"Committee of Engineers" warned the editor—then in New York
with the Wilson forces—that his paper "must not publish any more
matter in advocacy of Simmons, paid or otherwise." If Daniels did
not comply, the Committee was ready to resort to political blackmail: the Engineers would make affidavit about Daniels' overheated
talk during the White Supremacy Campaign, and reveal the details
of Henry Bagley's alleged philandering.[40] Daniels paid the Engineers no heed, and later Simmons won an easy victory. The only
unfortunate by-product was that the doughty Walter Clark felt that
Daniels had let him down, acquiescing in the victory of the conservative Simmons. The fact is, however, that Clark stood not a ghost
of a chance to win. Daniels' progressive and anti-Simmons views
had stood a chance of realization with Aycock in possible victory
but none with Clark in certain defeat. As a liberal and progressive,
Daniels supported—or at least did not oppose—the conservative Simmons just as he had supported the equally conservative Parker, and
for the same reasons of closing party ranks.[41]

The Woodrow Wilson campaign, on the other hand, was for
Josephus Daniels a labor of love. As early as 1886 Daniels had

heard his fellow-Wataugan Walter Page talk up the young professor's presidential possibilities. In 1897 Daniels had editorially commended Dr. Wilson for an article in Page's *Atlantic Monthly,* and in 1908 had given over the columns of his paper to excerpts from Wilson's baccalaureate address at Princeton. The Wilson biographer, Arthur Walworth, says that president-maker George Harvey sought to flatter Daniels on Wilson's behalf, that Harvey did so by giving over a page of *Harper's Weekly* in 1911 to Daniels' silver anniversary as editor of *The News and Observer.*[42] If so, Harvey could have spared himself the trouble, because more than two years earlier, on January 21, 1909, after Dr. Wilson spoke in Chapel Hill on Robert E. Lee, Daniels wrote for his paper a virtual promise of support for a Wilson presidential candidacy. By the time Wilson's pre-nomination campaign of 1911 brought him back to Chapel Hill to address a Commencement audience, Josephus Daniels was an all-out partisan for Wilson. And he went on from there, against great odds in the state convention, to get his state's Democrats to "endorse" Wilson after they balked at sending an instructed delegation to the Baltimore Convention.

The pre-nomination campaign gave Daniels a chance to show a nationwide audience his mediating skill in mending that breach between Bryan and Wilson opened by the notorious Joline Letter. In early 1912 the Republican *New York Sun* sought to weaken Wilson's prospects by publishing the embarrassing missive written by Wilson five years before to Adrian H. Joline, a railroad president and a Princeton trustee. It included the statement: "Would that we could do something, at once dignified and effective, to knock Mr. Bryan, once for all, into a cocked hat."[43] Fortunately for Wilson's hopes, Bryan was at the moment of publication a guest in Daniels' home. The editor calmed down the Commoner, who then gave cold comfort to the *Sun* correspondent seeking to exploit the breach. Then the two old friends entrained together for Washington where both attended the Jackson Day Dinner. Daniels urged Governor Wilson—who complied—to make graceful acknowledgment of Bryan's courage, wisdom, and past service to the party.

As a friend of both men Josephus Daniels was in a strategic position on the executive of the national committee. Bryan did not want the temporary chairmanship of the Baltimore Convention, but rather than give it over to Alton B. Parker and the domination of the conservative New York forces, the Commoner decided on a floor fight to defeat Parker. When Bryan wired the various presidential aspirants for their support against Tammany, Wilson was the only one who agreed with Bryan without quibbling. When Bryan was defeated in this fight, Daniels rightly viewed it as a Pyrrhic victory for the conservatives. Wilson's gesture later helped determine Bryan to withdraw his support from Champ Clark and throw it behind Wilson on fourteenth ballot.

Daniels served not only as an important Wilson floor manager but as dispenser of press passes with the help of Josephus, Jr. The editor was so busy that he interviewed callers while sitting in his tub and, after a subsequent fall in his bath, had to be taped so completely that he had to miss many another bath in steamy Baltimore. Daniels was one of those who steadfastly counseled Wilson by telephone not to release his delegates, as he had been advised to do at one point by his despairing campaign manager, McCombs. Wilson's eventual nomination which, as Arthur Link has shown, represented the culminating point of a progressive movement in the South, was for that very reason a disappointment to the candidate of the Progressive party, Theodore Roosevelt. "Pop is praying," Daniels later quoted Kermit Roosevelt, "for the nomination of Clark" [as the less progressive and therefore less effective competitor].[44]

The bitterly disappointed Champ Clark made up publicly with Wilson at Sea Girt, N.J., but Miss Addie, looking on, was not deceived. "Wasn't Champ horrid about everything the day he went to see Gov. Wilson," she wrote Daniels. Sea Girt was now the seat of power, and Governor Wilson requested nine aides, Daniels included, to meet there to appoint all campaign committees. "He calls the nine his confidential cabinet," Daniels wrote, not without pride, "—made up only of those with whom he can talk as to members of his own family." During the campaign Daniels headed the Publicity Bureau housed in New York's old Fifth Avenue Hotel, and there he remained except for a family bout of typhoid (Worth, Frank, and Miss Addie) that brought him to Raleigh in October. As the campaign neared its close, he wrote Miss Addie: "It seems certain that we will win our fight, but the very audacity and snap and vigor of the Roosevelt forces and the apparent inertness of the Taft forces causes some of our folks to have qualms." When the victory did materialize, Daniels emerged as one of Wilson's most deserving lieutenants, particularly earning the candidate's gratitude for keeping the feuding McAdoo and McCombs "from tearing headquarters apart."[45]

Daniels was North Carolina's acknowledged "candidate" for the Cabinet, but he bided his time in Raleigh and listened to all the talk while saying nothing. He confessed to William G. McAdoo that he was staying away from President-elect Wilson lest he be taken for a job-hunter. To McAdoo he also confided—and he did the same to Editor Henry Watterson—that Josephus Daniels might be unqualified for a Cabinet post. The most vigorous opponent of Daniels' appointment was Walter Hines Page, who had refused from the first to support Bryan and had conceived a great contempt for Bryan's admirers. To the question of whether he thought Daniels was Cabinet timber, Page fairly shouted: "He isn't a splinter!" and hurried off to New Jersey to try to talk Woodrow Wilson out of his resolve to appoint Daniels. Page claimed to have interceded with Wilson in late February, 1913, too late to head off Wilson's already mailed appointment letter to Daniels. Daniels knew better. He got from William Bayard Hale, a staff member of Page's own *World's Work,* an account that Page had entered his protest to Wilson in December, 1912, and had been turned down flat.[46]

At length came the confidential letter from the President-elect, dated February 23, 1913: "I have been sweating blood over the cabinet choices, and have decided to beg of you that you will do me the very great service of accepting the Secretaryship of the Navy. I know of no one I trust more entirely or affectionately, and I am sure that you will trust and believe me when I assure you that you will, in my judgment, best serve the party and its new leader by accepting the post. I cannot spare you from my council table." Daniels' acceptance went forward on February 25, 1913. To his mother-in-law he enclosed a copy of Wilson's letter, saying: "It was not dictated, but was written in his own hand. . . . I value it more highly than the position."[47]

When it came time to select an Assistant Secretary, Daniels first ascertained from Wilson that the President had no one in mind for the job and then suggested the name of Franklin D. Roosevelt, whom he had met at the Baltimore Convention. The seasoned Tar Heel ought to have an assistant, he told Wilson, "from another section, preferably New York or New England." Daniels was fifty years old and Roosevelt thirty. They made an oddly assorted pair, this provincial editor and the patrician from Groton and Harvard.

Roosevelt later confided to a Presidential secretary about Daniels: "When I first knew him, he was the funniest looking hillbilly I had ever seen."[48]

Young Franklin Roosevelt had a lot to learn about his "hillbilly" superior in the string tie and broad-brimmed hat, the man whom he, as long as he lived, was to call affectionately "Chief." He did not yet know that Daniels had, as Ray Stannard Baker later realized, "a gift of making warm, personal friends of men who at first regarded him lightly."[49] The energetic pugnacity of Daniels in his early years sometimes alienated people just as Roosevelt's early haughtiness did. Later, Justice Oliver Wendell Holmes was to hail Roosevelt for his "first-class temperament."[50] Similarly, as Daniels was maturing in the pre-Wilson years, it was discernible that he was developing a "first-class temperament" of his own.

Chapter three

Daniels and the New Freedom

It had been twenty years since Daniels had last seen a Democratic President inaugurated, so it is small wonder that President Wilson's daughter Eleanor found Daniels "twinkling and chatty" on that happy March 4, 1913, with the plumply handsome Miss Addie beaming alongside. At the first Cabinet meeting on the next day Daniels advanced exuberantly on Agriculture Secretary Houston, exclaiming: "Isn't it great" "Isn't it wonderful?"[1]

The new Navy Secretary's enthusiasm was not in the least dampened by the cancellation of the usual Inaugural Ball, for he did not—as a practicing Methodist—dance anyhow. More, the frugal Daniels had saved Miss Addie the cost of a new gown by correctly foretelling cancellation of the ball. On a pre-Inaugural social call on Ellen Axson Wilson, to whom he had described the glitter of the 1893 Inaugural Ball (observed from the gallery), Daniels had found the new First Lady confiding her distaste for commercializing such events. In any case the ushering-in of the Wilsonian New Freedom was tonic to the naturally buoyant Daniels, whose youthful optimism in his fifty-first year was as marked as ever. If he was provincial by some Washington standards, he was also capable of learning and growing. A "first-class temperament" and a capacity for growth go a long way toward explaining the success of this small-town editor in the Cabinet of a crisis-ridden administration. In his two full terms as Navy Secretary—matched only by another editor, Gideon Welles—Daniels left a record as a strong executive who revolutionized the Navy's attitude toward its enlisted men, whom he invested with new dignity. His predecessor, George von L. Meyer, was the only one of six previous Secretaries who had served a full four-year term, and Meyer warned Daniels to "keep the power to direct the Navy here," and significantly tapped the Secretary's massive desk. Daniels did so.[2]

Even when he was torpedoing hostile admirals, Daniels radiated a combination of common sense and amiability that his friends cherished—and none more so than Woodrow Wilson. In important ways they saw the world through the same peephole. As fellow-Southerners, Wilson and Daniels had shared the New South's growing pains and an inherited memory of the Civil War. As the son of a Presbyterian minister Wilson shared with his Methodist Navy Secretary an easy authority on Bible passages, and Wilson always enjoyed Daniels' ribbing him about Calvinistic predestination. There was a tangible warmth between the two men, undoubtedly bred of Wilson's sure feel for Daniels' loyal admiration. At the very first White House reception given by the Wilsons, Mrs. Daniels, who was chatting with the President, was horrified to see her husband unconcernedly sit down while the President stood. Miss Addie agitatedly clicked her heels together and looked daggers at her husband, who started to his feet just as Wilson intercepted the signal. He walked over to Daniels, smilingly pressed him back into his chair, and said: "Sit down and behave yourself."[3]

As for Franklin D. Roosevelt, it was part of his good fortune that his only administrative superior during a long public career was Josephus Daniels. The handsome young aristocrat, the Wilsonian State Senator with a record of mild insurgency against Tammany Hall, moved in an entirely different social world from that of his chief, and the two men represented two utterly different Americas. They were never as close and cordial, especially during Wilson's first term, as FDR's campaign biographers of 1932 tried to make out. Young Roosevelt fancied homself a disciple of Mahan in naval strategy and was greatly impressed with cousin Theodore Roosevelt, another amateur naval enthusiast. FDR thought Daniels too slow for words, and the young man's impatience—it often bordered on insubordination—would have cost the head of any admiral who had dared venture into such turbulent waters.

Daniels' toleration of FDR was later deemed "a miracle" by the latter's son James. Daniels himself said that it had been a case of "love at first sight," but the evidence shows that the mellow old memoirist was overstating the case. There was, to be sure, something akin to father-son affection on Daniels' part, and that partly helps account for the older man's invincible tolerance. But on the whole the two men were really wary of one another; Franklin energetically eager to show his administrative competence, and Daniels careful to give him just enough free rein. Daniels' attitude may be more justly likened to watchful waiting than to love at first sight. Elliot Roosevelt, whose father's personal letters included some derogatory of Josephus Daniels, conceded as an editor that those letters were "far more illustrative of the growth of F.D.R.'s personality than of Daniels' competence as Secretary of the Navy."[4]

Daniels quickly made his mark on the Navy Department by smilingly refusing to rubber-stamp letters prepared for his signature. Accustomed to long hours as an editor, he took naturally to working away until well after six despite a closing time of 4:30. He pursued his Navy education, studied past legislation, made his geniality serve him in learning through shop-talk. As he put a firm hand to the helm, he quickly met resistance to his vigorous assertion of civilian supremacy. The resistance came chiefly in the diminutive form of Rear Admiral Bradley A. Fiske, able enough but devoid of personal loyalty to the Secretary, who was Daniels' inherited Aid for Operations. The aggressive little Fiske was forever pressing for a General Staff system with himself on top. He was already ranking member of the Council of Aids, the first among four supposedly equal officers who made up the unsatisfactory Aid System that was Daniels' inheritance.

The new Secretary quickly gave notice of his independence. Finding himself unhappy with two advisers—Templin M. Potts, Aid for Personnel, and Philip Andrews, Chief of the Bureau of Navigation—Daniels got rid of both because, as he notified President Wilson, they "appear to hold together on every subject." As to Potts, Daniels said bluntly: "I have absolutely no confidence in him." As to Andrews, for whom Daniels had a ready replacement in the Spanish-American War hero Victor Blue, the Secretary wrote of needing an officer "to whom I feel confident I can express my wishes . . . knowing that they will be carried out to the letter and that I need not fear that anything brought by him to me for my signature is unjust or improper." Daniels rid himself of deadwood by his early-adopted Single Oak Policy (named by Navy officers after Daniels' first rented house in Washington) which required adequate sea duty of all officers and a single-term limit for the Staff Corps. That Daniels did not insist on yes-men is amply borne out by his suffering along two years with Admiral Fiske, whom he could have dismissed out of hand.[5] On the other hand, the Secretary let it be known that officers ought not to reject ideas simply because of lack of precedent. All this took place before Daniels served out his first month, by which time the energetic Secretary had witnessed the fleet target practice and had personally inspected every nearby Navy installation.

While Daniels was about to address an Associated Press Banquet in New York, little more than a month after taking office, he was given the dismaying news that *The News and Observer* plant had been destroyed by fire. The hard financial blow was eased, however, by the way Tar Heel friends rallied around. The rival *Raleigh Times* plant was put at the disposal of Daniels' paper so that not a single issue was skipped. Miss Addie's brother Henry, the paper's business manager, got up a campaign by which many readers volunteered to prepay their subscriptions in order to help meet the money crisis. Daniels wrote typically to his old friend, Judge Henry Groves Connor: "When I reached Raleigh on Friday and saw the ruins of a perfect plant, I felt very poor. But when I received such letters as yours from many friends I felt rich." Shortly thereafter, on the day following his fifty-first birthday, he addressed his home folks in Washington, N.C., who tendered the honored native son a banquet. There he embraced his old mother, and he and Miss Addie stayed the night at the Wiley Rodman home built on the site of Daniels' birthplace. In his speech, "The Love of Home is the Seed of Patriotism," the Secretary paid tribute to his mother and—for the benefit of those who credited the tales about alleged treason to the Confederacy—to the father whom he had never known, of the father who "came home broken in health and soon lost his life upon a mission of love—a mission that he was too unwell to have undertaken."[6]

Brothers Frank and Charles were proud of the Secretary too. While Frank remained on the Superior Court bench, Charles later got a Justice Department post in which he successfully prosecuted a number of Indian fraud cases. The close-knit family rejoiced not only in Brother Joe's good fortune but in his really beautiful home life. Outsiders admired it too, like President Wilson's comely daughter Jessie. Shortly before announcing her engagement to Francis B. Sayre, Jessie Wilson wrote to Miss Addie with whom she wanted to share her happiness: "When I saw you at the Palmers' luncheon just before your anniversary [the Danielses' twenty-fifth, in 1913] I felt that I could wish nothing better than to be so radiant and happy and happiness-giving as you are." The Danielses and their four young boys spent the first of their Washington years at Single Oak, their suburban home, and the remaining years in another big rented house—though without the same outdoor space—on Wyoming Avenue. With her ease in the social sphere, Miss Addie quickly proved herself a real better half to the Navy Secretary.[7]

Daniels had to face his first international crisis as early as May, 1913, in the form of a full-blown Japanese war scare. The restriction on Japanese immigration implicit in the earlier "Gentleman's Agreement" was now defiantly exacerbated by the California legislature, which enacted an openly anti-Japanese alien land bill. Too, President Wilson had broken up the exploitive banking consortium (Japan was a member) as if to rebuke the Japanese desire to expand at the expense of the new Chinese Republic. Still, did the Japanese Cabinet really want war? Wilsonians like Daniels guessed no, correctly as it turned out, and Daniels' Navy Department aides guessed wrong.

Believing that a Japanese-American war was imminent, the Army-Navy Joint Board urged the transfer of Chinese-based American warships to the Philippines. Not only did the Navy's General Board concur, but Admiral Fiske personally urged Daniels to order out the warships before it was too late. Fiske went on the record with two long memoranda to the Secretary, and expostulated further, but Daniels stubbornly held his fire. Nor could the aggressive War Secretary Garrison move him either. Daniels insisted on referring the Joint Board's recommendation to the President himself, and Wilson reacted as Daniels knew he would—he was outraged at the idea of such reckless provocation. Daniels' own opinion, voiced at Cabinet meetings, held that the Japanese would not only view the ship movements as warlike but could easily intercept the American ships in any case.

As if the President was not already angry enough at the Joint Board, he was exasperated further by its recommendations' being leaked to the press. The indignant Wilson at once directed his War and Navy Secretaries to order the Joint Board not to meet again without his express authorization. Many years later, while in Washington testifying in favor of armed forces unification and for civilian supremacy, Daniels put the blame for the near-war directly on Fiske and the political general, Leonard Wood. As might have been expected, the administration's gingerly handling of Japanese-American tensions infuriated the activist Theodore Roosevelt, who wrote sympathetically to Governor Hiram Johnson, who had signed California's anti-Japanese bill despite pleas from the President and Secretary of State. TR's Big Stick letter attacked the President's "literally criminal misconduct in entrusting the State Department and the Navy Department to Bryan and Daniels."[8]

Just as Daniels' "pacifism" and his Single Oak Policy on officers' berths made the admirals sit up and take notice, Daniels' well-known hostility to monopoly caused a stir among the Navy's suppliers. As early as May, 1913, the new Secretary, abetted in the Senate by one-eyed Ben Tillman as chairman of the Naval Affairs Committee, went on record as favoring a government armor plant. He had studied bids and found that armor plate contracts had been arbitrarily divided among the only three companies that could make the product, Bethlehem, Midvale, and Carnegie. Such open flouting of competitive bidding resulted in what Daniels indignantly denounced as a virtual subsidy. Later that year he urged the government establish an oil refinery to escape the alleged exactions of Standard Oil. Daniels consistently overruled those advisers who urged him to waive competitive bids, and on one such occasion in 1913 the high but favored bidder landed the contract behind the Secretary's back. Louis McHenry Howe, Man Friday to Franklin D. Roosevelt in the Navy Department, wryly reported that "there appears to have been some fancy figuring done and today a man who was low is haunting Mr. Danels' office with a complaint of some kind."[9]

Daniels never won his unequal fight with the privileged corporations, but he did fight them to a standstill. The classic encounter came in the summer of 1913, and Franklin Roosevelt recalled fondly how his old chief had faced the three identical bidders for armor plate. "So old Joe Daniels sent for them. I loved his words. He said, 'Gentlemen . . . this, I am afraid, is collusive bidding for you, all three, to arrive at exactly the same figure. I am afraid I have got to throw the bids out and ask for new bids.' And one of them stepped forward and said, 'Mr. Secretary,' with a perfectly solemn face, 'Mr. Secretary, it was a pure coincidence.' And Daniels said, 'Well, the bids are all rejected and we will open new bids at 12:00 o'clock tomorrow. Sharpen your pencils, think it over during the night and don't have another coincidence.'" And when the gentlemen came in with the same kind of coincidence next day, Daniels sent FDR off to New York to solicit the bid of a visiting British steel magnate. That competing bid brought the American Big Three to terms.[10]

Safeguarding the Navy's oil reserves occupied eight years of unremitting struggle by the Secretary. President Taft had set aside Naval oil reserves No. 1 and No. 2 in California (Wilson added the unimportant but more notorious Teapot Dome in Wyoming), and all during those eight years two administrative nightmares haunted Daniels and his aides. The first was to protect the government land from nearby drilling that might drain off the Navy's oil. The second was to protect the government's title against private claims, some legitimate and others unquestionably fraudulent. During the New Freedom days most of the oil men's pressure was concentrated on obtaining title to the lands. Later, when these men understood that Daniels had foiled them, they shifted to requests for various leasing legislation. It was an abuse of the latter principle that led to the later scandal of Teapot Dome. Daniels got the Justice Department to appoint special counsel to defend the government's oil against private claimants. Moreover, these attorneys were North Carolinians whom Daniels trusted: first, E. J. Justice, a fighting progressive, and after his death, J. Crawford Biggs, later Solicitor General under FDR. These Tar Heels consistently prevailed in the courts.

After the end of his first summer as Secretary, Daniels had visited every Navy installation from coast to coast. His attendance at spring target practice in Hampton Roads had merely whetted Daniels' eagerness to see more of the Navy. On that occasion, memorialized by a series of delightful photos, the Danielses played host to President Wilson's daughters, most of the Cabinet, and the young Franklin D. Roosevelt (the seasick-prone Eleanor Roosevelt hated naval reviews). That occasion was also marked by a Daniels-the-landlubber anecdote that FDR loved to tell. He and Daniels were sitting with the admiral after dinner when the latter's aide came in and addressed his superior: "I wish to report, sir, that all is secure." The admiral nodded a cue at Daniels who, not knowing he could have replied with a quiet "Very well," responded, in spontaneous cordiality: "Well, I declare! That's fine! I'm mighty glad to hear it!"[11]

After the Japanese war scare, Daniels set out on the first leg of his tour. In the course of it he took his first airplane ride, an eight-minute flight over Annapolis on May 21, 1913. Piloted by Lt. John H. Towers, the pioneer Navy aviator, Daniels wrapped himself in a borrowed overcoat for his open-cockpit aerial inspection of the Naval Academy. At the next Cabinet meeting President Wilson wanted to know why his Navy Secretary must risk his life, so Daniels explained: "I must sign orders for Naval officers to fly and I will not order any man to do anything I will not do myself." Postmaster General Burleson, not knowing that he would personally inaugurate an air mail service a few years later, murmured to Daniels, affectionately, "You are a damn fool."[12]

At Erie, Pennsylvania, on the centennial of the Battle of Lake Erie, Daniels spoke to a welcoming crowd in the shadow of the old brig *Niagara*. He left behind him, on that July 10, a characteristically moral "Declaration of Independence" that was later distributed by the local YMCA: "Resolved, That I will not be the slave of any habit, good or bad; . . . that I will cultivate my mind, and make it a storehouse for wisdom; that I will respond to the calls of conscience and duty. . . ." A few days later he left for a tour of the Pacific Coast bases, and at Seattle found himself acclaimed for the kind of flag-waving jingo he never was.

Seattle's respectable elements, Daniels' hosts, were then feuding with their mayor, whom they considered too indulgent to the radical I.W.W. Wobblies, the Industrial Workers of the World. On seeing a giant-sized American flag at the banquet, Daniels cast aside his Navy speech and patriotically set sail on a handsome apostrophe to Old Glory, an apostrophe which drew wild applause far beyond the oration's merits. The outcome was that some sailors aboard the *West Virginia*, where Daniels and Miss Addie were lunching, went ashore where they wrecked the I.W.W. Hall and burned its furniture. Daniels later saw to the punishment of the guilty sailors, and in some embarrassment made his explanations—as a well-known pro-labor editor—to West Coast labor leaders. In the meantime he persisted in his studies of Pacific Coast bases and bases-to-be, notably those at Mare Island and San Diego, mastering more Navy lore every day and making speeches less incendiary than at Seattle. At San Francisco he told the women of the Civic League: "We may as well get ready for the inevitable, for women are going to vote."[13]

Daniels never let up in his search for trustworthy officers whose gifts exceeded their rank, and on the record he did surpassingly well. One little-known salvage operation involved Richard E. Byrd, later the world-famous explorer. Byrd caught Daniels' eye when the Secretary inspected the Brooklyn Navy Yard in 1913 and found Ensign Byrd giving up his Sunday afternoons to teach a Sunday school class of newly enlisted sailors. Later, when an ankle injury threatened to cut short Byrd's Navy career, Daniels got the young officer transferred to Aviation where an inability to stand sea watches would not disqualify him.[14] The devout and "pacifist" Navy Secretary rejoiced that year as his friend Bryan brought forth the first of his thirty-odd conciliation treaties providing for "cooling off" periods. With Bryan he rejoiced at this beating of swords into plowshares, and took home from a treaty-signing one of the handsome little plowshare paperweights the Commoner was distributing to his friends.

Daniels was glad to echo Bryan's peaceable sentiments, and did so in his first Annual Report (December 1, 1913). There he enlarged upon the naval holiday idea recently put forward by Winston Churchill, Britain's First Lord of the Admiralty. Daniels contended that Churchill's projected one-year naval holiday was inadequate if the participants were restricted to two or even three great powers. Let there be, he said, a multi-nation accord on the limiting of competitive naval building so that navies might be "adequate" rather than gargantuan. "Ten years ago," Daniels' Annual Report said, "our largest battleship cost $5,382,000. The next dreadnaught will cost $14,044,000. When is this accelerating expenditure to be reduced?" He never got an answer.

By the time Congress reconvened in January, 1914, Daniels had already established himself as a virtuoso in the art of getting along with the legislative branch. The men on Capitol Hill liked Daniels and felt comfortable with this man who so thoroughly understood politics and politicians. The Southern Democrats, who dominated the chairmanships, quickly became his particular friends, men like Lemuel P. Padgett on the House side of Naval Affairs and Ben Tillman, and after his death Claude Swanson, on the Senate side. From

North Carolina itself there were Claude Kitchin, chairman of Ways and Means and Majority Leader, and F. M. Simmons, chairman of the Senate Finance Committee. The erstwhile coolly correct Simmons-Daniels relations became warmer now that the former partisan of the "Republican" Payne-Aldrich Tariff put his name on the Underwood-Simmons Tariff of the New Freedom. Even the Republicans on the naval committees generally got along with the Democratic Daniels, and in one case swimmingly—that of Thomas S. Butler, who became chairman of the House committee after the Republicans later regained control of Congress. Even Daniels' nominal adversaries in the congressional committees came to respect his concern for saving the government's money, for observing both letter and spirit of congressional intentions in statutes, and for the principles that underlay his naval reforms.

Daniels' frugal naval estimates in his first Annual Report found the House Naval Affairs Committee generally receptive. He got only perfunctory sniping for having asked for only two dreadnaughts instead of the four recommended by the Navy's General Board (he made the overruled Board's report an appendix to his Report). The Board had noted, quite correctly, the absence of a coherent naval policy, but the Committee paid more heed to Daniels' optimistic statement that never had the Navy been "in such a high state of efficiency as today." With the New Freedom proceeding under a full head of steam, the Committeemen were content enough to go along with Daniels' building program. Moreover, after questioning Daniels closely about his various first-year reforms, they found themselves much impressed.

The new Secretary had questioned the unnecessary duplication of Marines and Army in the Panama Canal Zone. He rehearsed in detail the collusion in armor plate bidding, including the saving of $378,261 plus one contract award to an English firm by advertising for bids on specially treated steel. He argued for more than the present token Navy manufacture of smokeless powder, showing that the "Du Pont Powder Trust" had charged the Navy anywhere from seventy down to fifty-three cents whereas the Navy was already making it for thirty-seven. He got authority to build ships at Navy Yards after bids to private shipbuilders had come back too high. He answered searching questions on his plan for introducing compulsory education in the Navy, his desire for more teaching officers, and he won unanimous praise for his plans for naval prison reform. He described as "worse than brutal" the situation at the Portsmouth, New Hampshire, Naval Prison where, he told the Congressmen, he had found more Marine guards than prisoners.[15]

Daniels' Navy reforms proceeded largely from his educational zeal, as enunciated on the first page of his initial Annual Report, saying that "the Secretary has given less thought to the guns than to the men behind the guns." His ambition was to make the Navy "a great university." He wrote: "Every ship should be a school, and every enlisted man and petty and warrant officer should receive the opportunity to improve his mind, better his position and fit himself for promotion." By the beginning of 1914 Daniels had set up a program of compulsory shipboard education, much to the disgust of some of the older officers who mourned the passing of the jolly (and illiterate) Jack Tar. Because the majority of shipboard instructors were to be young officers fresh from the Naval Academy, Daniels pressed his idea of Annapolis as the educational center for the entire Navy.

The *New York Tribune* reported, soon after, about the shipboard school aboard the battleship *Michigan* lying off Veracruz. The article described the enlisted men gathering between 1:15 and 2:30 for elementary grammar and arithmetic, plus a "daily composition" on a topic like "Why I Went Into the Navy" or "Secretary Daniels."[16] His well-marked concern for the dignity of the enlisted man buttressed the Secretary's long-held conviction that the very effort to learn something new rendered any man, even a simple coal-passer aboard ship, more self-reliant and self-respecting. Daniels sought to show that John Paul Jones had held much the same idea of shipboard schools and that there was nothing revolutionary in it. Nevertheless, the unmistakable Josephus Daniels stamp lay upon those recruiting posters of later years which read: "Join the Navy and Learn a Trade." He also saw to it that the Navy fulfilled its part of the implied bargain in "Join the Navy and See the World."

Daniels' lifelong concern for the Open Door of Opportunity led to his opening the gates of the Naval Academy to enlisted men. His distrust of a possibly self-perpetuating career officer caste led him to outlaw such favoritism in midshipmen appointments as he could unearth. "No accident or favoritism of 'adaptability' or 'probable efficiency' prevails there [the Naval Academy] or elsewhere in the service," he wrote in his first Annual Report. He had found that "adaptability" was too often a pretext for "an arbitrarily an-

cient protection to possible favoritism," and he discarded "adaptability" personally in appointing nineteen Marine Corps lieutenants
and getting the step confirmed by President Wilson. Too, Daniels
urged on his Congressman friends the use of fair competitive examinations in appointing midshipmen.

As irreverent of tradition as ever, Daniels not only cracked down
on hazing at the Naval Academy but began refusing to accept resig-
nations from newly commissioned officers. He was indignant at the
idea of the government's investing $20,000 in a midshipman's edu-
cation only to see him resign to take a better-paying job in private
industry. Unprecedented also was the Secretary's step of appointing educators to the Academy's Board of Visitors (later including
Edwin A. Alderman) and engaging civilians to teach non-naval sub-
jects. Nearly every member of the Annapolis establishment was hostile when Daniels later appointed the erudite C. Alphonso Smith,
who had taught at the Universities of North Carolina and Virginia,
as head of the Academy's English department. Smith was supposed
to be the kind of man who could never mix with Navy officers, but
in about two months he had charmed them so that the midshipmen
were calling him "Beefy" and he virtually owned the Academy.
Daniels undoubtedly could pick men. The "impossible" C. Alphonso
Smith began giving a postgraduate lecture on "Words" that thrilled
his audience and became one of the Annapolis legends.[17]

Daniels' reforms sometimes aroused amusement, resentment, or
outright misunderstanding. To the last-named category belongs the
order changing "port and starboard" to "left and right." The order
was one early in Daniels' administration, based on a study by the
Navy's General Board (Admiral George Dewey, president), which
had recommended the change in the interest of clarity for new re-
cruits. The daily press gave Daniels a spanking for his open flouting
of naval tradition, but it was Franklin D. Roosevelt who had really
signed the order. Daniels finally unearthed the original during
FDR's presidency and wrote amusedly to his former subordinate: "I
hereby transfer to you all the criticism which was heaped upon my
head. . . ." The Navy Secretary met predictable defeat trying to
get sailors to wear pajamas, but his basic concern for the enlisted
men led him to brave the officers' displeasure by setting up laundries aboard ship. Some officers thought the move subversive of
discipline, a pampering of the enlisted men, but Daniels persuaded
the brass to try it. A laundry was successfully pioneered aboard the

new battleship *Texas,* much to the enthusiasm of the seamen, and Daniels then ordered that all new ships should contain a laundry.[18]

Many of Daniels' Navy reforms were carried out in ships lying off the coast of Mexico, for it was there that he met his first big international crisis in April, 1914. The Veracruz episode of that year holds a special significance for the Daniels story because it set up an initial stumbling-block to the success of his later mission as Ambassador to Mexico. The Mexican Revolution, badly reported and misunderstood in the United States, found the Wilson administration as much at sea as that of Taft. Where Taft had used non-recognition of the usurping General Huerta as a bargaining weapon in pressing outstanding claims against Mexico, Wilson continued to "non-recognize" Huerta because of revulsion for his take-over from President Madero, in whose murder he had almost certainly participated. Wilson called his policy "watchful waiting," trying to wean away foreign support from Huerta, giving encouragement to the usurper's enemy, Carranza, and keeping the U.S. Navy on the alert.

Overt American intervention came in the wake of the notorious Tampico flag incident of April 9, 1914, in which a Huerta officer arrested an American shore party of the *U.S.S. Dolphin.* The arresting officer's superior quickly overruled the other and sent a personal apology to Admiral Henry T. Mayo off Veracruz. Instead of accepting it, Mayo demanded a twenty-one gun salute to the American flag and then issued an ultimatum for compliance. Despite its comic opera aspect the incident was of the gravest import, first because it was wholly unexpected and, second, because no American administration could lightly repudiate a flag officer in foreign waters, no matter how rashly he had acted. In fact, two years later when it could not be construed as a rebuke to Mayo, Daniels changed Navy Regulations to forbid commanders within telegraphic range of Washington to issue an ultimatum without first communicating with the Navy Department. The flag-salute ultimatum was extended by the pacific Secretary Bryan until April 19, but on the next day President Wilson—getting no satisfaction—had to appear before a joint session of Congress to seek a free hand in Mexico. His only opposition came from the super-patriots who thought he had already acted with too much forbearance.

The news reached Washington two hours before midnight on April 21, 1914, a message from the U.S. consul in Veracruz that the German ship *Ypiranga* was due there that very morning. The ship was carrying two hundred machine guns and fifteen million rounds of ammunition for General Huerta. Secretary Bryan telephoned the President, and Josephus Daniels joined them in the three-way conference call. When the President asked his advice, Daniels replied: "The munitions should not be permitted to fall into Huerta's hands. I can wire Admiral Fletcher to prevent it and take the custom house. I think that should be done." And it was done. Admiral Fletcher stopped the *Ypiranga* and seized the custom house that morning with no resistance. The Huerta general at Veracruz prudently withdrew his forces before an unequal clash, and active resistance was offered only by the cadets who held out in the Naval Academy and were quickly mowed down when the guns of the *U.S.S. Prairie* opened up at almost point-blank range. Street fighting and sniping before the cease-fire of April 25 resulted in the following casualties: Mexicans killed, 126, wounded, 195; Americans killed, 19, wounded, 71.[19]

Veracruz was forcibly occupied by the U.S. Army for most of 1914, while Daniels and other Wilsonians fought off demands at home that the United States go on and "take" all of Mexico. In one sense the Wilsonian Mexican policy was a reflection of the New Freedom at home. Certainly the opponents of the New Freedom reforms were the strongest foes of the too-pacifist "watchful waiting" in Mexico. It was no secret that Senator Albert B. Fall and Edward L. Doheny's Mexican Petroleum Company (foreshadowing the Teapot Dome) were impatient for American intervention, and Woodrow Wilson himself was convinced that the oil men had been among General Huerta's original backers. On the other hand, and despite their anti-imperialist principles, the Wilsonians ended by engaging in more peacetime intervention in the Caribbean than ever before in American history. To be sure, security of the Panama Canal, newly opened in 1914, was an anxiety later deepened by the war in Europe. But the repudiated Taftian "Dollar Diplomacy" merely gave way to what Arthur S. Link has aptly termed "Missionary Diplomacy," the missionary desire to do good.

So Secretary Daniels had to keep the American Navy and Marines busy in the Caribbean during the New Freedom days, in Mexico, in Santo Domingo, in Haiti. In each case the intervention—the natives perversely called it "invasion"—was supposedly for the natives' own good. Woodrow Wilson told a visiting British diplomat —and Daniels undoubtedly agreed—that the United States would "teach the South American republics to elect good men."[20] Even after serving as Ambassador to Mexico, Daniels confided to a high Mexican official the troubling thought that the Mexican people never "understood Wilson's deep sympathy for what . . . the revolutionists stood for." He insisted on distinguishing between the Navy operation at Veracruz and the "take Mexico" sentiment of the jingoes, a distinction too nice for any Mexican to draw. Not until Daniels got to Mexico as Ambassador did he first realize, and explain to President Roosevelt, that the Mexicans had been "apprehensive that our mission at Veracruz was not of helpfulness and peace." Later on, Daniels sent his old subordinate some Veracruz souvenirs for his stamp collection, a postal card and a revenue stamp testifying to American Occupation activities. FDR was delighted with the rare items, and admitted that he had never known of such activities by the Occupation. Confusing the Navy with the Army (or giving it a sentimental preference), President Roosevelt gaily noted to Daniels: "Verily, the United States Navy can and does do everything—ubiquitous and omniscient!"[21]

If not exactly ubiquitous and omniscient, the Navy under Josephus Daniels was taking new tacks and moving in unaccustomed directions. His own moral code led Daniels to press for more chaplains, and his first Annual Report noted reproachfully that the Navy had had forty-two chaplains in 1842 (with a Navy of 13,500 and still forty-two chaplains a century later (with a Navy of 65,000). He wrote of "leading men afloat to a recognition of the truth that man's first and highest obligation is to his Maker." His stern attitude against hazing and drinking at the Naval Academy led him to advise President Wilson against reversing a midshipman's dismissal for hazing. This errant midshipman was in the same room with the hazing, not taking part in the offensive act, but—what was worse to Daniels—adding to the victim's terror by silent acquiescence.

The Secretary's puritanical side came to the fore in his ban on the Navy's issue of contraceptives. "The use of this packet," his directive read, "I believe to be immoral; it savors of the panderer. . . . It is equivalent to the Government advising these boys that it is right and proper for them to indulge in an evil which perverts their morals." Where parasitic vice districts flourished near Navy bases, Daniels could be counted on to fight them. Although his most spectacular campaign came during World War I, he made a start on his first national inspection tour. Daniels found a sodden and disreputable area just outside the Marine Training Base at Port Royal, S.C., and he did not hesitate to let Governor Cole Blease know that the place must be closed up. The demagogic Blease tried to fight Daniels in the press, a self-defeating proposition from the start, even calling Daniels a liar. Daniels paid no attention, having in the meantime begun at Port Royal the prison reform he was to pursue more vigorously later. He restored to duty those men under the age of twenty-one for good behavior while at the Disciplinary Barracks.[22]

As stubborn as he was—and absolutely unmovable where he discerned a moral issue—Daniels could be persuaded to change his mind. For example, he reluctantly let himself be overborne on the anti-contraceptive order during World War I when public health needs supervened. No such arguments could be raised, however, against his order abolishing liquor in the Navy, and there the Secretary held his ground against all comers. His order became so much a part of Navy custom that many an Allied visitor to a World War II aircraft carrier would exclaim in amazement at the American seamen refreshing themselves at the ship's soda fountain. The original no-liquor order was the sensation of its day. When Daniels issued his preliminiary announcement about a dry Navy in April, 1914, some forgotten genius, bethinking himself of the "right and left" order, described Daniels' move thus: "At one swoop larboard, starboard, and sideboard have been jettisoned."[23]

For that matter the teetotaling Secretary always saw the humorous side of the liquor question. Almost a year before the Wine Mess Order the new Secretary inspected the library at the Navy War College and found a full-fledged saloon bar established therein. When asked his pleasure, Daniels stepped up and ordered White Rock, which each admiral in the party manfully ordered in his turn. One hard-drinking sea dog, stuck with his non-alcoholic drink, later averred to his mates—as Daniels recorded it—that "he would be damned if he would let other Admirals appear more temperate before the new Secretary."[24]

Nothing except war itself aroused the officer corps as much as the Wine Mess Order. Many perfectly temperate officers resented the implication that they were all drunkards. Admiral Fiske expostulated personally with the Secretary but met a stone wall, although Admiral Sims—later Daniels' blood enemy—came to praise the order. Daniels had prepared his case so carefully that his foemen never

had a chance. In announcing the new order to the press in April
he pointed out then and later that the order would impose the same
liquor regulations on the Navy as already bound the Army; that officers would now be subject to the same rule that had governed enlisted men since 1899; that the Navy's Surgeon General highly commended the reform; that the *Journal of the American Medical Association* did likewise; and that such foreign navies as the German
and Russian were initiating similar reforms. In the perspective of
time, and particularly in the context of the old peacetime Navy that
afforded plenty of leisure for quiet tippling, Daniels has come off
rather well. Admiral Richard L. Conolly has recalled his shock,
when on a midshipman practice cruise aboard the *Georgia* in 1913,
at having to report to an obviously drunken officer of the deck who
had no business being there.[25]

Daniels' own cup virtually ran over when his beloved University, from which he always regretted not having earned a degree,
conferred on him the honorary LL.D. at the commencement of
1914. Whereas the other recipients of honorary degrees wore serious miens—a state supreme court justice and Secretary of Commerce William C. Redfield—a contemporary reporter noted that
Daniels "wore the editorial smile that never fades."[26] Daniels' genuine smile made it easier for fellow-Southerner Woodrow Wilson,
himself usually dour, to confide in his Navy Secretary. On one occasion in 1914—the Trotter affair—the leader of a Negro delegation
protesting against the segregation of government workers engaged
President Wilson in a sharp exchange in which both men lost their
tempers. The ever-tactful Daniels recalled saying to Wilson: "Governor, you did not seem to get along very well with our colored
friends." Said Wilson, as Daniels recalled it: "Daniels, whenever
a man loses his temper he loses his judgment. That is what happened to me in the interview. What I should have done was to
have listened to what they had to say, asked them to leave their request, and promised to give it consideration. If I had done that the
incident would have been a passing incident. As it was, when I lost
my temper and unwisely ordered them to leave the executive offices, I lost my advantage and thereby I raised an incident into an
issue." The President paused, looked out of the window, and said
to Daniels, "I hope this will be a lesson to me."[27]

By contrast, the Franklin D. Roosevelt of 1914 was much less
open with Daniels. The outbreak of the European conflict excited

the frankly pro-British Assistant Secretary of the Navy, who could not begin to sympathize with the anti-militarist Daniels over the tragedy of war. On August 1, 1914, Franklin wrote to Eleanor that "Mr. D totally fails to grasp the situation," and next day he added: "These dear people like W.J.B. [Bryan] and J.D. have as much conception of what a general European war means as Elliot [then four years old] has of higher mathematics." FDR found that nobody at the Navy Department was sharing his excitement, and so he wrote his wife how he single-handedly set about preparing plans while Mr. Daniels was mainly sad that such a shock had been delivered to "his faith in human nature and civilization and similar idealistic nonsense. . . ." On August 5 FDR reported: "*I am running the real work*, although Josephus is here! He is bewildered by it all, very sweet but very sad!"

The European holocaust of 1914, toward which the great powers had been marching in lockstep for generations, caught an innocent and isolationist America by surprise. For his own part the saddened Daniels did what he had to do. In an increasingly efficient Navy Department, where he had already secured Victor Blue as Chief of Navigation, he installed William C. Braisted, David W. Taylor, and Samuel McGowan as bureau chiefs, respectively, of Medicine and Surgery, of Construction and Repair, and of Supplies and Accounts. All three were first-rate men whom Daniels retained by his side despite his own Single Oak Policy of one-year terms. Admiral Taylor, later Chief Constructor of the Navy, was probably the officer Daniels admired above all others. The Secretary also ordered that all officers, active or retired (the last would muzzle the pro-British Alfred T. Mahan) refrain from public comment on the European war. He also acted quickly to rescue Americans stranded in Europe by the "guns of August" 1914, including a little group shepherded in the Alps by his old friend, Edwin A. Alderman. One canard had it that Daniels had forbidden the singing of "Tipperary" in the Navy (Daniels had merely refused to overrule one C.O. who had so ordered). Woodrow Wilson came to Daniels' defense at a White House luncheon, a guest quoting the President: "Daniels . . . is surrounded by a network of conspiracy and of lies. His enemies are determined to ruin him. I can't be sure who they are yet, but when I do get them—God help them."[28]

The lights going out in Europe betokened the gathering gloom for the President, whose beloved wife Ellen was dying. When that good friend of the Danielses died shortly thereafter, Woodrow Wilson's note on the day after Christmas revealed the warmth of his feeling for Daniels and Miss Addie. The lonely President thanked them for the letter of Christmas greetings and for Miss Addie's cake, and added: "You are both of the sort that make life and friendship worth while. It is fine to have a colleague whom one can absolutely trust; how much finer to have one whom one can love! This is a real underpinning for the soul! And when marriage has united two of the same quality one can only wonder and be thankful that Providence has made them his friend." Their kindness had helped, the President wrote on his portable typewriter, "to keep the cloud from descending on me which threatened me all day." Both Danielses wept over that letter.[29]

The Secretary's second Annual Report, at the end of 1914, led to a much rougher reception for Daniels than his first. Even in the friendly House Naval Committee, he heard from the Big Navy men in full cry against him for following orders. For Woodrow Wilson's orders to Daniels had been to hold the line on the 1915 building program. The President's fears of a revenue deficit had been dispelled with the outbreak of the European war, but in the meantime the loyal Daniels was saddled with a budget request that again called for two dreadnaughts instead of the General Board's four. Admiral Fiske boldly testified that Daniels' program was ineffective and inadequate, that it reflected the views of economizers and civilians, that even the General Board had been browbeaten into scaling down its manpower requests. Daniels' reply to the Big Navy men was on this order: that no peacetime Navy could offer a "perfect war defense," that Congress should indeed spend more money on the Navy but not try to compete with militaristic nations; that the American people would not tolerate a great standing military establishment which would impoverish them.[30]

After anti-imperialists Bryan and Daniels had been mocked to their faces at the dinner given by the Order of the Carabao—the veterans of the Philippine Insurrection had sung a lusty version of "Damn, Damn, Damn the Insurrectos"—it was clear that the "pacifists" were in for it. To be sure, President Wilson had directed his Secretaries of War and Navy to reprimand the Carabao Dinner Committee[31] and the hold-the-line naval building program was carefully guided through Congress. But the bellicose General Leonard Wood had to be reprimanded for warlike utterances in public, and in a Cabinet meeting of January, 1915, Wilson directed Daniels to reprimand Admiral Austin M. Knight, who had publicly espoused the kind of General Staff that would undermine Daniels' authority. Soon thereafter began a barrage of ridicule and calumny frankly designed to drive Daniels out of the Cabinet. The malice of these attacks was all the more heightened because their target remained serenely unmoved and infuriatingly good-natured in the face of ridicule. As a journalist Daniels knew that his un-nautical physique and old-fashioned dress made him a caricaturist's dream. From the announcement of the previous year's Wine Mess Order, Miss Addie had been collecting cartoons satirizing her husband, and she applied to the artists direct for their signed originals.

Those who wanted a Navy on a war footing in early 1915 were headed by Daniels' enemy, Congressman "Gussie" Gardner, impressed by the pseudo-Darwinian exaltation of war as the vehicle of social progress. This son-in-law of Senator Henry Cabot Lodge began with an attack in Congress and then formed around himself the American Defense Society of preparedness enthusiasts. A virtual avalanche of propaganda emanating from the Society led to a demand for a Congressional investigation of the state of preparedness of the armed forces. Such a transparent political attack was easily evaded, but Senator Lodge sent copies of his speeches to his Big Navy friend, Theodore Roosevelt, to whom he confided that he had to restrain himself about Daniels who was, of course, "intolerable."[32] Lodge and Roosevelt did not have long to wait for the preparedness fever, spurred by U-boat sinkings, to soar. But in early 1915 the American people generally, let alone the peace advocates and anti-militarists, were unwilling to consider the kind of preparedness by which the Navy would be ready to fight its most formidable conceivable foe.

Daniels was less concerned with intervening in the European war than in mitigating the misery it brought with it. For example, the war had made refugees of thousands of Jews who were fleeing destitute from Turkish Palestine into Egypt, and in early 1915 a group of American Jewish leaders led by Louis D. Brandeis was trying to send relief to them. They appealed to Daniels, who was characterized all his life by his friendship for the Jewish people, and explained that the British and French had granted safe conduct for a relief ship. Sending such a ship was against Navy regulations, Daniels found, so he suggested to President Wilson the

solution that was adopted. So long as the American Navy was sending colliers into the Mediterranean for the coaling of American Navy
vessels there, why not reduce the space on the next two colliers and
give it over to Jewish relief supplies? Daniels dispatched the collier
Vulcan with nine hundred tons of food and medicines. A little later
he dispatched the collier *Starling,* which carried medicines and—
the Methodist Secretary had seen to it—*matzoth* for Passover.[33]

Woodrow Wilson knew perfectly well that Daniels was catching
the preparedness brickbats aimed at him and stood foursquare behind the Navy Secretary. When Wilson once caught a glimmer of
Republican opposition to the defamation of Daniels, he wrote to
him: "I did not need to have anybody tell me how entirely correct
and excellent your administration of the department has been, but
I want this evidence from the opposite party published." After reviewing the Atlantic Fleet at New York in May—the *Lusitania* crisis
then held center stage—the President told a banquet audience
there: "I want to take advantage of the first public opportunity I
have had to speak of the Secretary of the Navy, to express my confidence and to say that he has my unqualified support." The President was then courting Mrs. Galt, who later recorded her own "gor-
geous day in New York" and what a charming hostess she found in
Mrs. Daniels. On board the Navy Secretary's yacht *Dolphin,* at New
York, Miss Addie was delighted by the President's gift of a huge
box of flowers, ostensibly for her but really a token of regard for
her dinner guest, Mrs. Galt.[34]

By May, 1915, the impulse to preparedness had grown in the
American people, and during the debate Franklin Roosevelt had remained on guardedly friendly terms with Daniels' enemies. Not
only did the Big Navy men find an ally in FDR, but they could take
comfort in the words with which he seemed to contradict his chief.
Whereas Daniels, speaking to the Navy League, praised the Congress that had enacted Wilson's New Freedom, FDR told the same
Navy Leaguers: "Let us insist that Congress shall carry out their
[the Navy Board's] recommendations." The *Lusitania* was sunk on
May 7, 1915, and William Jennings Bryan resigned as Secretary of
State the following month rather than sign the strong second Lusitania Note that he believed would result in war. Daniels did not
think so, stayed on in the Cabinet, and loyally obeyed Wilson's directive to change course as regards preparedness. When the Commoner resigned, FDR exulted to his wife: "What d'y' think of W.

Jay B?" But he added thoughtfully—or was it regretfully?—"J. D. will *not* resign."[35]

In his most dramatically fateful move of 1915, Woodrow Wilson publicly declared for military and naval expansion, and on July 21 put Secretary Daniels on notice to prepare an expanded building program for Congress to consider in December. The attacks on Daniels now subsided a little, to the accompaniment of Wilson's stout support of his Navy Secretary, and in July George Harvey's *North American Review* wrote up "Mr. Wilson's Cabinet," in which Josephus Daniels came off surprisingly well. In any case Daniels was simply following the President's orders. The Navy General Board submitted a program approved by the President on October 15 that provided a five-year building program costing half a billion dollars. As Professor Link has said: "Even the Navy League had not asked for more."[36]

In September, 1915, while Daniels was readying his estimates for Congress, Colonel House was following out a Wilsonian directive to secure some easing of the press attacks on the Navy Secretary. House reported to Daniels that he had gotten an admission from the editor of the satirical magazine, *Life*, that he had treated Daniels unfairly and would now make amends. That promise—if, indeed, House reported it truly—proved unavailing, but Daniels did get considerate treatment from one to whom Wilson had appealed directly, Editor John R. Dunlap of *Engineering Magazine*.[37] Daniels' Annual Report for 1915, embodying his new estimates, wisely refrained from urging the ten-year program that would have given the United States parity with Britain by 1925. It was obvious that the European war was almost daily modifying Navy thinking. Because he was conscious of such change, Daniels deferred the laying of the keels of battleships forty-three and forty-four, already authorized.

In his own shrewd way Daniels took care of his own public relations. In the same way that he introduced civilian instructors at the Naval Academy, he prevailed on Thomas A. Edison to head a new Navy Consulting Board. At the end of the first year of the European war, when Daniels confidentially sounded out Edison, it was already clear how vulnerable were conventional navies to attack by U-boats. That was reason enough to set up a Consulting Board, but Daniels cannily seized upon the non-partisan Board to silence his Big Navy critics now that the Wilson administration had shifted to preparedness. When Daniels first went to call on Edison—it was pure hero worship as was the Secretary's regard for Admiral Dewey —the inventor counseled the Secretary to ask the scientific, and especially the engineering societies of the nation, to contribute their best brains. In acceding to the recommendations of Edison, who was something less than an effective administrator, Daniels overweighted the Board with engineers, which made the Board less a scientific than a popular triumph with the American people who adored Edison as their own inspired tinkerer. Elsewhere within his Department, Daniels made graduation from the Naval War College a prerequisite for promotion, and persuaded Congress to jettison the dread "Plucking Board" (which handed down no-appeal decisions on mandatory retirements) in favor of a Board of Selection.[38] When in 1915 Congress provided for a Chief of Naval Operations, Daniels naturally bypassed Fiske and carefully watered down any General Staff idea by replacing the Aid System with the Secretary's Advisory Council comprising the chief officials of the Department. Daniels also chose his own C.N.O. in the person of Captain William S. Benson, whom he jumped over a number of senior officers, a Catholic who got on extremely well with the Methodist Secretary. The solidly able Benson, loyal to the core, always reflected credit on Daniels' administration of the Navy. In Secretary Daniels the old-line admirals had found a civilian chief they could not manipulate or cajole.

The end of that year brought new distress to the Secretary, for *The News and Observer* plant was again destroyed by fire. Again that November, 1915, as after the fire two years earlier, the *Raleigh Times* plant was available to publish Daniels' paper. Again the friends rallied around to prepay their subscriptions and proffer new loans although Daniels had not been able to repay the money he had borrowed for the initial rebuilding. Again brother-in-law Henry Bagley took charge of the arrangements, but now a new source of distress was added to the other. For several years Daniels had been trying by every means to dissuade Bagley from divorcing his wife and marrying another man's wife. When Bagley remained adamant, Daniels protested against the decision as both cruel and wrong, then added: "If you are resolved in this course, no action should be taken and no lawyer consulted until you have made your home in some other place than Raleigh, North Carolina." Henry Bagley had his way, but he had to take up residence in Fort Worth, Texas; Josephus Daniels had had his way too.[39]

During late 1915, also, President Wilson's intentions toward Mrs. Galt became unmistakable. Daniels wondered aloud to Miss Addie whether the women of the country would turn against Wilson's re-election if he remarried. It appears that Postmaster General Burleson, the chief politician in the Cabinet, thought so. He and other Democrats had concluded that Wilson must be persuaded not to remarry until after the 1916 election and, moreover, that Daniels must be the one to tell him so. The Democrats had fastened on Daniels, they said, because of his closeness to the President and the friendship of the Danielses for the first Mrs. Wilson. With his usual good sense, Daniels wisely declined being selected to bell the cat. He later joked that he had no hankering to be "dragooned into a mission in which neither my heart nor my head was enlisted and in the performance of which my official head might suffer decapitation."[40]

The Daniels-Roosevelt relationship was easier now with the turn to preparedness. FDR jokingly forwarded "a requisition (with 4 copies attached) calling for the purchase of 8 carpet tacks," to which Daniels replied: "Why this wanton extravagance? I am sure that two would suffice." There were to be times thereafter when FDR's loyalty wavered, but he became increasingly secure in his subordinate role. Eleanor Roosevelt later observed that her husband conceived a "deep admiration for the qualities and character and to value the high ability of Mr. Daniels." The evidence has it that the Navy Secretary, for his part, increasingly valued Roosevelt as an idea man who could get things done.

As the presidential election year of 1916 opened, Daniels got his expected close questioning before the House Naval Affairs Committee. The Republican members tried to bait Daniels with Democratic responsibility for halving the General Board's earlier building requests. The Committee Democrats quickly made the record show that the leading Congressional Republicans had willingly agreed to the cuts, and Daniels retorted to Fred A. Britten (R.-Ill.): "If you wish to go into that, Mr. Britten" [criticizing the Wilson administration], "I am ready for you." So as Senator Lodge kept writing impatiently to Theodore Roosevelt about Daniels' too-small building program, the political guns were wheeled into place. TR got in touch with journalist Henry Reuterdahl, who began a new anti-

Daniels cannonade with his article "Josephus Daniels, Master of Errors," in the March 1916 *Metropolitan Magazine*. This attack pictured a Navy demoralized by Daniels' reforms, the article's main fire being directed at the Navy's "desertion" of the American refugees from Tampico, Mexico, in 1914.

Reuterdahl's article ushered in a greater flood of published abuse than any Secretary of the Navy ever had to endure. The attacks were quite unwarranted, of course, the few legitimate grievances being unconscionably exaggerated, but in an election year Daniels apparently was the chosen Democratic scapegoat. It all boiled down to a Republican campaign slogan coined by George Harvey: "A vote for Wilson is a vote for Daniels." The Democratic counterattack came in the New York *World*, in which George Creel, who had never met Daniels up to the time of their interview, published a point-by-point refutation of the anti-Daniels claims.[41]

It was not like the amiable fighter Josephus Daniels to speak "helplessly of the political outlook" as he was supposed to have done in the spring of 1916, according to Ambassador Henry Morgenthau's memoirs. Daniels himself scribbled a bold "no" in the margin of his copy of Morgenthau's work. Of course, a less buoyant soul than Daniels might have lost heart. Colonel House was now trying to ease the Navy Secretary out of the Cabinet. Then the June issue of George Harvey's organ carried a whole collection of reprinted newspaper attacks on Daniels, and the July issue of *World's Work*, Walter Page's magazine, carried the critical "Case of Josephus Daniels" by Burton J. Hendrick, later the anti-Daniels ally and amanuensis of Admiral Sims. Colonel House's alleged attempt to placate *Life* earlier also came to nothing because the September 14 issue showed up as the "Josephus Daniels Number," complete with a good ribbing of Daniels by that master of light verse, Arthur Guiterman.[42] Here is an example (p. 436), the opening stanza of Guiterman's "Sir Josephus Porter Daniels, K.C.B. (Solo from the new Gilbertian opera, 'U.S.S. Pantalette')":

> When I was a lad a kindly fate
> Preserved my morals in the Old North State.
> I shunned the flagon and the vile cigar.
> But I sometimes went a-boating on the raging Tar.
> I went out boating every now and then,
> So now I am Dictator of the U.S.N.

I went out boating every now and then,
So now I am Dictator of the U.S.N.

On the other hand, Woodrow Wilson was standing squarely behind his Navy Secretary. To Cleveland Dodge, with whom he
agreed in praise for Daniels, the President said of the other's Navy
administration: "It has been admirable." Wilson also intervened
with the editor of *Engineering Magazine,* whom he begged to
counteract "the partisan, puerile and most grossly unjust attacks on
Secretary Daniels." On Daniels' fifty-fourth birthday the President
wrote warmly of his support of the Navy Secretary "during the
trials you have had to go through to get the right established.[43]
At the peak of the anti-Daniels campaign of vilification Daniels
boldly took his stand with the vilifiers' other principal target, Louis
D. Brandeis, the "radical Jew" who had been appointed to the Supreme Court. Daniels went to work on his recalcitrant fellow Tar
Heel, Senator Lee S. Overman, who was acting chairman of the
Judiciary Committee where the Brandeis nomination was in trouble.
The two Tar Heels were guests aboard President Wilson's train
bound for Charlotte, N.C., where the President was to address a
patriotic celebration. The Presidential Special was scheduled to
pass through Salisbury, N.C., Senator Overman's home, and the
latter begged Daniels to intercede with Wilson on behalf of a
whistle-stop appearance so that President and Senator might pose
happily on the rear platform for the home folks. Wilson had already
refused Overman once, but Daniels' diplomatic urgings got the
President to relent and to make Overman happy. He also got Overman's vote for Brandeis' confirmation.[44]
That summer the Congress came through with a whopping Navy
appropriations bill that provided for completion of the five-year
building program in three. A happy Senator Lodge confided to TR
how he had persuaded Secretary Daniels "with all his bureau chiefs
around him." The bill also contained a "pacifist" rider, accepted by
Wilson and Daniels, that contained in embryo form the idea of a
League of Nations. This prophetic gesture authorized the President
"not later than the close of the war in Europe" to call a conference
looking to the inauguration of a world peace-keeping organization
and setting aside $200,000 for the purpose.[45]
That summer also brought the bitterest intramural fight among
the Wilsonians, with Daniels holding out against Interior Secretary

Franklin K. Lane's friendliness to the oil interests. Lane's proposed General Leasing Bill was pleasing to his fellow-Californian, Senator James B. Phelan, and to other oil-conscious Californians like Edward L. Doheny. Daniels had already committed the Navy to oil-burning vessels, and now he anxiously wrote to Woodrow Wilson to oppose his personal influence against Lane's bill.[46] Daniels had already fixed his suspicious eye on one oil claimant who would benefit from Lane's eagerness to please, the Honolulu Oil Company, claiming seventeen tracts inside Naval Reserve No. 2. Although Daniels liked Lane as a delightful companion, he raised enough out-cry among conservationists against the giveaway so that Lane's bill failed.

After twenty years as his state's Democratic national committee-man, Daniels quit the post so as to free his hands—as a whistle-stopping Cabinet member—for the 1916 presidential campaign. Be-cause "a vote for Wilson was a vote for Daniels," the Navy Secre-tary got a spirited personal defense from his party. On August 20 George Creel published in the *World* a new and thorough-going defense of Daniels by Admiral George Dewey. When Theodore Roosevelt repeated the Tampico refugee story in the New York newspapers, the Democratic national committee retorted the same day with a denial secured from Admiral Mayo, who had command-ed in the Tampico area at the time. For his own part Daniels was pressing on Wilson the progressive legislation needed to win West-ern votes, specifically a workmen's compensation law and a child labor law. Daniels also wrote to his old friend Bryan, now out of the administration, defending Wilson to him and by indirection urging Bryan not to let his silence comfort the enemy.[47] According-ly, Bryan got out and campaigned strenuously for Wilson.

Daniels' campaign trail was mainly in the North Central states, and in September he was keynote speaker at a great Wilson rally in the Coliseum at Bloomington, Illinois. The Navy Secretary was a house guest of the Stevenson family, and that night young Adlai Stevenson sat on the platform.[48] During October Daniels was in Indiana when he was recalled to New York by the national chair-man, Vance C. McCormick, who told Daniels that he had been se-lected to bail out the national committee by tapping Henry Ford for a large contribution. Thomas A. Edison and Ford had reserved space at the Biltmore, where Daniels invited them both to lunch thanks to his "in" with Edison, and where ensued the delightful kicking match that Daniels recalled for his memoirs. Daniels' admiration for Edison and Ford had to do not with their nativism or aggressive provincialism—qualities always foreign to Daniels himself—but rather with the attractive sides of their natures: their delight in rural and small-town virtues, their real native ability, and—when completely relaxed—their downright boyishness.

Said Edison to the auto magnate: "Henry, I'll bet anything you want to bet that I can kick that globe off that chandelier." So the two champions of rural American virtues fell to kicking like high-spirited boys, with the older Edison winning and crowing over Ford. McCormick himself gave Daniels an under-the-table kick when it came time to talk money. The auto king at once dashed their hopes by disavowing any and all campaign contributions, but the patient Daniels shrewdly began his counterattack by saying, "I think you are quite right, Mr. Ford." The result was that Ford, while acting independently of the national committee, paid for many an expensive full-page signed article in the big-circulation newspapers. In mid-November, after Wilson's narrow re-election, the *New York Times* was reporting that anti-Daniels hostility had largely disappeared because of the high caliber of the men Daniels had selected and his own coolness under fire. "Mr. Daniels is said to have suffered under the hard knocks he received but to have kept his temper with a sportsmanlike stoicism."[49]

What with the new Navy building program and the intensifying German U-boat crisis, Daniels and Franklin Roosevelt were making a much more harmonious team. Daniels handled policy matters and relations with Congress while FDR supervised Navy Yard and shipbuilding operations. The older man also exercised restraint on FDR in politically sensitive areas, almost as if he discerned something special in this young man and wanted him to pace himself. Daniels wisely got FDR to wait until after the Maine elections before using the Secretary's yacht *Dolphin* to evacuate the Assistant Secretary's family from Campobello, where lurked a deadly forewarning in the form of a poliomyelitis epidemic of 1916. From the campaign trail Daniels anxiously wrote the Acting Secretary to allow no postponement in the opening of shipbuilding bids. He need not have worried, because Roosevelt was now enthusiastically on top of his job, and Daniels' over-all patience with his aristocratic Assistant Secretary paid dividends. President-elect Franklin D. Roosevelt, on his way to be inaugurated in 1933, fondly introduced Rexford G. Tugwell to Josephus Daniels: "Rex, this is a man who taught me a lot that I needed to know. . . ."[50]

Chapter four

The First World War

After a Cabinet meeting in late 1916 Josephus Daniels stayed over to chat with the President. "I am glad, Daniels," the editor recalled the substance of Wilson's remarks, "that you do not permit yourself to be stampeded by the advocates of war. . . ."

> Every reform we have won will be placed in jeopardy or lost if we go into this war. We have secured many reforms: reduction of the tariff, establishment of the Federal Trade Commission, the Federal Reserve Board, a Merchant Marine. We have given a Magna Carta to labor, and begun the end of practices by monopolies, and in other ways unhorsed special privilege, which control ships, steel, coal, oil, and most of the instruments of war, and will regain control, and neither you nor I will live to see them ousted. We shall have lost all or most of that we have gained since 1913.[1]

The President's words were an echo of fears resident in many a progressive heart, Daniels' included, and the Navy Secretary acted on his near-pacifist convictions through 1916.

The Council of National Defense, set up at the same time as the stepped-up naval building program of August, first met with its Advisory Commission on December 6. After the meeting Daniels invited all hands to lunch at the Army and Navy Club, but first he voted a firm "no" when hands were called for on universal military training. On another occasion the Advisory Commission members put it quite bluntly to the six Cabinet members of the Council: what sort of preparedness could proceed from such foot-draggers as the "pacifist" Secretaries of Navy, War, and Labor? Daniels replied that the people were not convinced that force was yet in order, but that aggressors must of course be repelled by the Navy. The Council *Proceedings* describe him speaking "hesitatingly, his strong emotions not so well controlled as were those of the Secretary of War, confessed that he was morally, spiritually, and economically opposed to the practice of settling differences, individual or national, by physical encounter or warfare. He hoped, even yet, that we would not be drawn into the existing conflicts."[2] More characteristic of Daniels was his writing a delighted bravo to Bernard Baruch for his efficient procurement of copper and steel. More characteristic was the report President Wilson got about Daniels in late 1916. The Chief Boatswain in command of the only remaining American prison ship, a man who had served forty-three years in the Navy, delightedly informed the President that Daniels' reform would some day make naval prisons obsolete.[3]

President Wilson broke off diplomatic relations with Germany on February 3. Even at the previous day's Cabinet meeting he had hesitated over the step, recalling the issue of Asian policy raised by the Japanese war scare four years earlier, and he had found support in Secretaries Daniels and Baker.[4] But now the alternatives of the President, at once a realist and a moralist, had run out. He had been insisting on the maritime rights of a neutral in a war-maddened world that no longer tolerated neutrals. Daniels had congratulated the President on having made the Germans back down in the *Arabic* crisis two years before and on facing them down with a virtual ultimatum over the *Sussex* sinking last year. But the Americans, having committed themselves so strictly to maritime rights, were left with no room to maneuver once the Kaiser and his advisers opted to resume unrestricted submarine warfare. Imperial Germany, knowing full well that its defiance of Wilson's earlier warning would guarantee America's war entry, frankly counted on a knockout of the Allies before American help could become effective.

Secretaries Daniels and Baker conferred with the President on February 5, when Wilson directed them to put the armed services in a ready state. It must have been then, in the context of a Chief Executive cornered by the increasingly narrow alternatives left to him, that the President admitted despairingly to Daniels: "I can't keep the country out of war. They talk of me as though I were God. Any little German lieutenant can put us into the war at any time by some calculated outrage." That night the Daniels home was the scene of a dinner far more dramatic than usual. The Navy Secretary and Miss Addie sat across from one another at the center of the oval table in the company of Mrs. Bagley and Miss Addie's two sisters. It was the first Cabinet dinner for the President and the second Mrs. Wilson, the President personally approving the guest list as per custom. President Wilson sat on Miss Addie's right, Henry Ford on her left, and the guest list ran heavily to the Navy Secretary's newspaper friends. It was two days after the diplomatic break with Germany, and the Wyoming Street house was overrun with Secret Service agents.[5]

With Daniels' support, the President resisted the activists' importunities to arm merchant ships until February 25 when he got Ambassador Page's message from London with irrefutable evidence of a proposed German-Mexican military arrangement in the event of war (the Zimmermann note). That day's Cabinet meeting found Daniels still reluctant to risk war by convoying merchant ships, and on the following day Wilson went before Congress to ask for an armed ship bill. Daniels was already under press criticism for permitting "pacifist" messages to Germany from the Navy-occupied wireless station at Sayville, Long Island. Actually, the dispatches went to a German newspaper, but President Wilson took a personal hand in denying the transmitter to individuals and allowing it only to recognized news associations. In a contemporary letter Edmund W. Starling, whose Secret Service detail guarded all Presidents from Wilson through Franklin Roosevelt, described Daniels' mien while calling at the White House. "Starling," Daniels said, "these are tense times. The strain is awful. I don't know what I'd do if it weren't for that man upstairs." (Wilson) Starling ventured to remind the Navy Secretary that Woodrow Wilson himself had to look "higher than upstairs," and the pious Tar Heel brightened and thanked Starling for the thought.[6]

On March 9 the President got from Navy Secretary Daniels a rehearsal of three different sets of armed ship alternatives, and on the same day Wilson announced that he would put guns and Navy gun crews aboard merchant ships. Daniels was strictly enjoined to safeguard the secrecy of his armed ship preparations, the President using his own typewriter to urge on Daniels a court martial for anyone breaching security.[7] Wilson also set April for a special session of Congress to give him those expanded powers under the armed ship bill which the Senate's "little group of willful men" had talked to death. "Awful night," Daniels recorded in his diary of March 18: "Three American ships reported to be torpedoed by German submarines." The report was correct, and the great loss of American life led to an intensified demand for war. March 20, 1917, was the Day of Decision thereafter in Josephus Daniels' memory. On that day the Cabinet advised war, Daniels being the last to vote aye and doing so with tears in his eyes.[8] "It was a supreme moment in my life," he wrote in his diary that day. "I had hoped & prayed this cup would pass."

As soon as the arming of merchant ships was announced, steel prices advanced, and Daniels characteristically warned the President of this apparent exploitation of the national emergency. All during March the Navy Secretary carried on a spirited correspondence with Bernard Baruch, citing the Navy's steel needs and the companies' good profits but also praising the copper firms for their patriotic refusal to profiteer. The Secretary's old sparring partner, the now retired Admiral Fiske, hardly waited in telling the Navy League that "it is no small thing to ask men to join an unprepared navy on the brink of war." An indignant Treasury Secretary McAdoo fairly begged Daniels to court-martial Fiske, but of course Daniels said nothing. In later years Baruch testified to the Navy Department's alertness, recalling that a contemporary study showed that the Army "did not even know what materials were necessary to equip an army" whereas "the Navy was well organized."[9]

There was a note of sadness in the Navy Secretary's voice as he addressed the young midshipmen at Annapolis, their graduation accelerated by the war crisis. He was a patriot in the old-fashioned sense, holding fast, whenever ridden by doubts, to "my country right or wrong." He exhorted the young men: "Get you a naval hero" and then launched into a moving eulogy of Admiral Dewey who had died two months earlier. On the climactic night of April 2, when Wilson asked the Congress to declare war, young Jonathan Daniels was smuggled into the House Chamber (courtesy of the anti-war Congressman Claude Kitchin). Jonathan recalled the hoofbeats of Nip and Tuck, his father's carriage horses, as they trotted back through the streets from the excited Capitol. The boy, noticing a new grandeur attached to his idea of America, later recalled: "My own father, tired and serious in the carriage, seemed grand, too."[10]

So it was war. Josephus Daniels always insisted that Woodrow Wilson consented to war because of two factors only: Germany's unrestricted submarine warfare plus Wilson's belief that it would be a war to end war. On the twentieth anniversary of America's war entry Josephus Daniels conceded to a reporter that people in 1937 deemed it better to surrender temporarily their rights on the seas rather than be drawn into another war. He would not agree, however, that war entry in 1917 came because Americans were farsighted enough to fear a German-dominated world and that American security was imperiled thereby. Recent rethinking by scholars has led many to conclude that, for realistic reasons of national security, American intervention was justified in 1917—and better justified than made public at the time. Nevertheless, this was so much hindsight. It simply was not true, as Daniels correctly insisted, "that we entered the war for fear that Germany would strike us. . . . No such motive prompted President Wilson or the members of his Cabinet."[11]

The coming of the war was, of course, a tragedy for American progressivism, and it was brought home to Daniels in the personal travail of his anti-militarist friends from North Carolina. Congressmen Claude Kitchin and E. Yates Webb steadfastly opposed American intervention, and Robert N. Page had even refused to run for re-election in 1916. Robert Page, disagreeing with his pro-war Ambassador brother who needled him from London, gave up the House seat he had held fourteen years. He was the friend who had jollied bridegroom Daniels ("I will never marry") and had been a groomsman at Daniels' wedding. After the war Daniels asked the President to appoint the well-qualified Robert Page head of the Farm Bank for the Carolinas, but Wilson refused. In one of his rare criticisms of Woodrow Wilson, Daniels recalled: "Great as he was, sometimes Wilson had no forgiving spirit. It is a great tragedy that great men are not always great in magnanimity."[12]

The war crisis brought Daniels as much popularity as he ever enjoyed, for the loudest cheers for any Cabinet member went up when the theater screens showed the Navy Secretary's pleasantly plain face. He was now getting packets of laudatory clippings sent on by Joe Tumulty, that Wilson confidant who had helped get Daniels his Cabinet post in the first place. Even as 1917 opened, the House

Naval Affairs Committee was hearing from Daniels on the reform in naval prisons and of not permitting shipbuilders to pad their cost figures in cost-plus-percentage contracts.[13] The American war resolution found the Navy in good shape, considering that it was defending a typically unprepared democracy. Admiral Benson was the capable C.N.O., with top-notch officers at the critical posts, a good state of morale in the enlisted ranks, and Admiral Sims—for once reasonably happy—stationed in London. William S. Sims was the Navy's fiery petrel, that unquestionably able officer who had "taught the Navy to shoot" but who also was extremely difficult to live with. As an outspoken Anglophile—so outspoken that he had drawn a public reprimand from President Taft—he was eager to co-operate with the British in their hour of peril. On April 10 and 11 Daniels and his staff hammered out with visiting British and French admirals a preliminary policy whereby the American Navy would patrol the Western Hemisphere while giving what help it could spare to the British for the anti-submarine campaign. (Daniels' diary of April 9 recorded that FDR wanted to "go down to meet them [the foreign admirals] as an honor. I said no. He did not like it but—"). Two days later the diary reflected Daniels' heartfelt anguish over submarine sinkings: "O for more destroyers! I wish we could trade the money in dreadnaughts for destroyers already built." The large building program of 1916 was immediately suspended and new plans drafted for the construction of 250 destroyers and 400 sub-chasers.

Reducing the disastrous rate of submarine sinkings was the obvious order of the day, but in April, 1917, the British were still relying on dispersal rather than on the convoying of cargo ships. For his part Daniels had, as of the previous December, set Thomas A. Edison on full-time anti-submarine research that was to bear ample fruit before the end of the war. On May 4 the first American destroyers reached Queenstown, Ireland, but on July 2, after two experimental convoys from Gibraltar and Hampton Roads, President Wilson was still complaining to Daniels that the British Admiralty was dragging its feet as to convoying. With the assistance of Admiral Sims, who also was pressing convoying on the British, and a reinforcement of American destroyers in July, the convoy system finally was made general. Even before America's belligerency the President and Daniels had agreed that the British ought to be using convoys, and Daniels recalled saying as much to Admiral Sims on first posting him to London.[14] Any theoretical loss of efficiency occasioned by the slowness of the convoys was more than made up by the safety of the ships. The record is incontrovertible: two million American soldiers convoyed to France without the loss of a single man.

The longer view of defeating the submarine emerged as early as April 15, 1917, when the Navy's Bureau of Ordnance presented a plan for a mine barrage across the North Sea. The British Admiralty and Admiral Sims at first rejected the plan out of hand. The Navy Department kept at it until an improved mine so convinced the British that both navies undertook the following spring the ambitious project of laying a mine barrage between the Orkney Islands and Norway. The barrage was still incomplete by the time of the Armistice, but the mines probably helped make life almost unendurable for German submariners and helped provoke the German naval mutiny at Kiel. Among those pushing hardest for the Northern Mine Barrage, as it was known in the Navy, was Assistant Secretary Roosevelt. In October, 1917, urging reconsideration for the rejected proposal, he resorted to that lowest of all bureaucratic tricks, sending a memo to one's superior with a copy to their common superior. "I know you will not mind my sending a copy of this to the President," FDR sweetly wrote his chief, while on the same day writing to Eleanor Roosevelt that he had "given the Sec'y a very stinging memorandum and sent a copy to the President. Some day they will be interesting reading." Soon after the war Daniels had to admit that the insubordinate Mr. Roosevelt had been right all along. Daniels wrote: "Not laying that barrage earlier—in fact, at the earliest possible moment—was, in my opinion, the greatest naval error of the war."[15]

With America's war entry the activist FDR found his chief unbearably slow at making decisions. One typical FDR memo of the time begins: "Dear Mr. Daniels: *Do please* get through the vital things *today*." His impatience, while proceeding from the best motives in the world, did not always produce worthwhile results. FDR could rightly take credit for pushing the construction of the excellent 110-foot submarine chasers, for example, but he later forgot that he had harassed the entire Navy Department on behalf of the almost worthless 50-foot harbor patrol launches for which he had conceived an irrational enthusiasm. "How much of that sort of junk shall we buy?" Daniels complained in his diary of March 21,

1917, and later entries showed that Chief Constructor Taylor and other top-notch officers shared the Secretary's skepticism. It was like FDR to "sweat out" his chief and himself authorize construction—as Acting Secretary—of some of the 50-foot boats. He jokingly threatened to exile to Guam one unenthusiastic officer, and President-maker Louis McHenry Howe applied some pressure of his own. To the recalcitrant Captain Hugh Rodman, a member of the General Board who was anxious for sea duty, Howe intimated that it would be politic in him to favor the boats; whereupon the salty Rodman is reported to have cursed him roundly.[16]

In his President-making zeal Louis Howe stepped on so many toes that Daniels was convinced Howe "would have sidetracked both President Wilson and me to get Franklin in the White House." Shortly after becoming associated with Daniels in the wartime Committee on Public Information, George Creel recalled noticing a revival "of the old canards about Josephus Daniels' ineptitudes, rusticities and Billy Sundayisms. I put tracers out, and soon found that the whispers had their source in none other than Howe, whereupon I went over and let him have it right between the eyes. Of course, he insisted he was 'only explaining and defending Uncle Joe' but I told him if I heard any more of his phony explanations and defenses I would carry the matter to W.W. who had a very precise idea of what constituted loyalty."

FDR himself was far too busy to conspire in Howe's sophomoric whispering campaign, being genuinely distressed, during the "tooling-up" summer of 1917 with the Navy Department's rusty administrative machinery and with Admiral Benson's inflexibility as C.N.O. Roosevelt worked through the American novelist, Winston Churchill, to whom he gave the run of the Department and who could be counted on, as a fair-minded graduate of the Naval Academy and friend of President Wilson, to make himself heard in strategic quarters. FDR was right, for Churchill took an elaborate memorandum to the President himself, with the result that Wilson asked Daniels to see that younger men got a chance in both purchasing and operations.[17] Nevertheless, the really excellent Benson kept his job despite FDR. Daniels made it his business, too, to meet Churchill for a preview of the latter's report. In his diary of August 2, 1917, the Navy Secretary wrote relievedly: "I had heard he was going to criticize me rather severely, but I think not."

The Home Front in World War I, because it found him in a

position of leadership, posed perhaps the greatest challenge Josephus Daniels ever faced in his lifetime. Men in topmost posts were working themselves into physical and nervous collapse. There was no room at the top except for men who could measure up, and Josephus Daniels did indeed measure up. In the top-ranking Council of National Defense he energetically cracked heads on profiteering, kept predatory hands off the government oil reserves, helped shape the necessary propaganda effort, generally sided with labor, and raised hob over unsavory conditions near camps that housed young conscripts. He served gladly under the chairmanship of that progressive whom he most admired, Newton D. Baker, along with Secretaries Houston, Lane, Redfield, and William B. Wilson. Daniels learned much from rubbing elbows with the first-rate men on the Council's Advisory Commission: Chairman Daniel Willard, transportation and communications; Howard E. Coffin, munitions and manufacturing; Julius Rosenwald, supplies including clothing; Bernard M. Baruch, raw materials; Hollis Godfrey, engineering and education; Samuel Gompers, labor; and Franklin H. Martin, medicine, surgery, and sanitation. Among those he quickly learned to value was Baruch, from whose raw materials group one could expect fast action. On one occasion Baruch got Daniels a truckload of zinc during a shortage, with the metal ingots arriving literally hot from the mill.[18] Outside the Council Daniels worked with Herbert Hoover, head of the Food Administration; Harry A. Garfield, fuel administrator; Edward N. Hurley, head of the Shipping Board; William G. McAdoo, director-general of the railroads; and George Creel, chairman of the Committee on Public Information.

Daniels kept peppering Baruch with anti-profiteering ideas. For example, the Navy was getting copper below the inflated market price, so why could not Baruch arrange similar price advantages for small manufacturers using raw materials? How? Send to the President the actual cost figures obtained by the Federal Trade Commission. As 1917 progressed it became apparent to Daniels and everyone else that the General Munitions Board and its successor War Industries Board were not working well; the first director broke down under the strain, and then Daniel Willard left at the New Year. The ferocious winter of 1917-18 brought the home war effort almost to collapse, and the chaos in the mobilization effort—exposed in Congress—led the Republicans to demand a coalition War Cabinet. In reply Woodrow Wilson would demand, and get from Congress, unprecedented powers over the national economy, but first he called on Bernard Baruch to head the W.I.B. A month before Baruch's appointment, when the President asked Daniels' advice about the move, the Navy Secretary detailed the opposition to Baruch in the Cabinet and among businessmen and then stated his own confidence in Baruch's fitness for the post. With new authority Baruch made the W.I.B. the most powerful and most effective of the home front agencies. On the very day of Baruch's appointment Daniels wrote him confidentially that there was profiteering in the mills selling duck cloth.[19]

Daniels went after monopolists and profiteers with a zeal that bordered on joy. Even before American war entry—as early as January, 1917—he was making headlines by awarding a Navy shell contract to a British munitions firm. To be sure, the British government—itself locked in a desperate war—soon forbade the contract, but Daniels had won his point. The closely knit steel industry was shocked at his idea that a projectile factory might have to be built alongside the armor plate plant already authorized by Congress. "Had good time" was Daniels' diary comment of August 30, 1917, as he personally broke ground for the first government-owned armor plate and projectile plant at Charleston, West Virginia. Once America was in the war Daniels asked the editors of trade and technical publications to convince businessmen that it was criminal to make more than a normal profit out of war. Profiteers were spelling it "paytriotism," as Daniels expressed it, and he complained of the steel companies directly to the President, on whom he urged a profit-fixing policy by the Federal Trade Commission.[20]

Years later Daniels gaily reminded President Franklin D. Roosevelt of

> . . . the case in 1917 when the Steel Company was selling steel plates to the Navy at 1.90 and charging the Shipping Board 3.60 for the same plates and demanding that the Navy pay the higher rate. They never came in line until we told them, after conferring with President Wilson, that unless they made a price low enough to pay them a fair profit and not a penny more, the Government would take over the plant and operate it. The company officer asked me, "How will you operate the plant?" My answer to him was: "I will appoint you a Commander in the reserve force and give you the job as one of Uncle Sam's naval officers." The next morning he returned to the Navy Department and asked me to tell the President that his company was ready to do anything

the President desired done to win the war. You do not have
to use a gun if you have one loaded in sight.

A corollary was Daniels' wariness of the conflict of interest inherent
in the dollar-a-year status of some men recruited from the government's prime industrial suppliers. Daniels recognized that many
men of the highest integrity were serving at a dollar a year, but he
and others were to learn of many flagrant conflicts of interest. When
the War Industries Board was formed he got President Wilson to
outlaw dollar-a-year men in that group, even if the rich men among
them would (as they did) donate their salaries to charity. Not only
would dependence on dollar-a-year men deny the government the
service of all but the rich, Daniels held, but—as he recalled it to
son Jonathan on the eve of America's World War II entry—"Uncle
Sam ought to be under no obligation by getting free services and it
would create a caste that was contrary to American principles."[21]

The war made Daniels especially alert to its becoming a pretext for a private raid upon his jealously guarded oil reserves. Before American war entry he had carefully explained to the House
Naval Affairs Committee the status of private claims. That he was
not intractable is borne out by his willingness in 1917 to accept
Senator Swanson's compromise proposal which would extend rights
to certain oil men who had begun prospecting in good faith after
President Taft's withdrawal order. This leasing bill fell through,
not because of dissatisfaction with the foregoing compromise but
over leasing provisions outside the naval oil reserves. Later, in May-
June, 1917, a drive to force open the reserves was launched by
Gavin McNab, California's Democratic national committeeman, who
led an outcry against Daniels' allegedly "dog-in-the-manger" policy.
On June 14 Edward L. Doheny, of later Teapot Dome notoriety,
told the C.N.D.'s Advisory Commission about "the imperative necessity of utilizing all available sources of oil supply." Even the alert
Baruch was taken in, submitting a sympathetic resolution that the
Advisory Commission unanimously adopted. President Wilson, en-
closing McNab's four-hundred-word telegram of distress, asked
Daniels whether the oil situation could be relieved "without going
too far in opening the door to those who have been trying to get a
foothold in the oil fields in a way we cannot approve or sanction."
Daniels' reply fairly blew the oil men out of the water: nobody in
the administration could face him down. The Navy Secretary in-

formed the President that he had set the F.T.C. to investigating the claimants, that he had offered to accept the Swanson compromise, that the reserve in dispute contained less than 9 per cent of California's proven oil deposits, and that the claimants were clearly seeking to profit from the war emergency.[22]

Another area of Daniels' concern was public opinion and the war, for he was one of three Cabinet members—with Baker and Lansing—who comprised the Committee on Public Information of which George Creel was chairman. The progressive Creel, who had worked effectively for Wilson (and Daniels) in 1916, faced a formidable assignment. His easiest job was to avoid the pitfalls of the over-rigorous censorship already imposed by the warring European powers. His overwhelmingly difficult task was to "sell" the war to the American people, many of whom were unprepared for the idea. Many Socialists, who voted for Eugene V. Debs in 1912, were obviously hostile, as were many German-Americans, Irish-Americans, and other recent immigrants who had sought freedom from arbitrary conscription as part of a better life. Creel did not have the argument of national security to work with, for it had not been meaningfully invoked, so he did all he could with Woodrow Wilson's repeated calls for an idealistic crusade. On the other hand he had to wage a war of words against the enemy, so that his resultant lurid propaganda against the German menace led to an outbreak of spy hysteria and vigilantism. Generally Daniels' record was good— strong on the idealist crusade and playing down the hysteria. His own main effort was in the direction of a policy that was inconceivable in any other warring power of the time—voluntary censorship of the press.[23]

On April 10, 1917, Secretary Daniels, three days before the President's executive order setting up the C.P.I., issued an appeal for voluntary press censorship on news of ship movements. A month later President Wilson was taking nervous cognizance of that arrangement by sending Daniels a handwritten note: "I hope Creel will remind the newspaper men of their agreement *not* to publish news of the movements of our naval vessels." Indeed Daniels, as a newspaperman like Creel, put the emphasis on giving out the news rather than suppressing it, and as a result managed quite well with just two Navy publicists, John Wilber Jenkins and Marvin McIntyre. The Navy Secretary, moreover, was prepared to take his critical medicine just as he had spooned it out to public officials for a quarter of a century. Acknowledging the place of wartime criticism to the American Newspaper Publishers Association, he said, "There was never a time when I did not realize that it was the very life of our Republic that public men should be adequately criticized." Even in the face of great provocation he held his temper with the press. When, despite anxiety caused by a premature Associated Press dispatch before all elements were safely landed, the first convoy of American troops reached France safely, Daniels with genuine emotion exclaimed to Creel: "What a Fourth of July present for the people!" Creel got out a press release in Daniels' name describing too fancifully the convoy's beating off U-boat attacks, whereupon the A.P. correspondent in London cabled that the story was wholly false. Questioned by the A.P. in Washington and shown the cable, Daniels quickly killed the story, but not in time to keep it out of print in most cities. It turned out that the story was not made up out of whole cloth, that there was some firing at periscopes and real enough danger to the convoy. President Wilson got into a towering rage at the A.P. for what in the meantime had become labeled "The Fourth of July Fake," but Daniels took it all philosophically.[24]

Another "fake" enabled Daniels to emerge as benefactor of the later vitriolic anti-Roosevelt columnist, Westbrook Pegler. Pegler met Daniels on the day of FDR's first inaugural and recalled the story, which Daniels also remembered. In June, 1917, young reporter Pegler spent three days under open arrest in Queenstown and still more time under arrest in London on a charge of having faked a story about an American destroyer getting a "probable" on submarine patrol. Pegler sent his carbon copy stateside to U.P. chief Roy Howard, who hurriedly took it to Daniels. The Navy Secretary promptly reversed Admiral Sims and restored Pegler's accreditation. Pegler later mused: ". . . there was nothing in Sims' character to protect a young reporter. But in the character of Josephus Daniels there was."[25]

It was voluntary censorship—not in agitation for the Espionage Act of 1917 and the much more drastic Sedition Act of the next year—that remained Daniels' chief concern. To be sure, whenever voluntary censorship failed, Postmaster General Burleson would invoke wartime powers through the Espionage Act. He arbitrarily denied the mails to many a publication without a hearing, and his friend Daniels did not fail to protest such muzzling of the press.

The Navy Secretary argued that a future Postmaster General might suppress papers whose policies he did not like, and wreak havoc on the First Amendment freedoms. Daniels had no contact with disaffected or put-upon immigrants, but he was given many a pessimistic glimpse of wartime vigilantism by his old Tar Heel friend, Henry Groves Connor. As a federal judge with no-nonsense convictions on personal freedom, Connor protested against the arbitrary spirit of the Justice Department, against prohibition zealots who seized the pretext of food conservatism to press their cause, against the profiteering spirit. He mourned that the people did not understand why America had gone to war and why their government demanded such a sacrifice. After first encouraging Judge Connor to crack down on violators of the liquor law, Daniels wrote more philosophically:

> I entirely agree with you with reference to the punishment of men who ignorantly failed to carry out all the draft regulations. These days are days of tragedy to me, because of the demand upon our young men to leave their homes, their callings and dependents to go to war. Little did I think when I came to Washington that we would, in our day, witness a world war and I hoped and prayed to the last that the cup might pass from me. I think it is true, as you say, that a good many people do not understand why we are in the war. It is unfortunately true that they have not kept in touch with the spirit of Prussianism and do not appreciate that if it should succeed in its present undertaking, America would have to be armed to the teeth every day and every year and individuals would have to give way to autocracy.[26]

Daniels' two eldest sons wore a uniform in the war, and fifteen-year-old Jonathan tried to enlist secretly by a personal but futile appeal to War Secretary Baker. Jonathan's belligerency was perforce limited to bearding the renowned editorialist, Arthur Brisbane. The latter wrote a piece for the Hearst press sneering at Secretary Daniels for a nonexistent order banning tattoos in the Navy. Young Jonathan indignantly wrote a denial to Brisbane and loyally defended his overworked father, whereupon the youngster got Brisbane's apology complete with a grand luncheon. Josephus Daniels' diary records his pride in Josephus, Jr., who, as the Secretary of the Navy's son, insisted upon enlisting as a private in the Marine Corps. While his younger brother Worth donned a midshipman's uniform at the Naval Academy, Joe, Jr., later earned a commission and the regard of Old Gimlet Eye himself, General Smedley D. Butler. That two-time winner of the Congressional Medal of Honor was frustrated at not having been posted overseas, and he was delighted at the seeming portent of action when Joe, Jr., joined his outfit. The Danielses agreed that their son should see overseas duty, and it was young Daniels, as Butler recalled, who "literally dragged us overseas." The fire-eating Butler came to appreciate the elder Daniels as one of only two real Secretaries (he did not name the other) he had known in three decades with the Marine Corps. Smedley Butler deemed most of them figureheads manipulated by the admirals, "but not so with Josephus Daniels—he was boss of the Navy, and had enough brains to know what it was all about."[27]

As the bulk of American naval forces prepared to hoist anchor for Europe, Daniels persuaded President Wilson to make an unprecedented wartime visit to the fleet. Wilson slipped out of town on the *Mayflower*, Daniels on the *Dolphin*, and they met aboard the battleship *Pennsylvania* anchored with historic Yorktown in the background. With a Wilson-directed taboo on ceremony, Daniels introduced to the assembled officers: "Your Commander-in-Chief, the President of the United States!" It was a notable speech, a heart-to-heart speech, one later likened by David Lawrence to a fighting football speech at halftime. Woodrow Wilson spoke as a man on fire, and his inspiration probably was on Daniels when he proceeded to lower the boom on the Navy League. Shortly thereafter came a powder magazine explosion at the Mare Island Navy Yard, following which the Navy League charged Daniels with blocking an investigation. Daniels went straight to the White House. "Went to see W," his diary of August 14 reads, "about the charge of the Naval League & showed the stationery and letter." (Colonel Thompson of the League had suavely replied to Daniels' demand for his resignation with a suggestion that they both resign.) On the seventeenth Daniels forbade Navy Leaguers to set foot on Navy vessels or installations, and later got the Red Cross to assume direction of collecting relief supplies for the Navy. Investigation proved that the anti-Daniels leaders of the League had eagerly jumped to the wrong conclusion, and the League then withdrew its charges. Daniels was implacable, however, so that Colonel Thompson soon resigned and eventually—before Daniels left office—the Navy League underwent reorganization.[28]

On the home front, Daniels' well-known friendliness to orga-

nized labor consistently stood him in good stead. In the preparedness days he had worked on Congress for an eight-hour day, shrewdly getting the legislators to agree with him that "overtime is a very
costly proposition." Daniels' labor trouble-shooter was Franklin D.
Roosevelt, who was often put on his mettle during the hectic camp
construction being rushed on a cost-plus percentage basis. By August, 1917, it was clear that Army and Navy labor problems were in-
terconnected, so much so that a sympathetic strike was threatened
at the Army's camp at Yaphank, Long Island against a Navy can-
tonment near New York City. Louis B. Wehle who, as Secretary
Baker's special assistant, had negotiated the useful Baker-Gompers
no-strike agreement, got a sympathetic reception from Daniels.
First the Navy Secretary agreed, and Samuel Gompers concurred,
that a Navy officer should replace the Army's delegate on the Can-
tonment Adjustment Commission where Navy construction was involved. Shortly thereafter Daniels and Gompers informally extended the Baker-Gompers agreement to cover Navy construction,
the Navy Secretary scrawling longhand on the face of the original
document: "I agree to this policy for the Navy. Aug. 10, 1917. Josephus Daniels."[29]

Avoiding work stoppages without resorting to compulsory arbitration was the concern of those Wilsonians, like Daniels, who realized that American organized labor had come of age. In exchange
for treating labor leader Gompers as an equal, the administration
was getting not only an anti-strike commitment but a tacit agreement not to insist now on closed shop or union shop arrangements.
Daniels showed unbounded admiration for Newton D. Baker, whose
agreement with Gompers made such good sense, and the Navy Secretary also backed up Franklin D. Roosevelt in labor matters. When
FDR suggested V. Everit Macy for the public member of the Shipbuilding Labor Adjustment Board, Daniels heartily endorsed that
excellent nominee to the President. In that same August of 1917
Daniels heard with some anxiety Gompers' report of I.W.W. and
other labor troubles in the Southwest and Northwest. Daniels personally moved in the Council of National Defense, and it was so
voted, to request the President to appoint a commission of inquiry
and reconciliation. Tied in with Daniels' pro-labor attitude was his
lifelong antipathy for conscription. When President Wilson proclaimed the draft law on May 18, 1917, Daniels was already on the
record—as recently as March 24—as opposed to universal military

service, preferring a volunteer plan. More, he preferred an army of men older than the nineteen to twenty-one-year-olds first proposed.[30]

Protecting those young men against the evils of alcohol and vice was a task dear to Daniels' heart. He later looked back with satisfaction on the results of the wartime clean-up, saying: "It gave America the soberest, cleanest, and healthiest fighting men the world has known." From the public health standpoint, certainly, the armed forces' World War I record was notable. It is true that militant prohibitionists took advantage of the Draft Act's provisions to close the saloons in the larger cities, setting up five-mile "clean" areas around military camps. Military necessity, not morality, was the argument that finally weighed most in winning co-operation from local governments, but not before Seattle and Birmingham had been put off-limits to servicemen, and Secretary Daniels had posted a Marine patrol in the streets of Philadelphia. By the end of 1917 the logic of "Fit to fight" had impressed itself, so much so that Raymond B. Fosdick, director of the Commission on Training Camp Activities, could report that every red light district in the country (110 in number) had been closed and that the venereal disease rate was at an all-time low. He had had his difficulties with the Navy's high rate of venereal disease, owing largely to Secretary Daniels' principled refusal to give in on a Navy issue of prophylactic devices. At length Daniels reluctantly let his moral reservations be overcome, left on an inspection trip, and Acting Secretary Roosevelt signed the necessary order much to Daniels' relief.[31]

His anti-vice crusading has given Josephus Daniels the name in New Orleans of the "Johnny Appleseed of Jazz." Merry Puritan that he was, Daniels never heard himself called Johnny Appleseed during his lifetime, but he would have thrown back his head and laughed long and loud at the name. Since 1897 Storyville had been New Orleans' "restricted district," recognized by ordinance in the European manner. Storyville covered twenty-eight city blocks, gave employment to 750 women (according to the mayor's statement) and to uncounted jazz musicians who played from 7:00 P.M. until the dawn. Daniels opened his war on Storyville in September, 1917, with a two-page single-spaced letter sent simultaneously to the Governor of Louisiana and the Mayor of New Orleans. Daniels reminded them that the immoral conduct to which young servicemen were tempted by Storyville led to more casualties than enemy bullets, and implied, as he later stated explicitly, "Close Storyville or the Navy will close it for you." Mayor Martin Behrman put up a strenuous fight, making two trips to Washington to argue for "the God-given right of men to be men." Predictably, the Navy Secretary and father of four young sons was grimly unimpressed.[32]

Mayor Behrman gave in with a letter to which Daniels did not even reply for three weeks, paying no heed to the other's recital of alleged difficulties. Daniels did not reply until after New Orleans had passed the promised ordinance, effective after thirty days, abolishing Storyville. He coolly professed himself gratified that "you have acted in this matter so promptly that it has not been necessary for me to act under Sections 12 and 13 of the Act of Congress." Then the Secretary went off for his first visit to the Great Lakes Naval Training Station, speaking in Chicago to the Clinical Congress of Surgeons of North America. He told the surgeons: "Prostitution and its twin brother, drunkenness, must be fought vigorously and unceasingly until they have become anachronisms." A limited evacuation from Storyville began several weeks before deadline, most of its denizens staying on in glimmering hopes of a restraining order that never came. Storyville closed on midnight of November 17. To the nation it was proof of the administration's determined attitude, and even cities unaffected by proximity to training camps began to clean house. To the jazz musicians of Storyville, whose economic base had been destroyed, it was a removal order of first importance. They moved up the Mississippi to St. Louis, on to Kansas City and Chicago, where they developed those characteristic offshoots of New Orleans jazz in response to the "Johnny Appleseed" activities of Josephus Daniels.[33]

During this period the sedentary Daniels was fairly bursting with good health, while the energetic FDR fell prey to almost every germ that came along. Roosevelt, who had vigorously pioneered swimming instruction for Navy seamen, came down with appendicitis in 1915, with a severe throat infection in 1916, another in 1917, and double pneumonia in 1918, whereas Daniels, who never walked when he could ride, sailed serenely through it all. Walter Camp, the Yale All-American, was charged with keeping wartime America fit. He got Roosevelt and other Cabinet and sub-Cabinet officials to form an early morning exercise club, but he could not prevail on the Navy Secretary to join. Daniels sought the advice of Sterling Ruffin and Hubert Royster, Tar Heel physicians who had known him for years, and they agreed that the calisthenics and the running through Potomac Park probably would kill him. Walter Camp reluctantly conceded that Daniels' health was indeed holding up, but as a Parthian shot told the other that if he exercised he would live longer. Daniels had not exercised from the days he had played first base for the Swift Foot nine in Wilson, N.C., to that day he wrote in his memoirs: "Walter and his pupils have passed on, while I was strong and vigorous when I celebrated my eighty-third birthday."[34]

In the same summer of 1917, when Daniels was cracking down on vice conditions near training camps, FDR got the assignment to investigate conditions at Newport, Rhode Island. Governor Beeckman resented Daniels' having sent him a letter which he first released to the press—for the Navy Secretary as Puritan could be ruthless—but the personable FDR, newly made a Harvard Overseer, was really *persona grata* and a house guest of the Beeckmans. FDR had reason to remember Newport, because out of that trip grew the charge that he had condoned the entrapment of Navy homosexuals, a charge that greatly embarrassed him in the months before his grim and climactic battle with polio. But as a wartime Assistant Navy Secretary with political glamor, he could laugh delightedly at a wrong-headed report that linked Daniels with gambling. In his diary of July 26, 1917, Daniels wrote: "Secret service man in Newport wrote report quoting a gambler saying everything would be open soon for Gov. Beeckman had bought up Secretary Daniels—Roosevelt ha ha'd." At the inauguration of the first air mail next spring, Daniels got three letters from the air mail pouch. He gave one of the stamps to Miss Addie's mother and kept one for himself (after all, he had a stamp-licking background in his mother's front porch-post office). The third stamp went to FDR, who begged it for his stamp collection. "Of course he got it," Mrs. Daniels recalled. "Nobody could refuse Franklin anything."[35]

Undoubtedly the Daniels-FDR team worked best in the area of Navy procurement, where the caution of the Secretary and the impetuous zeal of the Assistant Secretary proved complementary. Daniels' attention to detail was proof, despite the unprecedented sums he spent, against any charges of wastefulness or improper spending. FDR's headlong attack on red tape, on the other hand, got things done without crippling delays. Herbert H. Lehman, a civilian Navy employee early in the war, quickly noted the difference in the two men's styles, and his admiration for FDR made Lehman later into one of Roosevelt's most loyal political followers. Still, Lehman's immediate superior was the brilliant Admiral McGowan, a shining example of Daniels' ability to pick good men (and was not FDR one of them?). McGowan did a notable job before the war of simplifying the Navy's supply functions, and he achieved an exceptional wartime record of maintaining competitive bidding, of absolute honesty, of keeping a high standard of subsistence for the enlisted men, of efficient cost-keeping. During demobilization McGowan saw to it that the first $70 million worth of government surplus fetched an actual profit of $3.6 million.[36]

Another of Daniels' appointees was FDR's friend, Thomas Mott Osborne, who as Warden of New York's Sing Sing had made a record of progressive penology. His sometimes abrasive manner made him less successful than McGowan, but Osborne's contribution to the Navy was not negligible. It proceeded from Daniels' personal dissatisfaction with the traditional naval prisons and his prewar emphasis on the return to duty of their inmates. When Thomas Mott Osborne reported to the Portsmouth Naval Prison during the summer of 1917, he found 190 Marines guarding 180 prisoners. He donned prison clothes, one of his regular inspection procedures, and engaged in the prisoner routine of cutting blocks of ice under the Marine shotguns. Many Navy officers were outraged at getting Osborne's "graduates" on their ships, but by and large the system won acceptance—helped on by the war emergency—and when Osborne left the service in the spring of 1920 he had sent back to active duty nearly 4,000 of the some 6,000 prisoners he had handled.[37]

Always a favorite with newspapermen, Daniels enjoyed good public relations once war was declared. The *Outlook* published "Josephus Daniels, The Man Who Democratized the Navy," the *Public* carried a eulogy on him by his longtime admirer, Professor William E. Dodd, and the *Forum* solicitously interviewed him: "Secretary Daniels Talks of the Submarine Menace." Strong common sense helped Daniels in many a situation, notably in setting precedent by enlisting women in the Navy and Marines. Early in the war, with a tremendous demand for clerical help—no men to fill the jobs and no money to hire civilians—Daniels promptly ascertained that there was no law saying that a Navy yeoman or a Marine had to be a man. Accordingly, he welcomed into the Navy no fewer than 11,000 Yeomen (F) and 269 Marines (F)—popularly known as Yeomanettes and Marinettes—whose handsome uniforms and fine record undoubtedly helped the postwar cause of woman suffrage. Meanwhile the old anti-militarist Daniels conceived a real love of the Navy, which he cherished thereafter as much as Franklin Roosevelt himself. Too, he learned new respect for the career Navy officers he had once distrusted as caste-conscious. "The big men in the Navy," he confided to Henry Groves Connor during the war, "I find very much like men everywhere and are men of the finest type that it has been a pleasure to come in contact with them since I have been in Washington. They are men loyal to their country, zealous, true and straightforward and forgetful of self and life."[38]

One such career officer was Miss Addie's youngest brother David—later decorated with the Distinguished Service Cross and still later an admiral—who came to say goodbye on the Danielses' twenty-ninth wedding anniversary, May 2, 1917. Now a lieutenant commander, David Bagley had command of the new destroyer *Jacob Jones,* and he took tender leave of Miss Addie, of the two maiden sisters, and of the mother who had lost Worth Bagley nineteen years before. One night in December the Navy Secretary got news that the *Jacob Jones* had been torpedoed and that David's name was not on the list of survivors. He delayed as long as possible telling Bagley's sisters and especially Miss Addie. Mrs. Bagley was not told until a doctor had been summoned, and the grim news went understandably hard with her. But near midnight came news that David Bagley, who had borne himself bravely, had been rescued, whereupon, as Daniels recorded in his diary of December 8, 1917: "Woke everybody up. Great rejoicing, telephoned to friends, & telegraphed & had regular thanksgiving." On the next day, according to the diary, President Wilson announced the good news to Daniels' newspaper friends at the annual Gridiron banquet, whereupon "everybody stood up and applauded." Characteristically, too, the Danielses had a clergyman come in (Miss Addie's Presbyterian minister) for prayers.

The devout Navy Secretary would sometimes startle his cosmopolitan dinner guests by his way of advancing a step, raising his hand, and asking an old-fashioned blessing. He carried off such international dinners with aplomb because of his unstudied simplicity, and on one such occasion in 1917 the heads of the British and French Commissions plus aides bowed their heads obediently (the French crossed themselves) and became temporary teetotalers. Their wine glasses were filled with Apollinaris water, White Rock, red and white grape juice—and somehow it all went off famously. The French, in particular, could later forgive Daniels for not having served them wine. In the spring of 1918 Clemenceau cabled desperately to André Tardieu, French representative in Washington, for more food to feed those made refugees by the German breakthrough. Tardieu applied to Herbert Hoover, the Food Commissioner, who refused because of a quota restriction. Tardieu recalled: "I went and found a kind old man [Daniels hooted at that ten years later!] who was Secretary of the Navy and was called Josephus Daniels. He immediately delivered the goods to me and the next day . . . he levied the equivalent from Mr. Hoover's stocks. The latter was enraged. President Wilson, who had a sense of humor, when he heard the story burst into laughter and said: "Fine joke!"[39]

In those days Daniels carefully noted in his diary the highlights of the sermons he heard preached at the Mount Vernon Place Methodist Church. He went further in January, 1918, during the Washington Revival conducted by Billy Sunday, and invited the evangelist to the Wyoming Street house for morning preaching. Mrs. Daniels reported a full house of Navy and other officials in attendance, covering the religious spectrum all the way from Franklin Roosevelt to Julius Rosenwald. Characteristically, the devout but fun-loving Danielses adopted as a family joke the fact of their not living in "The House of Truth." A religious society of that name was located next door, and a lady inquiring for "The House of Truth" was directed elsewhere by Robert Gaines, the family's Negro butler, who told the story with vast amusement. Gaines later was the beneficiary of two Presidential executive orders inspired by Secretary Daniels, one appointing him a messenger in the Navy Department and the other giving him the civil service status that enabled him to stay on until retired for age. The Billy Sunday campaign, to return to it, got the free use of the Navy and Marine bands from the Navy Secretary, who greatly enjoyed the luxury of listening to his "own" band. He was always glad that he had brought out of retirement John Philip Sousa, the famous bandmaster, and Daniels recalled: "I had the honor of welcoming him back into the Navy where his youthful spirit put life into the youngsters who loved his 'Marching Along.' "[40]

By the start of 1918 Daniels could report hopefully to Congress that the Navy's European patrols were cruising 516,000 miles a month and that the shipping tonnage sunk had declined steadily after the high of the previous April. Those patrols were directed by the difficult but able Admiral Sims in London, who was so much *persona grata* with the British Admiralty that he was offered an honorary membership in the Admiralty. Daniels' diary of November 26 said: "An emphatic *No.*" In January the campaign was renewed through Ambassador Page, who wired that King George V himself wished to confer the aforementioned honor on Sims. Daniels' diary of January 31, 1918, recorded a variety of collected opinions, but the one that really counted was Woodrow Wilson's. The President plainly indicated a no when he wrote for Daniels' opinion and Daniels responded with his own heartfelt negative. They both suspected that the Anglophilic Sims might thus be flattered against America's interests. Sims apparently never forgave Daniels for refusing to let him accept the Admiralty honor.[41]

No one, least of all Daniels, could deny that Sims's too-few destroyers were effectively killing submarines. His destroyers were too few mainly because more could not be spared from their compelling task of convoying American troops to France. Sims was all for vigorous action abroad rather than a timorous defense of the American coast, and in this he had Daniels' support even though it nearly cost the Secretary his political scalp. In the spring of 1918 a wave of German submarine attacks on American coastal shipping brought sharp and panicky criticism of the Navy Department. There was nervous talk about new German subs capable of crossing the ocean while submerged, plus much excited speculation in the press. Daniels firmly and wisely refused to weaken the naval forces in European waters, and he got support from—of all people—Henry Cabot Lodge. Leading Republicans like Penrose and Brandegee were heaping abuse on the Navy Secretary from the Senate floor, but the politically astute Daniels replied by inviting in for some straight talk the two top members of the Senate Naval Affairs Committee. So Chairman Swanson and ranking Republican Lodge got the facts. Lodge appeared on the Senate floor and launched into a defense of the Navy Department's policy and praise for the Navy's exertions that utterly silenced Daniels' critics. By implication Lodge justified the priority of destroyers for convoying troops rather than for submarine hunting, pointing out that "the chase of the submarine is something like searching for a needle in a haystack." No one could tell where in the vast expanse of the Atlantic a submarine might break surface. To be sure, Lodge's enmity for Woodrow Wilson made him a foeman of Josephus Daniels, but Daniels always kept a soft spot in his heart for the man who had stood by him in a critical hour.[42]

Because destroyers took so much time to build and cost $3 million each, Daniels was from the onset of hostilities committed to the substitute Eagle Boats later built at Henry Ford's River Rouge plant. The two-hundred-foot Eagle Boat was a good steel vessel and the Ford site made sense because Eastern shipyards were too crowded to make the boats. Unfortunately the preliminaries took too long and the work itself did not go fast enough. Daniels spent considerable time during 1918 trying to get Ford an additional East Coast plant, during which time the Secretary harassed Bernard Baruch for a site in power-short areas. The daring scheme to build ships in an auto plant was partially successful, Ford dispatching seven vessels to the Atlantic Coast by Armistice Day, but Ford met more difficulties than anticipated. They included a brief post-Armistice charge of profiteering levied by Senator Lodge, but disproved at the hearings by Navy officials.[43]

Both Daniels and Army Secretary Baker, who understood one another, knew they were handy civilian scapegoats for whatever went wrong in the armed services. Daniels had taken his turn in 1916, and Baker was due for his in the terrible wartime winter of 1917-18. The Senate Military Affairs Committee painted a damning picture of inefficiency in the war effort, laying particular blame on the War Department. The diminutive Baker fought back courageously and won general vindication, but he would have resigned first if Daniels had not dissuaded him. Daniels' diary of January 23, 1918, records a meeting with Baker: "I told him the President would not permit it [Baker's resignation], that the opposition would be satisfied with nobody except TR, Root or Wood, & the President would not name either & instead of composing & uniting, his resignation would have the opposite effect. Looks 5 years older. I told him that within a few months his critics would see how unjust they were."

Navy Department matters were running so smoothly, by comparison, that by April 5, 1918, FDR was petitioning his chief to allow him to inspect Navy installations in Europe. Actually FDR did not depart until three months later, so long did it take to put his political house in order. He had first to ease himself out of the New York race for Governor in order to make peace with Tammany. Louis Howe realized that FDR, while in Europe, would be beneficently sheltered from any intramural fights in the Democratic primaries. Accordingly, Howe advised Mrs. Roosevelt to get her husband to stay overseas until after the primaries, to hint to him that President Wilson and Secretary Daniels both thought it prudent. Daniels well knew about FDR's political glamor and had advised him before, in the fall of 1914, against offering for his party's nomination for U.S. Senator when the outlook was unfavorable. Daniels' advice went unheeded then, but in 1918 FDR did not come home from Europe until after the Democratic primaries in New York. He had had the grand tour and a grand time, delightedly and repeatedly exceeding his authority, and winding up with double pneumonia.[44]

FDR's recuperative power was matched by that of Mary Cleaves Daniels, now eighty-three years old, who was a regular visitor to Washington in the company of her namesake granddaughter from Goldsboro. Harry A. Garfield, the Fuel Commissioner and son of the Republican President, learned about her in detail. Garfield was shocked at one point to learn that his own revered father had somehow deprived the Navy Secretary's mother of her livelihood. His friend Daniels then good-humoredly told him the story of his postmistress mother and of her ouster because of her too outspokenly Democratic son and editor of the Wilson *Advance*. On his own birthday in 1918, the Navy Secretary hurried to Goldsboro on hearing that his mother had had a bad fall. When he got there on a Sunday morning she was unconscious and thought to be dying, by noon she was up and about, and two months later she was again in Washington to see her Joe and Miss Addie.[45]

All during 1918 Daniels kept fighting off raids on "his" oil reserves. In January Senator Swanson amended his then-current leasing bill so as to exempt the naval oil reserves, which left the California oil promoters understandably indignant. On the twelfth Daniels recorded in his diary his disagreement with Attorney General Gregory's idea that "innocent purchasers could get benefit of act." Daniels scrawled: "No! They would swear they were innocent & open door to recognize the fraudulent claimants." By June the American oil companies were trying to get armed intervention in Mexico under cover of aiding the war effort. Chaotic conditions in revolutionary Mexico did produce recurrent scares in the Tampico oil fields, largely owned by American and British firms, but Daniels produced a dispatch from his commander off Tampico saying that conditions were perfectly quiet. Also, Daniels had been burned by one Mexican intervention, and he now plainly told the President that such a move would be "an act of war against Mexico." On June 10 Wilson agreed with Daniels to let matters stand, to refrain from concentrating Marines at Galveston. Yet when he thought the oil companies had legitimate cause for redress, Daniels stated their case at a White House Conference in August. In the meantime, in July, Daniels had informed the President that California crude oil production was already ten thousand barrels a day in excess of need.[46]

Daniels let down when he wrote from the heart to his friend Henry Groves Connor that summer: "I feel something good must come out of all this suffering and travail." Eight American divisions, ferried to France by Daniels' Navy convoys, had just wiped out the German salient between Rheims and Soissons; a few days later Pershing's American First Army would take up positions before the St. Mihiel salient. It was the beginning of the end, about which conflicting alarms still circulated. Sir Eric Geddes and his Admiralty staff thought they had such vital news for Daniels that they came from England to the house on Wyoming Avenue to impart it in person and in secret. The Britons had intelligence of a massive German U-boat campaign to be launched in the spring of 1919. On the other hand, a returning American officer came to Daniels with a personal message from Ambassador William G. Sharp in Paris. Daniels must go to President Wilson personally with the information that the Germans would sue for peace within sixty days. The Navy Secretary delivered both reports to the President, and all hands had to act as if both were true.[47]

A similar confusion arose over the false Armistice news circulated by the United Press. Daniels knew, and said so, that it was an unnewsworthy practice to get "confirmation" of an armistice from Brest, far removed from the negotiating site at Compiègne. Nevertheless, when the A.P.'s Melville Stone tried to insist on official censure of the U.P.'s Roy Howard, Daniels would not be baited. "See her, Mel Stone," he recalled saying, "you and I have been reporters eager for scoops. If you had received the news as

Roy Howard did and had not rushed to give your paper the scoop, you would be no reporter and ought to lose your job."[48]

The war did not by any means cause Daniels to abdicate his involvement with politics; nothing could do that. His new-found popularity after Wilson's re-election had even evoked from Colonel House (who had confessedly worked for Daniels' ouster earlier) a specific denial that he was intriguing to replace Daniels. Well entrenched in the President's confidence despite the equivocal House, Daniels proceeded to recommend specific legislative goals to Wilson: a remedy for the break-down in rail transportation, extending the draft to non-citizens, and an extension of the price regulations. In the spring of 1918 the man who had welcomed Yeomanettes into the Navy took up the cudgels in favor of the Woman's Suffrage Amendment, successfully urging the President as head of his party to intervene with the Texas legislature to permit women to vote in the Democratic primaries there. By May he was anxiously working on details by which soldiers in the A.E.F. might cast absentee ballots. Seeing that the mountain district of North Carolina was politically precarious, Daniels solicited and got a Presidential letter to the voters on behalf of the Democratic incumbent, Zebulon V. Weaver, who did win re-election.[49]

With his eye on the 1918 elections and a precarious Democratic hold on the Senate, Daniels went to work on Henry Ford to be the party's senatorial standard-bearer in Michigan. The industrialist would not be persuaded. He was a nominal Republican who had voted for Wilson in 1916, so Wilson told Daniels: "Bring him over to the White House and I'll see what I can do." The quixotic millionaire could not deny his interest in peace-making, especially since his financing of the forlorn "peace ship" two years before and the dream of getting the soldiers out of the trenches by Christmas. Thus the auto magnate was successfully persuaded by the President he admired, but Ford took some of the bloom off the peach by stating that he was running only because Wilson wished it and that he would neither spend any money on the campaign nor sanction his supporters' doing so. Daniels took to the hustings on behalf of Democratic candidates generally, and called on the Michigan voters to elect Henry Ford, praising his building of Eagle Boats in the war effort. On the other hand the National Security League, Elihu Root and ex-Presidents Taft and Roosevelt urged that Ford be defeated, and Truman H. Newberry, Ford's Republican opponent, did not hesitate—as Daniels recalled—to pour out money like water. On election day the non-campaigning Ford lost by a narrow margin.[50]

The Ford candidacy was not an especially partisan move by the President, and specifically nonpartisan was his endorsement of the liberal Republican, Knute Nelson of Minnesota. Still, Woodrow Wilson crossed his Rubicon on October 28, 1918, by issuing a public appeal to elect a Democratic Congress in November. Most Democratic leaders (but not Daniels) considered it a mistake of the first order, an open invitation to disaster. Wilson was virtually repudiating those Republicans who had supported his war measures and, in dangerous off-year elections when the party in power usually lost votes, daring to ask for a vote of confidence. The Democratic defeat just before the Armistice of 1918, which defeat was certainly not caused by Wilson's appeal, nevertheless was interpreted—at his own invitation—as a personal repudiation. Daniels, for his part, never ceased to argue that the resultant Republican Congress offered nothing but a stalemate in domestic policies, and in the Senate managed to defeat the Peace Treaty. Certainly, no one could fault his arithmetic. If Henry Ford had won in Michigan, the Democrats could have organized the Senate, 48 to 48, with Vice President Marshall's deciding Democratic vote. If the Democrats had organized the Senate, the chairman of the Foreign Relations Committee would not have been Henry Cabot Lodge. If Lodge had not been in position, as chairman, desperately to block a Senate vote the following July, the then-strong public sentiment for the Peace Treaty might readily have generated enough pressure on the Senate to ratify it on the spot. All became an anguished might-have-been.[51]

So the Republicans organized the post-Armistice Congress because—as Josephus Daniels succinctly put it—"The Republican majority is out on bail." He was referring to the aftermath of the Ford-Newberry election during which Henry Ford, now mad enough to fight, secured some very plain evidence indicating that Newberry's primary and general election victories were bought. The Senator was convicted, in March, 1920, of violating the Federal Corrupt Practices Act, but the Supreme Court later declared the act unconstitutional. Nevertheless, a Republican-organized Senate in 1922 gave Newberry so clear an indication that it would expel him at the next session that he resigned in November of that year. Meanwhile, it was clear that Henry Cabot Lodge's undying enmity for "Wilson's League" and its author—warmly reciprocated, be it said—

were helping to create an irreconcilable attitude that would lead to the final tragedy. Daniels developed a personal theory to explain the Lodge-Wilson feud, saying that it originated in jealousy over literary rank. When Wilson was elected President, possessor of the Ph.D., Lodge was no longer *the* scholar in politics, but simply *a* scholar. Without consciously recognizing it, Lodge developed a rancor and hurt pride that first burst into open resentment over Wilson's Mexican policy. Daniels quoted from Lodge's writings to show that the senator had urged international agreements in the spirit of "Wilson's League" until the idea was broached by Wilson. By 1918, as Daniels saw it, Lodge was so consumed by a personal ambition for the Presidency that he saw no one in his way but a Woodrow Wilson who might be accorded an unprecedented third term after triumphantly winning ratification for the Treaty. "By all the rules of the game," Daniels later wrote, "Lodge deserved the nomination he coveted in 1920. That failure was gall and worm-wood to him."[52]

When Wilson set about choosing the peace commissioners, having announced his own intention of going to Paris, he got from Daniels a handwritten recommendation that he take along William Jennings Bryan. Of Bryan, Daniels wrote that taking part in the Peace Conference was "the crowning ambition of his life," but Wilson vetoed the idea "because it would be unjustly but certainly taken for granted that he [Bryan] would be too easy and that he would pursue some Eutopian scheme." No one today doubts that Wilson blundered over his choice of commissioners who would not pursue any "Eutopian scheme." Instead of the obscure Henry White he could have taken ex-President Taft or the near-President Charles Evans Hughes as Republicans who would have worked loyally for his purposes and also carried weight with their party. But, as Thomas A. Bailey has written, it was Wilson's tragedy to be "temperamentally incapable either of inviting . . . or of serving wholeheartedly" with opponents of such stature. Wilson did not take along a senator because, presumably, that senator would have had to be the distrusted Henry Cabot Lodge. Josephus Daniels later came to believe that Wilson erred and should have taken along a senator (he did not say Lodge) in the interest of getting the Treaty ratified. To be sure, Daniels said, Wilson was right in principle: "No Senator should have voice in negotiating a treaty over which he must act as a legislator." But in the context of the London Naval Conference a decade later, to which President Hoover appointed a senator of each party to the delegation, Daniels sighed: "After all, what is a question of policy in this day?"[53]

During Woodrow Wilson's ordeal, Josephus Daniels stood by him loyally. "I know," the President wrote him from the Europe-bound *George Washington*, "that you and all my colleagues will keep your eyes skinned against anybody getting the better of us while I am on the other side of the water." The President returned to the White House briefly in late February, 1919, and, when he boarded the *George Washington* to return to Paris, he was already sailing under the cloud of Lodge's senatorial "round robin" against the League Covenant. Aboard ship Wilson got a brave little Navy dispatch from Josephus Daniels telling him of a Democratic victory at a special election in Pennsylvania and assured him: "You have won first blood in the appeal to the people." The President replied to this and other like notes: "These are often days of very deep discouragement and anxiety, and it was an instinct of friendship which led you to write me as you did."[54]

False Dawn

As the dawn of the World War I Armistice approached, a false dawn as it turned out, Josephus Daniels shared in the general euphoria in which the postwar world was viewed. For example, not only did he share the widespread sympathy for the 1917 Balfour Declaration on Palestine, but Daniels became the premier Christian Zionist on the American scene. The stand was reinforced in him by a lifelong desire to liberate the Jewish people from the lands of their oppression. In New York's Carnegie Hall, on September 29, 1918, "to celebrate the victory of the Allied Armies in Palestine and President Wilson's statement approving the aims of the Zionist Organization," Daniels made an especially moving and heartfelt address. "In all my life," he recalled of the audience's response, "I have never seen deeper spiritual fervor." Yet a year later a saddened Daniels was back at Carnegie Hall speaking to a Jewish meeting called in protest against the vicious pogroms in the Ukraine, defiantly avowing "that the day would never come when America would fail to stand against injustice and oppression in any part of the world."[1]

By the same token, all Daniels' plans for a postwar Navy were based squarely on America's joining a League of Nations as per Wilson's Fourteen Points. He minced no words in telling the anti-League coalition that it must face up to America's pooling weapons with other peace-enforcing nations or face the alternative—the ruinous cost of unlimited armaments. So much was clear and logical. In fact, on Armistice Day itself Daniels and the Navy Department produced a secret plan for American participation in a League naval force. So much for idealism, but the plan also provided that the price for American participation would be naval parity with Britain. The secret was not revealed by the Navy Department until 1930 during the naval parity debate that engaged the London Naval Conference of that year. It turned out that twisting the lion's tail—in which Daniels and his top naval aides happily concurred—made vastly more difficult the task of winning over the European critics of American plans for a League. The American insistence on naval parity first alarmed, then alienated the British, who distrusted any threat to their traditional naval ascendancy. Unquestionably, the resultant failure of the two powers to cooperate bore tragic consequences for the future peace of the world.[2]

Not that Daniels was intransigent or dead set against a compromise that would save a League. As of the end of 1918 the Secretary was publicly committed to a resumption of the Navy's war-interrupted three-year building program, which included capital ships. In January Daniels wired confidentially to President Wilson that many pro-League Congressmen were hostile to navalism. "Unless conditions abroad dictate change," Daniels wired, "my own view is that three-year programme should be adopted with proviso that if Peace mission orders reduction of armament the President is authorized not to make contracts." He later repeated to the President his belief in a parity of armaments, and also advised against sinking the surrendered German warships at Scapa Flow. In Europe that spring the Navy Secretary compromised on both questions. He at least muted his objections to British naval predominance, and came around fully to Admiral Benson's view—shared by the British for reasons of their own—that it was the better part of wisdom to sink the German warships rather than distribute them among the victors. So as he stepped up pressure to get the Versailles Treaty ratified, Daniels would announce a peace offering to Britain—withdrawal of America's three-year building program.[3]

On the home front Daniels reluctantly yielded ground on the future control of radio, which the wartime Navy had helped to develop out of the earlier wireless telegraphy. The Navy Secretary's concern was for communications—not the unknown factor of radio entertainment—when he insistently held that radio should remain a government monopoly under the Navy Department, which had controlled it during the war. In a last-ditch effort for government control, Daniels set up a dramatic demonstration of the new radio telephone, and he called up President Wilson on Washington's Birthday, 1919, while the Chief Executive was approaching American shores aboard the *George Washington.* Daniels heartily assured the President of a warm welcome home on this brief return from the Peace Conference.

Nevertheless, Daniels' campaign for continued government control of radio had already been defeated. Having bought, under wartime powers, the systems of the Federal and Marconi Companies for $3 million, he appeared in late 1918 before the House Merchant Marine Committee in support of a government monopoly. "The special interests present opposed any government ownership," he recorded sorrowfully in his diary of December 12, meaning plainly that the great electrical manufacturing companies, which were now shorn of their war contracts, were eyeing future business. After the Republican victory in November, the G.O.P. leader in the House took a particularly dim view of Daniels' use of the Navy's uncommitted funds to buy up some of the privately owned wireless systems. Representative James R. Mann (R.-Ill.) loudly called for Daniels' impeachment in late January, 1919, whereupon the House deleted the radio-purchase money from a Navy deficiency appropriation. A few months later Daniels' final efforts, in which he made specific recommendations for a government monopoly, fell on unsympathetic ears in Congress.[4]

There was considerably more sympathy for the Navy Secretary in North Carolina, where during his Cabinet days Daniels showed a characteristic "style" that few people ever forgot. On one such occasion soon after the Armistice he stopped off a Pullman car into a Tar Heel community that had outdone itself to provide him a worthy reception. Alongside the train stood a rifle-bearing honor guard of recently demobilized seamen, and also close by waited a group of sword-clanking former Navy officers. Daniels smilingly took his time—he was not the kind of man you could hurry—and then put out his hand to the nearest enlisted man while the ex-officers fumed. Reporter Ben Dixon MacNeill recalled: "About the only printable item of their catalogue was 'demagogue.'" Then Daniels came around with the same affable smile to the stiffly saluting ex-officers, being fully aware—MacNeill swore that Daniels was shrewdly and amusedly aware—that the same ex-officers "had been calling him unprintable names in grisly whispers." Nevertheless, the Navy Secretary managed to convey in a twinkling that every Navy man was, individually, his personal concern, starting with the enlisted man. He carried this idea through to the townspeople, starting with the youngest men on the committee and later getting around to their elders, whom he disarmed by gently first-naming them.[5]

The Navy Secretary was listened to in his home state with understandable respect. In February, 1919, before a joint session of the General Assembly which gave him a personal ovation, he set out a whole catalogue of progressive ideas for the Tar Heel State's future. He declared for woman suffrage, a strengthened primary law, a revamped State Guard, a state income tax, a six-month school bill that would equalize educational opportunity in the poorer counties, even a state constitutional convention. Especially close to his heart was a Consolidated University of North Carolina, of which he was a pioneer supporter. His plan would include, besides the University at Chapel Hill, State College at Raleigh, and Woman's College at Greensboro, the teachers' colleges at Boone and Greenville.[6]

In furtherance of his plan Daniels called for "one institution, one board of trustees, and one president" in order to eliminate "duplication of effort." Thus his plea to the legislators was ostensibly geared to economy, but he revealed his desire to upgrade the teacher-training colleges where he "would emphasize those branches that give to women the best opportunities."[7] Although consolidation did not become a fact for more than another decade, and then primarily under the whip and spur of the Depression, Daniels was perhaps the best-situated spokesman to make so early a public plea for consolidation. As Secretary of the Navy he stood above the local battle: as an alumnus of the University and long-time trustee he could not be faulted as hostile to Chapel Hill, as a crusader for the establishment of State College he was equally secure there, and as a champion of Charles D. McIver in founding the Woman's College he was equally invulnerable.

Consequently, the name of Josephus Daniels was among the earliest to be advanced by those who were seeking a replacement for the late-lamented Edward K. Graham as President of the University of North Carolina. The terrible influenza epidemic of 1918 had claimed the life of Graham in October and that of his successor, Dr. Marvin H. Stacy, the following January. Chances are that Daniels' not being a professional educator—that plus his outspoken advocacy of consolidation with the "weaker" state colleges—would have worked against his candidacy, but he was interested. One of his diary entries that spring noted that Miss Addie, Worth, and Jonathan agreed with their friends that he "(say nothing now but not decline presidency of the University)." Daniels was eliminated by a decision of the state's attorney general that the University's Board of Trustees could not legally elect one of its members to the presidency. Later the Navy Secretary accepted with a perfectly good grace the election of Dr. Harry W. Chase, the Massachusetts-born chairman of the faculty, attended his inauguration, and acted as toastmaster at a banquet attended by representatives of other colleges and universities. As recorded in Daniels' diary, it became his duty to introduce none other than Professor John Spencer Bassett, formerly of Trinity and now of Smith College, who had been pilloried in *The News and Observer* seventeen years before as "bASSett." Navy Secretary Daniels was considerably less narrow than the old Editor Daniels, and he gave Bassett a warm introduction plus praise for his recent book on the war. Bassett's *Our War With Germany* (1919) had, in turn, given Daniels the highest marks: "As the political head of the navy during the war he made no mistakes and gained the approval of most of the men who had formerly found him unsatisfactory."[8]

Before retiring as Navy Secretary, Daniels used the immediate post-Armistice years as the occasion to travel more widely than at any other time of his life. As soon as he had completed his first postwar testimony before the House Naval Affairs Committee, Daniels left on March 15, 1919, for a three-month tour of Europe. He took along Admirals Griffin, Taylor, and Earle, chiefs of the Navy's three technical bureaus, but he also took Miss Addie and their Negro servant, Robert Gaines. They sailed aboard the *Leviathan*, the great wartime troopship now suitably decorated for the Secretary's use, and the Danielses took up quarters in the ship's handsome royal suite. After a week aboard, Daniels wrote a letter to his mother (to be copied for all the other Danielses and Bagleys): "My dear blessed mother:—This has been the happiest and quietest week I have known in a score of years." After describing the nineteen-gun salute and other pomp attending his embarkation, the son told the pious Mary Cleaves Daniels of religious matters including, the night before, a talk he gave at the shipboard Jewish services, the first he had ever attended. He then spoke of Sunday morning services:

> At ten o'clock, at the request of the chaplain I tried a lay sermon to the passengers, including a large number of welfare workers, a Red Cross delegation of eminent physicians and surgeons. That afternoon I talked to all the sailors—over 1,500 fine looking and clear-eyed lads who were so responsive and earnest I could almost feel that I reached their hearts. . . . Every night at sunset we go up on the bridge and as the sun sets, the chaplain makes a prayer for all on board. . . . During the war, going through the submarine zone, that prayer was said every night as the men were going to rest and ten thousand soldiers, upon the sound of the trumpet, would uncover as the chaplain prayed.[9]

At Brest, where it rained unremittingly on the sodden duck-boards of Camp Pontanezen, the Danielses picked up their Marine officer son Josephus. He was tactfully detailed as his father's aide by General Smedley Butler, who had not been permitted by Daniels—as it was forbidden to FDR, who had suggested it—to arrange an early discharge for the Navy Secretary's son. In Paris, between visiting President Wilson and conferring on Treaty matters touching naval affairs, Daniels was kept busy in a pleasant social whirl. "This is the busiest place in all the world, everybody working and conferring," he wrote his youngest son Frank, "and my little head is too small to carry the big problems they are trying to solve." In a lighter vein he wrote of Robert Gaines: "The French call Bob Ballon/de/nedge [*sic*], which means 'snow ball.' That is the word they use here when they refer to colored troops." Robert Gaines also was the center of attraction later in the Rhineland, where the German children collected around him so avidly that he good-naturedly avowed he might charge admission.[10]

A week in Italy was sandwiched in between the official business in Paris, during which the Danielses got an enthusiastic Southern welcome in Rome from Ambassador Thomas Nelson Page, who took the Navy Secretary to meet King Victor Emmanuel III. "He is short of stature," Daniels wrote son Frank, "well built; dressed like a soldier, with leather leggins and soldier officer shoes." Then, like the veriest Innocents Abroad, "We had quiet lunch with Ambassador Page & then went to St. Peter's and the Forum and felt that we needed a week more to see them fully." The father talked about the handsome dinner given by the Minister of Marine, on which occasion "I tell you your mother looked fine in her beautiful new black." He enjoined Frank, not yet fifteen years old, to "take care of all the girls at home [Mrs. Bagley and her daughters]. There are some beautiful ones here."[11]

It was a long way from North Carolina, this business of staying at the Ritz in Paris and going to the opera for the first time. As guests of the French Government the Danielses attended a performance of Saint-Saens' *Henry VIII* at which Admiral Benson, even more puritanical than Daniels, was scandalized by scanty costumes and allegedly off-color language. What scandalized the admiral probably was a ballet, typically introduced at Paris to enliven the tedium of an otherwise dull evening. Benson wanted the American party to walk out, but Daniels—although agreeing that the performance was in bad taste—overruled his Chief of Naval Operations. Besides, the Secretary was innocent of any French and could thus more easily overlook any allegedly objectionable language. He cheerfully admitted to Miss Addie's sister Ethel his embarrassment at knowing no French. "My lack of it," he wrote, "has been at times embarrassing, particularly when you take a beautiful lady out to dinner and she cannot say a word to you or you to her. The only thing you can do is make eyes at her and there is some danger in that method of communication in Paris."[12]

On Good Friday, 1919, Daniels, in company with General John A. Lejeune, reviewed some twenty-seven thousand American troops of the Army of Occupation. The Rhineland scene was the Kaiser's famed drill ground of Vallendar below a gigantic American flag floating from the tower of Ehrenbreitstein. After a river trip on the Rhine the next day, the Danielses went to a union Easter Sunday service and a luncheon with the Eighteenth Company, Fifth Marine Regiment. "Private Tucker of Va.," Daniels' diary of that April 20 recorded, "presented Addie with flowers & an insignia, colors of their shoulder piece painted on satin. She created great enthusiasm by her speech saying she outranked me." On the day of the review at Vallendar, Daniels found time to draw taut the reins on Acting Secretary Roosevelt back in Washington. He wired FDR that it was permissible for service personnel to make Victory Loan speeches, but "no reference must be made to questions past, present or future policies of the government, the Army or the Navy." That done, the

Navy Secretary wrote Miss Addie's mother: "We are having the best time of out lives. . . . We will see David [Bagley] at Brussels."[13]

Commander Bagley did join the party at Brussels, where all were invited to dine with Minister Brand Whitlock and his wife. The Danielses, Whitlock noted in his journal, "are not so bad; he a very intelligent and honest if narrow man, of good ideals, not lacking a certain distinction in appearance." Daniels lunched next day with King Albert, who was described in the diary of April 23: "Tall & spoke good English." Then the Navy Secretary recorded with undisguised admiration of King Albert: "Told my wife he was a teetotaler—did not touch wine." Before returning to the United States, Daniels wrote President Wilson in Paris to be sure to visit Belgium. At any rate the King of the Belgians fulfilled his desire to visit the United States, as he expressed the wish to Daniels that April 23, 1919. By the time King Albert reached Washington that October, the heartbreaking fight for the League had brought the President low. The visiting monarch was admitted to Wilson's sickroom to find the stricken President with a full beard grown white. No member of the Cabinet, certainly not the public, would see the President until he was again clean-shaven.[14]

To return to the Danielses, they were entertained royally—literally—in England. "Young men real boys," Daniels noted in his diary of April 30 of the three princes, including the Prince of Wales whom he was to greet in Washington later that year. Mrs. Daniels remembered how King George V joked to her husband at the Windsor Castle luncheon: "Your country is the only real autocracy, you know," to which Daniels replied: "But by choice, your Majesty." The Navy Secretary went up to Scapa Flow to view the still-unscuttled German fleet (on his return to America he told the press he agreed it ought to be sunk), and had a grand time in the Shakespeare country, leaving a wreath on the Bard's tomb. Lady Nancy Astor made a hit with the Tar Heel visitors that April of 1919, and even when Daniels disapproved her later Cliveden Set appeasement of Hitler, he always thought of her with personal affection as a "fellow Southerner." Lady Astor spoke up to Miss Addie at a dinner: "You had better smile at me, for I am the only other Democrat and Prohibitionist at this table." Those were delightful days, treasured in after years, such as that May 2 in London when Daniels recorded in his diary that he went out and bought a wedding present for Miss Addie on their anniversary.[15]

That May saw the aviation-minded Navy Secretary happily preside over the first flight across the Atlantic Ocean, that of the Navy's *NC-4*. In the immediate pre-war summer Rodman Wannamaker had sought two Navy aviators to pilot his large "aeroboat," the *America,* across the ocean. Skeptically eyeing the *America*'s two little 100-horsepower engines, Daniels had said: "The flight across the Atlantic is not in our line." After the war, however, such a project had become readily feasible, and in March, 1919, Daniels had told of the Navy's plan, a flight of three NC flying boats under his personal aviator of six years earlier, Commander John H. Towers. Newly returned from his European tour a jubilant Navy Secretary, on his birthday (May 18), announced successful completion (to the Azores) of the principal phase of the flight. The long flight, guideposted by a veritable bridge of Navy destroyers below, began at Rockaway, N.Y., on May 8 and proceeded via Nova Scotia, Newfoundland, the Azores, Lisbon, to Plymouth, England—a latter-day return of the *Mayflower*—on May 31.[16]

While the aviators were still in the Azores, the Navy Secretary had to make a Solomonic decision. Lieutenant Commander Albert C. Read's *NC-4* had made the successful flight from Newfoundland to the Azores, and Daniels ruled that he should have the undivided honor of flying on to Lisbon in the first aircraft ever to span the Atlantic. Under naval tradition Towers, as ranking officer, was entitled to transfer his "flag" from his disabled *NC-3* to the other craft, but Secretary Daniels—although he knew and respected Towers—ruled against him and in favor of Read. President Wilson was still in Paris, so the transatlantic flight was something of a diplomatic coup plus a victory over the British Alcock and Brown, whose nonstop flight (Newfoundland-Ireland, for the $50,000 offered by Lord Northcliffe's *Daily Mail*), occurred the following month. The flight of the *NC-4* probably helped Daniels in Congress. That body, seeing that Daniels had by now withdrawn the three-year building program, was determined to give the Navy Secretary far less than his $45 million aviation fund. Daniels made a rock-bottom plea for $36 million, and took the Senate's proffered $35 million, saying: "What's a million dollars between friends?"[17]

In July the President returned bearing the Treaty which he now considered to answer the objections in Lodge's "round robin." To be sure the Wilsonians found more Americans talking "reservations," but Lodge's counterattack had not yet gained momentum. As chair-

man of the Foreign Relations Committee, Senator Lodge could—
and did—delay a vote. Otherwise, a Senate vote in July probably
would have ratified the Treaty. So it was that in the yet-heady
July-September, 1919, Daniels again paid extensive visits to the
Navy installations in the Pacific area. At San Diego he set in motion
the expansion that was to upgrade the still-humble coaling station
and secondary port to the great base it was later to become. He
enthusiastically told the House Naval Affairs Committee later of his
plans for the Marine barracks, the first aviation base on the Pacific
at North Island, the new radio station. On August 8 Daniels and
Miss Addie reviewed the Pacific Fleet at San Diego and set sail
aboard the battleship *New York* for Hawaii. A minor triumph
awaited the Navy Secretary there, for he was to open the great new
drydock at Pearl Harbor.[18]

During Daniels' first year as Secretary, an earthquake-like un-
derwater movement at Pearl Harbor had destroyed the drydock
then under construction. Daniels had made his engineering experts
work long and hard on a drydock that could be built in stages and
thus avoid the seismic disturbances. His diary of August 21 recorded the destroyer trip around Ford Island to the site of the
new Pearl Harbor drydock, Miss Addie's pressing of the button that
let the water pour in, and the Hawaiian sacrifices to propitiate the
Shark God who had presumably destroyed the earlier dock. The
Danielses' two youngest boys, Jonathan and Frank, were understandably wide-eyed at it all, and especially at the great fleet review for their father on the return to San Francisco. Wherever
they went the Danielses were overwhelmed by courtesies and new
friends, but the Navy Secretary ended his tour with a major San
Francisco address on what was uppermost on his mind—world peace
and the League of Nations. Admiral Nathan C. Twining told Daniels—and the Secretary recorded it in his diary of September 5—"It
is the best speech I ever heard." It needed to be, for a belatedly
alarmed Woodrow Wilson was just starting out to carry his fight
to the people. The Danielses greeted the Wilsons at Seattle, an occasion made memorable by a naval review and one of the President's
most fervent appeals for support.[19]

The enemies of the League were now sparing no effort to poison
the wells of public opinion just as Woodrow Wilson was putting
his life in pawn. It was a time of anguish that Daniels would never
forget. The presidential train sped away from Pueblo, Colorado,

on September 25 with Woodrow Wilson in a state of incipient physical collapse, and on September 29 the anti-administration *Washington Post* carried a falsely slanted story about U.S. Navy activity in the Adriatic that was calculated to damage the League idea. Walter Lippmann used the episode as a case history in his notable volume, *Public Opinion*. The *Washington Post* writer shed some crocodile tears about Secretary Daniels' alleged embarrassment at seeing American Marines landed on the Dalmatian coast on the orders of the British. The implication was that, in the new League, American forces would be ordered about by foreigners. By the time Daniels could get an official report from the scene, the publicity damage was done. The Marines actually had been landed at the plea of the Italian government to help protect its nationals, and the British were not even involved. Lippmann wrote: "The picture of that scene in the senators' heads at Washington was furnished in this case, probably with intent to deceive, by a man who cared nothing about the Adriatic but much about defeating the League."[20]

Now, with the President prostrate from his paralytic stroke, Lodge's fourteen reservations—his own brand of Fourteen Points— were brought to bear on the ratification fight. These reservations mostly underlined what the League Covenant already provided, that the United States could take no decisive action without the consent of Congress. The real lion in the path was the reservation first suggested by Elihu Root, that the United States would not underwrite the anti-aggression Article X of the Covenant—binding member states to preserve world-wide territorial integrity and political independence. The President was seriously ill, but the stubborn man's mental faculties were unimpaired (after a visit to Wilson's sickbed even the hostile Senator Fall dropped the whole idea of the President's mental disability). Wilson's friends besought him to compromise, but he stood by his original plan of trying to split the "mild reservationists" away from the Republican phalanx of Majority Leader Lodge. Even after the defeat of November, 1919, and the opening of debate on reconsideration of the Treaty, Wilson would not yield to the kind of ratification he regarded as nullification.

In the midst of the heartbreak over Wilson's collapse and defeat, Daniels had to come to the defense of George Creel, head of the Committee on Public Information, who had run afoul of hostility from a Republican Congress. Creel was no diplomat, and many an old-line Congressman suspected him as a radical who was contemptuous of the legislative branch. Nevertheless, he was being given a rough time primarily because a Congress was fishing for data that might discredit the Wilson administration. In November, 1919, the Council of National Defense, named at last as the liquidating agent of the C.P.I., reported critically on Creel's financial management. Actually, Creel was at the Peace Conference during the first half of the year, and his agency had been unceremoniously wiped out by Congress as of the previous June 30. Daniels conceded in his diary of December 13 that Creel's first accountant had been negligent and had been replaced by an incompetent. However, the politically alert Navy Secretary quickly discerned the real object of the attack on Creel, and he accordingly warned Senator Overman of North Carolina that it was all a pretext for an attack on Woodrow Wilson. The Council of National Defense never did charge Creel with any dishonesty, and the irregular accounts turned out to be nothing more than the product of confusion incidental to a displaced agency's being left without an office to call its home.[21]

Defending fellow-Democrats was far more Daniels' style than engaging in intramural fights, so he was understandably unhappy with his party's divisions over the Red hysteria, prohibition, and racist-inspired demands for immigration restriction. His distress over these divisive issues was heightened because he realized that although they cut across party lines, these matters divided Democrats much more fundamentally than they did Republicans. Daniels did not belong to the fanatical wing of the prohibitionists, but he was embarrassed—and spent much time in the following decade trying to explain it—when on October 27, 1919, the bedridden President vetoed the Volstead Act that was to implement the Prohibition Amendment.

As to the Red Scare, it was invoked by the new Attorney General, A. Mitchell Palmer of Pennsylvania, who had been appointed as a sop to Northern Democratic resentment at lack of patronage and who was seized with a bad case of presidential fever. During the summer of 1919, after a series of bombings, Palmer at first resisted demands for drastic action against radicals, but he then seized upon President Wilson's illness to project his own image into the limelight. If the President had not been seriously ill, Daniels later maintained, the Chief Executive would have resisted Palmer's decision in October to enjoin the coal miners from striking. In November Palmer ordered a big roundup of radical suspects and feuded heatedly with Labor Secretary William B. Wilson over deporting the allegedly subversive workers. The Palmer Raids went on, 249 persons deported to Russia in December, more than 3,000 "radicals" rounded up on January 2, 1920, others held and finally released without ever having been arrested. Daniels steadfastly backed up Labor Secretary Wilson, a West Virginia coal miner, against Palmer. As Jonathan Daniels has recalled of his father: "To the end of his life he thought old man William B. Wilson was one of the greatest men he ever knew."[22]

At the very height of the Red hysteria fanned by Palmer, who was calculatedly doing what he thought most Americans desired, Josephus Daniels sounded a public warning. On January 8, 1920, grim in the aftermath of the crippled Woodrow Wilson's defeat in the Senate, Daniels told the Democrats gathered in Washington for their Jackson Day Dinner that Republican propaganda in the foreign language press had helped to kill the Treaty and the League. He warned that the existence of politically oriented German-Americans, British-Americans, Irish-Americans, Italian-Americans posed a danger in that American political contests might degenerate into ethnic divisions. But he added, in opposition to the philosophy that led to the later immigration restrictions: "But we must not shut doors to the men and women of other countries who have a mind to come to our shores by love of institutions and desire to share the blessings of liberty. The Democratic party was born in hostility to laws denying a haven to the oppressed of other nations. The narrow minded Alien and Sedition Laws of Adams damned and destroyed the Federalist party. Let all who would destroy the free press and deny public assemblage and proscribe liberty loving loyal foreigners take warning!" Later that spring the Daniels diary recorded the much-improved President Wilson's presiding over a Cabinet meeting at which Labor Secretary Wilson hotly continued his debate with A. Mitchell Palmer over the latter's policies. The President, Daniels reported, "told Palmer not to let the country see red." And by May Day, when the Palmer-predicted Red reign of terror failed to materialize, the hysteria began to abate.[23]

The Presidential election year of 1920 brought the predictable Congressional investigations into the conduct of the war—such as had occurred after the Civil and Spanish-American Wars—which turned out to be thoroughly partisan affairs. Daniels' turn came through the prickly Admiral Sims, who helped set in motion two separate but related probes, a minor one into medal awards and a full-dress naval investigation.

The opening gun sounded in the anti-administration *Washington Post* of December 15, 1919, whose Albert W. Fox wrote a page one feature article headlined: "Daniels Robs Naval Heroes of Honors. Secretary's Friends Replace Those Named by Board." Daniels' diary of that date noted that he was being urged to sue the *Post* for libel. "No," he wrote. "Gave facts." Next day the chairman of the Senate Naval Affairs Committee, C. S. Page, requested from Daniels a copy of the Board of Awards' original recommendations. Before the deadline for Daniels' reply, Admiral Sims joined the fray with a stiff letter of the seventeenth in which he refused a Distinguished Service Medal because some of his award recommendations had not been followed. He forgot to add what was also true, that he had for months been proclaiming his anger at the delay in giving him a wartime decoration. At the Harvard Commencement the previous June, the handsome and much-decorated Admiral Sims had appeared with his blue uniform bearing not a single ribbon. To Mrs. Theodore Roosevelt, Jr., who jokingly remarked that his unadorned uniform was now the height of swank, Sims had explained indignantly that he would wear none of his Allied decorations because of his lack of recognition by the United States. Daniels gave both documents—Sims's letter and the data for Senator Page—to the press on December 23 to the accompaniment of a storm of controversy. When hearings opened on January 16, 1920, with Admiral Sims as opening witness, it became clear that Sims's theoretical criticisms were the tail to a sensational kite of accusation—that Daniels had awarded a D.S.M. to his brother-in-law, David W. Bagley.[24]

The anti-administration press and the Republican majority on the investigating subcommittee played up the award to Bagley to the virtual exclusion of the real merits of the awards controversy. In keeping with his Single Oak Policy of 1913, Daniels had consistently put sea duty high on his list of priorities for recognition. That was his rightful prerogative, as was also his order awarding the D.S.M. (preceding that to Bagley) to captains who had conducted themselves gallantly under submarine attack. True, Daniels could be faulted for not having set up an invariable awards policy to guide the lower echelons, but the idea of nepotism in Bagley's case was ridiculous.

With the outbreak of the newspaper furore, Sims himself wrote a letter of regret to Bagley—whom he himself had recommended for the Navy Cross—and assured him that the hullabaloo was all Daniels' fault. Bagley replied correctly by cabling from Europe that he wanted to be considered only for the same award given to all destroyer captains in the war zone. Daniels took much of the sting out of Sims's attack by showing the admiral's own arbitrariness, not to say pettiness, in making recommendations for awards. Sims had put in for a D.S.M. every admiral who had served abroad except Henry B. Wilson, wartime commander in French waters, whom Sims had used rather spitefully and to whom he had given a much lower fitness report than had the Atlantic Fleet Commander during the same period. Whatever the true merits of the medal awards controversy, everything boiled down to a partisan trial of the Secretary of the Navy, as was amply borne out by the subcommittee's later report. The three Republicans and two Democrats divided on strict party lines, resulting in the kind of three-to-two history that FDR hooted at later.[25]

Another harassment was posed by revolutionary Mexico, where the smell of oil was as strong as ever. During the worst of President Wilson's illness, Secretary of State Lansing favored sending the Mexican government an ultimatum over the so-called Jenkins case. This latter involved an American businesman in Mexico, W. O. Jenkins, serving part-time as American consular official at Puebla. He had been supposedly kidnapped by bandits, and then arrested by Mexican officials who charged him with conspiring in a fake kidnapping. Lansing was all for an ultimatum, and in hot agreement was Senator Albert B. Fall of later Teapot Dome fame. Daniels and most of the Cabinet resisted Lansing's plea, and in any case another American businessman in Mexico paid Jenkins' bail so as to prevent imminent war. Daniels later wrote: "I am confident Jenkins kidnapped himself in order to bring about war between Mexico and the United States, something which Lansing and all the imperialists and concessionaires wished."[26] Daniels got an even sterner jolt at the time from friend William Jennings Bryan, an old anti-imperialist now turned jingo. Daniels recorded in his diary of December 17, 1919:

Took lunch with Bryan. He had plan for meeting Mexican situation without intervention. In brief take Lower California as hostage that Mexico pay for loss of American citizens by reason of lack of protection by Mexican authorities. Then take strip 15 miles on border to police and guarantee protection against incursions over the border. I suggested they might destroy the oil wells. Then, he said, take over & operate the wells because of the necessity of the oil. Guarantee every American the money invested but not speculative profits. In course of time Mexico would be unable to pay and we could trade by taking Lower California & Magdelana [*sic*] Bay. . . .

Oil men as a class never enjoyed Daniels' confidence, and if an oil man was Daniels' landlord in Wyoming Avenue it can be confidently assumed that the oilman-landlord won no influence thereby. Joseph S. Cullinan, an oil operator from Houston, bought the Danielses' rented house and allowed them to stay on at the same rental, a fact gratefully recorded in Daniels' diary. Moreover, Daniels did want to settle the minerals leasing dispute on an equitable basis and to do so before he left office. One of Daniels' undated memos to President Wilson on the subject is marked "To Europe," indicating that the Navy Secretary was suggesting provisions of a leasing bill even while the Peace Treaty was being hammered out in early 1919. Finally, in February, 1920, Congress passed a bill that Daniels could approve. He was impressed that such conservationists as Gifford Pinchot supported the bill, yet heard out carefully former Attorney General Gregory, who was opposed. "But," Daniels wrote in his diary of February 24, 1920, "the bill safeguarded better than any former bill the naval reserves & I wrote to the President that I would not ask him to disapprove because of naval reserves." Daniels suggested to Joe Tumulty that he secure for the President the written opinion of the new Secretary of the Interior, John Barton Payne. Former Secretary Lane, Daniels' amiable adversary on oil policy, had by this time accepted a $50,000-a-year job with Doheny's Pan American Petroleum Company of California.[27]

By now it was clear that the medal awards harassment of Daniels was no more than a sideshow preliminary to the coming performance in the main tent. This latter investigation took up where the medal awards hearings left off, extending from March 9, to May 28, 1920, filling—complete with majority and minority reports— 3,661 pages of testimony. The full-scale naval investigation pro-

ceeded theoretically from Admiral Sims's campaign for a General
Staff organization of the Navy, his arguments buttressed by alleged
wartime mistakes in the exercise of civilian authority. What it all
came down to was an attempt to drive Daniels from the Cabinet,
a maneuver that was seized upon eagerly in a presidential election
year. Sims was given a platform by his warm partisan, Senator
Frederick Hale, chairman of the Medal Awards Subcommittee. On
the first day of those hearings Hale—conveniently and with foreknowledge—asked Sims if he had had any other correspondence
with Secretary Daniels touching upon a critique of the Navy Department. The admiral just happened to have a copy handy, and
then gladly read into the record his letter of January 7, a comprehensive report entitled "Certain Naval Lessons of the Great War."
The report had already been allowed to leak in order to force Daniels' hand.[28]

Senator Hale's foreknowledge, and that of the public at large,
came in the same anti-administration *Washington Post* in a story
by the same Albert W. Fox who had sparked the medal awards
controversy. Three days before Hale put his convenient question
to Sims, the *Washington Post* informed one and all that Sims's private letter of January 7 "is a frank and fearless expose of the hopeless story of maladministration, mistakes, and blunders into which
the American Navy has fallen as a result of Mr. Daniels' policies."
The news leak could have come from any one of five of Sims's staff
officers who had seen the letter, and in any case the letter had to be
leaked if Sims's aim of arousing public opinion was to succeed. Sims
even admitted to the subcommittee that he been indiscreet in showing a copy to H. P. Davison, a wartime Red Cross official who was
a member of the J. Pierpont Morgan firm. Davison was, of course,
a prominent Republican, as was Mrs. Whitelaw Reid, in whose New
York home Sims had made his disclosure.[29]

Once Sims's letter had been read into the record, Senator Hale
got permission for his medal awards subcommittee to conduct the
comprehensive fishing expedition indicated by that letter. Sims's
principal charges were three in number: (1) that the Navy was
unprepared for war in 1917, (2) that the Navy had inadequate war
plans, and (3) that a "hand to mouth" policy had delayed for six
months the throwing of the Navy's full weight against the enemy.
To his difficulty of proving his point in the face of the Navy's fine
wartime record, Sims added to his troubles by failing to discrim-

inate—in the words of his biographer—"between rapping for attention and knocking his audience cold." Sims came forward with the
incredibly reckless charge that Daniels' "delay" had cost 2,500,000
tons of shipping, a half million lives, and fifteen billion dollars. When
his turn came to testify, Daniels could show—and caused to be
printed in parallel columns in the record—the striking similarity between these extremist charges of Sims and those made in August,
1918, by the *beau ideal* of Republican stalwarts, Senator Boies Penrose of Pennsylvania.[30]

From the time he had first become Secretary of the Navy, Daniels had had to keep a wary eye on Sims. In addition to Sims's abrasive type of ability was the factor of his restive tongue, the latter
attested by Sims's Presidential reprimand for the blatantly pro-
British sentiments in his London Guildhall speech of 1910. When
Sims was loudly critical about the Navy building program in early
1916, Daniels, while being cross-examined in Congress about Sims's
views, interposed that the other was "one of the brightest and
ablest men in the Navy," who had just been given command of the
new battleship *Nevada*. Later that year Sims wrote to Daniels recommending Robert E. Coontz for Chief of Navigation, whom Daniels reluctantly passed over in favor of his former naval aide, Leigh
C. Palmer. Nevertheless, Daniels shared Sims's regard for Coontz,
naming him C.N.O. in 1919 on Benson's retirement (ironically,
Palmer turned against Daniels in the Sims Investigation). Just before America's war entry Sims had been promoted to rear admiral
and given the post he himself desired, President of the Naval War
College. After his wartime service in Europe, Sims was reappointed
to head the War College, at which time he gratefully wrote Daniels:
"As you doubtless know, you are the first Secretary of the Navy who
has taken a really practical interest in the College."[31]

By now, however, the admiral already was gunning for Daniels.
The Sims-Daniels correspondence of 1919 was guarded; Daniels
had praise for Sims's paper on the Naval War College, Sims grumbled about the Navy's promotion system. Daniels wrote to Sims, as
to Benson, requesting a full historical account of his wartime command, adding sweetly: "I am sure this can be arranged so as not to
interfere, in any material way, with your book, which is certain to
have a large circulation and arouse wide interest." Sims had been
writing a series of articles on this very subject for *World's Work*, in
collaboration with Burton J. Hendrick, later to emerge in book form

as *Victory at Sea*. The volume was a surprise winner of the Pulitzer Prize for 1920, according to Hendrick, who recalled that the admiral wrote nothing published in the book and that Sims's resulting modesty was indeed well-founded. To Daniels' needling request for data Sims wrote in frank insubordination: "I am afraid that whoever prepared this letter for your signature very sadly misunderstands the nature and extent of such a task." Nevertheless, Daniels refused a demand that he discipline Sims for anti-Sinn Fein statements in *World's Work* articles, hotly protested by the Irish National Bureau.[32] In mid-1919 Daniels even put in Sims for promotion to full admiral, along with Benson, in citations to the Naval Committees of both houses of Congress.

Daniels' wartime diary bears abundant witness to his distress at the shortage of destroyers. Even Sims, on cross-examination, had to admit that nobody in the Navy could have anticipated the new warfare unleashed by the Germans. "If we could have imagined it we would have prepared for it and built destroyers galore, if we could have persuaded Congress to give us the money," Sims said.[33] A more philosophical Sims, not irritated by the frustrations he met in wartime London, would have conceded that the military leaders of each generation customarily laid plans for the kind of wars fought by their immediate predecessors. Sims might have gone further, with George F. Kennan, in likening America's chronic unreadiness to fight to a lethargic dinosaur, slow to anger, yet fearsomely destructive when finally and belatedly aroused.

A dispassionate set of conclusions has been drawn by Donald M. Mitchell, who approached the Sims Investigation as part of a lifelong study of Navy affairs. In his *History of the Modern American Navy* he has concluded that Daniels erred in trying to master details by himself, in too slowly following Sim's recommendations (although Daniels had Benson's counsel on them), and in retaining the Navy Department's ramshackle organization. Mitchell has concluded, nevertheless, that the Congressional investigation was thoroughly partisan and directed against Daniels personally, and—more important—that the wartime administration of the Navy "was characterized by ingenuity, vision, and energy." It was hard to rebut Secretary Daniels when he summed up before the subcommittee:

> . . . all knew that the fate of nations hung upon the ability
> to safely land American fighters in France. In comparison
> with that essential to winning the war nothing else counted.

And who in advance would have dared even to hope in those fateful days from June, 1917, when the first transports sailed, until November 11, 1918, when the signing of the armistice made the sea safe from undersea assassins, that of that vast army transported and guarded by the United States Navy on hundreds of Europe-bound transports not one life would be lost?[34]

While the Sims Investigation dragged on with Sims, Fiske (ret.), and allies testifying against Daniels' administration but a preponderant group of admirals supporting the Secretary, John Wilber Jenkins worked day and night to prepare Daniels' case. He had an eleven-page outline of investigative assignments from Daniels, and in any case performed a labor of love for the man he had known since the *State Chronicle* struggles back in Raleigh. When Daniels finally took the stand, and stubbornly refused to cut short his testimany lest anything be omitted from the record, he came up with evidence that hurt Sims in turn. Daniels exposed the amazing performance of Sims who, in the month before victory, had told three Southern Congressmen, Carter Glass, Richard S. Whaley, and James F. Byrnes, that the German armistice request would have to be granted because General Pershing's supply lines had broken down. In that harangue Sims had low-rated the American navy's performance like some spokesman for the British Admiralty, saying that only 3 per cent of the anti-submarine craft in British waters were American; that Britain had transported better than two-thirds of American troops and had escorted half of them. Daniels also brought forth abundant evidence that Admiral Sims had had the "slows" on the matter of the Northern Mine Barrage. The Secretary could also prove that his name was falsely affixed to a telegram in which Daniels supposedly expressed a preference for vessels with armed guards to sail separately rather than in convoy. Daniels challenged Sims to produce the forger as efficaciously as he had produced the spurious telegram.[35]

Sims's charges were so sweeping, so extreme, that they caused resentment in most of the American Navy's wartime leaders, notably Admirals Benson, Badger, Mayo, Rodman, Wilson, Niblack, Strauss, Fletcher, Pratt, and McKean. Daniels' diary also recorded Navy opinion opinion on the intramural significance of Sims's charges. The upright Chief Constructor, Admiral Taylor, according to the entry of March 8, 1920, saw the whole affair as a difference of opinion between admirals—Sims vs. Benson, rather than Sims vs. Daniels. Operations, over which Benson presided, ordered and allocated ships where needed. Daniels himself reflected that the chronic shortage of officers had caused him to break up the Office of Operations several times just to meet Sims's demands for staff. The diary of April 17 recorded: "Captain Ridley McLean said Sims had nothing personal against me. Rats. Mad because I did not let him belong to British Admiralty & get him full Admiral for life." Sims himself finally felt called on to temper his Anglophilia which had been exposed at the hearings. In the 1920-21 *Who's Who in America* he had recorded, in addition to his declining his country's D.S.M., that the Grand Cross Order of St. Michael and St. George had been conferred on him "by King George of England in 1918." In the next edition he decided to omit the king.

As the investigation droned along it became clear that Daniels' political opponents really had no case. Republican Chairman Butler of the House Naval Affairs Committee, who steadfastly refused to join the fishing expeditions of his party colleagues in the Senate, expressed the situation plainly enough, as recorded in Daniels' diary of April 22, 1920. "Butler said the Reps. were tired of the Sims business," Daniels wrote, "& if they knew how they would drop it. The House members are having fun with them." As Daniels was preparing to testify during the Sims Investigation, Mrs. Mildred Dewey, widow of the Hero of Manila Bay, took the Navy Secretary aside and told him: "Give them hell. That is the message George Dewey would give you if he were here." Daniels recalled that President Wilson, exasperated over Ambassador Page's Anglophilia, concluded: "Walter Page is the damndest fool we ever appointed." Daniels did not agree, saying: "I am committed to Admiral Sims."[36]

And what of Franklin D. Roosevelt during the investigations leveled against his chief? At first he wavered. Daniels did not know it, but in December, 1919, FDR congratulated Sims for his protest that led to the medal awards hearings. But FDR did not support the sweeping charges that Sims then levied against the Navy department, and in January he urged Daniels to reply at once when Sims reported the anti-British instructions he had been given in March, 1917: "Don't let the British pull the wool over your eyes." (Admiral Benson had given that prewar warning.) On February 1, 1920, FDR made a bad mistake when he virtually confirmed to a Brooklyn audience that Sims's charges of unpreparedness were true and that in any case he—FDR—had been more vigilant than Daniels or President Wilson. It marked the all-time low point of the Daniels-Roosevelt friendship. After the storm had been weathered and FDR resigned happily to run for Vice President, he wrote his chief a loving letter "wh. made me glad," Daniels wrote in his diary, "I had never acted upon impulse when he seemed to take sides with my critics."[37]

When the Navy Department counterattack first began and FDR appreciated how unjust were the sweeping charges against his chief, he rallied to him strongly. He quickly saw that the investigations formed a pattern of political attack on the Wilson administration, *his* administration. Moreover, he was now deeply involved in the charges—gleefully pounced on by anti-administration partisans—that FDR had condoned in wartime Newport the use of enlisted men decoys for the entrapment of sexual perverts in the Navy. While this Damoclean sword still dangled over him, he took occasion at the end of March, 1920, to remind a Democratic audience that the Republicans, despite ninety-seven postwar investigations, had failed to unearth a single embalmed beef or paper shoe scandal such as had plagued McKinley after the Spanish-American war.[38]

Later FDR cried out against "three-to-two history in Washington written by three Republican and two Democratic Senators." Roosevelt did not testify in person. Daniels' diary of April 21 gleefully recorded: "FDR—said he told [Senator] Hale if called he [Hale] would regret it." Invited instead to offer proposals for a Navy Department reorganization, FDR let Senator Hale have it straight: "Frankly, what is the most serious trouble with the Navy now, as it has been in the past, is Congress." He also refused to be taken in by the catch-all "giving more authority to the Chief of Naval Operations" because undefined in the context of civilian control of the Navy. The lessons of the Sims Investigation of 1920 stayed with FDR always; as President he would allow no tampering with civilian supremacy. In 1940 he appointed the Republican Frank Knox Secretary of the Navy rather than post him to the Embassy at London lest he turn into another Admiral Sims.[39]

Having paid an affectionate farewell to Admiral Benson on his retirement as the Navy's first Chief of Naval Operations, Daniels was not minded to forget him during the Sims Investigation. Not only was Benson called on to testify, but he served to remind onlookers of the civilian supremacy that he had embodied and of the

Navy's excellent wartime performance. Daniels and Miss Addie delightedly showed up at Baltimore on that April Sunday when the city's Cardinal Gibbons bestowed on Benson the Catholic Church's highest decoration for laymen. As usual when attending church, Daniels noted in his diary the sermon subject ("Render honor to whom honor—"), at noon lunching with the Cardinal and noted the prelate's courtesy and their exchange of anecdotes. With his usual light touch about alcohol, teetotaler Daniels told about North Carolina's Zeb Vance traveling with his law books in one side of his saddle bags. When asked what he carried in the other side Zeb grinned: "None of your business."⁴⁰

A lesser Navy protégé of Daniels' was the delightful Dr. Henry Van Dyke of Princeton, for whom the Secretary had waived the age regulations and let him have a reserve commission in the Chaplain Corps. When Van Dyke had first applied, Daniels waggishly called in a fellow-Methodist chaplain to examine this Princeton Presbyterian. "Do you believe in Calvinism?" was the question. Dr. Van Dyke replied: "I do not." The verdict: "You have passed." Dr. Van Dyke turned out a tremendous success with the Navy enlisted men and a frequent visitor in the Daniels home. When he accepted one dinner invitation glad that he had been "taken out of mourning," he was referring to that Daniels reform by which chaplains, paymasters and other staff officers were given equal rank and title with line officers. In consequence the staffers now wore the Navy gold braid instead of their old funereal (and discriminatory) black-braided uniforms.⁴¹

The reform of naval prisons had rockier sailing. Here the man in charge was Thomas Mott Osborne, that friend of FDR who shared Secretary Daniels' esteem. At the end of the war a bitter controversy cropped up between Assistant Secretary Roosevelt and Captain Joseph K. Taussig, director of enlisted personnel, who feared that Navy discipline was being undermined by the too-easy return to duty of inmates of the Portsmouth Naval Prison. The able and ambitious young Taussig, fearing that his career was being jeopardized by a controversy in the *Army and Navy Journal,* requested a Court of Inquiry. During the lull between the two investigations seeking to discredit Daniels, the Secretary appointed two rear admirals to the Court with FDR as senior member. After interviewing Osborne at length in what was anything but a whitewash, the Board found that the preponderance of evidence—including disproven charges by a lying ex-convict—showed that the prison was being run in an efficient and enlightened manner. By now the sensitive Osborne had served nearly three years and had had enough. His resignation was followed by another Daniels appointee who carried out the Osborne policies, but that trend was sharply reversed later in the Harding administration. Daniels remained a lifelong admirer of Osborne, and wrote him warmly at the time of his resignation, describing the work "to which you brought experience and enthusiasm which have borne fruit in the best prison system the Navy has known."[42]

Another abrasive type was Thomas A. Edison who took a dim view of career Navy officers running the proposed Naval Research Laboratory. "If Navy officers are to control," he warned Daniels after the war, "the result will be zero. . . . When you are no longer Secretary, I want to tell you a lot of things about the Navy that you are unaware of." Edison was much more intransigent about civilian supremacy than Daniels ever was, particularly in not wanting to locate the new laboratory in Washington for fear of Navy domination. The Wizard of Menlo Park later recalled: "I made about forty-five inventions during the war, all perfectly good ones, and they pigeon-holed every one of them. The Naval officer resents any interference by civilians. Those fellows are a close corporation." Nevertheless, he was unduly censorious. Daniels had put Edison on anti-submarine studies—and profitable ones—as soon as America declared war. And the Daniels-established Naval Research Laboratory came to be the center out of which emerged the scientific milestone of radar.[43]

In the midst of Daniels' ordeal with the Sims Investigation came the final ballot on reconsideration of the Peace Treaty. That tragic March 19, 1920, saw the Navy Secretary hurrying about the Senate floor and desperately buttonholing senators who might still be won for the lost cause.[44] It was only reluctantly that Daniels attended the San Francisco Convention (he was not a delegate during his Cabinet term), where the only hopeful glimmer he could discern was the political future of Franklin D. Roosevelt. During the Convention Daniels was quartered aboard the battleship *New Mexico*, part of the Pacific Fleet anchored in San Francisco Bay. So situated he enjoyed the beautiful weather of that hectic June-July fortnight but missed the ecstatic guzzling of fine bourbon supplied to the Democratic visitors by Mayor Rolph and remembered with such voluptuous nostalgia by H. L. Mencken.[45] Perhaps it was because of Mayor Rolph's fine whisky that the Platform Committee side-stepped prohibition, which had gone into force only five months before. Daniels—unlike Bryan—was only moderately unhappy about the platform's omission: he sorrowed more for Woodrow Wilson and the League of Nations and what was to become of the Democratic party.

Daniels had no ambitions for himself, although during the war he had gotten an occasional boost for the Presidency. In the very month of America's war entry Senator J. Hamilton Lewis had declared himself a Daniels-for-President man, and with a European victory finally in sight Editor John S. Cohen of the *Atlanta Journal* reported to Daniels a local consensus that it would be Daniels in 1920 if Wilson were not to run. Daniels replied only that he looked forward to getting back to his *News and Observer*, for which he had written a few *sub rosa* editorials as "managing editor of the Navy." At San Francisco, as perennial peacemaker among warring Democrats, the Navy Secretary stood unequaled as that rare bird who was agreeable to both Tammany and Bryan.[46] Martin Glynn, New York's former governor and a spokesman for the city bosses who held the Convention's balance of power, complained bitterly to Daniels of the party's failure to honor Irish Catholics with top-flight appointments. Daniels' diary of April 23 already paraphrased Glynn: "Frank Polk [State Department] & Frank Roosevelt carry no votes & no strength & yet they are recognized." Governor Glynn thought it might just be high time for a great defeat that would teach the Democratic party a lesson.

The Navy Secretary began his Convention chores by joining other Cabinet members in heading off the ill-timed move by Secretary of State Bainbridge Colby to give the nomination to Woodrow Wilson. The eager Colby, new to the Cabinet, had wired the President his intentions without telling anybody. Daniels and the other leaders were shocked when the President's message came through, a request to advise him about becoming a candidate. As diplomatically as possible they said no, without spelling out the specific objections of Wilson's partial paralysis and the humiliating rebuff which the Convention was sure to deal Colby's rash proposal. But Daniels could at least draw some solace from the emergence of Franklin D. Roosevelt as the party's Young Prince. FDR had come to San Francisco greatly strengthened by his recent fighting progressive speech to the Democratic National Committee. He had quite stolen the thunder of A. Mitchell Palmer and his tub-thumping Americanism—so much so that the Presidential nominee, Governor James M. Cox of Ohio, personally tapped FDR for second place on the ticket. Roosevelt was nominated by acclamation. Ignoring cries from the floor that he step up to the rostrum, FDR left the hall as dictated by the tradition that he be formally "notified," and let his old Navy Department chief pinch-hit for him. Josephus Daniels then advanced to the rostrum and joyfully shared his pride in his protégé, young Roosevelt.[47]

Daniels' next order of business, in July and August, was to slap down the oil men again via an inspection of the Navy's coal lands in Alaska. A threatening postwar shortage of oil had led Daniels to agree to the law of February, 1920, which was somewhat more lenient with claimants on oil lands outside the naval reserves. Inside the reserves, however, Daniels stood as unyielding as ever and had agreed to lease only producing wells and the land they stood on. The Navy Secretary then had asked Congress to allow him greater flexibility in the use of the reserves, securing such an amendment to the Naval Appropriations Bill of June 4, 1920. In effect the Navy Secretary could act, within a money limit of $500,000 in oil royalties, to use, store, exchange, or sell oil obtained from the offset wells that were now necessary to prevent loss of the Navy's oil through drainage. The disgruntled oil claimants, already held off for the seven years of Daniels' term, made his eighth year loud with complaints while he stubbornly continued to fight them off. Argued one of them: "You are a Democrat and we are Democrats; give us a break. If you don't just as surely as we stand here, before the snow flies in 1921 the Republicans will give us leases."[48]

That oil man was right. Danels' successor, Edwin Denby, naïvely agreed to transfer the naval oil reserves to the new Secretary of the Interior, Albert B. Fall. He, in turn, lost no time in secretly leasing the oil reserves and, with that accomplished, resigned from the Cabinet to take employment with one of the lessees he had just benefited. Daniels had resisted for eight years the mischief that was done in the first months of the Harding administration and which resulted in the Teapot Dome Scandal.

The Navy Secretary left no diary record of his summer trip to Alaska, but his usual buoyant attitude was reflected in the *New York Times* headline that marked his return: "Go North, Young Man,

Says Daniels." The Pacific fleet would benefit from Alaska's coal deposits, he added for the benefit of the California oil men. Moreover, Daniels had the like-minded Interior Secretary John Barton Payne for a traveling companion, just as amiable as Franklin K. Lane and far less reachable by the oil interests.[49]

Politically, the year 1920 petered out anti-climactically for the Navy Secretary. All during the tensions of the Sims Investigation Daniels had worked hard for the Woman Suffrage Amendment along with suffrage leaders like Mrs. Carrie Chapman Catt, Anna Howard Shaw, and Helen H. Gardener. In March the Navy Secretary had appealed to the Delaware legislature to ratify the Amendment, and in April he had wired Mrs. Catt assurances that his native North Carolina also would ratify. Mrs. Daniels meanwhile got the President's appointment as U.S. representative to the Eighth International Suffrage Alliance at Geneva.[50]

Miss Addie was reluctant to leave her husband during the very days he was testifying before a hostile Congressional committee, but Daniels had no doubt of vindication and insisted that she go. She went overseas in late May, having earlier planned for the family's return to Raleigh by buying "11 lots for $8,500 on the hill beyond the Methodist Orphanage." The Secretary's diary added, "We will build on the hill and be happy." That much, at least, was abundantly true. But it was a good thing that the practical Miss Addie had allies who could help thwart her sentimental husband's ideas about a house. He wanted a great rambling edifice, almost tent-like, where the four Daniels sons and their families could reside in four ells and use dining room, living room, kitchen, library, and outdoors in common. Admiral Dewey's widow punctured Daniels' plans when she briskly spoke up to him about his four ells: "You should call them hells."[51]

The Danielses hoped in vain to win for North Carolina the honor of becoming the final state needed to ratify the Woman Suffrage Amendment. Daniels' diary of August 14 recorded that Lodge's "round robin" device had been appropriated at the legislative session at Raleigh, where a majority of the House expressed opposition to the Amendment. Daniels wrote resignedly to his son Jonathan:

> Raleigh is hot in more ways than one. The anti-suffragists seem to have sewed up the situation in the House of Representatives and I fear we have no hope. It was what I both feared and expected. Your mother received quite an ovation

when she went down and we could win if there was to be no election soon. But the sentiment in the country districts has never been cultivated and seems so strongly against it that legislators feel they cannot safely vote for it. But the stars in their course fight for us and we will win. . . .

He was to say pretty much the same thing about the Presidential campaign, where he spoke loyally for the Cox-Roosevelt ticket in his old stamping ground of such North Central states as Ohio and Indiana. The old campaigner quickly learned "that practically the solid German and Irish and Greek vote was in the bag for Harding." The only man who would not believe the signs of certain defeat was Woodrow Wilson; even the buoyant candidate for Vice-President was convinced.[52]

When FDR left the Navy Department in August, succeeded by Gordon Woodbury, he carried away not only a loving cup that Daniels presented on behalf of organized labor at the Washington Navy Yard but also the prideful affection of his chief. On the day he left, FDR wrote Daniels a grateful handwritten letter that warmed the cockles of Daniels' sentimental heart: "Dear Chief:—This is not good-bye. . . . You have taught me so wisely and kept my feet on the ground when I was about to skyrocket. . . ." What Daniels "taught" FDR had little to do with his Navy Department duties— the young New Yorker had shown himself a first-rate official—but rather not to mistake Daniels' plain manner for weakness. Daniels replied to FDR with a long affectionate letter as "an older brother," which he followed with a formal note that he prepared for Woodrow Wilson's signature. It would not do, after all, to make Wilson's farewell to FDR too effusive, for the President's was not an easily forgiving nature. When informed of FDR's resignation, the President told Daniels: "I resent & deeply resent," in obvious reference to Roosevelt's Brooklyn speech of the preceding February 1.[53] That Daniels was cut from other cloth than Wilson is further borne out by their differing attitude toward Eugene V. Debs, the Socialist leader. At the Cabinet meeting of August 10, Daniels—and even the flag-waving Mitchell Palmer—supported a pardon for Debs, imprisoned under the wartime Sedition Act, but Wilson was implacable.

The day before that Cabinet meeting Daniels was in Hyde Park, N.Y., where a Committee on Notification waited upon the Vice-Presidential nominee. Daniels noted in his diary: "Both Mrs. R's spoke of my letter to Franklin & were pleased by it." The Navy Secretary sat with Mrs. Sara Delano Roosevelt during her son's acceptance speech (a good one, the diary noted), and chances are that even FDR's mother did not show keener pride in the Young Prince than his "older brother" Daniels. Even though quickly disillusioned about Democratic chances that year, campaigner Daniels sent wires of encouragement to campaigner Roosevelt, such as "You are hitting the bull's eye in every speech." It was a form of whistling in the dark, prelude to the impending defeat, but it betokened the Navy Secretary's faith that Franklin D. Roosevelt would be heard from again.[54]

While candidate Roosevelt was lightheartedly telling audiences how he allegedly had written a new constitution for Marine-occupied Haiti, his old chief was suffering acute embarrassment over the situation on that island. By the peak of the election campaign the *Nation* magazine completed a series of exposé articles documenting many abuses under the Marine occupation of the Negro republic. In September the Navy Department had had to deny the outspoken charge of Senator Harding, the Republican presidential candidate, that U.S. Marines had killed thousands of inoffensive natives.[55] In the midst of the election campaign Daniels had to continue probing the charges of cruelty and misrule while the investigating Marine Corps officers mostly protected one another.

General George Barnett had been painting a generally rosy picture of the Haitian occupation before he was supplanted on July 1 by General John A. Lejeune as Commandant of the Marine Corps. When Lejeune and Smedley Butler, who had earlier served in Haiti with distinction, were sent to investigate, they came home with a totally misleading whitewash. Then Barnett, by now hostile to Daniels and Roosevelt, confirmed a number of wanton killings of natives. In mid-October Daniels called in the press for a detailed briefing, and sent off a Court of Inquiry to Haiti. New information then showed that the *Nation*'s charges had been amply justified, and Daniels responded with courts-martial for punishment. The worst offenses in Haiti had begun in October, 1918, when a new revolt opened up against American authority. The flower of the Marine Corps was then in Europe, and in the following months many enlisted Marines became embittered at being kept on tropical duty after the Armistice while their buddies in France had been sent home. Daniels did his best to learn the truth that October of 1920, even while it was being kept from him: "I want everything—the good, and the bad—brought out, the responsibility fixed, and the whole thing cleared up once and for all."[56]

By the end of 1920, with Republican "normalcy" triumphant and Wilson's dreams in ruins, Daniels grimly proposed that the United States get on with its naval building program. He testified against the then-current Borah Resolution, which urged an American agreement with Britain and Japan to reduce naval expenditures by half during the next five years. Setting up an oligarchy of powers was not, in Daniels' view, the answer to world-wide suspicion thus excited in the excluded nations. Not only would such an agreement be arbitrarily exclusive, but Britain would be the chief beneficiary of any resultant naval holiday. Finally, in January, 1921, as spokesman for the repudiated administration, Daniels defiantly warned the House Naval Affairs Committee that a United States acting on its own in world affairs would have to complete the expensive ships now under construction and bear the expense of building many more in order to insure its security.[57] Isolation, he intimated, comes high.

At the end of the Secretary's term he got more than a little trouble from General William ("Billy") Mitchell, the pioneer exponent of air power. The general's prophetic testimony before the Senate Military Affairs Committee the previous year had so agitated Navy careerists that Daniels had had to write anxious letters of protest to War Secretary Baker. In the week before the presidential election the Navy's General Board conducted secret aviation bombing tests on the antiquated battleship *Indiana,* a test to which Daniels invited Mitchell. True, the *Indiana* was a sitting target, but the General Board did not advertise the extensive bomb damage wrought upon the battleship. Mitchell took care of that with some outspoken challenges when he appeared before the House Appropriations Committee in February, 1921. Then it was that Daniels was goaded into a retort that the cartoonists did not let him forget for many years. He was "prepared to stand bareheaded on the deck of a battleship and let Brigadier General Mitchell take a crack at me with a bombing airplane. " Of course Daniels meant a warship maneuvering in open waters and with all guns firing. But he had to give in shortly thereafter, and one of his last acts as Secretary of the Navy was to arrange a bombing test—with ex-German warships as targets—which later that year met all of Mitchell's expectations.[58]

Daniels' eight years in Wilson's Cabinet were to end on a gloomy and discordant note, but the Navy Secretary maintained his accustomed buoyancy and humor. To a newspaper reporter who interviewed him on the eve of his leaving the Navy, Daniels cheerily confided that he would have to work hard to make *The News and Observer* pay in a city numbering only twenty-five thousand persons and in a time of inflated newsprint prices. The reporter protested: "But with all your wonderful experience of the past eight years, Mr. Secretary, your services ought to be in great demand at big prices." Daniels replied, with a twinkle: "Yes that's so, no doubt. In fact ———— (mentioning a well-known politician) told me I ought to be able to earn $100,000 a year, but, you see, the only folks I know who could pay $100,000 a year are on the other side, politically and otherwise." Continuing, he said:

> You see, while I've been in office I've held up a good many fat contracts and prevented a good many gentlemen from making a good many millions out of our Uncle Samuel, and one way an another, I seem to have incurred their displeasure (another twinkle), and I'm afraid they don't want me, and, as I say, my friends, the folks I know best and like, haven't got any hundred-thousand dollar jobs, so I guess I'll have to go back to the editorial desk right away. Oh well, I love it; I love Raleigh, and I love the News and Observer, and I'm not so old either.[59]

When Daniels completed his eight years as Secretary of the Navy he had served longer than any predecessor save Gideon Welles (who had served the same length of time, 1861-69). Indeed, the Navy Department careers of the two men contain some surprisingly apt parallels. To be sure, there were obvious physical and temperamental differences; nobody could mistake "Father Welles's" serious and withdrawn mien, his bushy white whiskers and brown wig, for Daniels' cheery outgoing quality and his Bryanesque clothing. Daniels himself admired Welles's record, even to his predecessor's more complete diary, and the fact is that both compiled records during wars crucial to the nation's future and both have come to be regarded as strong Secretaries.

Welles and Daniels both presided over "unprepared" navies; Welles even more so, for the European powers had been building ironclads since the Crimean War while the United States had not a single one. Both men were editors, Welles of the *Hartford Times* and Daniels of *The News and Observer* of Raleigh. Both men were Democrats, Welles having been the pre-eminent Jackson supporter in New England and later becoming a founder of the Republican party via the slavery issue. (He returned to the Democratic fold as early as 1868.) Both men were deeply religious, Welles an Episcopalian and Daniels a Methodist; both were deeply loyal, Welles to Lincoln and Daniels to Wilson. Both built a reputation for economy in war and savings during demobilization.

Welles and Daniels both picked able Assistant Secretaries, although Welles's quiet style led his critics to assert that Gustavus V. Fox was the real Secretary of the Navy during the Civil War. Nobody said that about Franklin D. Roosevelt in World War I when Daniels was his chief. Both Secretaries made the mistakes inevitable in emergency situations, and both men had to submit to nuisance investigations by a hostile Congress. Indeed, both Secretaries were plagued by Senators named Hale; Welles by John P. Hale, chairman of the Naval Affairs Committee, and Daniels by his own Frederick Hale. In neither case did the frankly partisan investigations yield what their sponsors sought—evidence of inefficiency and fraud in the Navy Department. If Daniels had to curb such naval prima donnas as Admirals Fiske and Sims, Welles had to rebuke a whole catalogue of admirals including the redoubtable David D. Porter, whom Welles had to reprove for discourtesy. Both civilians refused to play the part of figurehead and, while not brilliant men, both mastered their jobs with competence and honesty.[60]

Like any outsider who questions traditional prejudices, Daniels met the predictable hostility of the Old Navy. Supposedly an indifferent administrator, he nevertheless attained the cherished dream of administrators—picking first-rate men and inspiring them to great heights of creativeness and devotion to duty. He changed for the better an enlisted man's Navy that was never the same once Josephus Daniels had put his hand to the helm. Particularly in his educational reforms was he far-sighted, leaving behind him a Navy in which increasingly there was reliance on the best brains wherever found. The illiterate old Jack Tar was no more, once it became possible, through Daniels' innovations, for virtually any high school graduate in the Navy to earn a commission. The number of enlisted men's appointments to Annapolis, which Daniels pioneered through competitive examinations, grew so that by the time of Daniels' death in 1948 more than 150 enlisted men a year were thus entering the Naval Academy.[61] The logic of Daniels' reforms led to the establishment at Bainbridge, Maryland, of a Naval Preparatory School to help promising enlisted men pass the Annapolis entrance exams. The success of that Regular Navy program led to a parallel one in the Naval Reserve. Daniels' "Join the Navy and Learn a Trade" was merely symptomatic of his larger insistence that the Navy must prepare for the new technical advances that lay in the future. It was, to repeat, in the Naval Research Laboratory established by Josephus Daniels that radar later came to be developed.

The dogma that every red-blooded seaman must execrate Josephus Daniels for having outlawed liquor aboard American warships simply will not stand up. Not only has Daniels' prohibition against liquor stood the test of time by surviving the coming and going of the Prohibition Amendment but, according to U.S. Navy historian Fletcher Pratt, it has come to be "fully approved by the vast majority of the service." Continuing, Pratt explains: "As ships grew more and more complex mechanically, lightning-fast unclouded reaction in handling them was obviously necessary."[62] However dense the propaganda smokescreen that was once intended to becloud Josephus Daniels' Cabinet career, any fair reading of the record must result in the verdict that he was one of the great Secretaries of the Navy.

ᴐᴠᴐᴠᴗᴐᴠᴗ *Chapter six*

Decade in Obscurity

Two days after President Harding's inauguration Daniels and Miss Addie stood misty eyed before some five thousand Raleighites who jammed the municipal auditorium. "I have not come from a larger job," the editor spoke extemporaneously, "but I am back to take up again the greatest work in the world—fighting for the man who has unequal opportunity." Daniels spoke proudly of having served Woodrow Wilson (a tempest of cheers from the throng), and of his own resolve "to fight, to be your comrade . . . to work with you, and to have your love, which I covet above all things." Back on the job Daniels wrote a simple "Home Again" editorial—he had already refused the offer of Adolph Ochs of a position with the *New York Times*—and quickly named himself his paper's correspondent at the forthcoming special session of Congress. Arrived back at the capital in late March, reporter Daniels called at the office of his successor, Edwin Denby. Daniels joked: "After an eight-year vacation in Washington as Secretary of the Navy, I am a plain country editor, scratching gravel to get an honest living. I think I'm going to miss that $12,000 a year." A rueful Denby replied: "After two weeks on your old job I have a very well defined idea of what kind of vacation you had."[1]

Daniels returned refreshed from his eight strenuous years in Washington to his never-failing Fountain of Youth, *The News and*

Observer. He set himself determinedly to reclaim his erstwhile title of the watchdog Mordecai at the Gate, to re-establish the local political influence he had exerted in the old days. Meanwhile he was enjoying the more relaxed social climate of Raleigh, where his old high-backed Cabinet chair had come home with the Secretary. The family was living in a rented house, Miss Addie in particular looking forward to the completion of their own big house where, as her husband's diary had noted: "We will live on the hill and be happy." Of his home arrangements Daniels wrote gaily as usual to his mother-in-law, who had gone to visit her son Henry Bagley in Texas: "Worth is a jewel at hanging pictures and together, with Frank's help, the house is well decorated with the pictures that came from Washington. . . . Before the car of furniture arrived Addie had been planting trees and plants on her hill, dressed in heavy shoes and brown sweater (tell Henry that wasn't all) and it was a task so big that I did my usual stunt—ran away and left her with the hard job to tackle."[2]

Daniels' gaiety lay in sharp contrast to the awesome ordeal that the summer of 1921 held for Franklin D. Roosevelt. Shortly before he was rendered a lifetime cripple through infantile paralysis, FDR got a political warning from his old chief. Daniels had gotten word that the two Republicans on the three-man Senate subcommittee investigating the alleged immorality at Newport—Roosevelt's wartime responsibility—was readying "a libellous report." FDR hurried off to Washington, but he got no satisfaction except permission to inspect the subcommittee's fifteen volumes of testimony. Before he could work up a statement of his own, FDR was hit by the majority report as released to the press. "LAY NAVY SCANDAL TO F. D. ROOSEVELT . . . Details Are Unprintable," read the headlines in the *New York Times.* The charge of using Navy personnel to entrap homosexuals had already been investigated by a court-martial that had termed FDR's actions ill-advised but no more. The minority report, issued by the subcommittee's lone Democrat, held the charges against Roosevelt (and Daniels) grossly unfair and, indeed, that was how the public saw the whole episode. The proceedings were so obviously partisan, so much akin to the three-to-two justice meted out in the Sims Investigation, that they were soon discounted and a happy Roosevelt was free to go to his deadly appointment at Campobello.[3]

Daniels' letter to the stricken Roosevelt is missing, but FDR acknowledged it with a whistling-in-the-dark "Dear Chief" letter, chafing at enforced idleness and talking "complete recovery." Whenever business took him to New York, Daniels came to the Roosevelt house in the East Sixties, usually accompanied by son Jonathan, then studying law at Columbia. The ex-Secretary recalled that on his first visit to see the convalescent, his old Assistant Secretary rose up in his bed, "hauled off and gave me a blow that caused me nearly to lose my balance. He said: 'You thought you were coming to see an invalid, but I can knock you out in any bout.'" Jonathan's recollection was more somber than that of his buoyant father. Mrs. Eleanor Roosevelt, anxious to keep her husband stimulated with a variety of callers, had invited young Daniels to Sunday dinner and asked him to bring along the young men who roomed with him. One of them found it impossible to spend an evening that could not possibly profit his career, and others claimed they were too busy, so Jonathan had to go alone.[4]

Somber, too, was the long-term outlook for world peace, although the Washington Conference for limitations of naval armaments now loomed ahead. During 1921 Daniels wrote a series of articles for the *Saturday Evening Post* in which he rehearsed the reform and growth of the Navy during his term as Secretary. He was openly skeptical of getting an effective pact—which, in his bitter regret over America's repudiation of the League, he implied to be impossible of achievement—and called instead for an American Navy equal to none. To his fellow-Methodists at Lake Junaluska, North Carolina, that summer, the best thing Daniels could say about the approaching Washington Conference was that it was scheduled "to meet on November 11th, an auspicious day to gather to carry out, if belatedly, the mission for which the American boys went to France." At the plenary session during which Secretary of State Hughes proposed the scrapping of the warships that Daniels had wrung from a Republican Congress, the ex-Secretary kept his seat while Columnist Mark Sullivan and William Jennings Bryan got up and applauded. Daniels recalled: "Mr. Bryan said 'get up Daniels, this is a great thing for peace.' I said, 'No, I see nothing very great in this; moreover, I am not disposed to applaud at my funeral.'"[5]

Shorn of national influence, Daniels nevertheless clung tenaciously to his power base in *The News and Observer* while writing and lecturing to help pay for Wakestone, the big new house on the hill. A one million dollar offer of William Randolph Hearst—accord-

ing to the recollection of Representative (later Senator) Estes Kefauver—was peremptorily refused by Daniels. To one broker in
newspaper properties who tried to talk price, Daniels explained
that he must just as well try to sell the State Capitol. "Just suppose
the paper was sold—what would we do?" the editor confided to son
Jonathan. "Where would be our forum? Where any lever? Where
any life?" During this period Daniels saw to it that every Democratic governor of his state, once the Democrat was inaugurated,
would find *The News and Observer* his severest critic. When asked
why so, by one political fledgling, the editor threw back his head
in one of his great laughs and explained: "Young man, you ought to
know that when any political party becomes dominant, there re-
mains only one source of criticism, and that's from within the
party."[6]

The Watts Scandal illustrates Daniels' gadfly status perfectly, being the highlight of the editor's chastisement of the administration
of Governor Cameron Morrison (1921-25). At the urging of his patron, Senator Simmons, and over the opposition of Daniels, A. D.
Watts had been appointed the state's first Revenue Commissioner.
Then came the explosion that erased Watts from public life. Two
Raleigh detectives and a uniformed policeman raided Watts's quarters and arrested him on charges of immorality after finding a Negro woman under his bed. Democratic leaders—in town for the 1923
legislature and abasing themselves in the cold as if at another Ca-
nossa—hurried out to Wakestone to plead with editor Daniels to
kill the story. After telephoning Frank Smethurst, his managing editor, who filled him in, Daniels turned them down flat. "When they
left," he recalled, "I told my wife that I could not have lived with
myself or looked Frank Smethurst in the face if I had acceded to
the request."[7]

The paper's then city editor, Robert E. ("Fleet") Williams, has
stated flatly that Daniels knew nothing of the episode until after
the party leaders arrived at Wakestone. Daniels' indignation was
private and not contrived for publication. To his writing-partner
son Jonathan he wrote: "They [the Democratic leaders] were in a
panic at the exposure of Watts—not over his offense, vulgar and
sordid and common." To his physician-son Worth he wrote: "The
chief indignation of the Governor and his crowd is not at the immorality of his appointee but because he was caught and exposed."
The search for the instigator of the entrapment of Watts—for it was

surely that—must shift from *The News and Observer* camp to that of Josiah W. Bailey, for the episode was clearly in his interest. With the help of his friend and Wake Forest law professor, N. Y. Gulley, Bailey was running full-tilt for Governor next year against the Establishment, and his friends were casting about for an issue. The conclusion is unavoidable, from both manuscript and confidential sources, that the Bailey forces—though not necessarily with Bailey's knowledge—set up Watts's arrest and tipped off *The News and Observer* staff.[8]

That spring brought the death of the editor's mother, in her eighty-eighth year, upon which the ailing Woodrow Wilson wrote Daniels: "I am glad I once had an opportunity of meeting your Mother and forming some conception of her strong character."[9] Old Mary Cleaves Daniels' character was indeed strong enough to have formed a conception—disapproving—of Wilson's too-sudden second marriage. Widow Daniels had declared at the time that it was the last time she would ever feel sorry for a widower. However, she could never really get over her fondness for the Woodrow Wilson who had honored her son Joe with a Cabinet appointment.

She was "Granny" Daniels to the Goldsboro people from the moment she had gone to live at the home of her son, Judge Frank. Never a big talker, she had the good reporter's knack of drawing out people and making them want to talk. Perhaps it was her reportorial instinct as much as pride in her son Joe that made her a great enthusiast for *The News and Observer,* which she had to see the first thing every morning. She was of that fellowship that went to church every time the church bell rang, and she could be found at the Goldsboro Methodist Church every Sunday morning under her grandson's escort. The latter found himself embarrassed by being so conspicuous, because he had to escort her to the very first row and later stand by for the innumerable conversations that marked her ceremonious departure. At her request she was buried at Wilson, N.C., where the townspeople thought of her burial as a homecoming. "When I recall how poor she was," her son Joe wrote to her grandson Worth, "when alone she had to work to earn the bread for her three small children, I am astounded that she accomplished so much. . . . She blessed every life she touched."[10]

A new generation of Danielses was emerging during the twenties, with the marriage of all four sons, and three of them—all save Dr. Worth—destined for careers with *The News and Observer.* In place of the two little girls who had died, Daniels delighted in four daughters—he would never hear of any "daughters-in-law" in his family. The parents lived in that fine house of Wake County stone that Miss Addie had named Wakestone. Its reputed cost of more than $100,000 made the ex-Secretary scramble for enough lecture and Chautauqua dates to pay for the home place. Having first conferred with Bryan, the champion of all Chautauqua lecturers, and with Vice-President Marshall, Daniels worked out arrangements—mostly with the Alber Bureau of Cleveland—whereby he got a lecture fee of $250, of which the bureau got 25 per cent commission and the speaker paid his own expenses. His robust constitution enabled him to take the one-night stands in stride, and his only regret was at the time away from his home folks. That regret is abundantly attested in affectionate letters in the all-but-undecipherable scrawl from such towns as Hebron, Nebraska; Wray, Colorado; and Blue Earth, Minnesota.[11]

Daniels was too busy fighting privilege to waste mourning the ascendancy of the reaction that he found implicit in the Coolidge era. The editor was four square for an effective State Corporation Commission to fix utility rates, for limiting issues of utilities stocks and bonds to actual money invested, for tying rates to such actual money invested instead of to inflated values based on watered stock, and for taxing such properties at their true value in money. He took as his motto a saying coined by Attorney A. L. Brooks of Greensboro: "Monopoly may carry on its schemes but it must do it in the middle of the street." Daniels opposed, from the beginning, the attempt to turn over Muscle Shoals (later a key element in the T.V.A. system) to private utilities, advocating that facility's completion and use. He encouraged the public power champion in the Senate, George W. Norris: "I wish to say how much I have been with you in the fight to control Muscle Shoals." Where the press bureaus of the utilities were planting at wholesale their inspired stories, signed by locally prominent citizens, in the nation's newspapers, *Editor and Publisher* reported one press agent as mourning that Josephus Daniels was "the lone enemy of utilities in the Carolinas."[12]

At home Daniels' *bête noir* was the redoubtable James Buchanan ("Buck") Duke. After having amassed his fortune in tobacco, Duke had made a brilliantly conceived entry into the utilities business. Daniels criticized the 1923 legislature for its truckling to rich men like Duke. Editorially, in "The Education of Buck Duke," Daniels scorned Duke's alleged attempt to blackmail the State Corporation Commission into a power rate increase. The editor was cheered on by Chief Justice Walter Clark in one of his last letters, saying that Duke sought more than an immediate profit—"by discriminating rates and by the part ownership he has already acquired in many mills, he intended gradually to absorb the entire mill interest of this State and South Carolina, if not more." Daniels was fated, however, to fret impotently at Duke, even to the latter's insuring his immortality by giving Trinity College a princely endowment on condition that the institution would now bear the name of Duke University. Of course Duke outwitted all his critics by tying the prosperity of the endowment—for hospitals and church work as well as for education—to the prosperity of his power system. Any move that curbed the prosperity of the Duke Power Company, like raising its taxes, would lower the value of Duke Power stock, and that stock (deposited in the Duke Endowment) was supporting many good works that would then suffer.[13] Daniels could only grit his teeth and fight on.

In those days the political dynamite inherent in the Teapot Dome scandal was being eagerly sniffed out by the nation's political leadership, with the Republicans warily on the defensive. After the death of the unhappy and betrayed President Harding an investigation was launched in October, 1923, by the Senate Public Lands Committee, in which Thomas J. Walsh of Montana probed relentlessly on behalf of the Democratic minority. The scandal was first set in train by Albert B. Fall of New Mexico, Harding's old Senate crony elevated to Secretary of the Interior, who persuaded the trusting President to do what Josephus Daniels would never do, transfer the Navy's oil reserves to the then business-oriented Interior Department. The essential features of the thievery were soon revealed: at the time Teapot Dome was being leased to Harry F. Sinclair, he was giving Secretary Fall $223,000 in government bonds, $85,000 in cash, and a herd of cattle for his ranch; at the time the Elk Hills naval oil reserve was being leased to Edward L. Doheny, he was "lending" Fall $100,000 conveyed to the Secretary of the Interior "in a little black bag."

As the presidential election year of 1924 opened, Republican leaders prevailed on President Coolidge to clean house before disaster overtook them. Coolidge subtly and cleverly stole the thunder from Tom Walsh, who had prepared a Senate resolution to annul the fraudulent leases. On Sunday, January 27, the day before Walsh's contemplated move, Coolidge proclaimed his plan to use special counsel of both major parties to prosecute the government's case in the courts. He thus carefully took the prosecution out of the hands of the Justice Department, whose head, Harry M. Daugherty, was notorious as the leader of the rapacious Ohio Gang and an intimate of Secretary Fall's. The next month, while the Senate committee's Republicans launched a counterattack that would tar the Democrats with the Teapot Dome brush, Coolidge appointed his special prosecutors, Democrat Atlee Pomerene and Republican Owen J. Roberts, later associate justice of the U.S. Supreme Court.

It was no great effort to identify some money-hungry Democrats with the scandal. Doheny, of the little black bag, himself a California Democrat, blandly announced that since the World War he had employed four one-time members of the Wilson Cabinet: Franklin K. Lane (at $50,000 a year), ex-Secretary of the Interior; Garrison, ex-Secretary of War; Gregory, ex-Attorney General; and Wilson's son-in-law and 1924 Presidential aspirant, William G. McAdoo. That was not all that the Democrats had to suffer in that dark February of 1924. Doheny testified that he had paid $5,000 to George Creel to persuade Secretary Daniels to loose his grip on the naval oil reserves (Daniels had turned him down flat). And the Democrats had to look on while another former Attorney General, A. Mitchell Palmer, sat in on the hearings as friend and attorney for Secretary Fall's intimate, Edward "Ned" McLean.[14]

Even Josephus Daniels, wholly innocent of any wrongdoing, came under enfilading fire. If innocent, he could at least be identified in the undiscriminating public mind with the Teapot Dome scandal. Meanwhile the Republicans were hastily removing the sources of their embarrassment. Secretary Fall had resigned the year before to accept employment from, of all people, Harry Sinclair. Navy Secretary Denby resigned in February, 1924, the unwitting victim of manipulators who had played on his loyalty to President Harding. Attorney General Daugherty, who was not above turning the F.B.I. on those who (like Burton K. Wheeler) were seeking to expose the rottenness, would resign the following month. At the same time ex-Secretary Fall's attempt to smear Josephus Daniels was falling flat. Fall told the investigators that he had asked Denby's Assistant Secretary, Theodore Roosevelt, Jr., to clear the

squatters from Teapot Dome with Marines, invoking a precedent
that Fall attributed to Josephus Daniels. It was a bold untruth; no
such precedent was ever located.[15]

But the lease of Teapot Dome had occurred two years before;
why had not Daniels followed out his accustomed role of watchdog
over the Navy's oil reserves? The truth is that nobody would listen
when he protested, that the time was out of joint for anyone who
would oppose "normalcy." To be sure, Daniels had been so busy
with his lecturing, writing a syndicated column (which paid rather
well) and *Our Navy at War* (which paid almost nothing), that he
hardly noticed the quiet transfer to Interior that occurred almost
as soon as he had turned his back on Washington. However, when
Senator LaFollette began to suspect skullduggery he promptly
confided his suspicions to Josephus Daniels and sought his advice
on how best to prevent a steal. And when the news leaked out
about the leases, the invalided Woodrow Wilson told Admiral Cary
Grayson: "Daniels will be outraged. He fought for that oil reserve
with tenacity all during his term and saved it to the country. He
will be heard from."[16]

Indeed, Daniels did all he could so that he would be heard
from. He hurried to Washington to confer with LaFollette, put
him in touch with the strategic Navy officers concerned, went on to
New York to intercede for publicity with his wartime friend Herbert Bayard Swope of the *World*. Swope told Daniels to forget it.
"We printed the news about the leasing but there was no response.
The people are not interested."[17] The crusading Paul Y. Anderson
of the St. Louis *Post-Dispatch* did sound the tocsin with his notable
exposé articles, and Daniels reprinted them in his *News and Observer*. In the main, however, the crusaders met a wall of indifference, and Daniels himself was treated first as a has-been and later
as a bigoted partisan. He fumed helplessly as successive federal
juries—one so flagrantly tampered with that Harry Sinclair served a
jail term as a result—refused to bring convictions in the face of
overwhelming evidence of thievery. At long last Albert B. Fall was
convicted of taking a bribe and he finally went to jail in 1931.

If all Democrats had been as incorruptible as Daniels, they might
have seized upon Teapot Dome as an election issue. Daniels could
and did show that, as Navy Secretary, he had sought a leasing provision to conserve oil in the ground and that he had counted on the
law's being honestly administered. True, his amendment of the Na-

val Appropriations Act of 1920 had been loosely framed to give the
Secretary a wide discretion, but it was a discretion that Daniels had
honored and that Fall had abused. Daniels showed that Congress
had appropriated only a half-million dollars for the Secretary's
anti-drainage program, so that the complete exploitation of the reserves—to the tune of $100,000,000 of the Navy's oil—was a flagrant
abuse of the law. Navy Commander H. A. Stuart, head of the Naval
Fuel Oil Board since 1916, testified: "To any of us who tried to get
Mr. Daniels to loosen his hold on the reserves in cases where we
considered it very essential to do defensive drilling it is highly amusing to see the apparent attempt to make him out as an 'exploiter'
of the reserves."[18]

At the height of the attempt to involve Daniels in the Teapot
Dome scandal came the death, in February, 1924, of Woodrow Wilson. By this time Daniels had already embarked on a busy career
of replying to every slur that was levied at his chief. With the postwar publication of *The Letters of Franklin K. Lane,* Daniels had instantly wired an answer—duly published in the press—to Lane's
charge (Lane was not yet revealed as Doheny's $50,000-a-year at-
torney) that Wilson and Daniels had dragged their feet on wartime
convoying. Admiral Sims also had attacked with his warmed-over
charges that had already been squelched during the naval investigation. With Wilson's death the ex-Secretary launched into a hurried biography of his late chief and made his own correspondence
files bulge with calls for quick information. Daniels' own signed editorial tribute was fully eight columns long, rehearsing Wilson's administration and stoutly defending it at every turn. He explained
Wilson's personal aloofness in the President's need to conserve his
limited strength. Wilson, according to Daniels, "was never a gre-
garious social animal and never at Princeton or elsewhere was he a
hail-fellow-well-met. . . . He did not understand that the average
American merely wished to 'pay his respects to the President.'" The
editor, who had called several times at the House on S Street, quoted
the last words he had heard from the lips of Woodrow Wilson:
"'We need not be doubtful of the issue. The things we have fought
for, the world peace we have tried to secure, will come, never doubt
that.'"[19]

Daniels exhibited his wonted resilience of spirit at the approach
of his first grandchild a few months later. To the expectant father,
Dr. Worth Daniels of Washington, Daniels told about reading the

welcome letter "on the lawn . . . to the assembled whole D family," who then speculated about the coming "launching." The editor's circumstances were comfortable during the twenties, for his *News and Observer* annual salary was $15,000, his reported income from lecturing and column-writing came to some $5,000 a year, and in those days his total annual income averaged around $25,000. So if he spoke of himself as "a poor man," and of the family car as "my wife's car," it was a throwback to the poverty of his youth as well as an adaptation of the then-fashionable attitude that only one poor man could champion the cause of other poor men. Though he never liked to spend money, especially on himself, and was thoroughly conservative in fiscal matters, Daniels actually was bored by business details. He joked to his auditors about his old *State Chronicle* days when he set up one cigar box for incoming money, another for outgoing, and any excess was looked on as profit.[20] He was far from naïve in money matters, however, and where he thought he was being victimized he could be an extremely tough customer.

Daniels outlasted the *New York Times* in their dispute over a series of the editor's articles about Woodrow Wilson. The original contract, dated March 22, 1924, conveyed to the *Times* the rights to a series of twenty-five articles by Daniels, "Woodrow Wilson as I Knew Him," in consideration of $13,000 on delivery of the completed manuscript and a like sum after publication. The dispute grew out of a claim by the *Times* that it had not been aware of Daniels' plans to write a Wilson biography for the John C. Winston Company of Philadelphia (although the *Times* itself had published a news story about this forthcoming biography in its issue of February 11, 1924). After advertising Daniels' articles on April 6, the *Times* announced withdrawal of the series a week later, just before the first article was scheduled to appear. Negotiators for the *Times* then sought Daniels' assent to a new contract by which the $13,000 already paid would be considered payment in full. Daniels stuck to his guns and held the *Times* to the original contract. He insisted (rightly, as *Times* counsel later conceded) that there was no real duplication between the articles and book in any case, and that the laborer was worthy his hire.[21]

Daniels had emerged so nearly the hero of Teapot Dome that a small-scale presidential boom developed for him in 1924, complete with a "Daniels for President Club" in North Carolina. He squelched it. Whenever anyone spoke of Daniels for President, as they occasionally did, the editor grinned and uttered the supposed truism: "The Democratic party is composed of Irishmen, Southerners and Jews, none of whom can hope to be elected President." An even more intriguing boom for Daniels involved a bid that he take second place on the Progressive ticket with Robert M. LaFollette. A *New York Times* story of March 18 first mentioned the possibility, and sometime later the noted journalist of the LaFollette camp, Gilson Gardner, came to Raleigh in a vain effort to persuade Daniels. Strangely enough, the same LaFollette, who a decade before had avowed that he knew of no progressives in the South, now came around to ask one of those nonexistent progressives to be is running mate. In any case Daniels loyally mailed a check for $100 on April 1 to Democratic National Chairman Cordell Hull.[22]

At the disastrous Madison Square Garden Convention, June 24 to July 10, Daniels looked on in dismay as his Democratic party grimly sought to commit suicide. Catholic against Klansmen, urban America against rural America, recent immigrants against older immigrants—the dissensions all were embodied in the principal contenders, Smith and McAdoo. As a columnist for the Hearst and other newspapers, Daniels bravely sounded a warning against party dissension and tried to direct his party's gaze, as he expressed it privately, at the main tent instead of the sideshows, "to clean up the mess at Washington." But the peacemaker never had a chance, for of all the divisive issues—prohibition, the League, Teapot Dome —none packed such emotional dynamite as the Ku Klux Klan. As a McAdoo man Daniels well knew that the anti-Klan resolution originated as a stop-McAdoo device of the Alabamians, and was a national projection of the conflict between Oscar W. Underwood and the Klan in Alabama. Nevertheless, Daniels would not accept the Klan's kiss of death—as did McAdoo and most of his followers— and the editor voted personally in the Resolutions Committee and on the floor to denounce the Klan as un-American. The anti-Klan resolution failed of passage by less than a single vote; Daniels contributed his one delegate vote to North Carolina's grand total of 3-17/20 (out of 24 votes) to condemn the Klan by name. Only his love for the nay-saying Bryan kept Daniels from playing an even more active role against the Klan. "I felt so strongly," Daniels said the next day to fellow-Democrat Claude Bowers of the *World*, "that I should have taken the floor and spoken in favor of the minority report [specific denunciation of the Klan], but I found it painful even to vote against Bryan."[23]

In the course of the marathon ninety-five ballots Daniels sought out McAdoo and begged him to withdraw so that the Convention might draft Tom Walsh, a Catholic, a McAdoo supporter, and the hero of Teapot Dome. But the unambitious Walsh had already eliminated himself, and so the Convention settled hopelessly upon John W. Davis. Then would Tom Walsh take second place, as Daniels and other leaders urged? In the Montana delegation Burton K. Wheeler, as Daniels recalled, asked with some bitterness why any friend of Walsh's would urge him to run on a doomed ticket. In fact, so disgusted was Burton Wheeler with the Democratic performance that he accepted that very second place on the Progressive ticket earlier refused by Daniels. Wheeler was already under a contrived indictment procured by his Teapot Dome foeman, Attorney General Daugherty. Josephus Daniels rallied with a group of fair-minded national figures who raised money and indignation against the obvious frame-up. A federal jury the following year easily acquitted Wheeler.[24]

In 1925, too, came the tragic end of William Jennings Bryan, tragic because it came to the accompaniment of ridicule for his sad performance at Dayton, Tennessee, in the Scopes "anti-evolution" trial. Bryan had been the first of Daniels' triumvirate of contemporary heroes, and there was a Bryan Breakfast—Daniels personally saw to it—at every succeeding Democratic national convention while Daniels lived. Unlike Bryan, Daniels had continued to study and grow; the editor had to refuse personally to join the anti-evolution crusade. In early 1925 Bryan had come to Raleigh to get Daniels' editorial support for a North Carolina law to ban the teaching of evolution in the public schools. The two old friends spent all of a long afternoon in the editor's sanctum, and at dusk the Commoner stalked out grim and silent. Daniels, the University trustee, at once proceeded to help kill the pending anti-evolution bill while Bryan, the anti-intellectual, made his way to his fatal rendezvous with Clarence Darrow and the iconoclasts in Tennessee.[25]

The third of Daniels' triumvirate of heroes (after Bryan and Wilson) was, as yet, only a hero-in-the-making: Franklin D. Roosevelt. Their friendly correspondence had risen to a crescendo on the eve of the 1924 Convention, FDR backing Al Smith and Daniels

his friend McAdoo. After the Convention the Man in the Brown
Derby was already mending his fences for another try four years
later, writing in cordiality to Daniels. After the election disaster
of November, 1924, the editor wrote FDR, Smith's lieutenant: "The
election in New York demonstrates that our friend, Al Smith [re-
elected Governor], is a wizard at getting votes." Because he believed that prohibition should not be allowed to become the
dominant campaign issue, Daniels tried to head it off with his customary humor. "I think you took only a light bath," he joshed
Franklin about his speech before the New York State Convention
of 1926. "From that speech nobody would call you an immersionist
like Al Smith; they would rather think you took yours by sprink-
ling or pouring."[26]

Just as the older political generation was passing, so was a
personal one in Daniels' life, and that same year saw the passing
of Miss Addie's mother. Unlike Granny Daniels, who wore the
same little bonnet and no-nonsense dress, Mrs. Bagley went splen-
didly attired always, and she would concern herself with such matters as social position and the graces (her pianistic feat of playing
simultaneously *Dixie* and *The Star-Spangled Banner* was well
known). A dominating influence on her unmarried daughters, Mrs.
Bagley always reserved a special affection for her son-in-law, Mr.
Daniels. On her deathbed she turned to him and said: "I love you
as if you were my own son." He reported, in his turn, that this
governor's daughter "talked about many things, not saying 'goodbye' but indicating it by everything she said. . . . It was a calm
and brave farewell."[27]

Only the year before, Daniels had sent to the "three girls" (Mrs.
Bagley and Miss Belle and Miss Ethel) a birthday check on *his*
birthday so they could trade in their old Ford on a new one. The
editor would send "love letters" to Miss Addie's spinster sisters,
who lavished their love on Brother Joe till the end of their days. To
his son Worth, Daniels sent a word picture of a happy family
Christmas at the end of 1926:

> We enjoyed reading about your Christmas and your thrill
> about playing partner of Santa Claus. There is nothing like
> it, and the joy of beholding the delight and wonderment of
> your boy opened a new source of pleasure never dreamed
> of before. . . .[The new baby, Jonathan's firstborn] is not yet
> old enough to have the real thrill over her stocking and the

Christmas tree, but . . . her big blue eyes opened wide in inquiry when the tree was lighted and Josephus officiated, as usual, in handing out the Christmas presents. John and Harriet and Jessie and Burle [Negro retainers] were all present and the old time flavor was there. Your mother and Ethel and Belle were teary around the lashes, thinking of the happiness of their mother last Christmas. But they knew she would have them brave and bonnie and we had an old time Christmas dinner and callers in the afternoon and a quiet evening at home, talking of you and wishing for you, and trying to imagine Worth Jr.'s state of mind.[28]

On the national scene, where he was in temporary eclipse, Daniels clung to his old Wilsonian mates and chastised their enemies. He greatly admired Newton D. Baker, carried on a lively political correspondence with Baruch, praised the benevolence of Julius Rosenwald, and upheld the arm of Smedley Butler, who had been euchred into taking on the impossible task of cleaning up the Philadelphia of that day. When Admiral Fiske returned to the wars with an attack on Woodrow Wilson, Daniels fired off complaints to the A.P. for giving "the old gas bag" so much prominence and credence. Melville Stone of the A.P. tried to placate Daniels by agreeing that Fiske was indeed a publicity-seeking humbug. Yet when Burton J Hendrick, Admiral Sims's ghost-writer, came to Raleigh, Daniels went out of his way to be kind to a fellow writer. Hendrick appeared around 1927, seeking material for his forthcoming Walter Hines Page biography. According to Ben Dixon MacNeill, Hendrick hesitated in his hotel two days out of indecision until Daniels, hearing of it, called on Hendrick, gave him much material, and invited him to supper.[29] Hendrick probably stayed at the new Sir Walter Hotel, which was Daniels' main civic promotion during the twenties, and one that was triumphantly realized. On the other hand, most of his national concerns fared badly during that decade, his editorials lamenting the defeat of the Child Labor Amendment, the presence of U.S. Marines in Nicaragua, the continued failure of the United States to join the World Court.

Daniels' fight against the Ku Klux Klan was a troubled one, troubled because he knew that his state's rank-and-file Klansmen were traditionally Democrats who must be carefully weaned away from their aberration. At the height of its power in North Carolina the revived Klan split the Democratic party down the middle in almost every city and town. So it was with an almost audible sigh of relief that Daniels greeted the resignation from the hooded order of its most respectable adherent, Superior Court Judge Henry A. Grady, North Carolina's Grand Kleagle. In the wake of Grady's resignation Daniels pushed, in the 1927 legislature, for an outright outlawing of the Klan. He did not get it, but he was satisfied that the hooded order would pose no further threat in that generation.

But if the Klan had been the divisive issue in 1924, would not prohibition be equally divisive in 1928? In their enmity to the Ku Klux Klan, Editor Daniels and his son Jonathan understood one another perfectly, but when it came to prohibition the two generations diverged. To Jonathan's generation, it was the disrespect for law brought on by unenforceable prohibition that was the palpable evil. To Josephus Daniels, who remembered the role of saloon keepers and distillers in dirty politics and commercialized vice, efficient enforcement of prohibition was the way out. Yet the elder Daniels was far from happy about the way prohibition dominated all other political issues as 1928 approached. He discerned early that fanatical prohibitionists were in fact sabotaging many overdue social reforms, that the issue of prohibition was swallowing up the reform and anti-big-business issues on which Daniels wanted his party to campaign.

It was Al Smith's "turn" for the Democratic presidential nomination, and he had the nomination clinched before the Houston Convention so much as met. Daniels, who long before had warned FDR that his man Smith could not be elected, arrived at Houston pledged to Cordell Hull. A Wet majority on the Platform Committee accepted as the price of the rural elements' acquiescence on Smith a dry plank written by Carter Glass and endorsed by Josephus Daniels. The plank was not as extreme as the Anti-Saloon League would have liked, but it was dry enough to enrage the brilliant but thirsty H. L. Mencken. He scolded prohibitionist Daniels as "one of the hollowest and dumbest of Southern politicians,"[30] a statement so laughably false that it can be understood only in terms of Mencken's own proclivities for the strong waters. No sooner had Governor Smith won the "harmony" nomination than he wired an acceptance that tore the harmony apart. Al Smith proclaimed himself a man still pledged to lead a movement to change the prohibition laws. Daniels mourned from Houston over this "inauspicious beginning of a campaign which promises to witness many surprises and unusual shifts in the voting."[31] Two weeks later he was thoroughly shaken when Smith made a surprise selection for chairman of the national committee: John J. Raskob, not only Catholic and Wet, but a high executive of General Motors, director of many corporations, and who only a year before had given his party affiliation as Republican.

On the evidence, Daniels opposed Al Smith's nomination only because of the prohibition issue; once Smith was nominated Daniels returned to his regularly maintained stand that prohibition was not, in any case, the main issue. He was well aware, of course, that many of his fellow-Protestants were concealing anti-Catholic bias under the cloak of prohibition. Daniels particularly resented the way "non-political" prohibition was being used as a pretext for anti-liberal and anti-Democratic sentiment. Thus it was that the editor denounced the "premium put upon hypocrisy" in the anti-Smith attitude of the prominent New York clergyman, the Reverend Dr. John Roach Straton. To the editor of the *Manufacturer's Record* Daniels finally confided that federal prohibition had been a mistake from the first, that local option bred less disrespect for the law and did less violence to states' rights principles. "If Smith can find any way of putting the matter to the States for decision," Daniels wrote, "I am for him."[32] In any case, Daniels loyally went down to defeat with Smith as bravely as he ever did with Bryan. Having campaigned and editorialized for Al Smith, Daniels remained proud always that his man had carried every single county in *The News and Observer's* circulation area. Those rural counties, unanimously opposed to Smith's nomination in the first place, nevertheless went down the line with Daniels for the losing candidate.

Franklin D. Roosevelt was Daniels' built-in complaint department during the campaign. Daniels did not hesitate to let FDR know how unhappy he was with Raskob. Franklin also confirmed a hunch expressed in a Daniels editorial, that Raskob's selection "was a bold stroke to try to end the 99% of business (big and little) preference for the Republican Party." Unhappy as was Daniels with the national issues, he could not restrain his joy at Franklin's nomination for Governor of New York. Daniels "pulled rank" on the younger man in a jovial telegram that ordered Franklin to drop anchor in Raleigh en route home from Warm Springs, Georgia. After the Al Smith debacle in November, Roosevelt's election as Governor helped ease Daniels' chagrin. "You have no idea how happy it made us all to see you come through in such great shape," he wrote Governor-elect Roosevelt. And when he told Franklin, "It was a great tribute to you," he said it mindful that this young comer had been elected Governor in a state that had denied its presidential vote to its former Governor, Al Smith.[33]

The undisputed paladin of the anti-Smith Democrats in the South was Methodist Bishop James Cannon, Jr., of Virginia, whose contribution to the Hoover victory made the bishop truly a power in the land. In the summer of 1929 the press exploded with the news that Bishop Cannon had for several years been speculating in stocks as patron of the New York bucketshop of Kable and Company, a firm since gone bankrupt and its principals penalized by the law. As a prominent Methodist and Southern Democrat, Josephus Daniels was subject to double arousal. Nevertheless Daniels' outrage was for Cannon the Methodist bishop rather than for Cannon the anti-Smith Democrat. Daniels said a gentle no to the other when Senator Carter Glass wanted to address to him an anti-Cannon open letter as from one prominent Methodist layman to another. They were both politicians, Daniels reminded Glass, and such a letter would be taken as the attempt of Democratic politicians to punish a Methodist bishop.[34]

Josephus Daniels joined other prominent Methodist laymen who went to the church's General Conference at Dallas, Texas, in May, 1930, and pressed for a formal church trial. But the Committee on Episcopacy, after voting for a trial, reversed itself after a week of politicking after which Cannon read to the entire Conference his letter of apology. Daniels and his friends were indignant that Cannon, who had previously proclaimed himself "Unspotted from the World," had apologized only when cornered and then allowed to get away with it. Daniels recalled the picture of Bishop Cannon at Dallas:

> After the testimony had piled up convincingly, one night Bishop Cannon came to the hearing, leaning heavily on a cane, either sick or pretending he was sick. He made a statement to the effect that he must confess before his brethren that he had been guilty of speculating but that he did not at that time properly evaluate the gravamen of his offending. He spoke most piously and contritely, weeping as he did, saying that he put himself on the mercy of his brethren of the Conference. He confessed his sin and promised in future he would have no part or lot in speculation of any

character. He did not use the word "gambling" but that was
what he was doing. . . . I expect most of the preachers in the
South voted against Al Smith and for Hoover, and nobody
criticized any of these preachers for exercising this right. It
was Bishop Cannon's gambling and his greed for money—
and that alone—that caused us to ask the church to find him
guilty of offenses unbecoming a minister of the gospel.

Having furnished the foregoing to Virginius Dabney for his Cannon biography, *Dry Messiah,* Daniels added: "The Conference
would not have been so gullible if the bitterness over the Al Smith
campaign had not survived the election."[35]

In his religion Daniels was a man of simple—often beautiful—
faith. His Sunday afternoon "open receptions" at Wakestone at-
tracted many Methodist clergymen and laymen, all of whom respected him for his record in the Cannon episode. Daniels' deeply
religious nature was troubled by the approaching publication, in
1930, of a religious satire of a novel, *Clash of Angels,* by his son
Jonathan. It represented the harmless kind of iconoclastic effort
that many young writers must get out of their systems. The father
was distressed lest any words of his add to Jonathan's new grief at
losing his young wife, but as it turned out the book was quite inoffensive. At the same time Jonathan's birthday present from his
father that year was a Bible.[36]

The prolonged bitterness of the Al Smith campaign and Hoover's
capture of North Carolina made inevitable a Tar Heel political
showdown in 1930. It was then that F. M. Simmons, in the Senate
nearly three decades and a party man of strictest sect, had to defend his desertion of Al Smith against Josiah W. Bailey, who had
led the state's pro-Smith forces. Between the two Daniels found
little to choose, having feuded with both before the Wilson era and
having made up with both during his Cabinet days. The huge
majority rolled up against Simmons bore witness to the premium
then placed on party regularity. But as a party regular himself,
Daniels cast his personal vote for the loser. "In spite of our differences over regularity in 1928," he recalled, "I supported Simmons
for re-election in 1930. I felt that for one lapse he ought not to be
repudiated by the party he had served so long and so well."[37]

To Daniels' mind a much more agreeable election contest took
place that year when a replacement had to be found for Harry
Woodburn Chase as President of the University of North Carolina.

The editor long had his eye on Frank P. Graham as another McIver, another "steam engine in britches," who had barnstormed the state in the early twenties on behalf of better public school education and whom Daniels had backed editorially as head of "North Carolina's conscience," the North Carolina Conference for Social Welfare. Graham's real reluctance to take the presidency was worn down by the pleas of the leading trustees, like Governor Gardner, Federal Judge John J. Parker, and Josephus Daniels, who confided to him the crisis the University was then facing. When the time came, Daniels personally moved—successfully—to make Graham's election unanimous. Judge Parker, a Republican, had just been defeated of confirmation to the U.S. Supreme Court in what was later deemed by the *American Bar Association Journal* a great mistake. Despite their political differences, Parker and Daniels remained the most cordial of colleagues. Moreover, a decade later, after FDR had appointed Republicans Stimson and Knox to his Cabinet, Daniels came up with the name of John J. Parker of North Carolina for a vacancy on the U.S. Supreme Court.[38]

The able Governor O. Max Gardner, elected triumphantly despite the Al Smith disaster, enjoyed only only the briefest of honeymoons with prosperity and with Josephus Daniels. The truth is that the great stock market crash acted merely as a punctuation mark in the story of North Carolina's deepening agricultural—and now total —depression. Having made himself heard during the honeymoon legislature two years before, Editor Daniels was a veritable flame during the marathon legislative session of 1931. In his seventieth year Daniels was at the center of every one of the sweeping reforms that the sorely beset state adopted. North Carolina now took over the county roads and schools, reorganized the three leading state educational institutions into a Consolidated University, and stabilized the credit of smaller governmental units through a Local Government Act. The revenue bill was a compromise that pleased nobody, least of all the crusading Daniels. For the one hundred and forty days of the Long Parliament of 1931, *The News and Observer* unceasingly proclaimed: "Taxes on property (meaning homesites) must be reduced." Governor Gardner agreed, but he and Daniels differed on procedure, the governor looked to retrenchment and Daniels to new sources of revenue. The lobbyists took care to insure that Daniels' battle cry: "Get the money where the money is" should go for naught.

That there arose much grass roots support of Daniels for Governor is amply attested by his collected papers. The editor had a long record of declining to offer for elective office, to be sure, but he was now tempted more than at any time in his life. Delegations came to visit him throughout the fall of 1931, and the surprise withdrawal of a leading competitor put even greater pressure on the editor to declare himself. But Daniels' serious injury in an automobile accident on January 13, 1932, turned the tide. A month later he made a formal withdrawal from the approaching contest, to the unanimous applause of Miss Addie and the other Danielses. He was now too old and battered, they thought, for hard political service.

The automobile injury might have daunted the will to recover of an old man who was not morally certain, as Daniels was, that 1932 was the year of destiny for Franklin D. Roosevelt. Daniels rode as a passenger—in fact he never learned to drive a car—in the automobile of a prominent Atlanta attorney when their car was sideswiped, forced down an embankment and into a tree. It occurred in an Atlanta suburb on the return from Mount Berry, Georgia, where Daniels had helped celebrate the thirtieth anniversary of the Berry schools for underprivileged youngsters. "I'm just a scarred soldier," he murmured to friends during the long wait, in good spirits, to enter the X-ray and operating rooms at St. Joseph's Infirmary. Actually his head was cut open, leaving that most vivid of several scars on his forehead, his left arm broken in several places between elbow and wrist (leaving the hand somewhat stiffened for life), and a bad glass cut on the left leg. Stitched up and X-rayed, the old war horse immediately dictated a letter to President Hoover on behalf of another try for a Supreme Court nomination for North Carolina's Chief Justice, Walter P. Stacy. To be sure, the Commercial National Bank back home had failed with the old editor's life savings, the very existence of his newspaper was in peril because of depressed business conditions, and now he was laid up in St. Joseph's Infirmary. At this juncture his wartime friend Bernard Baruch voluntarily came forward with a providential loan —truly a fortune in those days—of $25,000.[39]

"You have probably had occasion before to suspect that I had a hard head," Daniels wrote to FDR soon after the auto accident, and nothing was more tonic the the old editor than Roosevelt's chances to become President. FDR had to act more cautiously than Daniels in taking too-strong stands on divisive national questions, and although the editor generally understood FDR's temporizing on prohibition, he was troubled by Roosevelt's negative attitude on America's joining the League of Nations. The old Wilsonian said as much in March to Newton D. Baker, but he did it after first congratulating FDR on his sweeping victory over Al Smith in the New Hampshire primary. "Of course," Daniels wrote to William E. Dodd, "Newton Baker is the ablest man we have, but Roosevelt is clean and honest and I know him well enough to know that he would not be controlled by Tammany or anybody else." Later in the pre-Convention campaign Daniels assured Bernard Baruch: "I know Franklin very well and know his strong points and his limitations," but now happily reported to the other that FDR was certain of nomination.[40]

Daniels' later unpublished memoir puts the Baker-Roosevelt question this way: "In a contest between Roosevelt and Baker I would have had a hard time in taking sides. The test never came, for early in the year [1932] when Baker was in Raleigh appearing in the courts we had a heart-to-heart talk in which he said: 'Nothing would induce me to become a candidate. When I left Washington I had had enough and will never permit my name to be used for office. I will not be a candidate for President.'" Nevertheless, a strong stop-Roosevelt movement developed at the Chicago Convention and used Newton Baker's name as a rallying point. Here again is Daniels' recollection:

> As the delegates arrived there was a well oiled movement to draft Newton Baker, but no word came from him. Some people—not a few—felt that he was "a willin' Barkis," and there were quite a few delegates who preferred him. I had no reason to think he had changed his position from what he told me in Raleigh early in the year. But one day a New York leader, opposed to Roosevelt, aware of my admiration and affection for Baker, called at my room and outlined the matured plan that at the proper moment Baker's name would be presented for nomination, and solicited my cooperation in the plan. I repeated to him what Baker had said to me in Raleigh; that I was by choice and instruction for Roosevelt who would be nominated; and told him that he and others were doing Baker a disservice to bring his name forward to help the conservative element who opposed Roosevelt because of his liberal policies and principles.[41]

The Roosevelt-Daniels correspondence in the pre-Convention days clearly reflected an unquestioned mutual reliance and affection born of seven years together as comrades loyal to Woodrow Wilson. Their letters exchanged regards from Eleanor Roosevelt and Miss Addie, cordial invitations to visit Hyde Park and Wakestone, Daniels' congratulations on FDR's public utterances. Daniels liked particularly FDR's "forgotten man" speech of April 7, obviously reminded of the occasion thirty-five years before when the editor had introduced Walter Hines Page for his own "forgotten man" speech. "In this inability to carry on fully," the convalescent Daniels wrote FDR, "I have thought often of you and with increased admiration of your courage under all obstacles." The same letter congratulated FDR on his primary victories over Al Smith in Iowa, New Hampshire, and Georgia, in which Daniels saw evidence of Smith's lack of good sportsmanship, saying: ". . . it would require asbestos paper to print what I think about Smith." Daniels' advice to the presidential aspirant centered around defeating conservative Jouett Shouse for the Convention's temporary chairman, and he also begged FDR to rid himself of the embarrassment of the corrupt Mayor Jimmy Walker of New York City.[42] The Roosevelt luck held, for Walker resigned on September 1.

Now that the old editor's left arm was out of its cast and he had begun squeezing a rubber ball to exercise his weakened left hand, home affairs began to look up. Wakestone was then agog with son Jonathan's approaching wedding, as Daniels wrote the Misses Bagley and jollied them about their sister: "Addie has already bought her a hat and a pair of shoes and says that both ends are ready for the wedding but she has nothing to go between." He was away from Raleigh on his birthday, and when he got back he thanked O. J. Coffin for a gracious note the other had written for the *Greensboro Daily News*, Daniels adding: ". . . the boys did me a shabby trick to advertise me as seventy when you and I know that by every yardstick except Anno Domini I am not more than twenty-five." Jonathan was to leave *Fortune* magazine for the family paper that year, in response to encouragement from his father, who got son Frank to put plainly before Jonathan the paper's financial difficulties along with its real need for new blood on the executive editorial side. As business conditions approached the lows of the Bank Holiday, the paper's business staff often had to scramble for cash with which to meet payrolls, but Josephus Daniels' longtime aversion to going into debt now paid dividends. His largely debt-free business position, quite as much as Baruch's providential loan, helped *The News and Observer* to weather the storm.[43]

Although his state was electing a Governor and a U.S. Senator that year, Daniels found no candidate he could wholly back and so did not give his undivided attention to either contest. More congenial national politics occupied Daniels that spring as he met repeatedly with such local Democrats as Governors Gardner and McLean and Greensboro attorney A. L. Brooks. He was also in close touch with national leaders like Homer Cummings and Daniel C. Roper in addition to James A. Farley, Louis Howe, and others at Roosevelt-for-President headquarters. At the State Convention, Daniels and Brooks broke up a covert anti-Roosevelt movement and won through for an instructed delegation for Roosevelt. On getting Daniels' good news FDR wired back: "Perfectly delighted with good old North Carolina's action." The next day the ebullient editor wrote his son Worth: "We are busted but I made a contract to write daily reports from the Democratic National Convention at Chicago, to which I am a delegate-at-large, and so your mother and I are going to Chicago and let Mr. Hearst pay our expenses." Arriving early at Chicago, the personally dry Daniels quickly made news when he stated that he would not oppose a platform plank for resubmission of the Prohibition Amendment. As to President Hoover, already the Republican nominee, Daniels told the press: "Hoover is another Taft, an excellent gentleman, a hard worker, a fine man. But he and the Republicans are responsible for present conditions. The country needs the Democrats."[44]

Daniels' most anxious moment before Roosevelt's nomination came over the two-thirds rule, which had survived from slavery days as the South's veto over an unacceptable Democratic candidate. Some Southerners, and notably Governor Gardner of the North Carolina delegation, held to the rule out of genuine conviction that it was vital to the South's future within the party. However, the two-thirds rule was now embraced by the stop-Roosevelt forces. In vain did Daniels exhibit a resolution passed by his state's Democratic Executive Committee approving repeal of the two-thirds rule. His view of the matter in his unpublished memoir:

> If there had been no opposition to the repeal by the cabal to "stop Roosevelt," the two-thirds rule would have been repealed. His opponents knew that nothing could take away the majority for him, but they hoped to seduce a few dele-

gates to block his nomination by insisting upon the two-thirds rule. Even with this opposition of some to a change, the Roosevelt forces could have repealed the rule and nominated him on the first ballot. However, when the hullabaloo rose to a crescendo and fooled some people, the Roosevelt managers decided not to offer a repeal motion. That decision endangered the Roosevelt victory and might have prevented his nomination if public sentiment had not been so strong.

Now Daniels put on pressure for Roosevelt, on June 30 addressing the Convention in the high, penetrating voice that characterized him when excited, moving that seconding speeches for FDR be dispensed with in the interest of an early ballot. As to the trade by which Jim Farley got Roosevelt the votes of Texas and California, Daniels recalled: "I didn't like it; but, of course, like all Roosevelt supporters acquiesced because we had won the chief goal." The conditions were the nomination of John N. Garner as Vice President, and McAdoo to be consulted before any Secretary of the Treasury was named. If McAdoo had not been elected to the Senate that year he would have expected to be Secretary of the Treasury.[45]

From Lake Junaluska where Daniels repaired to "rest," he confided to FDR and to Louis Howe details of his forthcoming campaign article, a strategic one in the *Saturday Evening Post* entitled "Franklin Roosevelt As I Know Him." From Lake Junaluska to *The News and Observer* staff in Raleigh he sent detailed longhand instructions on how to raise a little advertising cash via a special Education Edition and an Auditorium Edition to greet Raleigh's new Memorial Auditorium. At this time Daniels was delighted at the surprise marriage of President Graham of the University, whom he already had privately fixed on as first President of the Consolidated University. When Graham later wrote the Trustees of his doubts of making an acceptable President, Daniels wrote him like a real Dutch uncle:

> I say to you now what I said to you on the day you were first elected President, that it is the duty of every man to serve where those who have the life of the University at heart think he can serve best. You were commandeered for the position when you were first elected President and when you were elected President of the greater University, and the only thing for you to do is to say, "Aye, aye, Sir!" and quit this business of being over-modest. I think a man ought to

be humble before his God but not before anybody else. Show
this letter to your wife and tell her what I say, and say as an
elder brother.[46]

In September Daniels made an extended Western campaign for
candidate Roosevelt. It began at the American Legion Convention
in Portland, Oregon, at which War Secretary Patrick J. Hurley was
roundly booed for opposing a soldier's bonus and Daniels cheered
for favoring it. He had already lambasted the Hoover administration for its use of force against that summer's Bonus Army in
Washington, writing: "The National Capital has been cleared of a
horde of ragged, hungry men, but President Hoover cannot wash his
hands of the affair by branding them as 'Communists.'" Daniels
was in top form. In Portland he had to share an overcrowded
private car with some ladies attending the Legion Convention. One
of them, costumed as Martha Washington for the Colonial Ball, sat
on Daniels' lap. The octegenarian Daniels later recalled his spright-
ly self at age seventy: "She wasn't heavy and she was good looking."
In California the editor spoke jovially on behalf of McAdoo's ability
to get things done for his state, saying "I never left Washington
during those [Wilson] days that I did not fear McAdoo would
annex Navy agencies. Every time I was out of the city I would
tell Assistant Secretary of the Navy Roosevelt: 'Do not leave your
desk while I am away, for if you do McAdoo will annex the Navy
to the Treasury Department.'"[47]

After campaigining for FDR in Oregon, California, Nevada,
Utah, Nebraska, Iowa—later in Ohio and Indiana—Daniels wrote
cheerily to Roosevelt about the sure capture of the first six of those
states (Daniels' report to Louis Howe was also cheerful, but more
guardedly so). By that time the September 24 issue of *Saturday
Evening Post,* containing "Franklin Roosevelt As I Know Him,"
was in the hands of readers and doing its work. Aside from a laudatory account of FDR's political record, the Daniels article described
Roosevelt's personality: "The two words that best describe Franklin
Roosevelt are 'eagerness' and 'determination.' . . . He has always
had a delightful eagerness in all things." In so writing, Daniels
may have put his finger exactly on the sort of personal qualities
which the frightened and Depression-ridden American people were
seeking in their President. Roosevelt did indeed carry every state

in which Daniels campaigned, and the delighted editor then reversed their traditional roles and now addressed the former "Dear Franklin" as "My dear Chief." But Roosevelt would have none of it. "My dear Chief:" he replied in turn, "That title still stands! And I am still Franklin to you."[48] And it was to "Dear Chief" and "Dear Franklin" to the end of their days.

Chapter seven

New Lease on Life

On the train from New York that March 2, 1933, Josephus Daniels rode happily into Washington with President-elect Roosevelt. Rexford Guy Tugwell, an early member of the Brain Trust, recalled how FDR, enthroned in the observation car, took his old chief's hand fondly in his and introduced him: "Rex," he said, "this is a man who taught me a lot that I needed to know." Inauguration eve was clouded with economic crisis, and the Democrats were shocked by the sudden death of the indomitable Tom Walsh, Attorney-General designate. Nevertheless, the party faithfully whistled up enough courage to sing their unintentionally ironic fight song, "Happy Days Are Here Again" at the Electoral College banquet. The festivities were in charge of Big Jim Farley, who was to be Postmaster General, and the principal speaker was the campaign publicist Claude Bowers, soon to be Ambassador to Spain. Farley had an announcement about Josephus Daniels. The President's old chief, the cheering diners were told, would be appointed to a post of importance in the new administration.[1]

The agonizingly long months between election and inauguration—which saw a frightening attempt to assassinate Roosevelt— were full of political move and maneuver in which Daniels played his customarily active role. He tactfully fended off most of the job-seekers who besought him to intercede with FDR, although Daniels did help the distressed widow of his old congressional friend, Claude Kitchin. He prevailed on House Speaker Garner (now Vice-President-elect), in the most appealing terms he could muster, so that Claude Kitchin's son did get a temporary congressional job. On the day before the Inauguration, Daniels was sitting in the office of Louis McHenry Howe when Raymond Moley came in, that most conservative of the Brain Trusters who was the first to arrive and the first to leave. From Daniels Moley got what he later called the "worse political advice I ever received." As an Assistant Secretary of State bound for the approaching London Economic Conference, Moley asked Howe and Daniels whether he should publicize the President-elect's statement giving Moley exclusive charge of the war debt negotiations. When asked, Daniels came forward—not with "the worst political advice" but with typically long-headed counsel—"If the President made such a public statement—and I do not think he should or would—and if Hull, who is to be secretary [of State], should acquiesce in it—and I do not imagine he would— it would be the worst possible thing that could happen to you."[2]

Eyewitnesses at the Roosevelt inaugural did not entirely agree in their descriptions of Josephus Daniels, except that his eyes were wet with tears at the sight of Roosevelt making his laborious way to the rostrum on the arm of his son James. One report had Daniels pounding his applause vigorously with his cane (undoubtedly true), another that the old editor "scrambled nimbly across the pine benches to his seat" (the "nimbly" is more likely than the "scrambled"). Thrilled by the new President's inaugural address, he could have laughed at fellow-Democrats Hull and Roper who had recently gotten Daniels to approach FDR about his too-conservative posture. Roosevelt had reassured his old chief "that he would make hard-boiled reactionism 'pop like a new saddle.'" In a Rhamkatte Roaster column back home, Daniels as the Old Codger reported on the inaugural address: "The biggest thing he said wuz that Fear wuz the only thing to be afraid of." The day after the Inauguration was a Sunday, and on that afternoon Daniels spoke at the tomb of Woodrow Wilson in the National Cathedral where he drew parallels between the two Democratic Presidents. He omitted to contrast Wilson's "missionary diplomacy" and that part of Roosevelt's inaugural which read: "I would dedicate this Nation to the policy of the good neighbor." Daniels had no inkling then of the key role he was to play in implementing that policy of the good neighbor.[3]

Once Daniels decided he wanted no part of any new-fangled Transportation Agency, first offered him by the President, he let it be known that he desired the Mexican Embassy. There was never any doubt that he would get it, although his own *News and Observer* was still publishing some A.P. speculation about the transportation post two days after the Mexican government had given its necessary assent to Daniels' being received. The formal White House announcement came on March 13, and on the eighteenth Daniels was sworn in by his elder brother Frank in the State Supreme Court Chamber in Raleigh, a happy group of Danielses and friends looking on. In thus honoring his old chief, Roosevelt freed himself from the understandable embarrassment of regular dealings in Washington with a superior-turned-subordinate. To Daniels' occasional hints in the thirties that he might like once more to be Secretary of the Navy, Roosevelt turned an understandably deaf ear; he could not possibly have been comfortable with Daniels in his own Cabinet. Daniels, for his part, was happy to be rid of the transportation post, a typically jerry-built agency that Daniels advised the President to place, with all such agencies, under an appropriate Cabinet department. Daniels later remarked of it: "My observations since then have convinced me that it was the best advice he ever received—and ignored." Daniels was happy, too, with the Mexican appointment. The salary was the same as for all embassies at that time—an exceedingly welcome $17,500 a year—but Mexico City was reasonably close to home, and the entertainment allowance would go further there than in some European embassy on the highroad of globetrotting Americans.[4]

Incredible as it may seem, Roosevelt and Daniels—the "aggressors" of 1914—claimed to have forgotten all about the Veracruz episode that had been the sensation of its day. "But you can't go to Mexico," Miss Addie explained to her husband in "recalling" Veracruz to him, and she also recalled it to the President at the White House a few days later. Now Roosevelt might possibly have forgotten the Veracruz episode, but not Daniels, for whom it had been the first international crisis of his Cabinet career. More likely, he simply did not consider the heritage of Veracruz any real bar to his success in Mexico. And he was right. By no means a vain man, Daniels still possessed that great self-confidence that marks so many successful men. He knew that he himself harbored a sincere friendship for the Mexican people, that he subscribed enthusiastically to all that the President had said about the good neighbor. Accordingly, he was perfectly confident that his own good will would surmount all obstacles—even memories of Veracruz—that barred the way to better relations. Moreover, many Mexican observers could not fail to notice that in the new envoy, the President's old and trusted personal friend, they had received an earnest of special consideration.[5]

The new Ambassador spent a three-week cram course in Washington preparing for his Mexican mission. Retiring Ambassador J. Reuben Clark was there to help, an able diplomat and a Mormon who had already instituted the "dry" entertaining at the Mexico City Embassy that Daniels was to continue. Herschel V. Johnson was helping, too, a fellow Tar Heel now in charge of the Mexican desk at the State Department and one who had served on Ambassador Dwight Morrow's staff in Mexico City. Daniels learned much about political realities in Mexico, and was exposed to some detailed briefing about such continuing Mexican concerns as anticlericalism and the still-living Revolution. As a graduate of the short course Daniels addressed the Pan American Society in New York at the end of March and was ready to depart for Mexico after some leave-taking in Raleigh. The trip would be by rail because the Ambassador reluctantly heeded Herschel Johnson's warning against another landing at Veracruz. Johnson later admitted he was wrong, that he had overestimated the lurking hostility, and that if the Danielses had debarked at Veracruz nothing untoward would have happened. Daniels left Washington after some good-natured ribbing at the President's press conference of April 5, all hands reminding the editor that he would miss the correspondents' party to distribute the first cases of legal beer.[6]

The Danielses got a grand send-off from Raleigh the night of April 11, riding in the private car of Eugene Bagwell, now general manager of the Seaboard but a former *News and Observer* carrier boy. Meanwhile the Mexican government was exerting itself to safeguard the Ambassador. Nevertheless, the Mexican escorts got the same answer from Daniels as the U.S. Foreign Service officers who vainly tried to keep him from leaving the train to greet well-wishers: "I did not come to Mexico," he said, "to be a prisoner." The precautions seem to have been well conceived. Julio Alvarez del Vayo, then Spanish Ambassador in Mexico and later one of Daniels' warmest friends, almost got mobbed by a Mexican crowd that was lying in wait for Daniels at one railway station. The Spaniard quickly showed himself to the excited crowd in the Latin American tradition of a man unafraid, and he heard the *mueras* intended for Daniels turn to *vivas*. The Communists at the extreme Left as well as the parties of the Mexican extreme Right already had raised an outcry against Daniels, including a demonstration against the U.S. Embassy that cost some broken windows. Daniels' heavily guarded train rolled slowly into the Mexico City station late on the Sunday morning of April 15, and he did not know until later that a section of track had been sabotaged. A powerful convoy of troops protected the Ambassador between railway station and Embassy, but Daniels shrewdly pretended to be honored by such attention and professed to be highly flattered. Safely arrived, welcomed by the Embassy staff, the Ambassador sat down to write President Roosevelt a long informal account of his trip. He wrote, he said, "agreeable to my promise to write you now and then something 'off the record.' "[7]

As an editor Daniels knew he had to clear the air and also knew that he could do so with the help of the newspaper reporters, among whom he felt at home anywhere. Accordingly, he called a press conference within thirty-six hours of his arrival in Mexico, and got Arthur Constantine, the I.N.S. bureau chief, to marvel: "Ambassador Daniels got off to an amazing start. . . . This was no slobbery goodwill stuff. . . . Here, his political experience and temperament stand him in fine stead." Next day every newspaper in Mexico City front-paged Daniels' remarks to the newsmen, and the sensitive Mexicans were both impressed and delighted with Daniels' words: "The principles of parity of sovereignty and of mutual respect between the two governments are so fundamental with the Peoples of the United States and Mexico that every right-minded man makes them his own. The two countries have common destinies. They should respect each others' territorial rights and seek to secure not only better understanding, but the closest association." The same reporter quoted the Mexican Foreign Minister, Dr. Puig Casauranc, on Daniels: "He doesn't take himself too seriously. He is human. He is simpatico. He makes a magnificent impression on me."[8]

The Mexican government still had to be won over, and Daniels

Courtesy of Frank A. Daniels

Mrs. Mary Cleaves Daniels, mother of Josephus Daniels. "Granny Daniels," as the neighbors of her old age knew her in Goldsboro, N.C., read her Joe's Raleigh *News and Observer* every morning, and she even held that newspaper as she sat for this portrait.

This photograph of his wife and their four sons, in 1912, was Josephus Daniels' favorite. The tallest boy is Josephus, Jr., and the others are, left to right, Frank Arthur, Jonathan Worth, and Worth Bagley.

The National Archives, courtesy of Dr. Worth B. Daniels

Josephus Daniels and Franklin D. Roosevelt, Secretary and Assistant Secretary of the Navy, smile down at the White House in 1914. Daniels joshed his subordinate about allegedly wanting to move in next door, to the White House, from his office in what is today the Executive Office Building.

Josephus Daniels with President Wilson and the second Mrs. Wilson at Washington's old Polo Grounds, where the first U.S. air mail flight (to New York City) took place. The date was May 15, 1918, but Daniels had taken his first airplane flight five years earlier, on May 21, 1913.

Worth Bagley, the family's hero killed in the Spanish-American War, was honored by a Navy destroyer named for him. At the ship's christening, October 19, 1918, Secretary Daniels stands behind the Bagley ladies: left to right, Mrs. Josephus Daniels; her mother, Mrs. Adelaide W. Bagley; and Mrs. Daniels' sisters, Miss Belle and Miss Ethel Bagley.

University Trustee Daniels was described as among those happiest to greet Sir Esme Howard, center, at the Chapel Hill Commencement of 1929. All hands recalled that Navy Secretary Daniels had dried up the U.S. Navy, whereas Sir Esme, British Ambassador in Washington, had just paid his respects to prohibition by banning further liquor importations to the British Embassy. At the right is University President Harry Woodburn Chase.

Courtesy of Dr. Worth B. Daniels

This candid camera photograph of Josephus Daniels is widely considered the most characteristic of all of his pictures. It was taken by Robert H. Davis, a columnist for the *New York Sun*, who used a simple folding camera to prove his contention that "man makes his own mask." The picture was taken on Davis' visit to the U.S. Embassy in Mexico City on January 6, 1935.

Josephus Daniels inaugurates the Navy Pre-Flight School at Chapel Hill in a ceremony in Kenan Stadium, University of North Carolina. The two civilians on the platform are, left to right, University President Frank P. Graham and Governor J. Melville Broughton. The date was May 23, 1942, five days after Daniels' eightieth birthday.

moved ahead despite artificial impediments. One such obstacle was presented by the U.S. Navy Department's insistence on staging naval maneuvers in Mexican waters just when Daniels was arriving at his new post. Only by dint of much persuasion did the State Department succeed in getting the ships moved from strategic Magdalena Bay to the serener Acapulco. Even so the Mexican government, probably retaliating, kept Daniels waiting a week to present his credentials and meanwhile held a medal-awarding cere- mony to honor the Veracruz defenders of 1914. But Daniels was not to be provoked. He broke precedent by insisting that Miss Addie and other Embassy wives attend while he presented his credentials in formal diplomatic attire (cutaway and striped trou- sers in place of the Bryanesque garb). As in talking to the report- ers Daniels addressed President Abelardo Rodríguez about their respective New Deals in terms that transcended the platitudes usual on such occasions. To "Dear Franklin" Daniels confided that President Rodríguez's reply could be likened to " 'We began this reform and we are glad Uncle Sam is following our lead.' "[9]

Daniels was quickly exposed to the importunities of visiting firemen from the States. One such, and a four-year headache for the Ambassador, appeared that first summer in the form of the quack medical healer, the self-styled Doctor Brinkley, who showed up under the impressive escort of former Vice-President Charles Curtis. On the strength of Curtis' ability to get an audience with President Rodríguez plus Mexican resistance to some arbitrary U.S. radio negotiators, Doctor Brinkley was allowed to go on broadcast- ing to U.S. audiences from his Mexican radio station. When Curtis informed Daniels that Brinkley was a native Tar Heel, the Am- bassador noted in a diary-letter: "Poor old State!"[10]

North Carolina politics predominated, in fact, with the Ambas- sador during his acclimatizing year in Mexico. As the inveterate foe of a general sales tax, Daniels had had to swallow just that bitter pill. As the even more inveterate friend of public education he had to concede that without a sales tax his state could not support the schools it had taken over from the faltering counties two years before. At the showdown of the 1933 legislature, Daniels had declared that he would "put a mortgage on this capitol" before he would "close the doors of learning to a single boy or girl in North Carolina."[11] Another bitter pill to Daniels, although he had reconciled himself to swallowing it, was the repeal of national prohibition. Nevertheless, he spent most of 1933 helping keep his own state dry.

After national repeal, a Wet-Dry showdown in North Carolina was arranged for November on the question of holding a convention to consider ratifiying national repeal. Those voting "for convention" would really be voting against the state's own prohibition law, the Turlington Act, and those voting "no convention" would register approval of state prohibition. All during that summer the mails from Mexico to North Carolina were heavy with encouraging messages from Ambassador Daniels to his friends in the United Dry Forces. The Drys won that November, and thus delayed for two years the first local option election which resulted in the first of many North Carolina-operated liquor stores. These Alcoholic Beverage Control stores (A.B.C. stores) were in later years invariably referred to by Daniels as "Alcohol Brutalizes Consumers." In his first year as Ambassador, Daniels could not resist trying to spur son Jonathan, now editor of *The News and Observer,* to wage an aggressively Dry editorial campaign. Jonathan did not agree with his troubled father and could not bring himself to write prohibition editorials in the style of Josephus Daniels. But he loved his father, and so Jonathan and his wife made a diplomatic visit to Mexico before the election. John Livingstone wrote the paper's editorials on the liquor question while Editor Jonathan sat out the election in the loving company of his parents in the Mexico City Embassy.[12]

Ambassador Daniels came home every summer except the first one, and without fail to the campus at Chapel Hill and to meetings of the University's Board of Trustees and the Board's Executive Committee. He had to miss the Chapel Hill commencement in 1933, still learning his duties in Mexico, and wrote banteringly to President Graham of not having missed a commencement since 1884 "except when I was in the Cabinet, in jail [the Yarborough House, 1904], or in Mexico."[13] To Dr. Graham, whose role in North Carolina he likened to that of Roosevelt in the nation, Daniels confided: "I told him [Roosevelt] before he was elected that . . . the people were going to select him as the receiver of a bankrupt corporation, sans assets and with overwhelming liabilities. That is what he inherited March 4th."[14]

Franklin Roosevelt's New Deal was to Josephus Daniels, as E. David Cronon has pointed out, the mature version of the less complex Bryan and Wilson types of progressivism. The Ambassador, aware that the "traitor to his class" in the White House had rescued American business, never failed to speak up for the New Deal and to discomfit Roosevelt-haters. One of the latter approached him early in Daniels' ambassadorial career and asked: "Do you approve all the policies which your friend Roosevelt is putting on the country?" Said Daniels: "I do not." The other rejoiced: "I am glad that you cannot stand for this radicalism." Replied the Ambassador: "What I object to in President Roosevelt is he is too conservative." When Columnist Drew Pearson reported this decade-old anecdote, he quoted the now-octegenarian Daniels: "I still think President Roosevelt is too conservative."[15]

Ambassador Daniels' voluminous correspondence with his "easy boss" in the White House and with other public figures makes him out an enthusiastic New Dealer. Before he even left for Mexico, early in the Hundred Days, Daniels lauded the President for his protecting investors with the Securities and Exchange Commission and depositors with the Federal Deposit Insurance Corporation. "The best thing you have done," Daniels wrote the President, "is to strike a body blow to *caveat emptor*. That hoary old inciter of fraud has encumbered the stage too long." The Ambassador was strong for the Tennessee Valley Authority (as a counterpoise to his old enemies, the private utilities), the N.R.A. (although he distrusted the waiving of the anti-trust laws), and the A.A.A. (which he regarded as a godsend to the depressed tobacco farmers). When the President made a speech attacking child labor, Daniels wrote his longhand congratulations from his still-new post in Mexico as from one who had fought the child labor evil for the past thirty years.[16]

The Ambassador's first homecoming was in the spring of 1934, when he reassured friends anxious for his health in Mexico City's high altitude that he was living as the Mexicans did: "I take a Sy-estah every afternoon." In mid-May he was in Washington where he made a presentation speech of the monument to William Jennings Bryan, President Roosevelt accepting for the government. Later that month the Ambassador joined his former Assistant Secretary at a fleet review off New York harbor and renewed old ties with Mayor Fiorello H. LaGuardia. In return, the Ambassador and Miss Addie entertained Mrs. Eleanor Roosevelt at breakfast at Wakestone, later escorting her to the Memorial Auditorium for a speech, and then driving with her to Durham where the First Lady spoke on world peace in the new Duke Stadium.[17]

In Mexico the Danielses played host to their sons' families and Miss Addie's two sisters, all of whom came in delightful relays bearing a touch of home. Anticipating one such visit the Ambassador wrote to his grandson Worth about the baseball game the old couple had attended in the President's box (but never a bull fight), about the little hunchback mascot of the Aztecas who brought his team good luck, and about the visiting U.S. tennis players who had autographed a tennis ball that Miss Addie was sending home in the diplomatic pouch. When the Misses Bagley came down in the summer of 1934 they had a chance to thank Brother Joe personally for having safeguarded their government clerkships by interceding with Navy Secretary Swanson and Interior Secretary Ickes. After Miss Addie's sisters had spent a delightful vacation in Mexico City they tried to reimburse Brother Joe; their papers contained two checks, each in the amount of $145 and each carefully shredded by scissors. "Dear Girls," the Ambassador wrote the maiden ladies:

> When I reached the Embassy this morning, returning from the train, and found your letter with enclosures, I was surprised that some vandal, armed with shears, had mutilated two perfectly beautiful checks. A secret service man has been put on his trail and you may be sure that if he is found the miscreant will be given the punishment he richly deserves. He may be led out and shot at sunrise as was Maximilian and others. . . . In view of this mutilation I have but one suggestion to make to the parties who signed the check. It would do no good to send another or others here. The same criminal would repeat the crime. Therefore the only thing to do is let the money remain in a bank drawing interest until you come back to Mexico.[18]

As to Daniels' mission in Mexico, he was fortunate in such predecessors as Clark and Morrow. Dwight Morrow, in particular, was Daniels' great precursor. A fine man of first-rate intellect, who studied Mexico and went there determined to understand and sympathize, Morrow won the confidence of Plutarco Elías Calles just as Daniels later won that of Lázaro Cárdenas. As a partner of J. P. Morgan, Morrow was at first attacked in the Mexican press as an agent of Wall Street just as Daniels ran into opposition as the aggressor of Veracruz. Morrow, like Daniels, did not know a word of Spanish (and neither one let it handicap him), and again like Daniels, enjoyed the personal regard of the U.S. President (Morrow was an Amherst classmate of Calvin Coolidge). Without Morrow's ushering in the first era of good U.S.-Mexican feelings since the Mexican Revolution, Daniels' work would have been twice as hard.

Unlike the unimaginative Secretary of State Frank B. Kellogg, who spoke in ignorance of the Mexican Revolutionary Party as a gang of Bolsheviks, Morrow quickly learned his homework. He found the Mexicans proud that their Revolution had antedated that of Lenin by nearly eight years. Morrow learned to discriminate between endemic anticlericalism and atheism, and he learned of the nationalist and sovereignty-conscious nature of the Mexican Revolution. To be sure, the Mexicans knew that Morrow was more than a superb negotiator. They knew that he spoke for American business and that he embodied the implied threat of American intervention. Still, Morrow recognized President Calles for the Strongman he was, but not all *caudillo* either, sensing that the nationalist impact of the Mexican Revolution could not be shunted aside as just another palace revolt in Latin America. On November 17, 1927, after Morrow had been in Mexico only a few weeks, the two nations concluded a truce on oil concessions that lasted a decade. The foreign oil companies got confirmation of their pre-Revolutionary concessions, and their fear of expropriation died down.[19]

When Daniels entered upon office Calles was still Mexico's Strongman, operating behind the façade of his personal and business associate, General Abelardo Rodríguez. Only waiting in the wings was Lázaro Cárdenas, governor of Michoacán, and from the start of 1933 Secretary of War and Navy. Daniels quickly attacked one prominent obstacle of good Mexican-U.S. relations, special claims of U.S. citizens for losses they incurred during the Mexican Revolution. Like his predecessor Clark, Daniels set himself to work out a lump sum settlement. Unlike Clark, however, Daniels could more easily sidestep the conservative influence of his nominal State Department superiors. Initial progress was so tedious, Daniels wrote his old friend the President, that "your son Franklin's grandchildren would be gray-headed before all these claims could be heard and determined." As Daniels' negotiations went forward with Foreign Minister Puig, as reported to Secretary of State Hull, it was clear that the Tar Heel Ambassador was far readier than the

State Department to take Mexico's poverty into account and meet the Mexicans halfway.[20]

When the Mexican Foreign Minister offered a lump sum settlement to be paid in fifteen rather than the thirty years earlier rejected, Daniels was all for agreement. But the State Department claims experts raised new objections because Mexico was excluding certain American claims of a kind that had been accepted in paying European claims. Not so, Dr. Puig retorted, pointing out that the Europeans had accepted payment in pesos without interest whereas the United States insisted on payment in dollars with interest. With the entire transaction in peril, representing a year's work and a total settlement of $300,000,000, Daniels wrote privately to Secretary of State Hull:

> I must say to you, my dear friend as well as superior officer, that I have felt that in some details insistence by the Department upon the strictly technical approach has been made paramount to the larger questions of policy which would affirmatively have shown that we are actually and practically practicing the generous good neighbor policy. . . . By insisting upon our point of view in debt collections for individuals (some of them questionable) I have feared that we might render it more difficult to reach agreements upon larger questions.

Shortly thereafter the State Department gave in. On the first anniversary of his presenting his credentials, Daniels happily joined Foreign Minister Puig in signing the special claims accord plus a protocol on future handling of general claims. The Ambassador had earned a "well done" from his admiring Embassy staffers, panting from their exertions in keeping pace with the "tired old ambassador."[21]

While the Good Neighbor Policy was undergoing its first testing elsewhere in Latin America, Josephus Daniels did not keep aloof. Across the Caribbean from Daniels' post lay Cuba, where in the fall of 1933 Ambassador Sumner Welles was speeding the exit of the unloved dictator, Gerardo Machado, and the installation of a conservative and hopefully pro-U.S. regime. Welles's reading of the Good Neighbor Policy did not rule out armed intervention under the Platt Amendment, which had been an original condition for Cuban independence. Thus when a revolt of army sergeants led by Fulgencio Batista overthrew the Welles-approved regime,

that envoy urged immediate intervention. Secretary Hull and President Roosevelt were decidedly chilly to Welles's suggestion, but if
they needed any encouragement they got plenty from Ambassador
Daniels in Mexico City. He telephoned Secretary Hull to convey
Mexican opinion, following the call with a letter: "It cheered me
greatly when you said, 'I would rather walk from here to the South
Pole than to have to intervene.'" Then Daniels wrote a longhand
note to the President, applauding his refusal to intervene, and his
resolve to invoke the Platt Amendment only in consultation with
the Pan American nations.[22]

"Wilson waited too long to invite A.B.C. participation," Daniels
reminded the President, his fellow-aggressor of Veracruz. Daniels
had his eye, as had the State Department, on the Seventh Pan
American Conference set for December 1933 in Montevideo. Hull
then and there learned a first-hand lesson about the fervor of Latin
American anti-Yanqui feeling, while President Roosevelt hastily
poured oil on troubled waters. He announced the coming recall of
Sumner Welles (who had been on leave from his post as Assistant
Secretary of State), offered to reconsider the Platt Amendment,
and joined in the Montevideo Conference's determination to re-
nounce armed intervention. After the President had recognized a
reasonably stable government in Cuba (and in El Salvador, which
had undergone a similar crisis) and had sent American food to feed
hungry Cubans, Daniels congratulated him for giving land reform
a chance to take hold. He also ventured a comparison—which is
intriguing in retrospect—between the situations in Cuba and Mexico, telling Roosevelt:

> At the bottom of the Cuban, and the Mexican, as well as
> most other revolutions, is hunger. . . . Here one half the land,
> originally ejidos for natives, belonged to the established
> church. Much of the best of the balance belonged later to
> the favorites of Diaz. The only hope of Mexico is dividing
> the lands so that those who live on them will be safe in their
> cultivation of the soil. . . . That and the public schools are
> the foundations upon which the leaders with vision are trying
> to rebuild the country after centuries of oppression and de-
> nial of the most fundamental rights to the great mass of origi-
> nal Mexicans.
> The same thing must be done in Cuba. Since American
> sugar companies became owners of most of the good lands
> in Cuba, the tillers of the soil have exclusively worked on
> sugar plantations. The old time cultivation of bread and meat

has fallen into disuse. Partition of land and raising home supplies is the essential for Cuban restitution. Mexico's safety
is that its people 'live home and board in the same place' and
are being given land.[23]

Meanwhile, Daniels' ear was more attuned to the political situation at home than in Mexico. The well-informed Ambassador deplored the fact that the New Deal policies looked too radical for
the more cautious of the old progressives. Some of the old Wilsonians had already gone sour; others, like McAdoo, were wavering.
When the latter paid Daniels a visit that fall, he got a plea from
Daniels to champion New Deal measures in the Senate. Daniels
wrote the President frankly about his unhappiness with such backsliders as Carter Glass, Henry Breckinridge, and Bainbridge Colby.
Such rigid constitutionalists as the last two, the Ambassador wrote
to Raymond Moley, whom he had greeted in Mexico City, were
having their views "financed by those who once having had their
arms in the treasury up to the elbow are seeking to get back their
old position." He was, in reality, commenting on the formation of
the American Liberty League, which was to make its ill-fated move
two years later.[24]

Daniels' initial insensitivity to Mexican politics was to cost him
dear. In the Mexican election campaign of summer, 1934, General
Calles made an anticlerical speech in Guadalajara. Not knowing
the real significance of the speech, Daniels used one unexceptionable sentence by Calles without knowing its context. "We must
now enter into and take possession of the minds of the children, the
minds of the young," the tough *Jefe Máximo* declared.[25] What
Daniels did not know was that Calles and the National Revolutionary Party were also promising to prohibit Church schools alto-
gether. All Daniels could see was that Calles, like Thomas Jefferson,
understood that "no people can be both free and ignorant"; that
Calles, like Aycock of North Carolina, was championing universal
public education. So the Ambassador inserted General Calles' sentence into "Universal Education," an address he made that July at
the Embassy to Professor Hubert Herring's annual American Semi-
nar. The visiting Americans listened appreciatively, but the Mexicans at first resented a foreign ambassador's meddling in Mexican
church-state relationships. By the time the Mexican press accepted
Daniels' explanations, the Catholics in the United States became
aware of the episode and therein lay trouble.

Even though the U.S. Catholic press was mostly restrained at the outset, commenting more in sorrow than in anger, the Mexican Congress kept debating the then-pending abolition of religious education. Then, in the fall of 1934, the U.S. Catholic press applied pressure against Daniels and against the Roosevelt administration's hands-off attitude. The mass of U.S. Catholics were understandably sensitive to events in Mexico, where some states limited the number of priests and otherwise harassed the clergy. Such Catholics remembered the open conflict between the Mexican government and the Church during the twenties, the Mexican Cristero Revolt, the Ku Klux Klan anti-Catholicism of the same period, and the injection of anti-Catholicism into the Al Smith campaign. But what they did not understand about the struggle for separation of church and state in Mexico, long an accomplished fact in the United States, was of little concern to the publicists who whipped up an emotional anti-Daniels crusade. Daniels' many Catholic friends, such at Patrick H. Callahan, Michael Francis Doyle, and Father John J. Burke (General Secretary, National Catholic Welfare Conference) rose to his defense, circulated copies of "Universal Education" to prove to fellow-Catholics what it really said, and otherwise reasoned that his detractors were unfair. The hue and cry rose to such proportions that in his press conference of October 17, President Roosevelt was asked whether he was going to recall his old chief from Mexico. The answer was, of course, no.

The Catholic crisis did not interrupt the Danielses' plans for their first "ambassadorial" Christmas at Wakestone. Miss Addie and the Ambassador were most particular about bringing souvenirs for every member of "The News and Observer family." Everybody from porter to editor got a gift of some sort at the annual Christmas party at which the old couple presided, and as the paper recovered from its business distress the annual cash bonuses grew in size. In any case, according to the recollection of contemporary staff members, the value of the gifts was less important than the ebullient spirit in which they were given. At the Methodist Orphanage, "one hill over" from Wakestone, the three hundred youngsters came to count on a Christmas treat from a naturally Santa Claus-looking man named "Mr. Daniels." The Ambassador, happily rocking on his heels, would make a little talk that always began, "I bring you greetings from the people of Mexico." Then he would distribute colorful little Mexican bags filled with Christmas goodies. A recipient of one of those little Mexican souvenirs remembered those Christmases as a gathering of 301 innocents, "300 orphaned children and kindly old 'Mr. Daniels.'" Naturally there were the festive Christmases at Wakestone, with a special one on Twelfth Night in January just for the grandchildren. Those youngsters were enthusiastically spoiled by the grandfather, who nevertheless puzzled them (for the children knew nothing about poverty) by greeting them at his door "Christmas gift! Give it to me!"[26]

As 1935 opened, the build-up of Catholic emotion against Daniels led to a spate of heated proposals in Congress for investigations or for intervening in Mexico's church-state conflict. What finally took the sting out of the anti-Daniels outcry was the presence of the fine Protestant hand of William E. Borah of Idaho. That premier isolationist now called for nothing less than a full-dress Senate investigation of religious conditions in Mexico. Such sudden concern of his for the rights of U.S. citizens in foreign parts and for intervening in the domestic affairs of a friendly nation looked suspicious in the extreme. Political observers of the time did not fail to note that Borah introduced his Mexican resolution two days after he had again blocked Senate approval of America's participation in the World Court. Was Borah's action a trade for "Catholic votes" against the World Court? Robert E. (Fleet) Williams of *The News and Observer's* Washington bureau certainly thought so, as Editor Jonathan Daniels relayed the news to his father. In Mexico now even the clerical press was horrified at the Borah Resolution. In the United States it earned a stinging rebuke from the newspapers and from most impartial observers. It was suitably buried in the Senate Foreign Relations Committee, unmarked and unlamented.[27]

Simpático was Josephus Daniels' favorite word in the Spanish language he could not speak. He really need not have concerned himself, as he did, about his ignorance of Spanish, because he quickly found that most high Mexican officials spoke English and were glad to lower the language barrier for him, as did President Rodríguez and Foreign Minister Puig from the first. Not being able to speak Spanish, the Ambassador never really had to say a word because what he *was* was written all over him. Daniels quickly learned to appreciate the special meaning of *simpático* as sincere, friendly, sympathetic, and yet more than the aggregate of all three. His principal Embassy interpreter, Stephen E. Aguirre, recalled how the Ambassador's new acquaintances beamed whenever he spoke through Aguirre's interpreting, their faces lighting up on recognizing his warmth. It was more of that same "first-rate temperament" that Daniels shared with Franklin Roosevelt.[28]

"This is an interesting and delightful country," Daniels had written an old Tar Heel friend on first arriving in Mexico. "The people are friendly and cordial." The truth of the matter is that the Mexicans and Ambassador Daniels quite simply fell in love with one another. It affected Mrs. Daniels equally and, unlike her thrifty husband, Miss Addie quickly became a lavish purchaser of decorative antique fans and Mexican silver. The old people were themselves decorative, Daniels beaming in his characteristic old-fashioned clothing, and Miss Addie, stoutly handsome with a radiance all her own. Her appearance surprised many young people who had never thought that an old woman could be a beauty, and it did those young people good to see how obviously the Ambassador and Miss Addie were in love. They read Mexican history together, Daniels re-reading Prescott's *Conquest of Mexico* and Miss Addie beginning with the nineteenth century memoir of Madame Calderón de la Barca. They even decided to write a novel together, Miss Addie conceiving the initial enthusiasm for the story of Malinche (the consort of Cortés) and then getting the Ambassador to collaborate.

By the start of 1935 Daniels and Miss Addie had their Malinche project underway. The Ambassador wrote home one of his diary-letters:

> We had a quiet week, with your mother and me delving into folklore and histories of Malinche. You know she was the Indian woman who was the interpreter, guide, philosopher and friend to Cortes and the mother of his son. Your mother has reached the conclusion that she was a sort of Joan of Arc and that without her aid Cortes might have failed in his conquest of Mexico. . . . You have rarely seen your mother so interested in anything and she wants me to help her "do" a book or magazine article on this remarkable Indian woman who she thinks has been neglected—or misrepresented—to the glory of the male Cortes. . . . [Then speaking of the hacienda Santa Monica given to Malinche by Cortes] It was a royal present and gives evidence of Cortes' gratitude to Malinche. I think he probably told her, "I would marry you, but my wife will not let me."

The end-product, the "Malinche" manuscript fragment of forty-four pages, lies uncompleted and unpublished, testifying to some of the naïve notions the Ambassador entertained about Mexican history but testifying much more to his love for Mexico.[29]

After an early rejection as a short story, "Malinche" was turned over for revision to son Jonathan, who got plentiful and imaginative advice from his father. Perhaps the most fanciful was the notion that Malinche had had a love affair with Cuauhtémoc before coming to know Cortés. In case son Jonathan could not identify Cuauhtémoc, his father spoke of him as "the Mexican hero, whose statue stands on Avenue Reforma and is the Aztec patron saint who refused to surrender to Cortes and whose feet were burned off in the fire." Later he speculated to Jonathan that Cortés was jealous of Cuauhtémoc as a prior lover of Malinche, and tortured and killed the Aztec ruler at least partly for that reason. Ambassador Daniels warned his son against assuming "that the reader knows more than he does about Cortes in Cuba." He also wrote to correct his son's mistake that involved the pre-Christian religious center of Cholula and Cortés' reputed zeal as a builder of churches to replace the idolatrous towers. Three years later the Ambassador referred to the then-forlorn "Malinche" manuscript: "Your mother and I worked so hard on this that we hate so to see it all lost." But it went into the discard, except as a testament to his love for Mexican history and culture, and despite his wistful thought: "I'd be willing to spend a thousand dollars to have it made a go."[30]

The Mexicans loved the Danielses too, and proved it many times over. Perhaps the episode that most convinced the Ambassador occurred in early 1935 when he and Miss Addie were visiting the fateful city of Veracruz. Their dinner host had a Cornell room in his home, so named because his sons' athletic trophies from the U.S. university were displayed there. In the Cornell room the Ambassador was moved to ask about the portrait of a handsome young man in Mexican naval uniform. He almost literally reeled back in dismay when told that the young man was his host's brother, one of those naval cadets killed when they futilely tried to resist the U.S. landing in 1914. But Sr. Martínez Zorilla gently patted the Ambassador on the shoulder and assured him that Josephus Daniels was not personally accountable for the fortunes of war. Later, in Mexico City, the Ambassador was honored by the Martínez Zorilla family in being asked to serve as official witness at their son's marriage, not as the U.S. Ambassador but as a cherished friend of the family.[31]

The same Daniels "style" was in evidence when the Ambassador came home, where he could be seen shaking hands with the Negro doorman at the Hotel Sir Walter or dropping in for an informal visit to the legislature. When he showed up at his first "ambassadorial" General Assembly, that of 1935, he was as a matter of course extended the courtesies of the floor and, according to his paper's "Under the Dome" column "had as much fun as a kid home from boarding school with a big red football letter on his sweater." At that year's Chapel Hill commencement, where Mrs. Eleanor Roosevelt got an honorary LL.D., the Ambassador introduced her as the "noble woman who presides over the White House but comes here in her own right as a leader of all causes that work for the betterment of mankind." That year marked the Golden Anniversary of Daniels' Class of 1885, but the class spokesman in Gerrard Hall was none other than Daniels' old enemy Marion Butler ("Butler, Booze, Boodle and Bonds"), and it would seem that the old battlers were still not speaking. Daniels addressed the alumni luncheon instead, ending his "Freedom in the University" address by exclaiming: "I am moved to suggest that all the alumni who feel to thank God for Frank Graham at this crucial hour, to indicate their gratitude by standing." [The assembly did so, to cheers.][32]

Daniels' public support of Graham was by way of anticipating trouble, for the next day the Trustees of the Consolidated University ratified Graham's controversial reorganization plan. Hostility to Graham had been building up, first for his allegedly too-liberal views, then for his de-emphasis of college football, and all these exacerbations now came to a boil. The original sponsors of consolidation, such as Daniels, O. Max Gardner, and Clarence Poe, were hoping to build up Woman's College (ideally, another Bryn Mawr) and North Carolina State (ideally, another M.I.T.) to academic parity with the more prestigious liberal arts University at Chapel Hill. Without the post-World War II ground swell of students clamoring for college entrance, President Graham set out to eliminate duplication in the three institutions. To that end the trustees ratified his various proposals, the most controversial being that to close the excellent School of Engineering at Chapel Hill and move it to State College in Raleigh (which appealed doubly to Daniels on the score of civic pride). Most of the Chapel Hill faculty members were opposed, as were many prominent alumni, and in the ensuing months the ideological foes of Graham—who were uninterested in the consolidation question—joined in the fray. At one point Ambassador Daniels even offered to resign and come home to fight shoulder to shoulder with Frank Graham. He had resigned his Interior Department post under Grover Cleveland to come home for a political fight and he could do so again.[33]

Daniels' resignation offer, undoubtedly rhetorical, still helped to enhearten Dr. Graham at a critical hour. Next the Ambassador was writing concernedly about an alumni questionnaire that had been loaded on the side of eliciting answers hostile to Graham's policies. But the Ambassador would be home again soon to confer with Dr. Graham privately: "The news in the Chapel Hill Weekly that the dogwood are in bloom makes me homesick." That year Daniels took the lead in the Trustees in speaking against reconsidering and in favor of Graham's consolidation plan. The "reactionaries" defeated, Daniels quickly agreed with his old friend Robert W. Winston on bringing together Trustee John Sprunt Hill and Dr. Graham. Hill was the leading opponent of Graham's plan for the School of Engineering, but a generous benefactor of the University and its dedicated friend. Daniels was ready, as always, to make peace within an institution he loved.[34]

Back in Mexico Daniels took Rexford G. Tugwell to a baseball game, and the visitor recalled: "The affection of both officials at the dinner, and the very different sort of Mexicans at the ball game was amazing. And he, I thought, was the man who had come here bearing the onus of Vera Cruz." Mexicans and North Americans alike delighted in the stories about the "dry" Embassy and Ambassador Daniels' battles against John Barleycorn. He himself told many such stories in his *Shirt-Sleeve Diplomat,* notably his famous Altitude story. This one dealt with a U.S. businessman who was a week late in coming in to see the Ambassador. It was the altitude, the tardy New Yorker explained, which had made his head swim and had put him out of action. Had not the Ambassador ever been adversely affected by this altitude? Daniels first sized up his caller and made sure that he could take a joke, and then replied: "I never drink it."[35]

The "God Damn Josephus" story was repeated to the Ambas-

sador at the insistence of the delighted Miss Addie, who knew that
her husband always enjoyed a joke on himself. The story involved
the American Navy captain who had become exhilarated by the
liquor with which he had been regaled aboard a British man-of-
war. As he returned unsteadily to the gangway, he had explained
to him the significance of the rumhead, inscribed "God Save the
King," from which the Jack Tars got their daily tot. "I am going
to get a barrel, fill it full of lime juice," the American avowed in
bitter resentment against General Order 99. "On the outside of
the barrel I will have printed in very large letters, 'God Damn
Josephus.'" Daniels got such a kick out of the story that he
straightway sat down and wrote it to Franklin Roosevelt.[36]

In those early years when Miss Addie could still get about, the
Danielses were eager tourists and saw much of northern and east-
ern Mexico. At the Presidential Palace *Grito* of 1935, the annual
September celebration of Hidalgo's sounding the tocsin of Mexico's
War of Independence, President Cárdenas told Daniels that his
desire to know more about Mexico was about to be gratified—
Cárdenas was putting the Presidential "Olive Train" at the disposal
of foreign diplomats for a "diplomatic tour" of West-Central Mexico. The ten-day trip, made in Pullmans bearing names like
Citlaltepetl and Xinantecatl, was only the first of three such Presi-
dental train trips. On this first one, as usual, the decorative Danielses were everywhere the center of attraction. At Uruapan, in
President Cárdenas' home state, the diplomats were treated to a
performance of the traditional wedding dance of the Tarascan Indians. At rehearsal the Indians were coached to change their ritual
in which the dancers give all their presents to the bride and groom,
this time distributing their gifts evenly among all the guests. The
Indians nodded their assent, but at the performance they did what
they had always done and piled all their presents at the feet of the
bride-and-groom Danielses. Miss Addie was especially delighted,
saying, "I have forty-two people on the News and Observer to give
Christmas presents to—now I'll only have to get two instead of
forty-two."[37]

As the election year of 1936 opened, the Democratic leadership
at home prevailed on Ambassador Daniels to forgo active campaigning this time and remain at his post in Mexico City. Always
the good party soldier, he willingly complied, although fears of
anti-Daniels sentiment by U.S. Catholics were grossly overesti-

mated. Through it all, Daniels had maintained his customary silence in the face of unjust criticism, certain that he had acted in good faith, and just as serene as during the anti-Daniels campaign in 1916 or the Sims investigation. Privately he explained to son Jonathan:

> The delicacy of the situation here grows out of a matter that some of the States have closed the churches and do not permit any priest to officiate. They say that this is done because the priests are in politics and are determined to dominate the schools and are fighting the Government. Of course there may be priests who are doing this, but the answer is not to deny the people of those States religious privileges which ought to be free to everybody. However, those who condemn such actions here would not feel that the United States had any right to dictate to Mexico than it has to Russia or to Italy or any other country.

When Cárdenas declared his independence of General Calles and threw out the entire Calles-appointed Cabinet, Daniels was relieved at the ouster of the aggressively atheistic Agriculture Minister Tomás Garrido Canabal. The Ambassador wrote the editor of the *New York Times*:

> The replacing of Garrido Canabal by Gen. [Saturnino] Cedillo seems significant. Canabal was a self confessed atheist and boasted "There is neither a church nor saloon in Tabasco." Gen. Cedillo as the man of power in San Luis Potosí has permitted no church to close or no priest to be troubled in that state. I hope that this change presages moderation leading to the full religious liberty we enjoy in the United States. [In the wake of the oil expropriation crisis in 1938 Cedillo, with Spanish Falangist, clerical, and industrial backing, staged an unsuccessful revolt.]

Always a good reporter, Daniels kept an eye on the relaxing religious tensions in the election year of 1936 and relievedly wrote President Roosevelt of Cárdenas' moderation in anti-clericalism:

> On Palm Sunday 30 Catholic churches were open in Mexico City, which is 15 more than have been open at any time since I came to Mexico. . . . I made it a point to drive through the city about midday Sunday and saw great congregations at all the Catholic churches. . . . I had unofficial information yesterday from Tiajuana that a priest gave instruction to children preparatory to Communion in the homes of the parishioners of that place with the knowledge of the authorities.

Repair work has been begun on a Catholic church in Mata-
moros which has been in bad repair for a long time. On my
trip to southeastern Mexico I found churches open at places
where they had been closed.[38]

An inveterate churchgoer with an abiding respect for all faiths,
Daniels often accepted invitations to attend Catholic services in
Mexico. Daniels' real humanity came to the fore in his personal
fight to secure honorable burial services when Archbishop Pascual
Díaz died the next year. On visiting the archbishop's mourning
household, Daniels learned that there could be no public funeral
procession because of the government's ban against wearing clerical garb in public. Daniels went first to the dean of the diplomatic corps, a Catholic, who could get no action, and then haled
the Foreign Minister out of a private party to notify him that the
U.S. Ambassador was going off to Cuernavaca to intervene directly
with President Cárdenas. So the archbishop was granted a public
funeral. The new archbishop, Luis María Martínez, gratefully inscribed to Daniels a souvenir album in celebration of the "Fourth
Centenary of the Apparitions of Our Lady of Guadalupe" (1938).
The album contains two news photos, which the news-conscious
Ambassador undoubtedly studied, pointing to the patriotic and national connotation of Our Lady of Guadalupe. The photos show
two contingents of Mexican revolutionary soldiers, one entering
Cuernavaca and the other (identified as Zapatistas) entering Mexico City, both bearing aloft the banner of the Virgin of Guadalupe.[39]

As to politics at home, Daniels wrote critically about the Liberty League to Newton D. Baker (who had already become too conservative for the Ambassador's taste: "It ought to be called the
Livery League because Shouse and others in it [Al Smith, John W.
Davis] wear the livery of plutocracy." Daniels deplored, too, the
political one-sidedness of the domestic daily press. "Hearst, of
course never did have any principles," he wrote son Jonathan, "and
is now the mouthpiece of Fascism in the United States. . . . It
distresses me to see the widely circulated press . . . being the
apologists and spokesmen for privilege in its worst form." He
mourned over once-progressive backsliders like Mark Sullivan,
Frank Kent, and David Lawrence. Early in that election year of
1936 Daniels made some tentative feelers about becoming Secretary of the Navy once more or U.S. Senator from North Carolina.

The other Danielses were unanimously opposed to an election race, however, and neither gesture turned out to be serious.[40]

The idea of the Navy Secretaryship hinged partly on the consideration that Daniels in Mexico City might prove an embarrassment before Catholic voters in a Presidential election. The idea hinged, too, on the ill-health of Navy Secretary Claude Swanson. But Swanson recovered after Daniels and Roosevelt discussed the matter, and there is no evidence that the President ever seriously entertained the embarrassing notion of appointing his old chief to his Cabinet. The main reason for Daniels' even considering a race for the Senate was the anti-administration conduct of Josiah W. Bailey, who had been making anti-New Deal noises even during the Hundred Days. To Santford Martin, editor of the *Winston-Salem Journal*, who was urging Daniels to run, the Ambassador confided, about Bailey: "If he is re-elected for six years he will vote like Glass, without the convictions of the Virginian." Commerce Secretary Roper broached the idea of Daniels' candidacy to Cordell Hull and to the President, but all hands agreed he should stay on at Mexico City. "Roper's letter," Daniels wrote son Jonathan, "sounds like you or Uncle Frank or one of the family had been talking to him." So the Ambassador gave in, although he was sure he could have been elected and that the political plunge would not harm his health. "On the contrary, it would be a tonic and make me young and vigorous," he declared shortly before his seventy-fourth birthday.[41]

While the Republicans were building up Governor Alfred M. Landon of Kansas, Daniels wrote Claude Bowers in Spain about him: "Before October the Landon myth will be so exposed that I do not think he could carry half a dozen States." Before leaving Mexico for the Democratic National Convention in Philadelphia Daniels wrote the President his agreement that now was the time to crush the two-thirds rule. He also furnished the President, on request, with an array of "kept" campaign promises for inclusion in Roosevelt's speech at the Convention, highlight of an otherwise unexciting affair. The newspapers were reduced to "color" stories: one reported that Daniels (who had long given up trying to lace his own shoes) "blocked traffic in the Bellevue lobby when he asked a bellboy to tie his shoe." The reporters also asked the Ambassador to comment on the walk-out of Senator Cotton Ed Smith of South Carolina. The violently racist Smith had declared he

would not abide having "a nigger to pray in a Democratic convention." Daniels said: "Standing in the need of prayer, O Lord,
standing in the need of prayer."[42]

One of those the Danielses prayed most for was that weakest
of the Bagleys, Miss Addie's brother Henry. He had failed to become the big-time publisher either in Texas or in Massachusetts
after his exile from *The News and Observer*. Now he was ending
his days in a minor federal treasury post in Little Rock. Miss
Addie loyally exposed herself to the emotional strain of staying
with her brother there in the fall of that year when it was known
that Henry was dying. Even so, the Daniels children brought their
Uncle Henry home to Raleigh in his last days, as the Ambassador
gratefully wrote them—"Dearest Boys and Girls"—so Henry Bagley
could be "made to feel the tenderness and care of those nearest
by blood and marriage." On the Daniels side of the family the
weak brother was Charles, whose law career in New York never
measured up to its early promise and who had been visited by
personal tragedy. Charles, Jr., had suffered a mental breakdown
and early death, and the talented writing son, James Robinson, was
a hopeless cripple. *The News and Observer* regularly ran James
Robinson Daniels' "Manhattan Kaleidoscope" column, his Uncle Joe
instructing Jonathan to pay for the columns even when they had
to be omitted for lack of space. Whenever he would extend his
brother Charles financial aid, as was the case through the years,
Josephus Daniels would deprecate it, murmuring, "He would do
the same for me."[43]

Visitors to the Embassy—and Daniels practically invited the
State of North Carolina in a body to visit him there—found him
delighted with the large Embassy residence, larger even than Wakestone. Across from the residence lay the Chancery, where the Embassy's routine work went on, and in between was a beautiful
garden that was the apple of Miss Addie's eye. (A small bomb
was exploded there in the early summer of 1935, but it did no
damage, frightened no one, and was an incident never repeated.)
The Danielses always served two kinds of water at table, plain and
bubbling, and the Embassy secretaries used to succor flagging
guests with a pre-dinner infusion in their office across the patio.
At dinner, as in the Cabinet days, the Danielses would keep talk
lively from seats opposite the center of the table. Their guests ate
from silver plates, were attended by impressively uniformed wait-

ers trained to serve in unison, the entire proceedings lighted by candles reflected by the mirrored walls. If Daniels could not personally greet every one of the thousands of Rotarians who crowded into Mexico City for a convention in the mid-thirties he come close to doing so, what with a formal dinner, a reception, and the attendant speeches. "Print rather fully," the father wrote Jonathan of a Rotary tie-in with *The News and Observer*.[44]

United States visitors were not nearly confined to Hollywood and show business people, as one might imagine from the photographs in Daniels' *Shirt-Sleeve Diplomat*. Having become fascinated by the ruins excavated at Chichén Itzá, the Ambassador formed a warm friendship with Sylvanus Morley, the archaeologist in charge. The diary-letters bear abundant testimony to the frequent visits from writers and scholars: Professor Frank Tannenbaum, who had won the confidence of President Cárdenas, and was investigating the Otomí Indian civilization; Waldo Frank, the author, who found Daniels full of penetrating questions about Latin America; Efrem Zimbalist, the concert violinist, who also found welcome at the Embassy. So did hundreds of young students who needed encouragement of whatever sort. The weeks were full of luncheons and teas at the Embassy aside from the formal dinners. In August, 1936, a lady visitor from Washington reminded the Ambassador that he and her little seven-year-old daughter had been on the same program for the previous year's Confederate Memorial Day ceremony at the Arlington National Cemetery. Daniels had been the speaker of the occasion and he had kissed the little girl, hoop-skirted and poke-bonneted, for reciting "Your Flag and My Flag." "Well then, I'll repeat that kiss—or I'll kiss her again," said the Ambassador, which he did.[45]

With the mainly conservative American colony, Ambassador Daniels got along quite well despite his personal friendship for "That Man in the White House." No matter how critical of Daniels' alleged liberality with other people's money, as they put it, most of the resident Americans could not resist the amiable Ambassador and the delightful Miss Addie. Daniels vastly enjoyed the discomfiture of those resident Americans who found themselves so far out of step with their countrymen in the 1936 election. A ballot taken at the American Club gave 117 votes for Landon to only 11 for Roosevelt. The Danielses were completely at ease at the American Club, however, which was the scene of their annual dance-reception on the Fourth of July. Carleton Beals recalled a striking instance of Daniels' diplomatic *savoir-faire* at one such:

> I was standing at his side when a tall elegant girl dancing near the long table with the food and refreshments had a little mishap; her panties came down about her ankles. Without a noticeable pause in her dancing, she stepped out of them neatly and with a little quick backward kick sent them under the table out of sight. I doubt if even a half dozen people noticed it.
>
> Mr. Daniels smiled and whispered, "See that! That's what I call perfect diplomacy. If I could be that clever and cover up so well, I'd really be a successful diplomat."

The American Chamber of Commerce invariably pulled a stunt at its yearly banquet that made everyone laugh, especially Daniels. At the prize drawing the teetotaling Ambassador invariably turned out to have won a bottle of liquor.[46]

The American Colony would have been scandalized if it had known the extent of Daniels' New Dealing. When the Supreme Court's conservative decisions threatened to undo the New Deal reforms, Daniels was as indignant as Roosevelt, and he went down the line for the President's "court packing" plan. On the very day that Roosevelt's plan to reorganize and enlarge the Supreme Court was sent to Congress, in February, 1937, the President got a telegram from Daniels, who had heard the message on the radio. Daniels wired: "More power to your arm in cutting the judicial Gordian knot."[47]

A state visit from President Manuel Quezon of the Philippines that spring presented, on the other hand, the kind of problem that Daniels handled so easily. Quezon was accompanied by the then Field Marshal of the Philippines, General Douglas MacArthur, whose routing of the Bonus Army had prompted Daniels to warn President Roosevelt against reappointing him Army Chief of Staff. But the really touchy question was that of protocol, because Daniels' instructions were that the Ambassador must take precedence over Quezon, whose country was then an insular possession of the United States. Daniels was wise enough to put the message in his pocket and ignore it. Courtesy always outranked protocol with Daniels, who insisted that an Ambassador must remember "that he was a gentleman before he became a diplomat." Waldo Frank recalled of Daniels: "As we chatted, I realized that this was the sort of American who manages to renew one's faith in one's country."[48]

When Leon Trotsky was given asylum that spring in Mexico, Daniels was urged by the U.P. bureau chief, William H. Lander, to interview the exile. As a journalist Daniels was fascinated by the story, but by the time Trotsky was murdered three years later Daniels still had not met the old Bolshevik. Arthur Sinnott of the *Newark News* was one of a group of visiting American newspapermen who had just interviewed Trotsky, and asked Daniels if he had seen him. The Ambassador replied that he must sacrifice his journalistic instincts. "It would not do for me to be seen talking to Trotsky. The Republican speakers called Roosevelt a Communist last fall [1936]. What would they call me if I confabbed with Trotsky?" Daniels' fascination with the Trotsky episode was never more manifest than when he sent word to Carleton Beals that he would like to hear his side of the alleged whitewash of Trotsky. Beals had bowed out of the so-called Trotsky Trial conducted by the committee headed by Professor John Dewey, and Beals now had a long evening interview with the Ambassador. When at length Beals asked Daniels what he thought about the Stalin-staged Moscow purge trials and Trotsky's alleged anti-Soviet conspiracy, the Ambassador observed: "When two men are trying to ride a horse, the one who is not the best rider gets shoved off."[49]

Daniels' most memorable trip of the thirties came that summer when he boarded the *S.S. Manhattan* as a member of the American Battle Monuments Commission. The trip was to take him not only to the battlefields in France, but to England and Ireland as well. At Brest, where he had trod the duckboards of World War I's Camp Pontanezen, Daniels would make a speech at the twentieth anniversary of America's World War I entry. By this time the former Captain Josephus Daniels, Jr., had newly completed a term as State Commander of the American Legion, and his old fire-eating general, Smedley Butler, was fated to die just as France was being overrun by the Nazis. So a scant two years before Europe would again be at war, Josephus Daniels spoke of America's war dead: "They lived and died in the hope that their sacrifice would insure a warless world." Newton D. Baker's untimely death had removed him from the scene, but General of the Armies John J. Pershing was there as head of the Commission as was France's

Marshal Pétain. They had barely time to memorialize the dead of the First World War before the Second was upon them.[50]

So all unknowing Daniels went to New York for embarkation, where he had to rebuke the anti-Semitism of his brother Charles. "Charles regaled me," the Ambassador wrote the other Danielses, "with his usual Jew-complex stories. I cannot imagine how any man can feel like indicting a whole race as he does . . . both nights I have been [to dinner and the movies] with Commander Newberger of the Navy Medical Corps—very intelligent and a Jew. . . . I rarely go anywhere without finding an agreeable Jew associate." Lawyer Charles C. Daniels, after World War I, had acted as head of a bureau of anti-Jewish investigation set up by automaker Henry Ford. Charles Daniels' family doctor had introduced him to the ring of the anti-Semitic Russian Czarist agent, Boris Brasol, and thence to the faked "Protocols of the Elders of Zion." With Charles Daniels' assistance, then, Ford's *Dearborn Independent* launched a violent anti-Semitic campaign based on those forgeries, the articles being collected in a pamphlet called *The International Jew.* Late in the decade Ford made an out-of-court libel settlement which included a public apology to the Jewish people and the destruction of every copy of the notorious pamphlet that Ford's agents could buy up. Charles Daniels was meanwhile publicly identified with some rather vicious anti-Semitism, which his openly pro-Jewish brother Josephus deplored in embarrassment. He could not then invoke the image of genocide.[51]

The Ambassador had as good a time as possible on that trip, considering that Miss Addie's arthritis did not permit her to go along. The trip started under the cloud of the sudden death of Senator Joseph T. Robinson of Arkansas, but at the captain's table the Ambassador found Jouett Shouse of Liberty League fame, and the light of battle came into Daniels' eyes. "We had a few passes at politics," he reported. Later a Washington broker spoke in derogation of Miss Frances Perkins, and the ship's captain had to admit he had never heard anybody speak well of the Secretary of Labor. "You now have one person who will speak up for her," the Ambassador retorted, and he proceeded to give them chapter and verse on Miss Perkins' excellent public service. It was at London that Daniels' political acumen really came to the fore. News arrived there that Senator Hugo L. Black had been named to the Supreme Court, whereupon Daniels hurried Lister Hill on his way back home in pursuit of the vacant Senate seat from Alabama. The then Congressman Hill, also a member of the Commission, telegraphed his intention of running on Daniels' advice, and lost no time beginning a long and useful career in the Senate.[52]

In Paris Daniels had dinner with Ambassador William L. Bullitt, who surprised him by his bitter denunciation of Russia and the Russians. In London Daniels found himself thoroughly at home with a fellow-publisher, Ambassador Robert Worth Bingham, a favorite cousin of Miss Addie's, and Herschel Johnson of the Embassy staff. Miss Addie had charged her husband to look up her Irish kin in the Emerald Isle, and so the Ambassador, in company of Irish friends from Mexico, was true to his word. A Dublin branch of Clarys, Miss Addie's kin, kept a shop dealing in wines and liquors. Knowing he would have to submit proof to his prohibitionist wife, prohibitionist Daniels bought a pint bottle with the autograph of shopkeeper Patrick Clary on the label. "It was the first money I had ever spent for liquor," he reported, "but I found on my return to Mexico that it was well spent, for without that 'Exhibit A,' my wife would have doubted what I told her of her Irish kin."[53]

Daniels' zest in life was rarely better expressed than in his description of his seventy-fifth birthday, which he had celebrated in Mexico that May. "In the early morning," he wrote home, "Miguel and other Embassy servants secured a marimba and woke me up playing near my room, and later the whole force of the Embassy and Consulate came over with some musicians and singers of the Tipica orchestra who played and sang Mexican music. All were very much amused when I danced the jarabe with the young lady in china poblana costume who was one of the singers." On his seventy-fifth birthday the Ambassador had told Embassy Secretary Aguirre: "Steve, my eyesight, my general health and my ability to work at seventy-five are as good as they were when I was twenty-five."[54]

Another "Well Done"

"It was my good fortune," said Lázaro Cárdenas "to be President of Mexico when Franklin Delano Roosevelt was President of the United States and Josephus Daniels was ambassador of the United States in Mexico." The stormy six-year Presidential term of Cárdenas both revived and institutionalized the Mexican Revolution. His leftist but strongly nationalist program forged a national unity unknown in modern Mexico, a national pride in economic independence, and the foundation of a political stability all but unknown south of the Rio Grande. Cárdenas' "Second Revolution" got some of the same theoretical approval from Roosevelt's New Deal that the Revolution of 1910-1920 got from Wilson's New Freedom. It is no accident, as Tannenbaum has said, that the domestic foes of Wilson and Roosevelt both wanted more direct action against Mexico.[1] As an exponent of both New Freedom and New Deal, Josephus Daniels added an extra dimension of his own. Despite his grounding in Southern white supremacy, Daniels never tried to transfer Southern paternalism—much less condescension—to his relations with the Mexican people. Instead, he sympathized with their aspirations just as if they were his own downtrodden and Trust-ridden Anglo-Saxon yeomanry of North Carolina. He saw the Mexicans, whether Indian or otherwise, as sovereign indi-

197

viduals in their own land, entitled to strive for a freer and a better
life.

Another dimension of Daniels' Mexican service is the absolutely
critical one of his personal friendship for President Roosevelt. To
be sure, the President's press conference remarks and his letters to
"Dear Chief" clearly indicate Roosevelt's reliance on Daniels' good
sense, patriotism, and wholehearted devotion to the Good Neighbor
Policy. More than that, however, Daniels' "Dear Franklin" letters,
especially the hastily scribbled longhand notes at times of crisis,
amply demonstrate that his was a key influence. He as much as
told "Dear Franklin" that distrust of old State Department hands
in the oil expropriation crisis made it necessary for Daniels to send
the President copies of the Ambassador's reports to his nominal
superiors. Daniels was on the same first-name basis with Secretary
of State Hull, too, and Daniels' special position did not go un-
noticed at the State Department. After the oil expropriation crisis
Cordell Hull told the *New York Times'* Frank L. Kluckhohn: "If
Josephus Daniels had not had the President's ear, I would have
handled the Mexican situation differently. Daniels went over my
head to the President."[2] In the perspective of time, it is just as
well that he did so.

By the time Daniels embarked on his European trip in mid-1937
President Cárdenas had been in office two and a half years, having
rid himself of Strongman Calles and taken personal command of
the dominant National Revolutionary Party. The President also had
become a good friend of Ambassador Daniels, so much so that
Cárdenas confided to a newsman who found him smacking his lips
over a Martini: "I pretend not to drink because it pleases Ambassador Daniels."[3] Things diplomatic moved along serenely, with
nothing more disturbing than the perennial *Jarndyce v. Jarndyce*
matter of the Chamizal dispute. This controversy involved a boun-
dary question at El Paso, owing to a change of the Rio Grande's
course in the days of the U.S. Civil War, a dispute not finally ad-
justed until 1963. But when Ambassador Daniels got back from
Europe, he found that several long-dormant problems had come
to a head.

A fairly manageable problem arose over Cárdenas' expropriation, in August, 1937, of the Yaqui Valley lands of U.S. landowners.
As a pragmatic socialist Cárdenas was trying to breathe new life
into the ancient communal *ejido* system of land tenure without

destroying private ownership of small landholding. The significance of his bold policy of land distribution was less important,
seen in retrospect, for its socio-economic impact (the land reform
created many uneconomic units) than for its role in a developing
Mexican nationalism. The Yankee wheat farmers there in Sonora
had made the Yaqui Valley bloom, and they had made generous
offers to fit their holdings into the land reform program expropriation. But Cárdenas was adamant. The expropriation in the Yaqui
Valley did not involve any threat of U.S. intervention, but Ambassador Daniels firmly set himself to assure fair compensation for the
property of U.S. citizens.

At the same time a wave of disputes and strikes broke out
against the two largest and most important industries in Mexico,
the railroads and the oil industry. A revolution in Mexican labor
had brought to the fore the C.T.M. (or Confederation of Mexican
Workers) with Vicente Lombardo Toledano at its head. He was a
self-proclaimed Marxist who followed the Stalinist line, but Cárdenas used the militancy of the C.T.M. to serve his own predomi-
nantly nationalist purposes. On June 23, 1937, Cárdenas expropriated the National Railways of Mexico, then all but moribund and
already 51 per cent government-owned. Even while the expropriation law was being debated the previous year, Cárdenas was
assuring Daniels that private property would be protected. Daniels
had gone out to the President's suburban home at Los Pinos (he
had refused from the outset to live in the presidential palace at
Chapultepec) for a frank talk about the expropriation policy. Daniels did not get an ironclad written guarantee, but he paraphrased
Cárdenas' conciliatory remarks: "He would not engage in any
suicidal policy. . . . He realized that it was necessary . . . to encourage and develop American investment in Mexico. The government would not be so childish or shortsighted as to engage in
any policy which would prevent this. It would not, for instance,
endeavor to take over the oil fields." In the face of Cárdenas'
express disclaimer against expropriation of the oil fields—and widespread agreement among students of the period that he was sincere
—he nevertheless did expropriate the foreign-owned oil industry on
March 18, 1938. The action had the usual Cárdenas abruptness,
and immediately plunged U.S.—Mexican relations into crisis at a
time already heaving with impending world war.[4]

A series of scattered strikes against the foreign oil companies

had led in early 1936 to formation of a unified Syndicate of Petroleum Workers, supported by the Cárdenas administration and af-
filiated with Lombardo Toledano's C.T.M. In mid-year the syndicate drew up a list of demands, some justified and some arbitrary,
that would have raised annual labor costs for the companies some
65.48 million pesos. The companies claimed they could not pay;
the workers amply proved that they worked and lived under conditions—even by Mexican standards of that day—of extreme misery.
When all parties negotiated through a Cárdenas-requested postponement of one strike without getting anywhere, he did not try
to prevent another strike in May, 1937. This time the government's
Board of Conciliation and Arbitration, to which the oil workers
had appealed, invoked the national security, suspended the strike,
and appointed a fact-finding commission.

This three-man commission was headed by the left-wing but
authoritative economist, Dr. Jesús Silva Herzog, and his exhaustive
report at the end of three months was a blockbuster against the
foreign oil companies. The commission found the companies in
top-notch financial health, well able to afford a sizable package
(about half of what the unions demanded), and censurable in being unmindful of Mexico's social progress and national interest.
The companies, which were already pressuring their home governments to intervene in their behalf, united in a cry of outrage to
Cárdenas about the allegedly impossible terms of the Silva Herzog
recommendations (which included a mixed commission to work out
a collective bargaining agreement). Even now, after the expropriation of the Mexican National Railways, the oil companies kept
harking back to their allegedly special status under the agreements
reached, under diplomatic duress, with President Obregón in 1923
and, thanks to Morrow's gentler pressure, with President Calles in
1928.[5]

A national revolution undoubtedly was underway in Mexico,
but the companies refused to deal realistically with it as they
learned to do later. A decade or so later the same companies would
be paying a 50 per cent oil royalty to Venezuela and to every
amenable Persion Gulf oil sheikdom, but in 1937 they were outraged at the idea of paying the Mexican Government what it now
proposed, a maximum royalty of 15 per cent. The State Department heartily agreed with the companies that an oil royalty arrangement would overturn the Morrow-Calles agreement in con-

ceding Mexico's property rights in its own subsoil. Even so, President Cárdenas agreed to shelve this entirely workable proposal until after the labor troubles had been settled. When Ambassador Daniels returned from Europe in September, 1937, the oil dispute was at an impasse. He explained to President Roosevelt that the U.S. oil men really wanted an Ambassador who would be their messenger boy, adding: "They are as much against fair wages here as economic royalists at home are against progressive legislation."[6]

Many U.S. and other foreign oil men then argued that the labor dispute was a pretext by which Mexico could seize their fields, an argument which Daniels rejected, but the oil men never made what might have been a convincing act of good faith—a concession, any concession. To the contrary, the companies provoked Cárdenas by withdrawing their cash reserves from Mexico and promoting a flight of capital at a time of financial crisis. In addition, when the Board of Conciliation and Arbitration handed down its oil award in December the companies not only appealed to the Mexican Supreme Court but bruited it about that they would not pay no matter what the Court decided. And after company spokesmen negotiated directly with the President to no effect, the Supreme Court on March 1 upheld the earlier award. Even now the deadline for compliance was extended to March 14 so that in a confidential meeting on the eleventh the companies finally did offer the union the 26 million pesos in the original award provided that the administrative clauses in the Board's ruling could be ironed out.

When the deadline of March 14 arrived, however, the companies again took up their defiant attitude of noncompliance with the Board's ruling. Their action clearly implied the companies' new attitude, that Cárdenas was bluffing and would not really expropriate. Daniels did not think he would either and, in fact, Cárdenas did try to avert it to the last. According to Pierre deL. Boal, Embassy counselor and Daniels' second-in-command, Cárdenas offered to give the companies the assurances they desired if they would comply with the wage award. What was the guarantee? Reportedly the proud Cárdenas said: "You have my word." The cold answer: "That is hardly sufficient." Thereupon the President summoned his Cabinet and announced expropriation of the foreign-owned oil fields, with compensation within ten years. To the patriotic Mexican March 18, 1938, thus became a landmark of national significance scarcely less important than September 15, on which Mexico celebrates its national independence.[7]

The oil expropriation dispute was not settled until the eve of Pearl Harbor, in the meantime putting the Good Neighbor Policy—and its ardent champion, Josephus Daniels—to a searching test. There developed an on-again off-again policy of varying pressure applied by the State Department, in which Daniels consistently played a conciliatory role. For example, the State Department urged upon a reluctant Treasury Secretary Morgenthau an immediate boycott of silver purchases upon which the Mexican economy depended. Next Cordell Hull sent off a stern protest note for Daniels to deliver, after which the Ambassador would be withdrawn to Washington. Being on the scene, Daniels knew that this was exactly the wrong way to proceed. He had had evidence of Mexico's new national unity on witnessing some 200,000 people parading their support of President Cárdenas on March 23. He had seen even the Mexican clergy, never at one with the government since the Revolution, join in raising funds to support the expropriation and to swell the unified pride in national sovereignty. In short, Daniels knew that the expropriation was irreversible.

Hull's telegram of March 26 directed Daniels not only to deliver the shockingly stern note to the Foreign Minister but to do so by a predetermined deadline. When Foreign Minister Eduardo Hay read the note he was dismayed by its strong language, including "confiscation," and President Cárdenas later asked that the note be "withdrawn and altered." The first thing Daniels did was to agree with Hay on keeping the note secret and "not received." The next thing he did was to telephone Washington and talk frankly with the Secretary of State, which he did on the twenty-ninth. Embassy Secretary Aguirre, who was present, recalled the Ambassador saying: "Cordell, if I comply with the instructions you have sent me, not only will my absence from my post at this time bring a revolution in Mexico, but it could possibly mean the assassination of the then President of Mexico." Daniels stayed.[8]

That same day the Ambassador got a letter off to President Roosevelt telling him of Mexican resentment at the silver purchase policy newly announced. That policy was a complete dud in any case, because its announcement brought down the world price of silver, hurt the silver-producing areas of the United States and, by a new Mexican export tax, the U.S. owners of the Mexican silver mines. Daniels had already written the President a longhand note saying that if things were quiet he would go home for his Golden Wedding in May. As to oil: "I sought in every possible way to prevent the impasse and feel that Cárdenas made a big mistake in the expropriation." In so saying, Daniels was reflecting the oil men's argument that the Mexicans were incapable of operating the oil fields, an argument echoed two decades later by the British and French who assumed that the Egyptians could not operate the Suez Canal. But the Ambassador was not sympathetic to the expatriate Americans. He wrote his son Jonathan, in the first week of the expropriation, about how the American Colony naturally lined up with the oil companies. "You cannot originate the Good Neighbor Policy, go the Buenos Aires [as FDR had done two years before] and declare that there can be no intervention 'direct or indirect in the domestic affairs of another country' and then try to force another country to disregard its Constitution. That is what the oil companies are doing." In the face of some excitable talk by the American Colony about revolution or military intervention, Daniels wrote longhand to Roosevelt reminding him of what the President's Cousin Ted had said to President Taft: "Never draw unless you mean to shoot."[9]

The Mexicans quickly learned to value their Good Neighbor in the Embassy. Said *El Nacional,* organ of the government party (now Cárdenas' Party of the Mexican Revolution), on April 6, 1938:

> But Mr. Daniels—a worthy friend of the second Roosevelt —is a good neighbor. He lives close by on one of the streets in the *Colonia Roma.* And he consumes no more gasoline than necessary for his car. He possesses no large estates, neither here nor in the United States. He is a good newspaper man. A journalist. And he is always analyzing. And smiling. He loves our Chapultepec Park. And he does not go to Cuernavaca [where the big money men dwelt in their mansions on the thoroughfare nicknamed Ali Baba Street].[10]

Oil did seem to be the Nemesis, as he confided to Jonathan, of Josephus Daniels' public career. He summed up his frustrating experience with oil in one of the outspoken letters to his editor son:

> The eight years I was in Washington I was in conflict with the oil men who were trying to get control of the Naval oil reserves, and engaged in a more or less friendly battle with Secretary Lane and the Senators from the oil States.

Only by sitting up all night when Congress was adjourning and in other ways did I manage to preserve those oil reserves. But I learned something about the machinations of such oil men as Sinclair, Doheny and company. Such men think the oil was put into the ground by God Almighty for their enrichment, and whatever they do to get it was all right. . . . The situation here is very delicate and difficult. . . . The trouble was that the Government here did not trust the oil men and the oil men did not trust the Government. It's pretty hard to negotiate when neither side has confidence in the other.

Daniels, after all, stood for something when it came to mutual confidence in the midst of labor disputes. At one pause in the oil crisis the printers of *The News and Observer* offered to accept the Ambassador as arbitrator of their wage dispute with the paper. Frank Daniels laughingly refused, on behalf of the paper, to appeal to his father out of concern that the Ambassador would as naturally sympathize with the printers as with the Mexican oil workers. And Josephus Daniels owned the paper.[11]

While the oil crisis was still building and the stateside New Deal was being rounded out by a more cautious Roosevelt, Josephus Daniels kept up his active political commentary from Mexico. When Senator Black had gone to the U.S. Supreme Court, Daniels quickly perceived that most of the hue and cry against the Alabamian as a member (largely *pro forma*) of the Ku Klux Klan in the 1920's came from conservative critics of Black's liberalism. As a veteran foe of the Klan, Daniels assured Black that his liberal views showed "an emancipation from the hardworn creeds which dominate the minds of our Southern public men." When, on his way to Europe, Daniels made a pinch-hit commencement address at Raleigh's Shaw University (Negro), he made a speech which, for a white Southern leader of that era, could be considered both enlightened and advanced. He likened the Good Neighbor Policy in Latin America to that subsisting between the races in Raleigh. Before the Danielses returned home for their Golden Wedding they had had to decline the offer of complimentary box seats for the Mexico City concert of the famous Negro tenor, Roland Hayes. The concert manager inquired whether the Ambassador would not go because the singer was a Negro. "We wanted to hear him anyway," Daniels wrote home, "but that settled it, of course, and we accepted the box." The Danielses later went backstage to congratulate Roland Hayes, who asked that he be allowed to sing them their favorite, "Swing Low, Sweet Chariot," which he did with fine effect.[12]

With the first break in the oil crisis of 1938 Daniels kept his date with Miss Addie for their Golden Wedding. The Ambassador went first to Washington, where the reporters—gathered to ask him anxious questions about the Mexican crisis—contained one young lady journalist who asked him the purpose of his trip. "I'm going to Raleigh to be married," he chortled. Thinking Daniels meant the Hotel Raleigh in Washington, she turned to another reporter and whispered, "Let's go to the hotel; it will be interesting to see an old man married." The Ambassador was tickled when he was told of it. Even at the height of the post-expropriation trouble, Daniels conceded only that Miss Addie might have to return home by train while he flew to the Golden Wedding he would not dream of missing. He did not hesitate to second-guess Editor Jonathan on advance news coverage for the great event, suggesting that the family paper use a picture of Miss Addie in her wedding dress and other family photos of a half-century before. "I hate to put you to so much trouble," the father wrote gaily, "but I'll promise never to have another Golden Wedding."[13]

The invitations—"The omission of gifts is requested"—were mailed only to out-of-towners, because *The News and Observer* let it be known that all Raleighites were invited as a matter of course. Wakestone was filled with flowers sent by plane by the Mexican government, and the central decoration was a three-tiered wedding cake surmounted by a pair of lovebirds and inscribed "A.W.D. and J.D." Miss Addie was radiant in a light blue gown with white orchids as her husband placed on her left hand a ring of Mexican gold. "It's an engagement ring for my bride," the Ambassador proclaimed with his famous twinkle. In the receiving line with Miss Addie and Mr. Joe were nine members of their bridal party of 1888, along with the aging family group. Miss Addie's two sisters were there, joined by poor Brother Henry's first wife and their financial cousin from Richmond, Herbert Jackson. Mr. Joe's two brothers were on hand, plus all of the second-generation Danielses and grandchildren.[14]

There was the expected long list of state and national dignitaries, Governor and Mrs. Clyde R. Hoey; North Carolina's Chief Justice, Walter P. Stacy; Assistant Navy Secretary and Mrs. Charles

Edison; Mrs. Nellie Tayloe Ross, Director of the Mint; F.C.C.
Chairman and Mrs. Frank R. McNinch; Mr. and Mrs. Michael
Francis Doyle of Philadelphia and Mrs. Norman Mack of Buffalo;
University President and Mrs. Frank P. Graham; former Ambassador (to Hitler Germany) William E. Dodd. There was music,
there was merrymaking, there were greetings from President Roosevelt and his whole Cabinet, from President Cárdenas and *his* Cabinet, and a couple of the Daniels grandchildren got sick from competing to see who could drink the most (unspiked) punch. Those
who celebrated that joyous anniversary would not soon forget it,
for Miss Addie had hired the Raleigh Memorial Auditorium so that
the city's Negroes could celebrate too. *The News and Observer's*
Negro employees and the Danielses' Negro house servants invited
their friends to the blowout, all expenses paid, plenty of surplus
food from the party at Wakestone plus a paid-up "piccolo" or juke
box for dancing.[15]

On his return to Mexico the Ambassador found the Mexican
press openly appreciative of his moderation during the oil crisis
and speaking of him with unabashed affection. Mexico City's *Hoy*
wrote: "The black suit, the narrow bow tie like those used by
rheumatic Yankee senators, the amiable smile and the big hands
of His Excellency Josephus Daniels, Ambassador of the United
States in Mexico, arrived in the Capital on Tuesday of last week
with their legitimate owner, Mrs. Daniels."[16] The time was thoroughly critical for Mexican-American relations, for already the
Mexicans had sent the British Ambassador packing after getting an
especially icy note on behalf of British oil firms. Some oil men
were predicting a revolution, Daniels wrote home, and that summer's Cedillo revolt was widely believed to have derived moral
and financial support from the oil companies. The companies
launched a boycott of Mexican oil by their tanker fleets and an
intensive propaganda drive in Jersey Standard's *The Lamp* and
many other sympathetic publications, including a notoriously
slanted special issue of the July, 1938, *Atlantic Monthly*. "I'm no
Santa Claus," Daniels reminded the Mexican reporters who crowded
to meet him, seeking some hopeful sign of accord on his return
to Mexico early in July.[17]

Instead, the situation worsened because the State Department
now hardened its attitude on general agrarian claims. Cárdenas
had offered to pay the Yaqui Valley landowners without delay,

but the State Department now insisted on prompt payment for *all* expropriated property. The hard-pressed Mexican government could do no such thing, and the oil companies and State Department experts knew it—their design was a reversal of the oil expropriation. Daniels fretted to Jonathan: "Hull's stiff note (too stiff and harsh for a good neighbor to write) has put things in a flutter here. . . . The Standard Oil is more powerful than governments." He added his own translation of Hull's note: "I am your Good Neighbor, you damn thief. . . . In the meantime Mexico is swapping oil for machinery, etc. from Germany, Italy, and Japan." Daniels' direct access to the President was busily invoked on behalf of the Good Neighbor Policy. A characteristic "personal and confidential" letter to "Dear Franklin":

> With a world on the verge of war, in fact portions of it at war, I feel that the success of your foreign policy and the good of our country depends upon the amity and friendship of the Pan American countries. . . . The goal of Cardenas is the same as your goal—to give people here, desperately poor, a living chance. They have erred in expropriating property without payment, and labor often makes excessive demands. . . . Today the Mexican masses as a whole are seeing daylight as never before. Given freedom from revolution and exploitation, another generation will be our best neighbors and best customers.

The logjam was broken that fall when Cárdenas made Daniels a new offer on agrarian claims, an offer that the Ambassador helped to survive various amendments, and on June 1, 1939, he accepted a one million dollar check from Foreign Minister Hay as a first payment.[18]

With this removal of the condition that *all* expropriations be compensated at once, the oil negotiations made their tortuous way forward. Throughout, as Allan S. Everest has observed,[19] Josephus Daniels "refused to act as a police-court lawyer for the oil companies," keeping the broader issue of U.S. national security in view. During 1939 he witnessed the efforts of Donald R. Richberg futilely negotiating on behalf of the oil companies as the first anniversary of the oil expropriation was celebrated as a popular holiday in Mexico. Later a "separate peace" was reached on behalf of Sinclair as worked out by Patrick J. Hurley, but further negotiations were postponed as national elections approached in both countries.

Daniels meanwhile rendered himself most *simpático* in people-to-people exchanges. To be sure, an ambassador does not have unlimited opportunity for meeting the plain people of the country to which he is accredited. Daniels therefore chose his occasions with care and with a sureness of touch that cannot fail to impress. One such case in point involves the time the seventy-seven-year-old Ambassador made his way to the village of Canonitas, in the state of Puebla. What took him there was a plane crash in April, 1939, in which two young U.S. students, Bronson H. Rumsey and Daniel S. Roosevelt (a nephew of Mrs. Franklin D. Roosevelt), were killed. Their passenger, Miss Tita Constantine, miraculously escaped death and was borne five tortuous and rocky miles on the back of a diminutive *campesino* and later removed to a hospital. When the Embassy staff reported the details to the Ambassador, he decided he must pay his personal homage to the villagers of Canonitas.

In his diary-letter of May 31, 1939, Daniels set down the story of his visit. The Ambassador's party spent the night at Puebla, and motored the next day to Guadalupe Victoria, where the village chief and villagers from Canonitas met them on horseback. Along a dry river bed and through the fields Daniels made his way until the party reached the village. Daniels described the primitive life of the villagers, who had no streets, no electric light or running water, and said of them: "and yet the most cultivated Christian in what we call the best civilization could not have been kinder or friendlier or put themselves out so much to care for people in distress than they had."

The church bells were rung, and the villagers crowded in front of the church where the young aviators' broken bodies had first been brought before burial. Ambassador Daniels told the assembled people of the United States' gratitude. He also recounted one of their own Indian legends and, reverting to his long years as Sunday school teacher, the story of the Good Samaritan. The village chief replied, saying he and his people had been deeply affected. After the brief ceremony, Daniels took aside the tiny Manvilio Islas who had rescued Miss Constantine and, telling him of the possible wish of the parents of the young people to reward him, asking what he would like best of all. "He first said that he was a very poor man," Daniels wrote, "and would like to have a piece of land and a mule, and then, lifting his four-and-a-half-year-old child in his arms, he said: 'But most of all I would like to make certain that my son will receive a good education.'" Thus the diary-letter; the later *Shirt-Sleeve Diplomat* tells us that Manvilio Islas got both his wishes.[20]

Characteristically, Daniels wanted to visit the village school in Canonitas. The three adobe houses of the school contained about twenty desks but no teachers. He asked some of the children if they would go to school if they had a teacher, and they spoke up enthusiastically as did several adults. Canonitas appeared a forgotten village to Daniels, and he proposed to do something about it. "I am going to take this matter up with the Governor of Puebla and see if something can be done that these children might have a chance. If they had a chance and others like them it would mean a different Mexico in another generation." Thus the diary-letter of May 31, 1939; the later *Shirt-Sleeve Diplomat* tells how the villagers got their school.[21] Mrs. Franklin D. Roosevelt and the Rumsey family contributed the funds, and on completion of the building Daniels returned to Canonitas in the company of General Eduardo Hay, representing President Cárdenas, and of the Governor of Puebla, Maximino Avila Camacho. The "House of the People" was duly dedicated, and this school was named "Fraternidad."

The year that followed the buoyant Golden Wedding nevertheless turned out heavy with depression for Daniels. In April came the death of his beloved elder brother Frank who, as one graybeard to another, would still call his younger brother "son." In May came the death of Miss Addie's sister Belle, the two surviving sisters comforting one another at Lake Junaluska with the Ambassador lonely in Mexico City. He had the opportunity of playfully shredding one more of Miss Ethel's bread-and-butter checks and to write her a few family love letters before she too died in October. The Ambassador was lonely and fearful for Miss Addie while she was at home seeing to the effects of her sisters. "A beautiful afternoon with warm sun," he scrawled a letter to her from Mexico, "and I longed for you to enjoy it with me." He awaited her return "so we can have some quiet and happy old evenings together. What happy hours we have enjoyed in the years since 1887, and we must have more, if not so many." Pope Pius XI had died earlier in the year, and in October a Solemn Pontifical Mass at the Cathedral in Mexico City was to take place. Not only did Daniels, as a friend of the archbishop, receive an invitation, but he was honored by a place in the procession that bore the Holy Eucharist. Still, the atmosphere was pervaded by gloom. Only his spare time preoccupation with his memoirs that year helped him to bear with the general gloom that was accentuated by the outbreak of war in Europe. The director of the University of North Carolina Press, publisher of Daniels' memoirs, asked the old Ambassador why the United States, between wars, seemed to wobble from one untenable foreign policy to another. Daniels replied, in effect, that if you couldn't really know everything, if you weren't God, you were doomed to wobble; and that if this muddling-through left you looking utterly absurd, you might then consider that this was your real situation.[22]

As war clouds began to gather, new refugees began to appear in the Mexico that was already sheltering thousands of Spaniards who had fled Franco Spain. But when the fugitive King Carol of Rumania "and his lady love—not his wife—Madam Lupescu" (as Daniels put it) were welcomed by Mexico City society, they were pointedly ignored by the U.S. Embassy. Daniels explained it later to Jonathan, saying: "I had a letter from Mr. [Ambassador George S.] Messersmith, at that time in Cuba . . . suggesting that I be friendly to Carol. He said they were very lonesome in Cuba, and he had entertained them. Your mother and I agreed they should never put their foot in the Embassy while we were there, and they never did." Carol later sought to enter the United States from Mexico, his being one of the few refugee visas that Ambassador Daniels did not endorse and, in fact, actively and effectively opposed. More than merely puritanical, Daniels knew how to distinguish between unemployed royalty and refugees whose misery he could do all too little to assuage.[23]

During the Hitler era Josephus Daniels was an especially outspoken friend of the persecuted Jewish people, and his Mexican diary-letters show that he did everything he could to mitigate the lot of the European refugee Jews there. His diary-letters of January and of October 22, 1938, voiced concern over the thousands of Jews who had come to Mexico after the First World War—barred from the United States by immigration quotas based on national origins—and had desperately described themselves as "agriculturists." Now there was agitation to deport them from Mexico, but where would they now find a haven? Two years later he wrote home in distress about the unfortunate eighty Jewish refugees who had arrived by ship at Veracruz from Portugal and were not permitted to land in Mexico. They all bore visas given them by the Mexican consul at Lisbon (by this time no longer an official of the Mexican government), and the poor people had been despoiled of $100 for each worthless visa. The Age of the Refugee, in all its tragic aspects, added greatly to the cares which burdened the old Ambassador.[24]

As an ardent supporter of the Spanish Republic, he had eagerly questioned all who had had news of the Civil War there (like Frank L. Kluckhohn, who reported from Republican Spain and was later expelled from Mexico). Daniels also was in constant touch with Ambassador Claude Bowers, first in Spain and then in Chile, a kindred spirit with whom he shared the bitter frustration of seeing Fascism triumphant. Nothing aroused Daniels' indignation as much as the manner (the so-called Nonintervention Policy of the West) in which the Spanish Republic was done to death, and he was in tears when his old friend Alvarez del Vayo appeared in Mexico as a refugee. By the time Daniels left Mexico, he had the partial gratification of knowing that some eight thousand Spanish refugees had been given a haven. Many of them were among the intellectuals and scholars whom he hastened to receive at the Embassy.

Since the Ambassador took an ardent personal interest in the plight of so many refugees, he suffered all the greater frustration at not being able to help those who wished to enter the United States. He had no power over the visa-granting U.S. Consulate General, which had State Department orders to screen applicants closely for Communist connections. However passionately Daniels pleaded with the career officers of the Consulate General, however sympathetic some of them might be personally, they could not disregard their orders. All refugees were not so fortunate as Alvarez del Vayo, whom a visa officer held up as a suspected Communist and who was cleared by Secretary of State Hull on Daniels' direct appeal. Daniels' emotional commitment to the Spanish Republic was so strong that he hailed the forlorn gesture in the immediate post-World War II days when Alvarez del Vayo, Juan Negrín and others went to Mexico City to establish a Spanish Republican government-in-exile.[25]

As the European war clouds gathered, Daniels took the long view as the only surviving member of Wilson's original Cabinet.

As long ago as 1934 Daniels had urged on President Roosevelt a unification of the army and navy under a Secretary of National Defense. He had given up on the battleship after his World War I frustration on seeing the British stationing some ninety destroyers—badly needed for antisubmarine warfare—to protect their dinosaur-like battleships at Scapa Flow. He worried to son Jonathan about the direction of the Navy building program in 1938, saying: "I became convinced that a dreadnaught was more of a liability than an asset—yet every officer in the Navy holds the opposite opinion." He urged his old subordinate, FDR, to channel more money into aviation, but he shared the President's love for the Navy and envied him the pleasure of attending fleet maneuvers in 1939. When the European war broke out, he took whatever comfort he could from the officially neutral posture of Mexico. The Ambassador confided to Miss Ethel, shortly before her death, that "last night the Government informed me that Mexico would unite for continental solidarity." To his old Navy second-in-command, Daniels scrawled a longhand reminder of a combined Woodrow Wilson-Franklin Roosevelt slogan: "The most adequate Navy in the world and 100 cents worth of efficient Navy for every dollar expended."[26]

Outbreak of the war in Europe made Daniels especially conscious of the strategic importance of the Caribbean area and the Panama Canal. He played an eagerly knowledgeable host at the Embassy to a group of five U.S. Senators and eight Congressmen in November, 1939, when they were making a tour of army installations in the Canal Zone and paying calls throughout Central America. Arriving in the afternoon, the legislators were immediately whisked off to a luncheon given by a committee of the Mexican Senate and Chamber of Deputies (the menu included turkey in honor of the impending U.S. Thanksgiving). Ambassador Daniels' dinner started, in the Mexican manner, after 10 P.M., with many courses and a great deal of highly informed talk that the then Senator Harry S. Truman found especially fascinating.[27]

All during Roosevelt's second term, Daniels spoke up for a more vigorous New Deal and upheld the President at every juncture. The Ambassador indignantly told the President of the "gall" of a Duke Foundation spokesman who had asked Miss Addie to use her influence with the President to block public power projects in South Carolina. Such projects would "compete" with the Duke

Power Company which, via the Duke Foundation, helped support Rex Hospital, of which Raleigh institution Miss Addie was board chairman. "But they didn't know," Daniels wrote the President, "that staunch Methodist that I am, I would not favor taxing all the people in excessive rates to help support orphans in a Methodist institution." Daniels bucked up the defeated Congressman Maury Maverick and urged him to keep on fighting for progressive causes. He supported the President's attempted "purge" of Democratic conservatives, fretting in a longhand note to "Dear Franklin" that every Cabinet and sub-Cabinet officer should be on the firing line, and what was Sumner Welles doing in Switzerland instead of trying to help defeat Millard Tydings in Maryland? Perhaps Daniels was already thinking of a third term for Roosevelt, having often said that the Presidency was an office that few men left willingly. He wrote Jonathan that the Democratic party would be defeated in 1940 unless it nominated a real progressive. "But," he scribbled his opinion, "we will have a Progressive."[28]

As he was about to leave Mexico for the domestic political wars in 1940, the Ambassador set down for President Roosevelt a "dream" in which Daniels predicted to his state convention that the Chief Executive would yield to a draft. "And I dreamed that the people cheered so loud," he reported of that dream convention, "that it woke me up!" In Washington he found Cordell Hull sleepless and harried by the impending fall of France and the emergency calls from Ambassador Bullitt. He learned that Governor Lehman was concerned over possible Fifth Column activities by pro-Nazi German elements in New York City. He found Harold Ickes unhappy at the administration's policy of placing "monopolists" like Knudsen and Stettinius in charge of defense production. In between times he sandwiched in a long political discussion with the President, and they dead-panned an exhaustive canvass of the prospective Democratic candidates (Roosevelt vetoed to Daniels all except Secretary Hull and Justice William O. Douglas). Of their personal meeting, Daniels recorded in his diary: "He addressed me as 'Chief' affectionately, inquired about my wife and 'your fine boys.' He laughed heartily when I told that, when the arthritis in my wife's knees compelled her to use a rolling chair, she said she could not go to an official dinner because she would have to be propelled in a rolling chair. I overcame her objections by saying: 'You and Franklin Roosevelt are the only two people in official life who ride in state to official functions.' "[29]

Daniels rejoiced at Roosevelt's third nomination, but he felt deep regret that the event should be the occasion of the break in the Roosevelt-Farley friendship. Six years before, Farley as national chairman was broaching to Daniels his idea of resigning as Postmaster General and reporting that Mrs. Farley had no taste for Washington life. Nevertheless, his strong Democratic ties and his own ambition conspired to put Farley in the race as stalking-horse for all the anti-Third Termers. Daniels recalled: "Carter Glass, who was then in failing health, made a brief speech and rather a tragic last appearance." More than a year earlier, the Ambassador had confided about Glass to the President: "He is a sad illustration of an old man who has lost faith in his early dreams and surrendered to the status quo." As to Farley's defense that he had gotten from the President a disclaimer of wanting a third term, Daniels believed that Farley should have unquestioningly stepped aside. "Conditions changed," he recalled, "and the need of the country and the party demanded the nomination [France had just been overrun and Britain's ordeal was soon to begin] and Roosevelt was not averse to heeding the call." The Ambassador flew up from Mexico for the Chicago convention, delegate-at-large from North Carolina, a member of the Platform Committee, and a hearty backer of Henry A. Wallace for Vice-President. Daniels reported to his family that his delegation, opposed to Wallace as a one-time Republican, had proposed to the Ambassador that he approach the President to withdraw his recommendation. Of course he did no such thing. "On the day of the nomination of Wallace," Daniels wrote home, "I took lunch with him and we talked about everything except his candidacy. . . . He told me he thought it was the proper thing for the Southern delegates to support Bankhead."[30]

In Mexico that year President Cárdenas was backing a man much more conservative than himself in an attempt to secure continuity in a national consensus, his candidate being General Manuel Avila Camacho. The opposition came from General Juan Andreu Almazán, supported mostly by the Right but also by those who had had enough of Cárdenas' "Second Revolution." The July election was preceded and accompanied by much bloodshed, with Avila Camacho declared the winner over a thoroughly unconvinced Almazán, and President Cárdenas—arbitrarily "counting" the votes

—sighed: "Mexico is not yet a democracy." The real question was whether the Almazanistas would permit the new President to take office on December 1, and the question disturbed Daniels who remained on the scene in order to put his presence on the side of stability. The Ambassador took no part in local politics, but he took care to be present at the opening of the Mexican Congress lest his absence be taken as support for Almazán, who was then making revolutionary noises outside Mexico. Almazán was the candidate of, among others, the Mexican adherents of the Axis Powers. Daniels was careful to warn Washington against overestimating the danger from Nazi or Fifth Column activities in Mexico, but the fact remained that the Cárdenas forces stood shoulder-to-shoulder with the United States in the international crisis now in progress, the fall of France and the disaster of Dunkirk. Cárdenas also rebuked the Communists by castigating the Nazi-Soviet Pact that then held sway and endured until Russia was attacked the following year. Ambassador Daniels advised Avila Camacho's aides against their man's visiting the United States, as Almazán had done. He also provided fellow-Ambassador Claude Bowers with a sophisticated briefing on not expecting a Mexican revolution because of the rural populace's not desiring one.[31]

Daniels happily scribbled a longhand note to President Roosevelt over the decision to send the U.S. Vice-President-elect, Henry A. Wallace, to attend the Avila Camacho inauguration. Other U.S. figures friendly to Mexico were invited as guests of the Mexican government. One of these was the aggressive Maury Maverick, now Mayor of San Antonio, who conceived himself insulted on not being met at the airport by Embassy staffers. Arrived at the Embassy, he angrily denounced all hands until a gentle voice from the next room commanded: "Bring Mayor Maverick in here." He was taken into Miss Addie's sitting room, where she was reclining on a sofa because of an arthritis attack. "You, Maury Maverick, sit down here," she motioned to a chair beside her. "You're a bad boy, Maury, I know you." Then she proceeded to pat his hand and the fiery Texan's wrath melted into a sheepish grin. Miss Addie had to be coaxed into attending the *Grito* at the Palace in September, having had to appear in a wheelchair. "But she got on very well," the Ambassador reported to son Frank, "everybody, members of the diplomatic corps and high Mexican officials treated her like the queen she is." Daniels also reported to his son the

100,000 people at the Zócalo in front of the Palace and the scattered cries of "Viva Almazán" that almost led to bloodshed.[32]

"Between you and me," Daniels wrote President Roosevelt, "it is a pity that the term of Cárdenas expires this year of war and confusion." Even after the collapse of the Almazán bid for power, his name was desperately seized upon by Fifth Columnists. The Mexican Nazis were prominent in launching an avalance of anti-U.S. propaganda together with a good-sized riot as Henry Wallace's car swung through the Embassy gate. The Wallaces were guests at the Embassy, where the Vice-President-elect and the Ambassador found themselves solidly *simpático*. Wallace had been briefed by his running mate, Roosevelt, to lay a wreath on the monument honoring the Mexican cadets who had defended Chapultepec against Winfield Scott's forces in 1847. (President Truman wisely followed suit when he visited Mexico in his turn.) When Wallace and Daniels appeared for the inaugural of Avila Camacho on December 1, 1940, the Mexican Congress rose in a spontaneous ovation, and the Congress later invited Wallace plus Congressman Sol Bloom and Mayor Maury Maverick to address that body. The Ambassador delightedly wrote a longhand note to "Dear Franklin" about Wallace's triumph and his fluency in Spanish, but Wallace himself recalled of Ambassador Daniels: "I never saw such a triumph of the human heart over the language barrier."[33]

Back in Washington within the month, the indefatigable Daniels helped see to the locating of the Marine base at Camp Lejeune in North Carolina. Having been briefed on the possible site by the Marine Corps Commandant, General Thomas Holcomb, the Ambassador "helped" President Roosevelt decide on locating the base on New River, Onslow County. The Chief Executive was won over, Daniels recalled, on being reminded of the pleasant hunting trip that Assistant Navy Secretary Roosevelt had enjoyed with Daniels' friends in coastal Carteret and Onslow counties.[34] One of those who saw Daniels in Washington was David E. Lilienthal, one of the T.V.A. directors, who described the Ambassador in his journal: "He is a wonderful little man, now approaching 80, but as perky and vigorous as can be, and none of the signs of age." Daniels talked animatedly about his forthcoming Wilson era memoirs, punctuating his sentences by jabbing Lilienthal in the chest, and vowing to give an eternal comeuppance to those who had served Wilson badly, notably House and Lansing. "And so," Lilienthal wrote, "his head looked down in that funny one-side way he has of inspecting the floor as he walks, he went down the hall, wishing me a Merry Christmas. A grand old man."[35]

President Roosevelt wrote an especially affectionate letter to his old chief on being reminded, by Daniels' Electoral College speech of January, 1941, of his own efforts to see active Navy service during World War I. "Did I see the world leader in the young State Senator from New York?" the Daniels speech went on. "Of course not. But I did see young strength, young ardor, young courage, young energy and intelligence. I saw in the finest form I know the young American." Later in the year Wendell Willkie, Roosevelt's defeated opponent, joined a growing clamor for some supreme leader of the defense effort. The equalitarian Daniels indignantly reminded the President in longhand of Woodrow Wilson's reply to such a demand: " 'There is no such Superman as you demand. It is a God you want and I am sorry to say I have no Gods at my disposal.' " But ever mindful of politics, Daniels used the same letter to express his joy prematurely for the supposed victory in the race for the Senate of Lyndon B. Johnson of Texas (Congressman Johnson did not become Senator Johnson until 1948).[36]

To Cordell Hull the old Ambassador confessed his distress at the apparent necessity to soften America's strict neutrality and to repeal the arms embargo. He held back from the total pro-Allied posture of his old friend, William Allen White, but agreed with him in mutual discomfort at the subterfuge of Panamanian registry for U.S.-owned ships. During the period of the "phony war" he urged the President to renew their old drive for a democracy of merit in the armed services. Indeed, before the Battle of Britain reached its height, Daniels' tinge of old-fashioned Anglophobia had reappeared; he would have liked to see the war terminate with an end to British imperialism and all its works. Like FDR, he was prone to exaggerate the vitality of that "imperialism" which had never really recovered from the First World War. Daniels added, to Jonathan, a wish that the war's end would see "the aims and policies of Nazism, Fascism and Communism—Hitler, Mussolini, Stalin—all dead and damned." At first he was in a very agony over the President's adoption of Lend-Lease, but when both houses of Congress passed the bill he told Jonathan they had to accept it. In the "Great Debate" over American isolation, Daniels consistently took refuge in Stephen Decatur's "Our country, right or wrong." To Roosevelt, Daniels scribbled his "prayers that you may have divine guidance in these tragic days, for human wisdom will not suffice." But to his son Jonathan, the Ambassador waxed gloomy about labor troubles, about profiteering in defense contracts, with Republicans like Stimson and Knox in the Cabinet and acting "in sympathy with monopolists. I am sick at heart, but impotent."[37]

Impotent or not, it was not like the buoyant Daniels to despair or turn sour. Those pre-Pearl Harbor months saw an active correspondence between him and the one old friend who did later go sour, Robert W. Winston. Old Judge Winston, who had been Daniels' chief defense lawyer in the contempt-of-court episode of 1904, lived to become bitterly disillusioned and convinced that America's participation in the Second World War was due to a Roosevelt conspiracy. In 1939 he was an isolationist par excellence, but the two old friends were not too far apart for some mutual soul-searching. Daniels wrote "Dear Bob" of the many unexpected turns his own career had taken, turns without any discernible causes, and of the two old men being caught up in events they had no power to influence. "And now," he wrote,

> I, as you and all of us, am walking in a confused world, fearing the worst and hoping for the best, having only one crumb of hope in the faith that Right will triumph over Might and the prayer that out of the welter, democracy in politics, in industry, in a better division of the rewards of brain and arm will eventuate. . . . Even walking through a graveyard, I try to whistle, and my optimism makes me believe that "far off, good will come to all."[38]

Daniels had argued for—Winston against—Roosevelt's domestic program. "If I have been inconsistent," Daniels wrote when the Judge criticized him for supporting the "court packing" proposal, "it is the sort of inconsistency that Jefferson practiced in the Louisiana purchase. . . .

> I have the faith, sometimes no larger than a mustard seed —that one day we shall not have to fight the devil with fire. The courts became the refuge of Privilege. It was absolutely necessary to stop the packing by methods that were the only ones which God and nature permitted us to use. Roosevelt lost his fight but won the war. The agitation did a world of good and woke up many judges who hardly knew they were converting this government into one of privilege, by privi-

lege, for privilege. The recent decisions show that there was
need for a right-about-face.

In that pre-Pearl Harbor summer he wrote Winston of his disappointment at not being able to come to Chapel Hill for Commencement, duty to the Good Neighbor Policy keeping him at his post.
He added:

> If I could serve my country and promote world peace I
> would gladly make any and every sacrifice. My great and
> good friend Bryan thought if he resigned and went to the
> country, he could keep the United States out of war. He did
> his best and no man could have done more, but he had little
> more effect than King Canute had in driving back the waves
> of the ocean. . . . The sun is darkened, and yet I dare to hope
> that God is in His Heaven, though I cannot say with Brown-
> ing "All's well with the world." Let us pray for light and
> peace.[39]

In the worsening Pacific crisis Daniels sent along for President
Roosevelt's "confidential reading" a plan that sought a basis of
peace between China and Japan. Dr. Stanley Jones, whom Daniels
identified to the President as "one of the greatest preachers in the
world" was author of the enclosed memorandum indicating that
the time was ripe for American meditation between the warring
Asian nations. On the family side was the Ambassador's concern
for Miss Addie's worsening arthritis and failing eyesight. Of course
he loved to indulge her in everything, even while his thrifty soul
protested at her "spendthrift" ways. He wrote son Frank—and directed him to "read and tear up" the letter (which, happily, Frank
did not do)—that "your mother can lie in bed and think of more
ways to spend money in a day than I could evolve in a year." He
grumbled to Frank that Miss Addie had her heart set on a new
car to use at home (it had come to that), and that "my feeling is
that this is no time to be buying a new car." On the contrary it
was exactly the right time to buy a new car, with production shortly
to be curtailed, and the new 1942 Buick served Josephus Daniels
well for the rest of his life. On top of everything else, the Danielses
had been using in Mexico the Lincoln limousine they had bought
from Mrs. Dwight Morrow for a bargain $300 eight years before.[40]

On September 29, 1941, the Ambassador wrote to the President
in longhand explaining that Miss Addie's arthritis was worse and
that he must ask for an interview. In October the old couple re-

turned to Raleigh, Miss Addie to rest in the more comfortable lower altitude, and her husband to entrain for Washington and an appointment with the President. Daniels' official resignation was dated October 30 and the President's acceptance the thirty-first. Roosevelt had known of Miss Addie's progressively worsening health, but the time of parting officially with his old chief still came as something of a shock. The President's voice was husky with emotion—the newsmen at his press conference could not help but notice it—as he announced that he was "very, very regretfully" accepting Ambassador Daniels' resignation. "I don't know that the country as a whole realized," the President pointed out, "that of all of the people in the last eight and a half years who have been in foreign posts in Central and South America . . . Mr. Daniels has probably done more to encourage and live up to the Good Neighbor Policy than anybody else I know."[41]

In his private talks with the President, Daniels entreated for an immediate end to the frustratingly long oil dispute. Daniels' argument, repeated in a follow-up interview, evidently helped tilt the balance, for just three short weeks before Pearl Harbor the United States and Mexico agreed to abide by the compensation award made by a two-man mixed commission. Morris Llewelyn Cooke and Manuel J. Zevada were the oil experts for their respective countries, and their award, although unpalatable to the oil companies, was to be insisted upon by a United States already at war. Remembering the World War I jitters over an unstable and revolutionary Mexico south of the border, Daniels had taken a long view of the oil expropriation. He had shown the vision to prize a stable and friendly neighbor to the south in the event of war, and indeed a few months later the Mexican government itself declared war on the Axis.

President Roosevelt persuaded Daniels to go back to Mexico for a proper leave-taking, insisted that the resignation would not become final until the Ambassador had completed his accrued leave, and gave him a personal greeting to hand to President Avila Camacho. At Raleigh's Union Station Miss Addie and a happy group of Danielses awaited Daniels. "Hello, beautiful," he greeted her, and Miss Addie replied, "Hey, precious." To a reporter who wanted to know if he would compete against Senator Bailey next spring, Daniels broke into his usual contagious laugh and replied: "I don't even think about politics; all I am thinking about is my next book." But he *was* thinking about North Carolina. While awaiting his appointment with Roosevelt, Daniels had paid a deferred visit to the land of his forebears, flying over the Outer Banks in a Coast Guard amphibian. At Nag's Head he had had his picture taken with his kinsman, Captain John T. Daniels, then the sole survivor of the men who had helped the Wright brothers on the morning of their first flight. Daniels had assured members of his clan that he wanted to set up a Daniels Night at *The Lost Colony,* the outdoor historical drama on Roanoke Island.[42]

He flew back to Mexico City for a week of affectionate farewells from those of high and low estate. Those of low estate might have been typified by Patricio Suárez, the bibulous Embassy gatekeeper whose name had somehow become permanently anglicized as Patrick. He it was who had opened the door of the Ambassador's slightly frayed Lincoln and, when Patrick was full of *pulque,* flung open the Embassy gates as if they were the flimsy doors of a *cantina.* Miss Addie had made Patrick know her displeasure when he had been drinking. She had scolded him like one of her naughty grandchildren, and would not let him help her into the house despite her arthritic lameness. But the prohibitionist and teetotaling Ambassador had always casually overruled the orders to fire Patrick for being drunk on duty. When Daniels returned to Mexico for his last goodbyes, Patrick was desolated and marched out of the Chancery straight into the nearest *cantina.* As the Ambassador was clearing up his last papers, an aide came to tell him—as recorded by Jonathan Daniels—that it had been found necessary to fire Patrick again.

> "Well," said the ambassador. "Don't you think. . . .?
> And the young man laughed aloud.
> "Certainly, Mr. Ambassador," he said. "I've already arranged it. I gave him hell. And he'll be restored to duty when he sobers up."
> My father looked at his papers. "That seems to me a very diplomatic way of handling the matter," he said. "It shows the qualities that will bless our country when you're a chief of mission."[43]

Daniels would still return to Washington and plead with President Roosevelt for an oil settlement (it was reached on November 19), but for now—from the moment he again set foot on Mexican soil until he emplaned for home—Josephus Daniels walked in triumph. On November 5 came the luncheon of the American Press correspondents, along with assorted compliments from the Rotary Club, Lions Club, and Chamber of Commerce. On the seventh came a dinner in Daniels' honor by the American Colony, and at a luncheon that day came a sincerely eloquent exchange between Foreign Minister Ezequiel Padilla and the Ambassador. Padilla's gift was an excellent oil portrait—the Ambassador had sat for it as painted by artist Armando Drechsler—and that portrait now hangs in the Josephus Daniels Junior High School in Raleigh. The diplomatic corps, also invited to honor Daniels as their dean, presented him with an inscribed silver service. The Daniels family, a decade later, presented that service to the U.S. Embassy in Mexico City after clearing the idea with President Miguel Alemán.[44]

Daniels lunched with President and Mrs. Avila Camacho, exchanged *abrazos* with them, and did not forget to send an admiring telegram of farewell to Lázaro Cárdenas. At the Embassy the staff and U.S. consuls from all over Mexico gathered for a grand send-off. There was a telephone hook-up, amplified so that all could hear, with Miss Addie in Raleigh. All Embassy and Consulate hands had contributed to the purchase of a Spanish colonial *bargueño,* a delicately handsome secretary in fancy inlaid gilt, which thereafter reposed in the Mexican room at Wakestone. At the airport, "teary around the lashes" as he would have said, the Ambassador turned to the crowd with a rare try at an utterance in Spanish: *"Que Dios os bendiga"*—"May God bless you." Arias Bernal responded by drawing a famous farewell caricature for *Hoy* entitled "Goodbye, Boy!" That magazine carried a center-spread of photos showing *El Embajador* exchanging *abrazos* with the Mexican first family, *Hoy* speaking of the departing Tar Heel as "the most beloved of U.S. ambassadors in Mexico." The editor of *Hoy* got a final interview with Daniels, whose eight years in Mexico he described as *"los más felices de mi vida."* Those "happiest years of my life" were a far cry from the Veracruz of 1914 and his anxiously guarded arrival in Mexico City in 1933.[45]

Daniels' "onus of Veracruz" could have turned his appointment into the most spectacularly inept one that Franklin D. Roosevelt had ever made. Instead, the President had wrought better than he knew in sending Daniels to Mexico. The *simpático* Ambassador, who stayed at his post longer than any other U.S. envoy to Mexico, exemplified the policy of the Good Neighbor to perfection. If

Daniels appraised the Mexican scene intuitively, he also brought his native shrewdness to bear. He well knew that whereas the majority of ordinary Mexicans esteemed him, his name was anathema to all those who yearned for their erstwhile privileges under Porfirio Díaz. He knew that many oil men bore him ill will, but he knew better than they that their intransigence had cost them dear and that the oil expropriation was simply irreversible. Even the redoubtable William Randolph Hearst was won over at last, a man whom Daniels had long opposed in politics and who had owned much Mexican land lost to expropriation. Hearst nevertheless wrote in his syndicated column in 1941; "Folks at home, you should be proud of your diplomatic representation in the Republic of Mexico. Ambassador Daniels is a splendid man for you. Able and experienced and popular—attentive to the interest of his country and genial in his intercourse with the people of Mexico and of his homeland."[46]

In the judgment of observers more competent than Hearst, Josephus Daniels had indeed measured up. His ambassadorial mission was marked by his unfailing good humor, his deep understanding of the age-old divisive issues in U.S.-Mexican relations, and—not to put too fine a point on it—his old-fashioned moral courage. It all provided one more instance—like that of his Cabinet career—in which he would succeed where his critics insisted he must inevitably fail. For his was a triumph of temperament over inexperience, of character over "qualifications." So doing, he played a key role in paving the way for Mexico's later industrial revolution accompanied by a new political stability. So doing, he played a key role in paving the way for the Mexican-U.S. era of good feelings that followed his mission. Indeed, since his day U.S.-Latin American relations generally have followed a course rocky enough to have caused more than one observer to wish for more United States diplomats in the Daniels mold—liberal, democratically inclined, *simpático.*

Editor at Eighty

Josephus Daniels enjoyed a brief retirement those weeks before Pearl Harbor, and certainly Raleigh's affectionate Welcome Home Celebration was meant to augur a newfound serenity for the indefatigable old work horse. On a November Sunday afternoon a friendly and sentimental audience gathered in the Memorial Auditorium to honor Miss Addie and Mr. Joe. Dr. Frank P. Graham presided, introducing for brief remarks such friends as Governor J. M. Broughton, Dr. Thurman D. Kitchin, president of Wake Forest College, and Neil Hester, longtime telegraph editor of *The News and Observer*. The invocation was by the Danielses' neighbor on the next hill, Albert S. Barnes, superintendent of the Methodist Orphanage, and the musical serenading ended with the entire audience singing "Blest Be the Tie That Binds." The honored Danielses—the printed program recorded—"are now as ever our unpretentious fellow citizens, neighbors, and friends with whom we shall again delight to have daily fellowship." But the Danielses had no more than settled down in Wakestone when the attack on Pearl Harbor galvanized the "retired" editor into action, a challenge that probably helped to prolong his life. Captain Joe, Jr., again put on his Marine Corps uniform, Dr. Worth donned the uniform of the Army Medical Corps, Jonathan was called to an official post in Washington, and only Frank was left to supervise the business side of the newspaper while his father, now in his eightieth year, again occupied the open-door office on West Martin Street.[1]

There was no time, even if Daniels had been so inclined, to sink into any sentimental decline surrounded by mementoes in his Wakestone "museum" atop its gentle hill with the naval gun commanding the front lawn. The big house contained souvenirs of the three Democratic Presidents he had served (every one between the Civil War and World War II). From the first period came the large oil painting of the little girl who had died in her second year of life more than a half-century before, the cherished first-born who had borne the beloved name Adelaide. From the second period came the great welter of photos of shipmates and other comrades of the Wilson era with the autographed originals of Berryman's Daniels cartoons drawn for the *Washington Star*. From the third period came the mementoes that crowded the library, where Daniels retreated every time he felt like "going to Mexico." On the library wall opposite the entry one encountered a large Mexican flag that Daniels carried away as a gift from President Avila Camacho so that the Ambassador might always "live under the Mexican flag." There, too, was the diplomatic corps' silver service, the *bargueño* from the Embassy and Consulate staffs, serapes from Saltillo and a special one from Zacatecas as a gift from President Cárdenas. This one was decorated by a border designed in the national colors of both countries, with the center bearing a woven likeness of Ambassador Daniels. Mexican labor's two top officials, shortly after Pearl Harbor, showed up at Wakestone. Lombardo Toledano, now president of the Latin American Federation of Labor, and Alejandro Carrillo, head of the Labor Bloc in the Mexican Chamber of Deputies, were taken to visit the Duke and Chapel Hill campuses, feted by the ex-Ambassador in the company of Governor and Mrs. Broughton. The Mexicans were en route home after conferring in Washington with U.S. labor leaders on joint plans to combat Axis efforts to divide the two Americas. Carrillo was later to part company with Lombardo Toledano over the latter's taking Stalin's side in the Cold War, but with Soviet Russia then a wartime ally of the United States the atmosphere was different. Daniels did not fail to write Vice-President Wallace of the significance of Mexican labor's efforts to promote hemispheric solidarity.[2]

Miss Addie was now confined to her wheelchair by the heart trouble that had speeded her return from Mexico City's high altitude, but she got around Wakestone quite well thanks to the special elevator that had been installed for her. She was, as her granddaughter Lucy recalled, "a too-plump pigeon of a woman with soft white hair and the blue eyes that could either sparkle or go deliberately blank. She had a smile of sunshine and a will of iron," cherishing and worrying over "Mr. Daniels." For himself, he was a man of no hobbies, who lived for his work and his family. He delighted in reading to Miss Addie of an evening.

At this time Mr. Joe did not look like anybody else in the world because of the way he dressed. Having worn exactly the same sort of clothes for about sixty years, much of his archaic raiment had now to be made to order. This was true of his semi-pleated stiff-bosomed white shirts with stiff cuffs and collars (gold studs), the marvelous high-topped shoes that laced part way up and then hooked the rest of the way to the bowknot, even handmade long underwear that had his white socks pinned at the ankles. His hat was a custom Stetson affair, the Josephus Daniels trademark of a picturesque broad-brimmed black felt with a flat crown, making him look as if William Penn had become a Southern planter. His string tie was another trademark as was the long black ribbon that dangled to his pocket. From the ribbon hung a watch instead of the spectacles he was proud of never having to wear, and when he went abroad he carried a gold-banded cane. His height was recorded on his passport, accurately enough, as five foot, eight and one-half inches, but—as Dr. Worth observed—Josephus Daniels showed old people's tendency to "shrink" somewhat with age, and his old head bowed forward from the effects of his auto accident. As the old editor himself expressed it, Spurgeon Fields was "a true friend through the years, my chauffeur and help in all ways, 'a gentleman in black.'" Spurgeon Fields dressed and undressed old Mr. Daniels (who insisted only on tying his string tie and shaving himself with his safety razor), gave him an alcohol rub twice a day, even put him into his bathtub and lifted him out.[3]

Now that he held no official position and in the midst of war, Daniels was more hesitant in writing to President Roosevelt. He did wire the Chief Executive on Jonathan's behalf right after Pearl Harbor, and in Washington during those feverish December days Daniels dined with Vice-President Wallace, who told him that

Jonathan was indeed slated for a government appointment. The post that took Jonathan to Washington in February was that of Assistant Director of Civilian Defense.[4] The post that seemed to beckon his father, however, was the elevated one of the U.S. Senator from North Carolina. There were many friends, Josephus Daniels recalled, who urged him to make the race against Josiah Bailey in 1942 "when I could have attained the nomination"[5] (read "election" in one-party North Carolina). The octegenarian wisely resisted the idea, much happier in his editorial sanctum than he could ever have been in elective office. On his eightieth birthday he went on record once again as an optimist, happily quoting to reporters Browning's "Grow old along with me/The best is yet to be."

Not the U.S. Senate but his beloved cause of public education was then engaging the old editor's interest. The past legislature had added a twelfth grade to the state's public schools but had balked at financing a nine-month school term also. Representative John W. Umstead of Chapel Hill had introduced the bill providing the nine-month term and he got ample support from *The News and Observer,* but the bill had died in committee. Daniels quickly realized that somehow a fire had to be built under the conservatives in the legislature. As one of the architects of one-party dominance in the state, Daniels set out to make the nine-month term part of the Democratic state platform in 1942 and thus virtually shame the forthcoming legislature into enacting it. Daniels got himself named to the Platform Committee, helped get the plank adopted there by a 7-5 vote, then personally read the plank with happy emphasis while the State Convention cheered. At the ensuing General Assembly, Representative Umstead offered to Daniels what amounted to a trade, the vote of the Wets in the legislature if *The News and Observer* would temporarily relent in its demand for a statewide liquor referendum. The old editor snapped at Umstead: "Liquor's bad, liquor's bad," but his real love was public education, and so the trade was effected and North Carolina got its nine-month school term.[6]

In the first wartime spring Daniels started his Victory Garden at Wakestone, and when his friends needled him about not doing the work himself he said: "All right, then, if you don't believe it, you come by here sometime between five and six o'clock in the morning and you'll find out." He was the friendliest of car-poolers in those gasoline-rationed days, one day happily alighting at his office from the cab of a garbage truck. To be sure, he never walked when he could ride, and he adopted to his own use the retort of the exercise-shunning William Allen White to the effect that he kept busy acting as pallbearer for his golfing friends. There was a certain sweetness about his personal relationships, even with total strangers, that was affecting to observe. Of course he anxiously inquired of his "daughters" what would be appropriate presents for the grandchildren, whom he enthusiastically spoiled. Grandson Frank, Jr., and Grandson Edgar Foster (son of Joe, Jr.) came over to Wakestone to serenade their grandparents on Mother's Day— which followed hard upon the Danielses' fifty-fourth "wedding day"—to sing them the Marine Corps hymn. "Their sweet young voices," Daniels described the scene for Jonathan's family in Washington, "gave a lilt and a swing to that favorite of your mother and the old man." Sometime later, newscaster Cedric Foster observed Frank Daniels saying goodnight to his father after an evening at Wakestone. Frank, tallest of the sons, gently bent over and touched his lips to his father's old head, and the venerable editor turned slightly and placed his hands in Frank's.[7]

As always, Josephus Daniels stood ready to assist the University of North Carolina, and President Graham credited him with helping bring to Chapel Hill its World War II Navy Pre-Flight School. When the University of Georgia was awarded the School earmarked for the "South," the decision went counter to the recommendation of a nation-wide survey committee that had voted for Chapel Hill. So President Graham drafted a protest letter that went to the Navy Department via the White House, with an assist from Josephus Daniels. Chapel Hill thereupon got the Navy Pre-Flight School for the "East," and Daniels served as chairman of the commissioning exercises in Kenan Stadium in May, 1942. He was a familiar figure in town during the Pre-Flight days, beaming proudly on all hands and oblivious to the ritual muttering of curses among the World War I brass at the sight of "the man who dried up the Navy." He probably got some of them apoplectic with rage at the closing exercises of the School when he boldly declared for unification of the armed forces. The Navy was never far from his mind in those war years and, as he wrote Jonathan in the summer of 1942: "It would run me crazy, the U-boat sinking on this coast, if I were Secretary of the Navy." Unable to sit passively in the

Junaluska resort he went off to the annual Governors' Conference in Asheville, where he and a group including Governor Lehman of New York joined David Lilienthal in a flight over some of the newer dams in the T.V.A. system.[8]

During the war Daniels worried to O. Max Gardner, now in Washington, that President Graham's enemies were behind the effort to set up three "presidents" at the component units of the Consolidated University, that real consolidation precluded multiple "presidents." Gardner, Daniels, and their trustee allies met, at length, with Clarence Poe in the latter's Raleigh office. Instead of letting Charlotte publisher David Clark and the Graham-haters downgrade the President by making him "Chancellor," Gardner unveiled his scheme of providing *three* chancellors under President Graham. Daniels got so tickled and laughed so hard that tears rolled down his face. "Max," he gasped, "I always knew you were smart but not that smart." (Gardner's plan eventually won out among the trustees.)[9]

In this latter period the old editor enthusiastically helped set the stage for the state's Good Health Program that came later, in 1947. *The News and Observer* was early enlisted in the fight that culminated in the proposed rural clinics, the hospitalization for the needy, and expansion of Chapel Hill's two-year Medical School to a four-year unit complete with teaching hospital. Daniels and his friends had to settle first for half a loaf, when the legislature set up machinery to receive any federal funds that might later be forthcoming (as they were, eventually, in the form of Hill-Burton grants), agreed to expand the University's two-year Medical School to four years, but postponed the building of a hospital at Chapel Hill until a Rockefeller Foundation group could survey alternate sites. Characteristically, Daniels wanted to fight against any delay. But President Graham, the Medical School's Dean W. Reece Berryhill and others persuaded him to hold his fire, that any outside survey, would as they saw it, inescapably be led to favor the Chapel Hill site for the teaching hospital (as indeed happened).[10]

Daniels' friendliness to organized labor, particularly his refusal as an employer to be baited by anti-labor propaganda, was marked during the war. He editorialized "Treat All Alike," against a Raleigh speech by H. V. Kaltenborn that Daniels found slanted against labor. Kaltenborn said nothing about American industrialists who had acted in collusion with Nazi patent cartels,

Daniels wrote, and instead advocated nothing newer than that old tax on poverty, the sales tax. Most of the time Daniels acted as labor peacemaker. On one occasion when Dr. Graham asked Trustee permission to negotiate a labor contract with the University's janitors and other unskilled help, he ran into a barrage of opposition. Daniels moved an unprecedented recess for lunch so that all could cool their tempers, and when Graham apparently became convinced that he should resign over a show of no confidence Daniels poured oil on the troubled waters. In January, 1943, A.F.L. Vice-President Matthew Woll came to Raleigh to present a forty-year button to Josephus Daniels in token of his honorary membership in the International Typographical Union. Daniels had been an honorary member since 1889, cited by the I.T.U. as "the only publisher to hold honorary membership in the International Typographical Union," and his paper's longtime cashier, Miss Mary Horton, pinned the forty-year button on the editor's lapel.[11]

Wartime travel restrictions and the demands of his newspaper kept Daniels fairly close to home, but he did manage a few trips. He was in Washington with the American Society of Newspaper Editors in February, 1943, where he joined William Allen White in speaking a kind word for the "journalism of the sticks." On the twelfth he attended a special A.S.N.E. press conference with President Roosevelt, newly returned from Casablanca, who jovially twitted the editors on his having given them the slip. He had not fooled Mrs. Josephus Daniels, he admitted, for she had a virtual sixth sense about such matters and had correctly told her husband that the President must have gone to North Africa. Jonathan Daniels was at the White House, delighted with how well his father looked, and—he reported to his mother—"I wish you could have heard the President . . . telling the story about your gift of intuition and how you found Admiral Fiske's document in the left tail of Father's jim-swinger coat." Miss Addie's sixth sense was then working overtime, because she correctly directed to the city of Monterrey, Mexico, her husband's April telegram of greetings to the U.S. and Mexican Presidents "meeting somewhere."[12]

About this time Jonathan Daniels came to the White House staff via a circuitous route. He had been appointed Minister to New Zealand, but to everyone's great surprise Senator Josiah Bailey made it known that he would oppose confirmation. Superficially, Bailey's motive seemed to be resentment at a jibe at him in Jonathan's book *Tar Heels* (1941), in which political gazetteer the author described Bailey as a man who "struts even when he sits down." President Roosevelt had a good laugh over the contretemps and noted to Secretary Marvin McIntyre that people had said much harder things about FDR than Jonathan had said about Bailey. Meantime Josephus Daniels was shocked and indignant that Bailey, whom he had declined to oppose in 1942 when convinced he could have beaten Bailey, should now act with such "malevolence." The consensus of the Danielses was that Bailey's action was the result of an accumulation of political and personal differences that had animated both families for years. In any case, it took the President less than a week to bypass the Senator's veto with an executive appointment of Jonathan Daniels as a presidential administrative assistant. There was great rejoicing at Wakestone, where his father happily scrawled to Jonathan advice to keep a wartime diary for later publication. If Bailey had been smart, he wrote, the Senator would have confirmed Jonathan and then explained how happy he was to have him as far away as New Zealand. From Mexico City came *Novedades*, which happily identified the new White House aide as son of the beloved Ambassador, better known to his admiring bluejackets of World War I as "Tio Joe."[13]

Daniels' old Nemesis of oil returned to haunt him in the face of the wartime need for increased petroleum production. The Navy's reserves in the ground were again imperiled, this time by a contract in which Navy Secretary Frank Knox granted Standard Oil of California authority to drill in the Elk Hills Naval Reserve. The contract of November, 1942, was to many people of Daniels' generation a virtual alarm bell in the night, a dread reminder of Denby, Doheny, Sinclair, and Fall. Six months later the Congress began to investigate and found that the Justice Department had never sanctioned the agreement. Norman M. Littell, Assistant Attorney General, followed up with a searching memorandum in which he branded the Navy's explanations as "incredibly naïve" and the whole transaction a "shell game." During June, 1943, Daniels kept the mails busy with letters to such key people as Kent Cooper of the A.P., urging more intensive news coverage of the dispute, and to Drew Pearson, putting that columnist on the alert. To James F. Byrnes, then head of the Office of War Mobilization, Daniels conveyed the warning that the contract would impair confidence in the war effort. Knox ought to have more sense than to have even considered the lease. . . . My experience in the last war was that ninety per cent of the 'dollar-a-year' men were working for their corporations and not for Uncle Sam." When confronted with accumulated evidence of open irregularity, including opinions from Littell and Comptroller General Lindsay C. Warren, Secretary Knox voided the contract and Daniels rejoiced. His editorial, "Should be Knighted," paid tribute to Littell, "whose wisdom and courage compelled the annulment of the illegal, invalid and indefensible lease of the Naval oil reserves in California to the Standard Oil Co."[14]

But a working agreement went on between the Navy Department and Standard Oil of California. Littell sent Daniels a memo about it, hoping through him to get action from the President. Daniels did write the President on July 7, not only warning him of the arrangement but of its possible dangerous effect on election issues next year, and Roosevelt replied: "I think you are absolutely right. The whole thing is stopped in California." But the whole thing was not stopped in California. Daniels quoted to White House aide Jonathan a letter he had gotten from the House Public Lands Committee to the effect that that group was stymied in its effort to probe the "working agreement." Jonathan reported, in reply, a talk he had had with Adlai Stevenson, then Special Assistant to Secretary Knox, who insisted that the Navy was trying to keep its reserves and that the real danger lay in any possible transfer of them to the Interior Department. Now Admiral H. A. Stuart wrote his old chief along the same lines, whereupon Daniels expressed surprise that the officer who had fought the Teapot Dome battle with him should now make a "truce with the bear." A new contract was reached in the months ahead and the still-suspicious Daniels considered it almost as bad as the earlier one. He wrote the President repeatedly, preferring to go into condemnation proceedings rather than into co-partnership with the oil company, citing arguments put forward by Congressmen Carl Vinson of Georgia and Jerry Voorhis of California. But the wartime need for oil, plus suitable safeguards for the Naval Oil Reserves, argued for the new contract. President Roosevelt was in the main exquisitely patient with his old chief, reassuring him that there would be no Teapot Dome scandal and no corruption. Replied Daniels to the President: "I hope you are right, but I 'hae me doots.'"[15]

The Office of War Information was only one of many wartime agencies that the old Democratic partisan felt to be overweighted with Republicans. He confided to Mark Ethridge of the Louisville *Courier-Journal* his unhappiness with a switch in O.W.I. domestic directors; Gardner Cowles had resigned to work more closely with Wendell Willkie only to be replaced by a Pacific Coast Republican. (This was E. Palmer Hoyt, then of the Portland *Oregonian,* and by no means as die-hard a Republican as Daniels a Democrat.) To fellow-Democrat Bernard Baruch, Daniels fretted that the nation had not listened to Edison about synthetic rubber before World War II any more than it had listened to Woodrow Wilson about winning the peace after World War I. Baruch's sitting out the war on the sidelines (he had not supported Roosevelt in 1940) struck Daniels as another waste. "He is a fine man. I love him very much," the old editor confided to Jonathan of Baruch, "and I wish he had a little less money and [was] a little more liberal." A really "backslidden" liberal to the old editor was George Creel, who had disappointed him by accepting a position in the Almazán election campaign in Mexico. "He told me the last time he saw me that he had cancelled his contract with Collier's [Magazine] because he could not write what they wanted. "I see he has now capitulated." But he kept up his correspondence with Ambassador Claude Bowers, who was extremely critical of his successor (Carleton J. H. Hayes) for his open approval of Spanish Dictator Franco. The old editor sent Bowers' letters along to Jonathan, adding of their countrymen: "We held the clothes of Franco while he was stoning the prophets."[16]

"Stoning the Prophets" was the title of a "Rhamkatte Roaster" the old editor had written in 1942 when Norris of Nebraska lost his Senate seat to Kenneth S. Wherry. Daniels sent his column to the President. A progressive, liberal Republican of the Norris stamp had become a contradiction in terms, Daniels mourned, and he observed that Nebraska had produced only two great men (Norris and Bryan) since statehood, and had stoned both prophets. He elaborated on this theme in the obituary editorial he wrote on Norris' death two years later. Keeping his eyes glued to Washington like a hawk, Daniels probed anxiously into the reported rift between Cordell Hull and Sumner Welles, and Daniels was not sure he approved when E. R. Stettinius, Jr., was later appointed to replace Welles as Under Secretary. Stettinius nevertheless thanked

Daniels for commenting editorially on his appointment, whereupon the old editor confided to Jonathan: "Mr. S. is a real diplomat." Jonathan had written earlier that the editorial might have been kinder if Editor Daniels had known that Stettinius had "the same trouble that you have" (hemmorhoids). The old editor was inclined to agree: "I sympathize deeply with Mr. Stettinius because sitting on a red hot stove is not any pleasure." He wasted no time in informing Stettinius that ex-King Carol, now furnished with a press agent, was again seeking entry to the United States and that the country was better off without such discredited ex-royalty. He was even more indignant when a young F.B.I. agent came in to see him in search of wartime stenographers for that government agency. "I asked him how old he was," Daniels reported, "and he said 25 years and looked strong and vigorous. I told him he ought to be ashamed of himself."[17]

Son Jonathan kept his father informed about U.S.–Latin American affairs, especially through canvassing them with Nelson A. Rockefeller, then Co-ordinator of Latin-American Affairs. When Rockefeller addressed a panel discussion, "The Future of Pan-American Relations," without mentioning the Good Neighbor Policy, and said that good relations would continue no matter who was the next President, Daniels was already sniffing out a future Rockefeller career in politics. Elsewhere in Latin America Juan Domingo Perón was later elected President of Argentina, and Daniels pointed the old lesson of Latin resentment against even the appearance of outside interference. Perón had been allowed to oversimplify the election issues, Daniels editorialized, into a choice between himself and Spruille Braden, the former U.S. Ambassador in Buenos Aires who had boldly charged the Argentine regime with ties to the Nazis. Braden's charges were probably true enough, Daniels wrote, but Braden and his superiors should have known that Latins will not stand for even the hint of outside interference. Daniels' own wartime lines of communication with Latins were maintained through a steady stream of such visitors to Wakestone as Mexico's Foreign Minister Padilla and Ambassador Castillo Nájera.[18]

The University of North Carolina was celebrating its Sesquicentennial in 1943, and Josephus Daniels was there on University Day—October 12—when Miss Addie's illness relented just long enough. He described for Jonathan the pageantry by which the

cornerstone-laying of Old East building was re-enacted in the costumes of 1793, the speech-making, the luncheon at President
Graham's. But all was not well at Chapel Hill, where the Pre-
Flight School now overshadowed the University, where Dr. Graham
was spending more and more time in Washington as member of
the War Labor Board, and where a postwar renovation would be
very much in order. As always Daniels was the stout arm that did
battle for Frank Graham, for Daniels considered him more valuable
in Chapel Hill than anywhere else. In the early months of the
war Daniels had said no when it was suggested by W. Kerr Scott,
then State Agriculture Commissioner, that they back Graham for
U.S. Secretary of Labor. "There is a very good reason," Daniels
wrote. "It is that we cannot spare him as President of the University. He is more valuable there than he could be in any other place,
though I quite agree with you that he would make an ideal officer
in any position." With the removal of Daniels' restraining hand,
the late Governor Scott did appoint Graham to the U.S. Senate
only to have him defeated in a McCarthy-style smear campaign.[19]

In 1943 Miss Addie was living the life of a shut-in, persistently
brave in the face of a fast-weakening heart. She had gotten used
to the radio news commentaries of Cedric Foster, and timed "Mr.
Daniels'" lunches so they could both listen. Foster and Daniels
had exchanged letters in which it came out that Foster had the
Navy Secretary's autograph of a quarter-century before, still legible.
Daniels' surgeon friend, Dr. Hubert A. Royster, snorted: "There
never was a worse handwriting in the world, if it was well done it
was a forgery." The bluff bantering tones did not conceal the
gloom as Miss Addie suffered the first of a series of heart attacks
that summer. Son Worth, now stationed at Fort Bragg, was on
hand and warned of a probable recurrence. In August, Daniels
wrote Jonathan about Miss Addie: "She rules the roost and knows
every seed that goes into the ground, every ear of corn and every
tomato that grows, and keeps her telephone going pretty strong.
Her right arm gets plenty of exercise, as David [Admiral Bagley,
her younger brother] wrote her. She is like Mrs. Blodgett, a character in Paul Leicester Ford's novel, 'persistently thoughtful and
affectionately domineering,' but it is always for the good of others."
Later that month the old editor's trouble with hemmorhoids kept
him home from the office, where he reported eating "good lamb
chops, and rice, and spoon bread and milk, and I am living like a

king!" He was concerned that he was a great burden on Miss Addie, who would insist on coming to his room and looking after him. Son Jonathan meanwhile cheered his parents by delving into the Worth family genealogy and teasing them with findings that kinsman Aaron Worth of Indiana was a Republican, but with the saving qualities of adhering to Methodism and prohibition. There was a respite in Miss Addie's illness during September so that Daniels could go to Fort Bragg and greet the Chinese Ambassador whom he had personally invited to the nearby town of Dunn.[20]

The old editor took to staying with his sick wife every afternoon, writing his editorials morning and night. Of the servants in the house he reported: "They are very good, but I try to make it easier for her by reading and talking to her." Miss Addie herself wrote to Jonathan, quoting his father: "'I always long to know what Lucy and Jonathan are doing on Saturday night.'" By December Miss Addie was barely clinging to life, and Daniels quoted her words to their son, Worth: "I would not be sorry to go. I'd be more sorry for your father than for myself." On December 18 Daniels wrote a longhand note to President Roosevelt, home safely from Teheran and Cairo, of "your great adventure for victory and peace." Daniels would run to Washington, but "my dear wife is very, very ill, and I am living anxious and fearful days." Miss Addie died on the next day. In her last days, occasionally delirious, she called out for Ana María, her maid of the Mexico City days. Otherwise she insisted on talking frankly with her husband, telling him she wanted him to keep on living at Wakestone just as though she was there. She made the servants, and especially Spurgeon Fields, promise to stay with Mr. Daniels all his life and to leave his souvenirs and papers undisturbed. Her last conscious thought was of her husband, to whom she turned and murmured, "I love you dearly." Robert McGregor, to whom Daniels described Miss Addie's last days, was on hand at Wakestone representing the State Department, and this "Aztec" (as the Mexico City Staffers called themselves) described the scene in a letter home:

> When I got to the house Joe Jr. told me that Mr. Daniels was waiting and anxious to see me. He was upstairs in the sitting room, and family and close friends were gathered downstairs. I found the "Chief" his grand old self; composed and deeply grateful for all the messages that were being received and with none more than those from Mexico which I

later translated: Camacho, Padilla, Torres Bodet, Beteta, Or-
tiz Rubio, Portes Gil, Suarez, Aleman, etc. He also was so
touched with the one that the messengers and former servants in the Residence sent. . . . When he said goodbye he
was just a little saddened but I came away with the feeling
that his faith plus his memory of Mrs. Daniels' desires for
him will sustain him for some years to come.²¹

That Christmas was the dreariest one that Daniels had ever
known. He took what little comfort he could from the great out-
pouring of consolatory messages. Acknowledging one to Dr. Thurman D. Kitchin, Daniels recalled that his anti-war brother Claude
had, in his mortal illness, told Daniels he would still recover and
work to make Miss Addie Governor of North Carolina because
"she'd make a better Governor that you would." President Roosevelt sent a consolatory telegram, particularly asked Jonathan
whether his mother had been in great pain, and sent word that he
wanted his old chief to come up and visit him. Mrs. Roosevelt
remembered Miss Addie in her "My Day" syndicated column: "No
one could have been kinder to young people than she was to us
when Mr. Daniels was Secretary of the Navy and my husband's
chief in Washington. . . . She gave out a great deal to those around
her and I think she was always the tactful and unifying influence
which someone must be in every big family." Shortly after the
turn of the new year Daniels sent a congratulatory wire to Miss
Addie's brother David on his wartime promotion to Vice-Admiral,
assuring him that he had gladdened his sister's last days by ful-
filling her fond ambition for him. To all his sons the old father
wrote, as he did to Frank:

> I am sure as long as you live you will cherish almost the
> last words of your dear mother and be true to her wise coun-
> sel: "Love is the only thing worth while in the world. I want
> you boys to love one another and stick together, and take
> care of your father." I know you will always be true to that
> last admonition. . . . You, my dear boy, have no enemies, and
> our family is unified by the only cement that holds—the love
> your mother spoke of when the lights were low in the world
> before passing to the Better Land—but each of us will do
> well to bear in mind her counsel if ever tempted not to love
> each other and stick together.²²

When the old editor received from the *Saturday Evening Post*
Miss Addie's memoir articles published after World War I, he re-

joiced to Jonathan at "the best day I have had since your mother's going made this house little more than an empty shell." As a labor of love Daniels assembled and edited Miss Addie's memoirs, had them privately published later as *Recollections of a Cabinet Minister's Wife,* and sent autographed copies "only for those she esteemed." On his first May 2 "wedding day" without Miss Addie, Daniels wrote nostalgically to Jonathan: "This is a beautiful day, just such a day as your mother and I were married on May 2, 1888." A few months later the Liberty Ship *Addie Bagley Daniels* was launched at Savannah, and the father described the scene to son Worth, now with the Army in New Guinea:

> Your mother—exactly 44 years ago—had gone to Bath, Maine, to christen the first of three destroyers named for your uncle Worth Bagley. It moved me to see that another ship with the name "Bagley" was to be christened. . . . In a very brief talk I said if it be given to those who have gone before to know what transpires in this sphere, no honor so dear to your mother's heart could have pleased her more. You know how true that was. I think she loved the Navy better than either of her Navy brothers. . . . I knew all this would have interest and sacredness to you and your brothers and all the family, and that is why I am writing of a day and an event that made me wish to cry and rejoice.[23]

For his "daughters," Daniels copied out—working on his memoirs—the details of what Miss Addie had worn the night of the banquet and reception for the Prince of Wales in 1919. "I can see your mother's radiance," he wrote, "as she charmed all who came within the circle of her grace and beauty." In sending a copy of Miss Addie's privately published memoir to Lady Nancy Astor, he joked in addressing her as "Dear Fellow Southerner" and assured her that "I am still your companion on the water wagon," but referred somberly to Miss Addie: "I am living without her radiance." After her death Daniels could never mention Miss Addie's name without his eyes filling with tears. As he told Cedric Foster: "When Addie Worth Daniels died my heart went with her. But I am finishing out my life in the knowledge that one day we will be together again and that is all I wait for."[24]

The "Aztecs" did their best to enhearten Daniels, and he enjoyed their hospitality in Washington the following April. The Foreign Service hands entertained him and themselves by digging up an old State Department dossier, which portrayed some amusing wool-gathering that went on during Daniels' Cabinet days. A minion of Secretary of State Bryan had sent an invitation to the nonexistent Swiss Navy to attend the celebration set to mark the opening of the Panama Canal. The contemporary press had had a great deal of fun with Secretaries Bryan and Daniels at the time, and it all made nostalgic reading now—in the midst of a Second World War—of a celebration that had been canceled because of the outbreak of the First. But the "Aztecs" had to play second fiddle to the old editor's real mission in Washington, as it was every year around that time, which was to attend the annual meeting of the American Society of Newspaper Editors. In the first postwar A.S.N.E. meeting, Daniels was to be instrumental in getting the Society to postpone what he considered a too-hasty approval of the State Department's take-over of the functions of the O.W.I.[25]

Like the oil Nemesis, another echo of the past—the Bishop Cannon controversy of the early thirties—came back clamoring for Daniels' attention. One day he had a caller named Harry Golden. In those days, long before he had won fame by writing *Only in America,* Golden did much traveling to make financial ends meet, and on that occasion he bore an invitation for Daniels to speak at a Zionist meeting. The old editor was charmed by Harry Golden, and he began making a rule of inviting the younger man to his home. About the third meeting, Golden recalled, he felt compellel to reveal the secret of his prison record to his host. Golden was concerned lest Daniels hear the story from someone else, that it might then be taken as a reflection on Jews generally. He identified himself as that Harry Goldhurst who had conducted the stock speculations for Daniels' intramural Methodist foeman, Bishop James Cannon, Jr. Did it now make any difference to Josephus Daniels? Not in the slightest. He gave a great peal of laughter, patted Harry Golden on the back, and never revealed his secret. It was that old feudist, Carter Glass, now anticlimactically rounding out his career in the U.S. Senate, who had warred on the Bishop for political reasons. Such old political warfare was dead for Josephus Daniels, who was far more concerned with the political shape of the future.[26]

With the nomination of Roosevelt a foregone conclusion in 1944, Daniels began the year by making a characteristic closing-ranks plea to fellow-Democrat Jim Farley (to no avail). There was, like Farley's, a scattering of protest votes against the Fourth

Term nomination, but the real excitement at the Chicago Convention centered on what many Democratic insiders correctly took to be the presidential succession. Daniels personally was for the old ticket of Roosevelt and Wallace and in the previous December had met Wallace in Raleigh. He had tendered Wallace a breakfast attended by Governor Broughton and others and had gone over to Chapel Hill where the Vice-President addressed the Carolina Political Union. At the State Convention, with the word from Washington that there would be no White House preference, the Tar Heels instructed their delegation (including Daniels as perennial delegate-at-large) to support Governor Broughton. Daniels thought highly enough of Broughton to stay aloof from the Wallace-Truman contest at Chicago, where he found a coalition of city bosses and Southerners arrayed against his old visitor at the Avila Camacho inauguration in Mexico. The city leaders, distrusting Wallace's liberalism, argued that the nomination would cost the ticket several states; the Southerners, still smarting from the last time when Wallace was given the nomination over Bankhead, joined in on the fight against the "one-time Republican." In his heart Daniels wanted Wallace to win, but he was quite content with Senator Truman, whose yeoman efforts to expose profiteering in war contracts he especially admired. Daniels recalled of the Vice-presidential fight: "But the sores, if concealed, remained, and stories galore of how Roosevelt had promised Byrnes the nomination, had wanted Wallace, had suggested Douglas, encouraged Rayburn, said Broughton or Pepper would be agreeable . . . under cover worked overtime. Only the Roosevelt wave kept it under the surface, but some scars were never healed."[27]

The old editor was "chaperoned" at Chicago by Mr. and Mrs. Jonathan Daniels, who had an adjoining room on the twenty-third floor of the Stevens. One hot July evening, while Jonathan and his wife took an excursion on Lake Michigan, Daniels enjoyed the cool breeze in their parlor overlooking the lake. "I had a number of visitors and so had a nice evening," he wrote home to son Frank. "So I was free to do as I pleased, except to keep the promises made." His work on the Platform Committee and the renewal of old political ties were too much fun to miss, and indeed Daniels outlived the doctor who was about to order the old editor home because of a slightly twisted foot. Kent Cooper of the A.P. relied on Daniels for getting the Democratic platform to include a plank regarding world-wide freedom of the press (Cooper proposed the same to the Republicans), which the eighty-two-year-old editor zealously saw adopted. Daniels also helped defeat the efforts of resurgent Southerners who wanted to restore the two-thirds rule that they had once wielded as a veto in national conventions. At a Convention press conference at which Daniels voiced his support for Governor Broughton, he pointed out that a North Carolinian would face fewer embarrassing questions than aspirants from the deeper South; that the Tar Heel state had had no poll tax for twenty-four years, that it paid white and Negro school teachers equal salaries, and that generally his state was the most progressive in the South.[28]

The "white supremacy" plank sought by the Dixie delegates in 1944, foreshadowing the walk-out four years later, found no friend in Josephus Daniels. On getting back to Raleigh he told the Kiwanis Club that this minority, with its threat of a bolt, had rendered a disservice to the South. He knew, too, that antiliberal elements were again using the Negro issue as a mask for reaction, confiding to a friend: "The more the reactionaries fight him the bigger will be F.D.R.'s majority." To be sure, Daniels reminded his Kiwanis audience, some Northern Negro Democrats were unhappy at not securing all their platform demands, but had they not quit the Republican party long before and with cause? Besides, he reassured his neighbors, the Vice-presidential nomination went—in the face of threats that no Southerner should get it—to a "Southern Senator whose father was a Confederate soldier." The sought-for white supremacy plank was championed by men who in 1944 stood about where Daniels had stood in the white supremacy days nearly a half-century before. He now openly regretted the anti-Negro excesses he had encouraged in his paper, and he was now widely sought—as the foremost among friendly white Southerners—as a speaker in Negro churches and colleges. For example, he was invited to introduce Under Secretary of State Sumner Welles at a wartime Commencement at the North Carolina College for Negroes in Durham (on that trip Welles had the grace to credit Daniels for cordial U.S.-Mexican relations, which his own course in Cuba would have undone).[29]

It would be inaccurate to describe Daniels as a race relations liberal in the context of the civil rights struggle that followed the climactic Supreme Court school desegregation decision. But although

he often fretted that his son Jonathan was too advanced in his
racial attitudes, the old editor seems to have been deeply troubled
privately by the racial malaise of his native South. A former resident of Raleigh recalled Josephus Daniels' confiding to him that
"the Negro is helpless and his case is hopeless," except that the
South would never be the same after enough Negroes acquired an
education and insistently pressed for their rights. Two years later
Daniels got radio news commentator Cedric Foster to come to
Raleigh on behalf of the campaign for the (Negro) Shaw University Development Drive. At Wakestone after the dinner, Foster recalled talking alone with Daniels until near midnight,

> . . . discussing the negro question and the problems raised
> in desegregation. For at least two hours he poured out his
> heart from his liberal point of view. Then suddenly he pulled
> out his watch, looked at it in surprise at the lateness of the
> hour and then said abruptly: "Cedric, I never discuss the
> negro question. I never discuss it." He smiled as he said this.
> Despite the fact that he had discussed it for several hours
> I followed through with the query he must have known was
> coming, one that he had, indeed, invited.
> "Why is that, Mr. Daniels?"
> He said, with a somber, clouded face and no trace of a
> smile: "The answer, sir, is simple. There is no solution, Cedric.
> There is no solution. Time to go to bed."[39]

The 1944 motion picture "Wilson" (Tar Heel actor Sidney
Blackmer portrayed Josephus Daniels) served as a virtual reminder
that Daniels must redouble his efforts to help his country avoid
repeating the tragedy of 1919. Of the motion picture itself, the
premiere of which he attended in New York, he conceded that
"some of the things detract from dignity—but dignity is the bunk.
People had rather have a little love than all the dignity in the
world." Shortly thereafter, his testimony was given to the House
Judiciary Committee on behalf of a proposed constitutional amendment to permit ratification of treaties by a majority vote of both
houses of Congress. Another ghostly echo came in the premature
flashing of the World War II German armistice. Daniels protested
the ensuing punishment of the A.P. for ignoring the news blackout,
holding that Edward Kennedy of the A.P. was no more guilty of
wrongdoing now than was Roy Howard in 1918.[31]

Before the war was over, Daniels testified in Washington against
peacetime compulsory military service. To the Select House Com-

mittee on Postwar Military Policy, Daniels argued that the draft propaganda was based on the false premises of fear, cynicism, and imperialism, and that volunteers would fill military quotas if the armed services were made sufficiently attractive. He asserted that the Nazi victories had been achieved by air superiority, by mechanization, by advanced technology—not by conscription. Like Roosevelt, Daniels counted the absence of Russia a fatal flaw in the World War I peace-making effort and, again like him, would have made almost any concession to forestall the already looming Cold War. Thus it was that Daniels did not appreciate Winston Churchill's historic "iron curtain" speech later at Fulton, Missouri. The old editor agreed there was menace in Soviet imperialistic communism, but the United Nations was now the proper world forum for discussion "without the rattling of sabers which echoed through Mr. Churchill's address." Instead, Daniels turned to a personally more grateful postwar concern, federal aid to education, and urged North Carolina's Graham A. Barden of the House Committee on Education and Labor to start the ball rolling. He used on Barden the only argument that had a chance of arousing Southern Congressional support: "Those who criticize us for being backward ought to remember that the obligation of educating the Negro is a National one."[32]

The old editor's long working hours in those years never imposed added strain because he made sure to get plenty of sleep. His indignation was of the moral type only, for it would be hard to find Daniels' superior for equable personal relationships. His journalistic slogan was: "Righteous wrath is as essential to editorial influence as keen interest in all that goes on in the world." With Daniels on the job there was always a plenitude of copy for the editorial page, as he busily went through the exchange newspapers with the scissors he always kept in his pocket. He was a great one for turning out copy, writing so voluminously—without editing— that he would regularly scribble at one sitting enough editorials to fill two or three editorial pages. Deciphering what he had written was another matter. Only Will Alford, composing room foreman; Jim Hayes, Daniels' "personal" linotype operator; and Fleet Williams, his editorial page colleague—in that order—could decipher his script. With the Rhamkatte Roaster and its dialect, only Jim Hayes could cope, but Roasters and editorials continued to pour out on every conceivable wartime subject.[33]

Early in the war Daniels decried talk about the "Yellow Peril" as applied to the Japanese, denied that fighters for their country must also be haters, fought against unreasonable censorship and the red herring activities of Congressman Martin Dies. Daniels was indignant at General Patton on hearing of the soldier-slapping incident, at loan sharks, at profiteering, and at the services having been caught napping at Pearl Harbor. At the end of the war he was horrified to hear from Atlanta of a revived Ku Klux Klan. A few of his clipped-out "It is To Laugh" editorial page items were somewhat on the racy side, and when questioned about them Daniels said he derived from Justice Holmes this sentiment: "Every gentleman has to have a touch of the vulgar." And when a seventy-two-year-old reader complained that a *News and Observer* story had called him "elderly," Daniels, who was eighty-four at the time, agreed wholeheartedly that his paper had exaggerated.[34]

At Christmas, 1944, with the clouds gathering more quickly now for Franklin Roosevelt than for Daniels, the President gaily wrote: "Dear Chief: You guessed wrong in thinking that neither Eleanor nor I could snatch time to read that personally inscribed copy of your latest book: The Wilson Era—1911 [1910]-1917." Now Daniels was talking of visiting Washington again, which gave his sons a chance to conspire against their father's thriftiness. Frank wrote Jonathan in Washington that their old father would not be persuaded that he badly needed some new clothes, "so will you, Joe, Worth and wives work on him about some new clothes when he is in Washington. . . . You might sell him on getting one suit and being measured for it and just tell the tailor to make three or four more." When the President returned in March from the Yalta Conference looking shockingly worn, Daniels sent him one of his editorials recommending that Roosevelt be accorded a vote of confidence just as Parliament had given one to Churchill. In longhand he scrawled: "They ought to have broken an old precedent. You know I love to smash them and traditions too."[35]

President Roosevelt appointed Jonathan Daniels his Press Secretary on March 24, and on the following day Editor Daniels wrote in longhand to jolly his old Assistant Secretary about his ignorance of Scripture, quoting the plea—with unintended but terrible irony —in Jeremiah 37:20, ". . . do not let me be taken back to the house of the secretary Jonathan, or I shall die there." On the thirtieth Daniels, always ready to twist the British lion's tail, wrote the

President of his concern lest the British Commonwealth acquire undue voting preponderance in the assembly of the planned World Organization (Press Secretary Jonathan marked his father's letter "File"). The President wrote on April 3 to reassure his old chief, who had expressed his concern lest Philippine independence be delayed, adding: "I do wish you could have been in my office the other day when Jonathan was sworn in." On the afternoon of the fatal twelfth of April, author John Gunther was in Raleigh getting from Editor Daniels a precise and comprehensive account of "who runs North Carolina." Gunther recalled: "At almost the exact moment of Roosevelt's death, Daniels started talking about him and about how the three greatest things of life—birth, love, and death— were mysteries beyond control."[36]

After the Roosevelt funeral services in the East Room of the White House, Daniels' noble old face would be a sight that Robert E. Sherwood would never forget. On the train returning the mourners from the Hyde Park burial, Jonathan brought his father into Francis Biddle's compartment where Mr. and Mrs. Ickes, Frank Walker, and Frances Perkins were exchanging memories of FDR. There was some liquor in evidence, but Editor Daniels said he did not mind if they didn't care about poisoning themselves, and then—Biddle recalled—"we laughed and joked and felt more normal." There was what amounted to a funeral wake aboard that train, Reporter Frank Kluckhohn recalled, with many Roosevelt people lamenting the death of their ambitions even more than that of their Chief. "The one sincere mourner, to me," Kluckhohn recalled, "was Mr. Daniels who invited me into his compartment and then burst into tears in talking about 'Franklin' and what a 'fine boy' he had been. The tears streamed down his face and I was most touched."[37]

Despite the pall cast by Roosevelt's death, the Woodrow Wilson Foundation decided not to call off its scheduled dedication of the Woodrow Wilson House. So on the seventeenth Daniels was there in New York addressing the assemblage about the many parallels between Franklin Roosevelt and Wilson, and presenting to Mrs. Woodrow Wilson the keys to the edifice. Daniels had greeted Navy Secretary James V. Forrestal at the East Room services and commiserated with him over the coming demobilization and its pressures. Later in the month Forrestal dined with three ex-Secretaries of the Navy, Charles Francis Adams, Charles Edison, and Josephus

Daniels. Forrestal recorded in his diary of Daniels: "I offered him a glass of sherry before dinner but he said that so far as he was concerned General Order No. 99 was still in effect. However, at the end of the dinner, he did drink a toast to the memory of President Roosevelt."[38]

It is some measure of the love that Daniels bore Franklin Roosevelt that when the President died the Old Man lay on his bed all day and sobbed his heart out just as he had done when Miss Addie died.[39]

Coda

"Coda. 1. Music. A concluding passage, the function of which is to bring a composition . . . to a cogent and well-proportioned close. . . ." *Webster's New International Dictionary*, 2nd Edition.

During 1947, the last full calendar year of his life, the Old Man of *The News and Observer* stayed busier than ever. Son Jonathan, now returned from Washington, contented himself with supervising the news columns while his father stayed in full control of editorial policies. Callers would always find him in his office with the door open, but they had to settle for a no-nonsense reception. Their conversational gambits, while returned, would not interrupt Josephus Daniels' scribbling away at copy or snipping items from newspapers, which he tossed over his shoulder like the movie image of Henry VIII discarding so many gnawed chicken bones. As he wrote by day so did he read by night. Time had begun to blunt the edge of his loneliness at Wakestone, and he padded around the great house alone except for the servants. At least one of them was supposed to "sleep in," but the Old Man would often give them all a night off and sit up reading—always without spectacles—into the wee hours.

He lived within hailing distance of his three Raleigh sons. After 5:00 P.M. the old teetotaler would say to his visitors, by that time dying for a drink, "Don't you want to go down to see the boys?" (meaning his non-teetotaling sons). Of the grandchildren Adelaide was something of a favorite, apparently because of her name. The Old Man spoiled them all, but Adelaide got most of the rides downtown with Grandfather and played most games of stop-light baseball (three red lights retired the side, and the winner—meaning Adelaide—got a dollar). The grandchildren would come in to see the patriarch, wondering to see him there alone, a smallish rotund figure with the scarred forehead, the stiffened left hand, the archaic clothes, and his white hair. Seeing him eating alone at the end of the big table, the youngsters were apt to overrate his loneliness and underrate his excellent digestion. He would eat almost anything while away from home, but stayed in training by eating his invariable supper of two lamb chops and two pieces of extra-hard toast. The toast at the Hay-Adams House, where he stayed when in Washington, was never crisp enough to suit him. One day he got his cook to prepare a brick-hard sample, which he proceeded to seal in an envelope and mail to the hotel. The Old man was—and was not—lonely at Wakestone, where he sometimes rather courted solitude. On the other hand, "If you aren't seen," he chortled in explanation of his almost compulsive traveling, "people will think you're dead."[1]

He was happily going off to Mexico again at the end of 1946, but before going he left with Jonathan one intimation of mortality —a list of last requests, not really a will, in case anything should happen to him. First on the Old Man's list was "a simple present for every member of The News and Observer family each might wish to keep." Next was a reminder to continue to help Spurgeon Fields pay for his house, as Miss Addie had wished. The Methodist Orphanage deserved continued help, he wrote, as did the crippled James Robinson Daniels. The Old Man hoped—his was not the dead hand to guide the living spirit— that *The News and Observer* would remain in the Daniels family. As to the disposition of material things the Old Man expressed preferences, not commands; Jonathan to keep his father's books and papers, the family to get first choice of the Mexican souvenirs, and the future of Wakestone itself he commended to "your sound judgment."[2]

On the first day of 1947 the Old Man sent his thank-you notes to ex-Presidents Cárdenas and Avila Camacho, who had entertained him in Mexico City during the previous month. His return there for the inauguration of Miguel Alemán was a triumph during which he was almost smothered with affectionate *abrazos* as he again appeared with Stephen Aguirre, whom the State Department considerately detailed as his old chief's escort. The Old Man revealed in the whirl of that week-long fiesta that is a Mexican inauguration, and regretted only that "I tried to do in one week what I should have done in one month." He was not too busy, however, to bring back six silver loving cups in his baggage. He had been asked by his state's Society of Mayflower Descendants to seek out sources of (but not to buy) silver trophies then unobtainable in the shortages-plagued States. Recent winners of the Mayflower Cup, a best-book-of-the-year award, had been given fifty-dollar checks in lieu of the customary miniature replicas of the big Mayflower Cup. The Old Man had refused to accept his check when his first volume of *The Wilson Era* won the award a year before, and now he had triumphantly brought back his own trophy from Mexico.[3]

His editorial correspondence from Mexico City spoke of the crowded days full of ceremony, parades, processions, operas, illuminations, and historical pageants. His brief chats with old friends kept him in the capital city, and the time was all too brief "to enable me to revisit many places which had in other days given friendly welcome." He would have been glad to visit more of Mexico, as indeed he jokingly applied to Foreign Minister Torres Bodet for an Ambassadorial assignment to the Utopia of Sir Thomas More. Torres Bodet avowed he would like to go himself, as did General Jonathan Wainwright, the hero of Bataan and Corregidor, who was also present for the inaugural.[4]

Daniels told his Tar Heel readers, with satisfaction, that Mexico was inaugurating in Alemán its first non-general since the twenties. He also enjoyed the innovation, which he had seen inaugurated six years before, of having all living ex-Presidents attend the inauguration. The Old Man was happy in being something of a good-luck charm for Alemán, too, because he had been present at Alemán's installation as Governor of Veracruz, as Minister of Gobernación, and now as President of the Republic. But the Old Man was happiest, as always, in people. "It heartened me," he wrote, "to foregather with literally hundreds of old friendly associates and partake of a hospitality which I always called Mexican and Southern and to recall the happy days spent in that beautiful country." He further recorded of his visit:

At a reception in the American Embassy, where I had spent nearly nine years, when greeted with kisses by lovely senoras and senoritas and lady friends from the United States and other countries, Ambassador Walter P. Thurston asked "How do you rate all this lipstick? The ladies do not accord these honors to me."

My answer was "These ladies are very discriminating. They do not give their favors except to very young and very handsome men. You do not qualify."

Life truly begins at seventy![5]

"Life Begins at Seventy" was, in fact, the title of the latest volume of memoirs on which the Old Man was embarked now that the manuscript of *Shirt-Sleeve Diplomat,* his Mexican memoir, was in press. He busily queried Senators Robert F. Wagner, Claude D. Pepper, and former Senator Bennett Champ Clark about their recollections of the stormy Platform Committee sessions at the 1940 Democratic national convention. He set researchers the task of determining exactly how North Carolina voted in all of the presidential elections since Washington's time. Just as there would always be an unfinished memoir at hand, so would there always be plans for the future. Four years before Daniels had gaily replied to Stephen Aguirre's request for information about his prospective biography: "There will be time enough to do this about 20 years from now when I begin to get old." But after once again visiting Mexico, the Old Man sent Jonathan a $1,000 check (never cashed) with the message: "When I pass on to rejoin your mother in the better land, you may wish to write a biography of the 'Congenital Non-Conformist Crusader.'" But 'non-conformist' Josephus Daniels never left himself time enough to feel tired, and Mexico—rejuvenator of his old age—continued to figure in his looking to the future.[6]

That last trip to Mexico included a visit to the American School in Mexico City, and the result was a written plea, accompanied by blueprints and photographs of the school, seeking an old friend's intercession with the Rockefeller Foundation on behalf of a grant. Always ready to put things educational first, Daniels had visited the school "and was impressed with its magnitude and its possibilities." As always, Daniels read widely about Mexico and never ceased yearning to go back. During 1947 he reviewed for his paper Sylvanus Morley's authoritative *The Ancient Maya,* Frances Toor's collected *Treasury of Mexican Folkways,* and Hudson

Strode's travel account, *Now in Mexico*. "You cannot follow Dr. Strode," the Old Man wrote, "without a yearning to trek the scenes he makes real to you."[7]

When President Truman journeyed to Mexico that March, the old Good Neighbor ambassador applauded editorially. And when President Alemán arrived in Washington the following month on a return visit, one of the first persons he greeted—and with an *abrazo* —on alighting from his plane was Josephus Daniels. Invited to Washington by President Truman, the Old Man rode in the motorcade to the White House where he was a dinner guest. On the next morning he was at the Mexican Embassy reception, where he had his picture taken with President Alemán and Mrs. Woodrow Wilson, taking luncheon later at the Pan-American Union. With so much of Mexico in his blood, Daniels could ignore—if, indeed, he was aware of it in the first place—a slighting comment in a *Saturday Evening Post* article. In the course of an otherwise unexceptionable piece explaining to American readers "Why Mexicans Don't Like You," the point was made that a certain "well-meaning statesman" (undoubtedly Josephus Daniels) had once mistakenly applauded a Mexican senator's anti-American speech through his inability to understand Spanish. Instantly taking up for Daniels was William H. Lander, former U.P. bureau chief in Mexico City, who informed the *Post* editor first, that the "incident" was far from the dramatic or significant episode portrayed in his pages, and second, that the magazine was unfairly disparaging the man who had given real meaning to the Good Neighbor Policy. Himself fluent in Spanish, Lander told the *Post* editor: "Linguists often make good doormen."[8]

The year 1947 dawned gray with the disappointment it was to bring to an anxious humanity, dismayed at the scope of rebuilding a ruined Europe in the context of a worsening Cold War. Daniels could express his unease in private; in public he was the invincible optimist. The New Year was bringing a biennial session of the legislature, a new session of the Republican-controlled Congress, a general meeting of the University trustees where President Graham increasingly needed Daniels' help against hostile critics. Like the old war horse, which Daniels called himself after Job's description, the Tar Heel Editor sniffed the battle from afar and shouted among the trumpets, Ha, Ha. Winter might chill the bones of other old men, but this one had work to do and causes to champion. His

Rhamkatte Roaster column on New Year's day set forth his resolutions for 1947: to uphold the United Nations in keeping the peace, to fight for his state's Good Health Program, and, like his fellow-journalist Benjamin Franklin, to do good.

The legislative fight in 1947 was over the critical appropriation that would implement the state's Good Health Program and make it come alive. Josephus Daniels was not minded to see North Carolina backslide. No one attending the legislative hearing on the appropriation failed to mark that the sturdy octogenarian Daniels rose to his feet and quoted the proverb: "He who has health has hope, and he who has hope has everything." When the University's vice-president, W. D. Carmichael, Jr., and Medical School Dean W. Reece Berryhill drafted editorial ammunition for the Old Man, they noted how invariably he blue-penciled every qualifier, every "possibly" or "probably." He delighted in the zeal of Kay Kyser, a Tar Heel newly retired from a Hollywood career, who had prevailed on many of his show business friends to lend their names, via recordings for North Carolina radio stations, to the Good Health Program. At a banquet in Greensboro honoring Kyser, Editor Daniels made the introduction with such vigorous enthusiasm that Kyser jokingly avowed that he must repay the kindness by subscribing to *The News and Observer.* Momentarily diverted from the Good Health Program, the Old Man popped to his feet and grinningly announced to one and all: "That will be five dollars!"[9]

Daniels *knew* that good health was the third in that trinity of great advances he would live to see in North Carolina, following upon good roads and good schools. Once again, as in other forward looking measures, the old reformer found himself in some pretty conservative company. If some "spokesmen for privilege" wanted to support the Good Health Program, well and good; for himself, Daniels was giving support to two of his oldest loyalties. The first was to spread opportunity through rural North Carolina, which had received the most dramatic benefit from good schools and good roads. The second was to benefit his beloved University, which he had served as a trustee from 1901, and his equally beloved Frank P. Graham.

It was, in fact, President Graham's supposed need of protection that kept Josephus Daniels at home that winter. He sent Josephus, Jr., off to Minneapolis in his stead and deputed him to read the Old Man's speech of tribute at the Thomas A. Edison Centennial

celebration there. If the Old Man "could not make the trip," as
press dispatches had it, it was not for any lack of physical vigor.
It was rather that Frank Graham was "in trouble" and Daniels
decided to stay in Raleigh and "protect" him.[10]

In February the trustees gathered in the Hall of the House to
consider an extremist resolution that would (1) forbid a certain
"too-integrationist" professor to continue teaching social anthro-
pology in the University, and (2) return the "pro-Negro" Rosenwald Fund to the Foundation. The Board—providentially composed
of one hundred members so that extremists could be included and
outvoted—arranged for two old white supremacist leaders to reply.
Ex-Governor Cameron Morrison, age seventy-seven, opened the defense of President Graham, and was joined by Josephus Daniels,
age eighty-four. One anti-Graham specification had it that his
dangerous faculty colleague had urged some Greensboro residents
to write their friends in Georgia in support of Eugene Talmadge's
opponents. Josephus Daniels replied with some warmth about Talmadge: "He tried to make a political machine out of the University
of Georgia." That was a damning indictment in the Old Man's
eyes as was the entire proposal that "could not only hinder the
freedom of our University but"—and here he emphasized what he
considered self-evidently despicable treatment of his old World
War I colleague Julius Rosenwald—"it would be Jew-baiting." The
pending resolution was beaten decisively.[11]

Daniels was virtually the only businessman in the state who
would come forward with a kind word for organized labor that
February of 1947. At issue was the enactment (successful) of a
"Right to Work" bill as a foreshadowing of the Taft-Hartley Act.
Daniels fought a dogged rear-guard battle, for he was virtually
the only "respectable" prolabor spokesman in the state. His opening salvo rang out against the bill as a misnomer and a cloak for
antiunionism. "Elimination of the closed shop," he then warned,
"will not create a single job." When University Trustee Daniels
and President Graham threw their personal weight against the bill,
the two crusaders were roundly cheered by the union members
who crowded the chamber in trying to create an impression of labor
militancy and strength. However vain the effort before a business-
oriented group of legislators, Daniels gave it all he had. He warned
the committeemen not thus to inflame state politics by setting class
against class, and he added: "For more than fifty years I have

operated with the closed shop. No one ever made The News and Observer have a closed shop."[12]

As the fight intensified, the Old Man felt it time to invoke his personal credo, Jefferson's equal rights to all and special privilege to none. Wherein lay the special privilege? Daniels listed for his readers the then twenty-one special state licensing boards, all self-regulating, and empowered by the state to "exclude all not desired by the closed membership," ranging from accountants to photographers and barbers. Either abolish these boards, he argued, or forbear from making the closed shop illegal. Otherwise the "Right to Work" bill would divide people into two classes, "the preferred class of employers and white collar men and the inferior class of workers who labor with their hands."[13] Now Daniels did not labor with his hands and could not, in fact, drive a nail. His father did labor with his hands, however, and Josephus Daniels—in his consistent support for organized labor—never allowed himself to forget it.

Another legislative defeat, not unexpected, came in the Old Man's lifelong concern to extirpate the liquor evil. More a personal teetotaler than prohibitionist, he was nevertheless so emotionally involved in the question that the distinction often lacked clarity. The legislators were, as usual, under strong pressure from the Allied Church League to provide a statewide referendum on the liquor question, the assumption being that such a statewide canvass would result in a Dry majority. Most legislators covertly gave the proposal the silent treatment, while the veto-less governor made a brave show of prodding the reluctant lawmakers. Daniels was all for the Allied Church League, against the local option system that bred A.B.C. stores ("Alcohol Brutalizes Consumers," in Daniels' phrase). But Daniels would not dream of imperiling his cherished Good Health Program, so he wrote little and late upon the issue of a statewide liquor referendum. "We will not end drunkenness and drunken driving," he warned at long last, "until we have a state system as to alcoholic beverages."[14] By that time, however, the Good Health Program was out of danger, and the liquor question could no longer divide the progressive forces.

A Republican Congress was in session, and such occasions found Daniels alert for fancied mischief. This time he became far more exercised at the action of the U.S. Supreme Court which did violence, as he saw it, to his cherished principle of church-state separation. It was "The Camel's Nose Under the Tent," as his editorial proclaimed it, this decision to permit the use of tax monies to provide transportation to parochial schools. It was wrong, Daniels maintained, because "it is the heaviest blow at public education that has been struck in all the years where it has been the strength and hope of democratic governments." To Senator Lister Hill the Old Man wrote a hot letter in criticism of Hill's fellow-Alabamian, Justice Hugo L. Black. Daniels found it hard to understand Black's siding with the majority in the Ewing decision, for it constituted a "dagger thrust at the heart of the separation of church and state and the American public school system."[15]

A senatorial confirmation battle was underway, too, this involving the appointment of David E. Lilienthal to be Chairman of the Atomic Energy Commission. Daniels did what he could—and it was considerable—on Lilienthal's behalf, writing editorials and pressing senators. In one instance he wrote his state's Senator Clyde R. Hoey and reminded him that many Jewish leaders would resent the anti-Semitic overtones of the Lilienthal fight just as they had in the fight to confirm Justice Louis D. Brandeis. The Old Man's analysis of the dispute conveys a good sample of the shrewdness that made him a political virtuoso. "My opinion," he wrote a friend, "is that the fight on Lilienthal was stressed by some Senators . . . to serve notice on Truman that he must not appoint anybody but reactionaries to office if he expected to get them confirmed. . . . They are running true to the 1918 form, and, if history repeats itself (though I think that old saying is a lie), we will have another Harding in 1948."[16]

The Old Man duly congratulated his state's Representative John H. Kerr on winning approval for the Bugg's Island Dam that would control the Roanoke River, but his main congressional contact was his fellow Tar Heel octegenarian, Robert L. Doughton. As a long-time chairman of the House Ways and Means Committee, "Muley Bob" was now in minority opposition, and as the session opened he got a suggestion from Daniels. Let the record show, this graybeard wrote to the other, that the history of the graduated income tax is a mark of credit in the Democratic party. Daniels later wrote Doughton anxiously about the Reed-Bulwinkle Bill, which he saw as an aggravated instance of the Republican–Southern Democratic championship of privilege. The bill in question would exempt railroads from the antitrust laws so far as to permit them to fix freight rates by agreement. "It is the worst bill that has been mentioned in Congress since the Harding complete surrender to monopoly. . . . Can't you induce him [Rep. Alfred L. Bulwinkle of North Carolina] to withdraw?" The editor also wrote the budget-minded Congressman that the then-astronomical defense budget of $11.2 billion was indefensible in peacetime. As to the political rumblings about Doughton's retirement, Daniels bade him not to commit himself and, in any case, to stay put.[17]

Yes, Daniels assured his old friend, Judge Abram L. Elkus of New York, he was still actively managing the editorial policy of *The News and Observer.* "Plenty of work helps to keep up the zest of youth. Of course, I have made many mistakes but, being a good Methodist (he jollied his Jewish friend), I have reserved the right to fall from grace and get up again." That good health was all the more striking by contrast with the obituary editorials he wrote for his friends. The most dramatic loss was that of ex-Governor O. Max Gardner, who died on the eve of his departure to his new ambassadorial post in London. Another loss was marked in the obituary editorial on March 11 for Mrs. Carrie Chapman Catt, the woman's suffrage pioneer, to whom Daniels had only recently sent a telegram on her eighty-eighth birthday. Closer home he initialed his "J.D." on a black-bordered editorial on the death of Leroy Alford, the beloved Uncle Jimmie of Daniels' newspaper family. Alford had been the Old Man's back-shop associate of nearly sixty years, beginning on the *Wilson Advance,* and the Old Man sorrowed: "I truly feel the loss of a brother beloved." Nevertheless, his contemplating the deaths of old friends had a way of inspiriting him too. What he remembered of Edison on the centennial of his birth was that "he always had the heart of a boy." And what if Max Gardner, a younger man than Daniels, had worked himself to death? The Old Man wrote: "I would not live and be happy unless I exerted myself most of the time, but I am always careful to get enough sleep and enough rest; therefore I expect to celebrate my one hundredth birthday."[18]

To be sure, the usually buoyant Daniels was oppressed by the failure to adjust differences between the Powers, by the burden of European reconstruction falling to America's lot. To Fiorello H. LaGuardia, now a radio commentator whose death Daniels would lament later in the year, the Old Man wrote in approval of of his commentary opposing military men in civilian positions. The resignation of Secretary of State James F. Byrnes early in the year puzzled the troubled Daniels, who appreciated Byrnes's abilities. The editor was a great admirer of Byrnes's successor, General George C. Marshall, but did not like the affront to the Jeffersonian principle of civilian supremacy. Still the Old Man was in good heart as winter passed into the hopeful spring. He was writing book reviews and scribbling away at "Life Begins at Seventy." He had enthusiastically reviewed for the paper, among other books, Editor Ellery Sedgwick's autobiography, Brandeis' biography by Alpheus T. Mason, and a monograph on the history of prohibition in North Carolina. For "Life Begins at Seventy" he wrote nothing less than "My Confession of Faith."

> If I were asked what term would best describe my faith and action throughout my life my reply would be that I am a congenital Non-conformist. If I had lived in England I would have opposed the established church, gone to jail with John Bunyan, emigrated to America with Joseph Gales, and gone to Wesleyan meeting houses—not so much because I accepted all their beliefs (though I was at least a fellow traveler with them) but chiefly because I have always herded with those men and women who refused to conform in dress and opinions and have demanded to live my own life, select my own dress regardless of fashion, express my own convictions—often not in line with the majority—and have refused to be regimented in thought, word, or action. I have been and hope always to belong always to the company of Dissenters who at first were given that name as a term of reproach.[19]

There was much in the anxious spring of 1947 to give pause to the self-styled Dissenter. The unprecedented American response to the Cold War threat made Daniels more than a little uneasy, and not only the irresponsible calls for preventive war; but also the loyalty investigation of all federal employees, the Truman Doctrine of military aid to Greece and Turkey, the imminent enactment of universal military training. As he viewed these developments in the context of domestic reaction, Daniels clung grimly to the patriotism that had seen him through other dark days, the patriotism of Stephen Decatur's "Our country, right or wrong!" In addition to Decatur the Old Man added Franklin Roosevelt, who wrote, on the night before he died, "The work, my friends, is peace." Daniels wrapped it up in a letter to his old Wilsonian comrade,

James W. Gerard, and the old patriot signed himself, "Sincerely yours in the spirit of Decatur."[20]

Unlike many publishers, Daniels did not invoke a Decatur-like doggedness when the American press came under criticism. In fact, he greeted the principal contemporary criticism with his editorial called "Bias of the Press." In it he expressed agreement with Dr. Robert M. Hutchins and his colleagues who had, in *A Free and Responsible Press,* called for a greater measure of press responsibility. Although that report was received in some journalistic quarters with much asperity and bitterness, it called forth from Daniels: "The report truly points out that 'the bias of owners' who have large incomes, is responsible for the loss of influence of the press . . . [and] endangers the position of the press as 'the tocsin of the people.' "[21] The Old Man preferred to act his own tocsin, not to hire syndicated columnists to sound his alarm bell. He said as much when he got to Washington when the milder weather at the end of the legislative session permitted his attendance at that year's meeting of the American Society of Newspaper Editors.

On being recognized by the session chairman, Virginius Dabney, as "a grand old gentleman who gets younger every year," the Old Man rose from his front row seat and avowed that newspaper columnists flourish and proliferate because editors are lazy. For himself Daniels published only the columns written by Mrs. Eleanor Roosevelt, because of who she was, and by Drew Pearson, because a publisher could not dispense with Washington gossip. The editors were somehow warmed and cheered to have Josephus Daniels there, "the dean of newspaper editors in America," full of the old twinkle and radiance. The charm was even more noticeable when the editors converged on the White House, where everybody from the President down delighted to do him honor. The Negro servants greeted him warmly, and the Old Man remembered them too and shook their hands with his usual easy unaffectedness. Ever mindful of his readers back home, Daniels wrote a column from Washington entitled "Health and Education." On the one hand he was inquiring into chances of the Hill-Burton Act, upon which his state's Good Health appropriation of ten million dollars was contingent. On the other, he spoke up for federal aid to education and cited Senator Robert A. Taft and Walter Lippmann in its support.[22]

On such trips to Washington, the Old Man would ride up front with chauffeur Spurgeon Fields, who would drive at the fast clip that Daniels enjoyed. When the Old Man tired, Fields would stop and put him on the back seat of "Miss Addie's 1942 Buick," helping him out of enough clothing for a comfortable "Sy-estah." On longer trips the Old Man went by train, and the lack of help with his personal needs never stopped him. Nothing could keep him from visiting the U.N. at Lake Success, where he eagerly questioned his host and fellow Tar Heel, Herschel V. Johnson, then alternate American representative to the special General Assembly session on Palestine. Daniels' newspaper column of May 7 from Lake Success was entitled "The Parliament of Man," and— despite his fears for the U.N.'s future—he was his usual energetic and forthright self in print. "It was my good fortune to be here," he wrote from Lake Success, "at the time the interest was centered on Palestine and the promised homeland of the Jews." Always ready to twist the lion's tail, he called on Britain to make good on its Balfour Declaration pledge or stand aside and let the U.N. do so. A Wilsonian mood was upon him when the Old Man attended a meeting of the Woodrow Wilson Foundation in New York, where he recalled that the group had been organized twenty-five years ago in the resolve that Wilson's vision of a successful world organization should not vanish from the earth.[23]

He was back home for his eighty-fifth birthday. It was almost as if the Old Man had contrived to be absent from the great empty Wakestone earlier in the month. May 2 was his wedding anniversary, and the idea of spending such a day at Wakestone without Miss Addie probably spurred his going. But May 18, his birthday, was something else again. Newspapers all over the country published Drew Pearson's "Washington Merry-Go-Round" of that day, one long tribute to Josephus Daniels. Said Pearson: "When the last surviving member of the Woodrow Wilson cabinet achieves the lusty age of 85, and when on that birthday he still writes a daily editorial and keeps his sense of humor and his same sane philosophy of life, and when he is just as great an inspiration to his neighbors and to his family and the nation as Josephus Daniels—then that's news." The Old Man twinkled his gray eyes at the young reporters who came to interview him, laughing gaily as they took down his every word. How did he feel? "I feel as well as I did when I played first base and captained the Wilson Swiftfoot baseball team when a boy." What about retirement? "When I retire it will be in six feet of ground." What about "Life Begins at Seventy?" "After that," he mused, "I may turn out volume No. 7. Maybe we can call it "How it Feels to Be a Centenarian."[24]

Shirt-Sleeve Diplomat, the Old Man's fifth volume of memoirs, was newly published and reviewed by George Creel in *The News and Observer* of June 1. Creel was enthusiastic about the ambassadorial role played by Daniels in Mexico and likened him to Benjamin Franklin in France. The Old Man's historical interest was engaged, at the time, by Mrs. Lyman A. Cotten, a North Carolina friend from his Navy days. She was having trouble convincing a naval researcher that John Paul Jones really got his surname from the Jeffersonian disciple, Willie Jones, of Halifax, North Carolina. "There is a cult," the Old Man complained to her, "that declines to accept anything about the early history of North Carolina which is not documented in the English Archives or in the Congressional Library in Washington. This is true not only about John Paul Jones coming to North Carolina, and about the Mecklenburg Declaration of Independence being signed on May 20th [1775] at Charlotte, but about a dozen other incidents that give glory to the state."[25]

But Josephus Daniels was never long for the backward glance. On the first of June chauffeur Spurgeon Fields had driven him to Lake Junaluska, where the Old Man appeared in his familiar role as principal speaker for Haywood County (N.C.) Day, the opening of the Methodist summer season at the mountain resort. To some three thousand in the audience Daniels made an anxious plea for world peace, in the course of which he bade President Truman hold fast to the Atlantic Charter and Stalin to abandon his U.N. vetoing of all constructive proposals. The speaker told of the American Indian who asked, after having been taught the Ten Commandments, why the white man had not become better after so many centuries' exposure to holy writ. Back in Raleigh, Daniels stood before the young women graduates of Peace College to introduce Congresswoman Helen Gahagan Douglas. Appearing at Peace was a labor of love to the Old Man, for Miss Addie had been an alumna of the college. Mrs. Douglas rose to the occasion to say of him: "Mr. Daniels has managed to stay young, despite his years, because he has never stopped studying."[26]

"Studying war no more" was in fact the theme that helped bind Daniels to Henry A. Wallace during those uncertain days after

Wallace had been dropped from the Cabinet and was serving as editor of *The New Republic*. Daniels had written admiringly of the former Vice-President that spring on reviewing *The Wallaces of Iowa*. After Wallace's sensational speech of April 12 in Manchester, England, in which he blasted the Truman policy as imperialistic, Daniels wrote an editorial critical of Wallace. Still, the editor wrote, Winston Churchill had also erred in making his provacative "iron curtain" speech, and Churchill had no more right to call Wallace "a crypto-Communist" than Daniels would have to call Churchill "an imperial Fascist." Besides, to Daniels, Churchill was an imperialist sinner beyond redemption, while Wallace was still proclaiming his loyalty to the Democratic party and its ideals.[27]

The Wallace Crusade of Peace was then on the road as the former Vice-President's attempt to feel the public pulse. His forthcoming speech in Raleigh's Memorial Auditorium was sponsored by the Southern Conference for Human Welfare, suspect in respectable Southern quarters, and the speech was to be made to an unsegregated audience. Not only did Josephus Daniels bespeak a kind reception for Wallace in a welcoming editorial, but he insisted that the visitor stay at Wakestone as his personal guest. The burden of Wallace's speechmaking (he also spoke at the University in Chapel Hill) was that the Truman Doctrine was dangerously warlike. But Wallace's most newsworthy remark came at a morning press conference during which he said that he would not support President Truman in 1948. The whole episode was painfully embarrassing to the Old Man, this former Vice-President virtually bolting the Democratic party while his house guest. The Old Man's editorial, entitled "An Iowa 'Idee,'" spoke in whimsical embarrassment of Wallace's "idee" (antimilitaristic) being too nonconformist nowadays to contend against the prevailing "idee" (a reactionary and Republican-controlled Congress). Not a word did the Old Man say in public about Wallace's bolting of Truman; after all, he had not bolted the party as such. Wallace responded in a *New Republic* eulogy of Daniels, saying "if his great voice is heeded there may be a chance to save the Democratic Party."[28]

On the Sunday (June 8) following the Wallace speech, the Old Man was making a speech of his own, this one sponsored by the Allied Church League in an effort to defeat legalization of alcohol in a forthcoming A.B.C. election. The following Saturday the Wets were victorious in Mecklenburg County, despite Daniels' own editorial distress over the "Million Dollar Bribe" (in liquor revenues) dangled before the voters. "Today," he wrote grimly, "the voters of Mecklenburg, directed to vote on A.B.C. joints by the Legislature without any petition from the people, will vote on whether to go into the liquor business."[29] His note of frustration was understandable; the same legislature that gave the silent treatment to the idea of a statewide liquor referendum (presumably Dry) quickly sanctioned an A.B.C. election in an urban county (presumably Wet). His native state's growing urbanization, of which Wet sentiment was only a symptom of changing values, was a development that the Old Man recognized with something of a rueful shake of the head.

Still, his beloved state university stood boldly for what was really best and abiding, and the Old Man took particular satisfaction in that year's commencement award of an honorary degree to Herschel V. Johnson. Himself a University trustee who had happily voted for Johnson's LL.D., Daniels gave a luncheon in Raleigh in honor of this "Aztec" from Charlotte, N.C.[30] The Old Man was not only returning Johnson's hospitality of the previous month at Lake Success but also pointing the younger man to their beloved alma mater and the twilight commencement exercises in the pine-encircled stadium at Chapel Hill. This year's commencement address would be made not by some visitor but by President Graham, and the old survivor of the Class of 1885 was warmed by the anticipation of again seeing his presidential protégé. Too, Herschel Johnson's current role as United States spokesman at the United Nations General Assembly was wholly consonant with Daniels' editorial approval of that recent speech at Harvard in which Secretary of State Marshall enunciated that Marshall Plan of historic import.

As the hot Carolina sun warmed his old bones, Josephus Daniels moved his travel schedule into high gear. Except for Lake Junaluska in the mountains earlier, and the Pinehurst area in the Sandhills, he would concentrate his travels in his beloved home country of Eastern North Carolina. Thousands of his fellow Tar Heels, seeing Spurgeon Fields at the wheel of the Buick or seeing the Old Man wearing his suit-coat despite the heat, could bear witness that he was still very much with them. Daniels roamed his home country as energetically as any Antaeus, renewing his strength by contact with the earth.

First the Old Man entrained for Warm Springs, Georgia,

where FDR's Little White House was to be dedicated as a national shrine on June 25. At Atlanta Ralph McGill of the *Constitution* joined the party and went into the Old Man's Pullman bedroom to pay his respects. The Old Man was struggling into his clothes as best he could, and McGill helped him with the tricky shirt studs, kneeling wordlessly to tie Daniels' high-topped shoes.[31] This was not a day for light banter, but for a serious address by Basil O'Connor and what Daniels described as "an inspiring message from the President," read by White House aide William D. Hassett.[32] But there was something of a consensus among the scores of congressmen, judges, and other state and federal officials that Josephus Daniels somehow stole the show. The nation's newspaper readers could glimpse it in the photograph of the group, including the Old Man, huddled around the chair in which Roosevelt was sitting when stricken. No one's speaking at Warm Springs carried more conviction than that of Daniels, who remembered Franklin Roosevelt as a "beautiful" young man.

He reminded his hearers that, like Roosevelt in the early 1920's, a world also once beautiful "in its purposes for democracy and for peace, was crippled with the paralysis of bitterness at home and abroad." Today, after a terrible second world war, the wartime alliance shattered, our "great and beautiful nation, equipped as no nation ever was for the leadership of mankind, is a cripple. . . . And in a sick world we seem more concerned with contagion than energetic in cure." The Old Man defiantly hammered home his optimistic credo: "We need not be the captive of our fears. Only the already lost can think of our future as besieged. We have more to give than to guard." Was not this faith hard to hold? Yes, and he admitted that to "an old man, who has seen many years, these times seem dark. But this place is lit with courage. Indeed, it is illuminated with faith. At Warm Springs today our task is not to dedicate a shrine, but here and now to rededicate ourselves.[33]

Three days later the Old Man was at Atlantic Beach, N.C., helping his fellow journalists celebrate the seventy-fifth anniversary of the state press association. His rambling editorial correspondence from Carteret County paid tribute to the beauty of the seashore, mentioned many editors by name, and included an irrepressible anti-Republican jibe. It had been jokingly regretted by the Press Association president that on the diamond jubilee a diamond could not be given to each member, "due to war and postwar conditions." A pretext, Daniels hooted in print, "a favorite excuse for everything in these days of soaring prices in spite of the promises of the GOP (Grab Oil Profits) that prices would drop if the OPA were sent into innocuous desuetude."[34]

The seaside trip enabled the Old Man to pay prideful visits to the Marine Corps bases, the Cherry Point Marine Air Station, and the great encampment at Camp Lejeune. In reporting his visit to the former, Daniels recalled North Carolina's pre-eminence as the site of the Wright brothers' first flight. At Camp Lejeune the Old Man waxed especially eloquent. He recalled reviewing, on his previous visit, a drill parade of women Marines headed by the commissioned daughter of General Lejeune, and why were there no women Marines this time? Now he recalled "helping" FDR select the present site on New River, Onslow County.[35] From the Marines, as a crack professional fighting unit, to mass levies raised by conscription, was too extreme a step for the old antimilitarist. Within the week of his visit to the Marine Corps bases, Daniels had joined twenty Americans of national stature, most of them educators or churchmen, in signing a statement opposed to universal military training as part of a disastrous arms race. Along with such signers as Robert M. Hutchins and Senator Edwin C. Johnson of Colorado, Daniels warned against provoking "a titanic showdown conflict" with Russia. On the next day Daniels' additional statement was released to the press by the House Armed Services Committee, to which the Old Man had written characteristically: "If half the cost of the proposed universal conscription (estimated at over $2 billion a year) was appropriated to the public schools, the youth would be far better trained than in any system conducted with the chief emphasis upon training for war."[36]

As alert as ever to injustice wherever he found it, the Old Man was no less decisive for finding it at home. On July 15 *The News and Observer* carried the first story that had appeared in a daily paper, plus Daniels' editorial, about the injustice in the Ahoskie episode. It happened that a young Negro war veteran, who held the winning ticket in the Ahoskie (N.C.) Kiwanis Club's raffle for a $3,200 Cadallic car, was denied the prize. The pretext was that Negroes were barred from the dance at which the drawing (an illegal lottery in the first place) was held, and the result was that a retired physician, who already owned a Cadillac, was awarded the prize. Daniels editorialized: "The Automobile Belongs to the Negro." He wrote: "Here is one case in which, without reflection, a Negro was treated unjustly. . . . The wrong should be righted!" And, after nationwide publicity and direct action by Kiwanis International, the wrong was indeed righted. The young man received a check for $3,200 in lieu of the Cadallac he could not use, and the new president of Kiwanis International (from North Carolina, as it turned out) wrote Daniels in appreciation of the fairness with which he and his newspaper had treated the episode.[37]

Late July and August saw the traveler in action again, first to the Sandhills at the height of the peach harvest there. Chauffeur Spurgeon Fields drove off with the Old Man and four youngsters, three of them Daniels' grandchildren. The good lady who had invited Josephus Daniels for lunch had not bargained for the extra guests—and the Old Man, naturally, had neglected to warn her—so she hurriedly and in dismay suggested that they lunch after first touring the peach orchards. Later, when the grandchildren trooped back, their hands and arms itching mightily from handling peaches, they almost tore apart their hostess' bathroom in their efforts to scrub themselves clean. The Old Man paid no attention, for he was too busy with the details of how things stood in Moore, Montgomery, and Richmond counties. His lengthy editorial correspondence recalled the history of the Yankee immigration, how promotion ads for Sandhills property were placed in New England papers with homesites offered in payment for the ads. The Old Man recalled how James W. Tufts, the Boston soda fountain manufacturer, visited the Sandhills out of curiosity and put the place on the map, buying land, building hotels, and making Pinehurst a winter resort.[38]

The first week in August saw Daniels back in Eastern North Carolina where, at New Bern, he recalled to a group of advertising executives his old hat-in-hand approach to potential advertisers without whom his paper could not have survived. His hat was still off to advertising as an institution, and he took note that the once-adless newspaper, *PM*, recently "was improved in content and interest by its advertising."[39] A few days later he was in tiny LaGrange, N.C., for the eighty-fifth birthday celebration of a younger man, James Yadkin Joyner, the Grand Old Man of North Carolina education and long-time Superintendent of Public Instruction. A page one picture in the August 8 *News and Observer* showed both grand old men on the platform, Daniels presenting the other with a scroll on behalf of Joyner's town, county, and state. On hand were the Governor, both U.S. Senators, Congressman John Kerr, and Dr. Frank P. Graham. The scroll bore the names of Joyner's friends, but that of Daniels led all the rest, being signed: "Josephus Daniels, comrade and friend of three-score years."

Roanoke Island was the scene of a meeting of the University alumni on Saturday, August 16, and the Old Man revealed in the fellowship, in the luncheon talk by Lenoir Chambers of the Norfolk *Virginian-Pilot,* and in the speech by Dr. Graham before that night's performance of Paul Green's *The Lost Colony.* The alumni attended the performance in a body, and if the Old Man ran true to form he must have shed a tear for John Borden and the other vanished colonists. Monday was Virginia Dare Day at Manteo, and there the Roanoke Island Historical Association met and re-elected the Old Man honorary vice-chairman, while he sat and beamed proudly at the principal address made by his son Jonathan. The next day some three hundred Danielses of five generations met in a family reunion on the grounds of the Methodist Church in the island village of Wanchese. With Dr. and Mrs. Graham as guests of honor, the Old Man brought forward a resolution that the next legislature rename Croatan Sound as Daniels Sound. The resolution was adopted with a whooping cheer, and all then fed on ice cream furnished by Josephus Daniels. He also renewed his urgings on Dr. Graham to accept as his "duty" the proffered assignment as U.N. mediator of the dispute between the Netherlands and Indonesia. Dr. Graham did so, a peacemaker after Daniels' own heart.[40]

When he got back to Raleigh, the Old Man took occasion to size up Dwight D. Eisenhower, then president of Columbia University but already the subject of energetic political speculation. Daniels had already written in approval of Eisenhower's appointment at Columbia (was it in relief at seeing him out of political contention?), and on the last day of August wrote an admiring editorial, "Come Again, General." Eisenhower had been feted at the Governor's Mansion after making a talk at State College, and Daniels was a shrewdly observant dinner guest. The same editorial page that proclaimed "Come Again, General" carried a Rhamkatte Roaster in which the Old Codger did some political thinking out loud. If the Republicans nominated Eisenhower, he mused, the only way to beat him would be with General Marshall. The Codger didn't like the look of it, for Andy Jackson was the last military leader who had been all for the interest of the common man. At the same time, the Old Man wired the American Legion convention in New York, in regretting his inability to be present, begging the Legionnaires "to pour no oil on the fire of hysterical prophecies of war, but to call a halt to the disturbing war hysteria." Explaining his strategy privately, the Old Man said: "I sensed that all the invited speakers would sing the militarists' tune."[41]

The Old Man's long-standing concern for organized labor came to the fore that Labor Day, which he called "the saddest Labor Day since it was made a holiday." He referred, of course, to the Taft-Hartley Act, which had been passed over President Truman's veto. Shortly before, when the bill first became law, Daniels described the original bill as one intended "to put labor in its place and to take away all the rights labor won under Wilson and Roosevelt." Daniels did not deny that the Senate had amended Taft-Hartley to make it less objectionable, but he labeled it a political move inspired by "supporters of [Thomas E.] Dewey who want to make it appear he is not as much an enemy of labor as [Robert A.] Taft." Thus, the Old Man's Labor Day message was of Labor as People. As People, he said, they were entitled to "just compensation, a voice in working conditions and wages, and collective bargaining. No party or individual can be trusted who wish to see Labor reduced to the old days when it was a commodity."[42]

He had anticipated Labor Day with an editorial prepared in advance, for on that day itself he was in Swan Quarter to take part in Hyde County Farmers' Day. He had invited himself, the Old Man wrote, to do honor to his mother's family, the Seabrooks. It was the counterpart, he felt, to his attendance on the Daniels Day he had created to honor his father's family. While he was at it, the Old Man took the occasion to do some editorial reminiscing about the section he was visiting. He rehearsed the efforts of the wealthy August Heckscher to drain Lake Mattamuskeet until, giving it up as a bad job, he made a present of the lake to the United States for a Wildlife Preserve.[43]

"I am glad to be back on *The News and Observer*," Jonathan Daniels wrote a friend, "but I am only dealing with the news columns. Father is still robustly able to handle the editorial policy. . . . I am constantly amazed at his physical powers." The Old Man was still mourning the deaths of younger men, and wrote an editorial eulogy of Fiorello H. LaGuardia. He recalled that one of LaGuardia's last regrets dealt with "too few men in Washington fighting for the little man." In early October Daniels was in Goldsboro for the opening of a week-long centennial celebration. The Old Man's job—in that town of Aycock, Alderman, his brother Frank, and his mother's last years—was to crown the queen and give the keynote address. He did so, as always with éclat, speaking on "Goldboro's Pauline Revere," the intrepid Mary Hooks Slocumb, whose midnight ride came in 1776 at the Moore's Creek battlefield. The speech was, in a measure, a final bow to the Old Man's feminist sentiments, centering ostensibly on the young centennial queen but in reality on the women who had blessed his long life, his mother and Miss Addie.[44]

That fall nothing gave the Old Man more concern than President Truman's stand on Negro civil rights and the presumed Southern Democratic revolt that it might inspire. The majority recommendations of the President's Committee on Civil Rights— made public that fall—alarmed and offended him. He was concerned not only as a paternalistic white Southerner, not only as a Democrat seeing his party endangered, but also as that kind of progressive who feared that the civil rights remedies might prove more dangerous than the disease. Entrusting the enforcement of civil rights to federal agencies, he fretted, would enhance the kind of government that Alexander Hamilton had envisaged, and besides, since when did federal law enforcement become so effective anyway? (look at the antitrust record). What bothered the Old Man most of all was the scheme to deny federal aid-to-education funds to states that supported segregated schools. It was, he declared, "a proposal which the members know is equivalent to a denial of needed assistance for the children of both races."[45] In 1947, seven years before the U.S. Supreme Court was to speak out, Daniels spoke truly. Experience was to prove, however, that civil rights remedies could be enforced—including school desegregation—and that enforcement would bring eventual acceptance.

"No man who understands the situation," Daniels continued, "and would have better schools for both races, would advocate the policy recommended by a majority of the committee. The report should have printed the names of the members who did not favor giving aid to schools in States whose Constitutions compel separate schools for the races." Daniels' concern was all the more insistent because Dr. Frank P. Graham, a friend of federal aid to education but a signer of the minority report, had to be "protected." He must be portrayed as a Southern moderate and not a sponsor of what the irreconcilables would call "forced race mixing." Daniels' own moderating influence made him reject the suggestion that he now republish the old scare stories, vintage 1901, over Booker T. Washington's taking lunch in the White House with Theodore Roosevelt. The Old Man deplored "the attitude of the [Eugene] Talmadges on the one hand, and the people in Boston on the other hand."[46]

Daniels had no idea of returning to the old implacable white supremacy days, but he quickly published three editorials in support of the old Aycock Negro education policy. In the first Daniels recalled Aycock's insistence that there be no discriminatory racial division of taxes for the public schools as between white and Negro. In his second editorial, "Aycock Charted the Way," the Old Man held Northern opinion mistaken in attributing anti-Negro feeling to the majority of Southern leaders. In his third, he recounted Aycock's favorite speech, that to an audience at the Negro State Fair in 1901: "If you can equal the white race in achievement . . . you will find no generous-hearted white man who will stand in your way, but all of them in the South will insist that you shall accomplish this   high end without social intermingling. And this is well for you; it is well for us; it is necessary for the peace of our section." Like so many men of his generation, the Old Man conceived a phobia against "social intermingling," which he feared must surely follow upon the extension of Negro civil rights. The Old Man's fear of possible civil strife was real enough, for he took the trouble to send tear-sheets to fellow editors and to political leaders like Senator Hoey, to whom he wrote that "the matter is one of great importance and should give us pause and . . . we should speak out plainly."[47]

Putting aside his troubled civil rights concerns, the Old Man went off to the northeastern corner of his state for the annual Methodist Conference, this year held at Elizabeth City (called "Betsy" by old timers like Daniels). He was pleased to see peace and youth dominate the Conference, and he reserved his highest praise for an address on the "World Peace Commission" by the new head of Duke Divinity School, Dr. Howard A. Bosley. As the Old Man's former pastor, Bishop W. W. Peele called on Daniels to address the young ministers who were being received into the

Conference. The great church auditorium and its balcony were jammed to capacity with visitors who saw Daniels, as one witness recalled, "going as smoothly, as efficiently, as impressively as far as this thrilled audience could see." The Old Man reeled off to the young men a list of eight admonitions, each beginning: "Don't be afraid." He caught a ride back to Raleigh with Robert B. House, Chancellor at Chapel Hill, and on the trip along the Roanoke river valley Daniels remained alive to every association, talking tirelessly about such landmarks as the old home of General Matt Ransom. Those Methodists at Elizabeth City evidently felt real confidence in the Old Man's vigor, for they elected him a lay delegate to the General Conference at Atlantic City for the following spring.[48]

Off again, this time to Hyde Park, of which he had been reminded while reviewing a recent book, *Franklin D. Roosevelt's Hyde Park.* The Old Man was on hand for a late buffet lunch, and then Elliott Roosevelt drove his mother and Daniels over to the big house and the grave and the library. The Old Man wanted to see the farm, too, and the party did not get back to Mrs. Eleanor Roosevelt's home until around five o'clock. Mrs. Roosevelt recalled of the Old Man:

> When I asked him if he wanted to rest, his answer was: "Certainly not, my dear. Elliott has just given me this interesting book of Franklin's letters when he was a boy, and I shall sit down right here by the fire and read them." I went to do a little work, but my other guests, Joe and Trude Lash, later told me he read little bits aloud to them and told them stories right up to supper time.
>
> After supper, we started for New York City. Mr. Daniels sat beside Joe Lash, who was driving, and talked to him about politics and the world in general. We left him at his hotel after 10 P.M., quite as chipper as when I had met him early in the afternoon.
>
> The next evening at the Woodrow Wilson Foundation Dinner we met again, and it seemed to me that his speech was one of the best of the evening.[49]

The scene was the Empire Room of the Waldorf-Astoria. The Old Man looked particularly distinguished in tails that night, and took his seat between Mrs. Franklin D. Roosevelt and Mrs. Woodrow Wilson. Some lighthearted speculation, based on the frequency with which the two were thrown together, had given it out that Josephus Daniels might marry Mrs. Wilson. The old editor laughed heartily at that one: "Mrs. Wilson won't give up her name, and I won't give up my freedom." At the Empire Room's head table sat Mrs. Eleanor Wilson McAdoo, daughter of Wilson and widow of William G. McAdoo. The surviving Wilsonians were introduced, and each spoke briefly.[50]

The Old Man rose to his feet in his turn, smiled benignly on members of the Foundation (notwithstanding their often being too conservative for him), and told them: "If it be given to those who have gone before to know what transpires in this sphere I am sure the heart of Woodrow Wilson is gladdened at this hour that the foundation bearing his name has given its highest honor to his dear friend and comrade—Bernard M. Baruch." There is a charming word-picture in Jonathan Daniels' memoir of his father homeward-bound from New York—of the Old Man visiting his brother Charles and having to hurry lest he miss the train, of his switching taxis to escape a traffic jam, of his making directly for Pennsylvania Station and counting on the Hotel Plaza to forward his luggage. The younger Daniels reminisced: "He felt triumphant over time as he boarded the train, an old man without bag or baggage but in high spirits going home."[51]

Back in Raleigh the Old Man's health took a turn for the worse; he caught a bad cold, developed a pain in his back, and suddenly looked frail and failing. He fretted at the absence of Jonathan, who was now in Geneva as the American member of the anti-bias subcommittee of the United Nations Economic and Social Council. So indestructible had his father appeared that Jonathan thought it safe enough to leave on this particular overseas mission. Thus it was that through November the old father impatiently awaited his son's return, and yet when Jonathan debarked at New York in mid-December he got an additional mission from his father. Jonathan was instructed to inspect the artist's model of the proposed statue to the three North Carolina-born Presidents (Polk, Andrew Johnson, and Jackson, the claim to the last-named of whom Josephus Daniels stoutly maintained). The Old Man was a member of the state commission that was planning for this statue (since erected) on Raleigh's Capital Square, and Jonathan duly inspected the model on his way home.[52]

Shortly thereafter, the Freedom Train and its cargo of priceless historical documents was welcomed in Raleigh, and by none more enthusiastically than Josephus Daniels. He gloried, of course, in the original of the Constitution. Still, recalling North Carolina's early refusal to ratify, he wrote: "Without the Bill of Rights, the Constitution was a compass for the mariner, but it was like a body without a soul." Who had inspired the insistence on a Bill of Rights? Jefferson, to be sure, but give due credit to Willie Jones of Halifax. The Old Man, convinced that Willie Jones had conferred his name upon John Paul Jones, was still busy on that tack. He had just recently urged Mrs. Lyman Cotten to write a book entitled "John Paul Jones—the North Carolina Captain." The book "should deal only with his North Carolina affiliations. . . . This is an S.O.S. . . . I never went to Annapolis without uncovering before the tomb of John Paul Jones"[53]

With the Freedom Train enroute to Raleigh, the Old Man planted himself on the front row of the seats in the ballroom of the Hotel Sir Walter for the speech December 5 by Dr. Julian P. Boyd on Daniels' hero Jefferson. Dr. Boyd addressed the State Literary and Historical Association on "Thomas Jefferson and the Police State," the speech being aimed against the spirit that later came to be called McCarthyism. The Old Man beamed and twinkled as he congratulated the speaker afterwards, confiding to Boyd, as an alumnus of Trinity College, that his speech would have caused that old Jefferson-hater Bishop Kilgo to read young Boyd out of meeting. Indeed, *The News and Observer*'s peppery columnist Nell Battle Lewis tried to do much the same thing, but the Old Man— ever tolerant of Miss Lewis, who had turned reactionary with age —wrote his own approval of Dr. Boyd's speech and quoted with relish the specifically "anti-McCarthyism" part of the address.[54]

The Old Man did not even break stride that December. In Richmond, where he had gone to a family wedding that his sons could not attend, he was described: ". . . and the father said, with that famous twinkle in his eye, 'It looks as if I am the only member of this family who is young enough to make this trip.'" On the tenth of the month he was in the Governor's office for his last meeting with the executive committee of the University's Board of Trustees. Josephus Daniels moved, and his motion was approved unanimously, "that the Board proceed, without further delay, to carry out the instructions of the General Assembly of North Carolina in expanding the two-year Medical School into a four-year school, and in building the teaching hospital at Chapel Hill." The eve of the Jewish Sabbath, December 12, saw the long-time Methodist Sunday school teacher, a skull cap on his head and a Zionist message on his lips, exhorting the congregation of the House of Jacob Synagogue in Raleigh. That Friday night was set aside to celebrate the United Nations' recent decision to partition Palestine. Another Christian visitor described the scene: "Mr. Daniels was as much at ease in the Jewish synagogue as he would have been in a church of his own Methodist denomination." In a way he resembled those "beautiful" old men who are the cherished elders of Israel.[55]

During the following week the Old Man was in the nation's capital, eagerly sniffing the political winds, and understandably concerned about Democratic chances in 1948. At a presidential news conference on December 18, the Old Man amusedly learned that President Truman still looked upon him as a dollar-a-year "special adviser." Later he had a personal chat with the President, and emerged to tell newsmen his heartening conviction in Mr. Truman that ultimate world peace would be achieved. "I'm tired of hearing these warmongers," Daniels told the reporters. "They ought to talk about peace. If you talk about war people will think war. If you talk peace they will think peace." He had no doubt that President Truman would compete in 1948, for the Old Man told the National Women's Democratic Club that night: "I am not sure Franklin Roosevelt would not have responded to a fourth encore, and there is not room to doubt Herbert Hoover liked it [the White House] better as a residence than salubrious California's beloved Stanford University, and Harry Truman finds the White House more attractive than Independence, Mo."[56]

That the Old Man was concerned for the solidarity of the Democratic party is borne out by the company he kept. For one of that weekend's luncheons he joined Democratic Senators Hill and Sparkman of Alabama with J. Howard McGrath of Rhode Island, the Democratic national chairman. "In spite of his 85 years," Hill recalled, "he was as vital, as vibrant, as joyous as ever, interested in all about him, concerned with all the momentous events and problems of the world today." He was anxious lest a Deep South revolt wreck the Democratic party in 1948. Lister Hill recalled that Daniels spoke of "how the Republican party, as the instrumentality of the Big Interests of the North and East, had through the imposition of unfair, discriminatory freight rates, unjust taxation, unfair tariffs and financial policies denied the South economic and industrial development." A revolt by the Deep South against the Democratic party would therefore be tragically short-sighted and self-defeating. Mrs. Woodrow Wilson had placed her car at Daniels' disposal while he was in Washington that trip. The Old Man was a little tired, so in Washington's Union Station he announced to the porters, "I'll ride," and boarded a baggage cart on which he rode in style to the train carrying him home.[57]

Daniels had dealt with revolt on the Left as early as his Fourth of July editorial, "Third Party in 1948." After rehearsing the failure of other third party attempts and recalling Wilson's saying that the Democratic party contained 75 per cent liberals, 25 per cent conservatives and the Republicans just the opposite, the Old Man had written: "If it caters to the so-called conservative vote, it [the Democratic party] will invite the same fate that defeated it when it nominated Parker, Davis, and other candidates who received the kiss of death from some of the Big Boys." Party divisions had Daniels worried. In reviewing James F. Byrnes's *Speaking Frankly,* Daniels took note of Byrnes's demand for Wallace's head as the price of his own continued service as Secretary of State. But why, after Wallace had left the Cabinet, had Byrnes resigned in his turn? At year's end came that third party bid that Daniels had foreseen and had tried to anticipate, that of Henry A. Wallace. On December 30 the Old Man wrote of Wallace: "Most of his friends will regret his ill-advised candidacy, which is foredoomed to failure and will lessen his influence."[58]

His editorial, "Christmas, 1947," was a grave plea for peace, and on New Year's Day he quoted Franklin D. Roosevelt: "Let us move forward with strong and active faith." The Rhamkatte Roaster of January 2 carried the Old Codger's "Forecast for 1948." It was not an optimistic one, predicting, among other things, no relief from high prices, continued need for American foreign aid, a continuation of name-calling attacks on political opponents as Communists. Still, the old humor flashed forth. "It bein' Leap Year, the motto ov the gals will be the new look before ye leap." The Old Man had prepared plenty of Rhamkatte Roasters in advance, so that Josephus Daniels' words might appear in *The News and Observer* even as he lay on his deathbed.

At the turn of the New Year, the Old Man caught cold. Thinking, as always, that *The News and Observer* could not possibly go to press without him, he slipped off downtown on a day when the faithful Spurgeon Fields was not around to chauffeur him. Perhaps for the first time in his life the Old Man rode on a city bus, minus his overcoat and with his untied shoelaces trailing. The trip probably accounted for the cold's worsening. He was plainly unwell on Sunday, January 4, and Spurgeon Fields tried to talk him out of going to church. No, the Old Man's mother would have wanted him to go to communion on this first Sunday of the New Year, so he had himself driven to the Edenton Street Methodist Church, where the Old Man established himself in his regular second-row aisle seat and where he sang the good old hymns loudly and out of tune. He stayed in bed most of that day, but got up and dressed for supper which he took with grandson Derick, Dr. Worth's boy, whose last conversation with his grandfather made an indelible impression on him as a fledging journalist.

The next morning the Old Man telephoned son Frank, who usually got the sick calls, to report himself not feeling well. Going to the hospital was out of the question of course, and the Old Man wanted Spurgeon Fields (whom he remembered in his will) close by for those personal attentions that nurses could not properly perform. The Old Man worked in bed, fussing with books and papers, until he became too weak. The cold developed into pneumonia as the doctors stood by helplessly, Dr. Hubert Haywood (son of an earlier family doctor) and the Old Man's son, Dr. Worth B. Daniels, who had hurried in from Washington. The Old Man drifted into a coma, and his bodily functions ceased almost in unison like the breakdown of the wonderful one-hoss shay.

As he lay in a coma on the day of his death, January 15, 1948, his newspaper carried the Old Man's Rhamkatte Roaster in which he warned against bellicose war talk in the press and on the air. "I air a good mind" Daniels wrote as the Old Codger, "to fly to Moscow an' Washington an' Lake Success an' tell those fellers who air ablastin' to recommember that wise saying': 'A soft answer turneth away wrath.'" On that note, having lived a life free of anticlimax, the good man died.

Notes

The following abbreviations are used throughout:

LC   Library of Congress, Washington, D.C.
SHC   Southern Historical Collection, University of North Carolina, Chapel Hill, N.C.
FDR   Franklin D. Roosevelt Papers, Franklin D. Roosevelt Memorial Library, Hyde Park, N.Y.

Initials only will be the rule throughout for the names of Woodrow Wilson, Mr. and Mrs. Franklin D. Roosevelt, Mr. and Mrs. Josephus Daniels, and Mary Cleaves Daniels. *The News and Observer* (Raleigh, N.C.) appears throughout as *News and Observer*.

Chapter One

1. Source for genealogies, Frank A. Daniels, "The Daniels, Seabrook, and Cleaves Families," appendix to Josephus Daniels, *Tar Heel Editor* (Chapel Hill, 1939), pp. 513-24.
2. *Ibid.*, p. 513.
3. A valuable source of material on Josephus Daniels, Sr., in addition to his son's accounts in *Tar Heel Editor*, is the MS "Josephus Daniels, Sr.," which contains notes compiled c. 1928 by Jonathan Daniels, now in the Jonathan Daniels Papers, SHC.
4. Mary Cleaves Daniels, undated statement presumably dictated to another writer, in Charles C. Daniels Papers, SHC.
5. Jonathan Daniels, "Josephus Daniels, Sr." MS, Jonathan Daniels Papers.
6. JD, *Tar Heel Editor*, p. 98.
7. Interview, Mrs. P. L. Woodard, Wilson, N.C., Apr. 19, 1963, who is also the authority on Mary Cleaves Daniels' personal appearance.

8. See also "Josephus Daniels Was Once a Potential Babe Ruth," *Literary Digest*, July 17, 1920, pp. 72-73.

9. Frank A. Daniels to JD, Oct. 15, 1878, Daniels Papers, LC.

10. Josephus Daniels, "Life Begins at Seventy," unpublished memoir, Jonathan Daniels Papers.

11. *Ibid.*

12. JD holograph will, Feb. 13, 1882, Daniels Papers.

13. JD, *Tar Heel Editor*, p. 210.

14. JD to MCD, [late May, 1885], Daniels Papers.

15. See article by Clarence Poe, historian of the Watauga Club, "Club Boosted State Progress," *News and Observer*, May 30, 1954.

16. JD, "Charles Duncan McIver," *News and Observer*, Sept. 23, 1906.

17. JD to MCD, [1886], Daniels Papers.

18. *State Chronicle*, Jan. 14, 1886.

19. JD to MCD, Mar. 22, 1886, Daniels Papers, LC.

20. Robert Menzies, article on JD, *Hickory* (N.C.) *Daily Record*, Jan. 15, 1948; *State Chronicle*, Jan. 26, 1887.

21. JD to Ashe, Sept. 14, 1887, Samuel A'Court Ashe Papers, N.C. Dept. Archives and History, Raleigh; JD, *Tar Heel Editor*, p. 434.

22. JD to MCD, [Sept., 1887], Daniels-Bagley typescript copies, Jonathan Daniels Papers. The aforementioned letter of May, 1887, is in the same place.

23. JD to Addie Worth Bagley, Mar. 27, 1888, *ibid.*

24. Frank A. Daniels to JD, Apr. 13, 1888, Daniels Papers; Worth Bagley to Mrs. JD, May 1, 1890, Bagley Family Papers, SHC; JD to Jonathan Daniels, Jan. 31, 1938, Jonathan Daniels Papers.

25. JD to Mrs. W. H. Bagley, May 8, 1888, Bagley Family Papers; Mrs. W. H. Bagley to Belle Bagley, Sept. 6, 1888, Daniels-Bagley typescript copies, Jonathan Daniels Papers.

26. JD, *Tar Heel Editor*, p. 493; Mrs. W. H. Bagley to Belle Bagley, Nov. 20, 1889, Jan. 22, 1891, Daniels-Bagley typescript copies, Jonathan Daniels Papers.

27. JD to Ransom, Dec. 19, 1888, Matt W. Ransom Papers, SHC.

28. McIver quoted in JD, *Tar Heel Editor*, p. 459.

29. *Ibid.*, pp. 406-9.

30. Worth Bagley to Mrs. JD, May 1, 1890, Bagley Family Papers, SHC; Mrs. W. H. Bagley to JD, June 6, 1891, Daniels-Bagley typescript copies, Jonathan Daniels Papers; Worth Bagley to Mrs. W. H. Bagley, June 14, 1891, Bagley Family Papers.

31. Mrs. W. H. Bagley to Belle Bagley, Apr. 13, 1892, Daniels-Bagley typescript copies, Jonathan Daniels Papers; JD, *Tar Heel Editor*, pp. 436, 489-92.

32. JD to Mrs. JD, [June, 1892], Daniels Papers; JD to MCD, June 18, 1892, Daniels-Bagley typescript copies, Jonathan Daniels Papers.

33. JD to Ransom, Feb. 28, 1893, Ransom Papers, *ibid.*

34. JD to S. L. Patterson, Jan. 31, 1894, Samuel F. Patterson Papers, Duke University Library.

Chapter Two

1. David Worth to Mrs. W. H. Bagley, Dec. 13, 1894, Bagley Family Papers, SHC.

2. MCD to JD, Aug. 6, 1894, Daniels-Bagley typescript copies, Jonathan Daniels Papers, SHC.

3. *News and Observer*, Mar. 6, 1895.

4. *Ibid.*, June 27, 1932; JD to WJB, June 1, 1895, William Jennings Bryan Papers, LC.

5. JD to W. E. Christian, July [10], 1896, Daniels Papers, LC.

6. Josephus Daniels, *Editor in Politics* (Chapel Hill, 1941), p. 192.

7. JD to Mrs. JD, [Sept. 27, 1896], Daniels Papers; placards quoted in JD, *Editor in Politics*, p. 196.

8. JD to Francis B. Lassiter, Oct. 16, 1896, Lassiter Papers, Duke University Library.

9. Quoted in *News and Observer*, Oct. 18, 1896; *Raleigh Gazette*, Oct. 31, 1896; Mrs. W. H. Bagley to Belle Bagley, Nov. 1, 1896, Daniels-Bagley typescript copies, Jonathan Daniels Papers; JD, *Editors in Politics*, p. 199.

10. Recent biographical studies of Bryan give the Commoner full credit for his role in the Progressive Movement. One such study is Lawrence W. Levine, *Defender of the Faith: William Jennings Bryan* (New York, 1965), p. 364. Another is Paolo E. Coletta, *William Jennings Bryan* (Lincoln, Neb., 1964–), pp. 438-45.

11. *News and Observer*, Feb. 10, 1897.

12. *Ibid.*, July 29, 1897, quoted in JD, *Editor in Politics*, p. 225.

13. JD to Marion Butler, Nov. 9, 1896, Marion Butler Papers, SHC.

14. On Ensign Bagley, see JD, *Editor in Politics*, pp. 265-75.

15. Josephus Daniels, "Life Begins at Seventy," unpublished memoir, Jonathan Daniels Papers; *Biblical Recorder*, Oct. 26, 1898; JD, "Life Begins at Seventy" MS.

16. *News and Observer*, Nov. 11, 1898.

17. J. Fred Rippy (ed.), *F. M. Simmons, Statesman of the New South* (Durham, 1936), p. 29.

18. C. Vann Woodward, *Origins of the New South, 1877-1913* (Baton Rouge, 1951), p. 369.

19. JD, *Editor in Politics*, p. 145.

20. JD to Mrs. JD, Sept. 6, 1908, Daniels Papers.

21. Interview, Jonathan Daniels, Raleigh, N.C., Sept. 10, 1959.

22. For additional detail on this period of North Carolina's struggling Progressivism, see: Louis R. Harlan, *Separate and Unequal: Public School Campaigns and Racism in the Southern Seaboard States, 1901-1915* (Chapel Hill, 1958); Oliver H. Orr, Jr., *Charles Brantley Aycock* (Chapel Hill, 1961); Joseph F. Steelman, "The Progressive Era in North Carolina, 1884-1917" (Unpublished Ph.D. dissertation, Department of History, University of North Carolina, 1955).

23. Woodward, *Origins of the New South*, p. 406.

24. H. G. Connor to MCD, June 1, 1904, Bagley Family Papers.

25. See the chapter entitled "Daniels and the John Spencer Bassett Episode," in the writer's *Josephus Daniels Says . . .* (Chapel Hill, 1962), pp. 121-48.

26. Daniels proposes Parker for President, *News and Observer*, Nov. 9, 1902; calls Parker "a dead one" in 1912, JD, "Fifty Years of Attending National Conventions," *ibid.*, July 14, 1944.

27. JD to Mrs. JD, Aug. 22, 1904, Daniels Papers.

28. JD to Mrs. JD, Aug. 31, 1904, *ibid.*

29. John A. Livingstone, article on JD in "Romances of American Journalism" series, *Editor and Publisher*, Nov. 17, 1928, p. 16.

30. JD, "Life Begins at Seventy" MS.

31. *Ibid.*

32. Ensign David W. Bagley followed a lifetime Navy career, fought in both world wars, and retired as an admiral. Brother Henry Bagley generally

played the grasshopper to Brother Joe Daniels' toiling ant. Henry became business manager for *The News and Observer* shortly after the turn of the century.

33. Interviews with the four sons of Josephus Daniels, Raleigh, N.C., month of November, 1962, and Washington, D.C. (Dr. Worth B. Daniels), June 14, 27, 1962.

34. JD to the Misses Bagley, Oct. 7, 1911, Daniels Papers.

35. Interview, Mrs. Mary Cleaves Daniels Stenhouse, Goldsboro, N.C., May 1, 1963.

36. Interviews with the four sons of Josephus Daniels, Raleigh, N.C., month of November, 1962, and Washington, D.C. (Dr. Worth B. Daniels), June 14, 27, 1962.

37. JD to Mrs. JD, Sept. 26, 1908, Daniels Papers.

38. JD to Mrs. JD, Aug. 18, 1908, *ibid.*; JD to Mrs. JD, Oct. 21, 1908, *ibid.*

39. For a monograph that illuminates the political warfare that was fanned to new heights by the South Dakota Bonds controversy, see Robert F. Durden, *Reconstruction Bonds and Twentieth Century Politics* (Durham, 1962).

40. Committee of Engineers to JD, Sept. 3, 1912, *ibid.*

41. To the angry charge by Judge Walter Clark that Daniels had somehow made a deal with Simmons so the editor could remain the state's Democratic national committeeman, the best answer is that Daniels had overwhelming delegate support at the Baltimore Convention of 1912 without any help from Simmons. See the discussion of this point in Morrison, *Josephus Daniels Says. . .* , pp. 272-73.

42. Arthur Walworth, *Woodrow Wilson, American Prophet* (New York, 1958), p. 208, n. 5.

43. Wilson quoted in Josephus Daniels, *The Wilson Era, Years of Peace, 1910-1917* (Chapel Hill, 1955), p. 31.

44. JD, "Wilson and Bryan—What Brought Them Together in 1912 and What Separated Them in 1915," *Saturday Evening Post,* Sept. 5, 1925, p. 48.

45. Mrs. JD to JD, July 14, 1912, Daniels-Bagley typescript copies; JD to Mrs. JD, Sept. 6, 1912, Daniels Papers; JD to Mrs. JD, Nov. 1, 1912, *ibid.*; interview, Jonathan Daniels, Raleigh, N.C., Sept. 10, 1959.

46. JD to William G. McAdoo, Dec. 30, 1912, McAdoo Papers, LC; JD to Henry Watterson, Feb. 4, 1913, Watterson Papers, *ibid.*; Charles Seymour (ed.), *The Intimate Papers of Colonel House* (Boston, 1926), I, 113; JD, *Wilson Era, Years of Peace,* p. 99.

47. WW to JD, Feb. 23, 1913, Daniels Papers; JD to Mrs. W. H. Bagley, Feb. 27, 1913, Bagley Family Papers.

48. JD, *Wilson Era, Years of Peace,* p. 126; Jonathan Daniels, *The End of Innocence* (Philadelphia, 1954), p. 54.

49. Ray Stannard Baker, *Woodrow Wilson, Life and Letters* (Garden City, 1927-39), III, 444.

50. Justice Holmes, quoted in James M. Burns, *Roosevelt: The Lion and the Fox* (New York, 1956), p. 157.

Chapter Three

1. Eleanor Wilson McAdoo, *The Woodrow Wilsons* (New York, 1937), p. 208; Daniel F. Houston, *Eight Years With Wilson's Cabinet* (Garden City, 1926), I, 35.

2. Addie Bagley Daniels (Mrs. JD), *Recollections of a Cabinet Minister's Wife* (Raleigh, 1945), p. 708; Josephus Daniels, *The Wilson Era, Years of Peace* (Chapel Hill, 1944), p. 119.

3. On the biblical citations, JD to WW, April 2, 1914, Daniels Papers, LC; WW quoted, Mrs. JD, *Recollections of a Cabinet Minister's Wife*, p. 27.

4. James Roosevelt, *Affectionately, F.D.R.* (New York, 1959), p. 61; Elliot Roosevelt (ed.), *F.D.R., His Personal Papers, 1905-1928* (New York, 1948), p. 243.

5. On Fiske's insubordination, Innis L. Jenkins, *Josephus Daniels and the Navy Department, 1913-1916*, xerox print of Ph.D. dissertation, University of Maryland, 1960 (University Microfilms, Ann Arbor, Mich.), p. 55. On JD's naval administrative reforms, see this dissertation, *passim*.

6. JD's speech, *News and Observer*, May 20, 1913.

7. Jessie Wilson quoted, Mrs. JD, *Recollections of a Cabinet Minister's Wife*, p. 100.

8. JD on Japanese crisis, JD Diary, LC, May 16, 1913, and JD, *Wilson Era, Years of Peace*, pp. 163-67; Fiske's memoranda, E. David Cronon (ed.), *The Cabinet Diaries of Josephus Daniels, 1913-1921* (Lincoln, Neb., 1963), pp. 54-64; JD on Wood and Fiske, U.S. Congress. Senate. Military Affairs Comm. *Hearings, Dept. of Armed Forces*, 79th Cong., 1st Sess., 1945; TR on JD, quoted, Elting E. Morison (ed.), *The Letters of Theodore Roosevelt* (Cambridge, Mass., 1954), VIII, 846.

9. JD on armor plate subsidy, *New York Times*, May 22, 1913; on Navy oil refinery, *ibid.*, Nov. 13, 1913; Howe quoted, Lela Stiles, *The Man Behind Roosevelt: Louis McHenry Howe* (Cleveland, 1954), p. 46.

10. Donald Day (ed.), *Franklin D. Roosevelt's Own Story*, told in his own words from his private and public letters (Boston, 1951), p. 23; contemporary report, *New York Times*, Aug. 29, 1913.

11. FDR anecdote, Edmund W. Starling, *Starling of the White House* (New York, 1946), p. 82.

12. JD to Louis Graves, undated [1935], Josephus Daniels Papers, SHC.

13. *Men of Erie!, A Message from Hon. Josephus Daniels* (Erie, Pa., YMCA [1913]); on the Seattle disorders, *New York Times*, July 19, 20, 21, Aug. 21, 1913, and JD, *Wilson Era, Years of Peace*, pp. 303-6; JD quoted on woman's suffrage, *Sacramento Bee*, July 26, 1913.

14. Byrd anecdote, JD, *Wilson Era, Years of Peace*, pp. 294-96.

15. U.S. Congress. House. Comm. on Naval Affairs. *Estimates Submitted by Secnav*, 63rd Cong., 2nd Sess., 1914, *passim*.

16. "Bluejackets Ashore and Afloat," *Literary Digest*, May 16, 1914, pp. 1194-1200.

17. JD, *Wilson Era, Years of Peace*, pp. 264-67; on Smith's "Words," Admiral R. L. Conolly reminiscences, Oral History Project No. 365, Columbia University.

18. JD to FDR, Dec. 15, 1938, Daniels Papers, LC; on Navy laundries, JD, *Wilson Era, Years of Peace*, pp. 261-62, and JD to R. S. Grant, Aug. 24, 1943, Daniels Papers.

19. JD quoted, Josephus Daniels, *The Life of Woodrow Wilson* (Philadelphia, 1924), p. 182; casualty figures, JD, *Wilson Era, Years of Peace*, p. 197.

20. Arthur S. Link, *Woodrow Wilson and the Progressive Era, 1910-1917* (New York, 1954), p. 119.

21. WW on Huerta's American backers, JD, Diary-letter, Apr. 16, 1938, Bagley Family Papers, SHC; JD to Ramón Beteta, Apr. 30, 1945, Daniels Papers; JD to FDR, Apr. 19, 1933, *ibid.*; FDR to JD, Nov. 19, 1938, *ibid.*

22. JD to WW, May 28, 1913, Daniels Papers; on anti-contraceptive order, JD to all C.O.'s, "Venereal Disease in the Navy," Feb. 27, 1915, in *Social*

Hygiene, I (1914-15), 480-85; on Port Royal, JD, *Wilson Era, Years of Peace,* p. 324; on Blease's attack, *New York Times,* Apr. 24, 1914.

23. Jonathan Daniels, *The End of Innocence* (Philadelphia, 1954), p. 128.
24. JD, *Wilson Era, Years of Peace,* p. 270.
25. Admiral R. L. Conolly reminiscences, Oral History Project No. 365, Columbia University.
26. JD's honorary degree, *News and Observer,* June 4, 1914.
27. WW quoted on Negro episode, JD to Frank P. Graham, Nov. 5, 1936, copy in Jonathan Daniels Papers, SHC.
28. WW quoted, Ray Stannard Baker (ed.), *Woodrow Wilson, Life and Letters* (Garden City, 1927-39), VI, 15.
29. WW to JD, Dec. 26, 1914, copy in Bagley Family papers and published in Jonathan Daniels, *The End of Innocence,* p. 157, in which he recalls his parents' weeping over Wilson's letter.
30. U.S. Congress. House. Comm. on Naval Affairs. *Estimate Submitted by the Secnav,* 63rd Cong., 3rd Sess., 1914, *passim.*
31. The Carabao dinner occurred on Dec. 11, 1913. The *New York Times* reported JD's displeasure on Dec. 16; WW's directive on a reprimand was sent on Dec. 22.
32. Lodge to TR, Jan. 20, 1915, in H. C. Lodge (ed.), *Selections from the Correspondence of Theodore Roosevelt and Henry Cabot Lodge* (New York, 1925), II, 453.
33. On the Jewish refugees, Alfred Lief, *Brandeis: The Personal History of the American Ideal* (New York, 1936), pp. 324-25, and Josephus Daniels, *The Wilson Era, Years of War and After* (Chapel Hill, 1945), p. 219; on JD's friendship for Jews, J. L. Morrison, "A Southern Philo-Semite: Josephus Daniels of North Carolina," *Judaism,* XII (Winter, 1963), 78-91.
34. WW to JD, Jan. 17, 1915, Daniels Papers; WW quoted in N.Y.C., *New York Times,* May 18, 1915; Edith Bolling Wilson, *My Memoir* (Indianapolis, 1938), p. 66; Mrs. JD, *Recollections of a Cabinet Minister's Wife,* pp. 39, 93-94.
35. FDR quoted in Jonathan Daniels, *The End of Innocence,* p. 172; FDR on Bryan, FDR to Mrs. FDR, June 10, 1915, in E. Roosevelt (ed.), *FDR, His Personal Letters, 1905-1928,* p. 270.
36. Link, *Woodrow Wilson and the Progressive Era,* p. 179.
37. House to JD, Sept. 29, 1915, Daniels Papers; WW to Dunlap, Sept. 15, 1915, copy in Bagley Family Papers.
38. For these and others of JD's administrative reforms, see Jenkins, *Josephus Daniels and the Navy Department, 1913-1916, passim.*
39. JD to Bagley, Dec. 28, 1915, Bagley Family Papers.
40. JD, *Wilson Era, Years of Peace,* p. 454.
41. Mar. 26, 1916.
42. On JD's alleged despondency, Henry Morgenthau, *All in a Life-Time* (Garden City, 1922), p. 235; on JD's marking "no" in Morgenthau's book, Jonathan Daniels, *The End of Innocence,* p. 187; on Colonel's House's cabal, see *ibid.,* p. 188. The suggestion that the second Mrs. Wilson was engaged in an anti-Daniels plot was specifically denied by her, *ibid.,* p. 191; the involvement of Bernard Baruch was specifically denied by him to Jonathan Daniels, May 25, 1953, Jonathan Daniels Papers, SHC.
43. WW to Dodge, undated [late June, 1915], copy in Bagley Family Papers; WW to Dunlap, Sept. 15, 1915, copy in *ibid.*
44. The anecdote is in JD, *Wilson Era, Years of Peace,* pp. 546-47.
45. *U.S. Statutes at Large,* Vol. 39, Pt. 1, p. 618; for JD's role as the Wilson administration's conferee with the House antimilitarists, see JD's

letters to Alex M. Arnett in the latter's *Claude Kitchin and the Wilson War Policies* (Boston, 1937), especially pp. 94-102.

46. JD to WW, May 13, 1916, Daniels Papers.

47. JD urges progressive program on WW, JD to WW, July 17, 1916, Daniels Papers; JD to Bryan, July 8, 1916, *ibid.*

48. On JD in Adlai Stevenson's home, Kenneth S. Davis, *A Prophet in his Own Country* (Garden City, 1957), p. 88.

49. On Edison and Ford, JD, *Wilson Era, Years of Peace*, pp. 464-66; McCormick's account is in Morgenthau's *All in a Life-Time*, p. 243, and he makes Ford the winner of the kicking contest; *New York Times*, Nov. 15, 1916.

50. R. G. Tugwell, *The Democratic Roosevelt* (Garden City, 1957), p. 105.

Chapter Four

1. JD personally dated this Wilson quote in the fall of 1916, JD to Alfred Lief, Feb. 15, 1938, Daniels Papers, LC. A similar JD quote of Wilson seems to refer to the fall of 1914, that being in Ray Stannard Baker, *Woodrow Wilson Life and Letters* (New York, 1927-39), V, 77. However, JD gave Mr. Lief the 1916 date in specific answer to the latter's query about the quotation in Baker's book. JD gave substantially the same quotation to Harry M. Ayers of the Anniston, Alabama, *Star* also indicating the fall of 1916, in a typescript statement, undated, in Mr. Ayer's possession.

2. On meeting of Dec. 6, 1916, F. R. Martin (ed.), *Digest of the Proceedings of the Council of National Defense During the World War* (Washington, 1934), p. 59, hereinafter cited as *Proceedings, C.N.D.*; JD described, *ibid.*, p. 68.

3. JD to Baruch, Apr. 13, 1917, Daniels Papers; W. L. Hill to WW, Dec. 20, 1916, copy in Bagley Family Papers, SHC.

4. David F. Houston, *Eight Years with Wilson's Cabinet* (Garden City, N.Y., 1926), I, 229.

5. WW's conference Feb. 5 with JD and Baker, Newton D. Baker to JD, Mar. 3, 1921, Daniels Papers; JD's quote of WW, R. S. Baker, *Wilson Life and Letters*, VI, 258; the guest list, as approved by the President, is in Mrs. JD, *Recollections of a Cabinet Minister's Wife* (Raleigh, 1945), p. 41, and in WW to JD, Jan. 4, 1917, Daniels Papers.

6. JD in Cabinet Feb. 25, Anne W. Lane and Louise H. Wall (eds.), *The Letters of Franklin K. Lane* (Boston, 1922), pp. 239-40; on Sayville wireless, JD to WW, Feb. 7, WW to JD, Feb. 8, 13, 1917, Daniels Papers; Starling to his mother, quoted in E. W. Starling, *Starling of the White House* (New York, 1946), p. 85.

7. JD to WW, Mar. 9, 1917, Daniels Papers; on security, WW to JD, Mar. 12, 1917, Baker, *Wilson Life and Letters*, VI, 488-89.

8. Arthur Walworth, *Woodrow Wilson, World Prophet* (New York, 1958), p. 85.

9. JD to WW, Mar. 14, 1917, Daniels Papers; JD to Baruch, Mar. 14, 16, 21, 1917, *ibid.*; Fiske quote in New York *World*, McAdoo to JD, Mar. 31, 1917, Daniels Papers; Baruch's testimony, U.S. Senate. *Hearings, Special Comm. Investigating the Munitions Industry*, 1935, 74th Cong., 1st Sess., Part 22, p. 6203.

10. JD at Annapolis, U.S. Senate. *Addresses to the Graduating Class, USNA, Annapolis, Mar. 29, 1917*, 65th Cong., 1st Sess., Doc. No. 58 (Washington, 1917); JD on Apr. 2, Jonathan Daniels, *Frontier on the Potomac* (New York, 1946), p. 3.

11. JD, Apr. 4, 1937, interviewed by John P. McKnight, A.P. Bureau chief, Mexico City, from clipping in Mr. McKnight's possession; JD to Charles A. Weil, Sept. 19, 1938, Daniels Papers.

12. JD to E. Y. Webb, May 14, 1941, *ibid.*

13. JD's popularity, Baker, *Wilson Life and Letters*, VI, 283 n.; JD to Congress, U.S. House Naval Affairs Comm. *Hearings on Estimates Submitted by Secnav, 1917*, 64th Cong., 2nd Sess., pp. 780, 708-9.

14. WW to JD, July 2, 4, 1917, Baker, *Wilson Life and Letters*, VII, 140, 146-47; JD to WW, July 3, 6, 1917, Daniels Papers; on convoying, JD to M. P. Andrews, Mar. 10, 1927, *ibid.*

15. Origin of mine barrage, Baker, *Wilson Life and Letters*, VII, 21, 22 n.; details, U.S. Navy Dept., Office of Naval Records, *The Northern Barrage and Other Mining Activities*, Pubs. No. 2 and 4 (Washington, 1920); FDR to JD, Oct. 29, 1917, in Carroll Kilpatrick (ed.), *Roosevelt and Daniels* (Chapel Hill, 1953), pp. 39-40; FDR to Mrs. FDR, Oct. 29, 1917, in Elliott Roosevelt (ed.), *FDR, His Personal Letters, 1905-1928* (New York, 1948), p. 363; JD, *Our Navy at War* (Washington, 1922), p. 130.

16. FDR to JD, Apr. 1917, Kilpatrick (ed.), *Roosevelt and Daniels*, p. 34; fifty-foot boats, Frank Freidel, *FDR, the Apprenticeship* (Boston, 1952), pp. 311-12.

17. JD quoted, Lela Stiles, *The Man Behind Roosevelt* (Cleveland, 1954), p. 56. Creel quoted, Jonathan Daniels, *The End of Innocence* (Philadelphia, 1954), p. 226; FDR and Churchill, Freidel, *FDR, the Apprenticeship*, pp. 308-10.

18. Margaret L. Coit, *Mr. Baruch* (Boston, 1957), p. 168.

19. On Baruch's purchases, U.S. Senate, *Hearings, Special Comm. Investigating the Munitions Industry, 1935*, 74th Cong., 1st Sess. Part 22, p. 6263; JD to Baruch, June 1, Aug. 27, 1917, Daniels Papers; JD to WW, Baker, *Wilson Life and Letters*, VII, 522; JD to Baruch, Mar. 4, 1918, Daniels Papers.

20. JD's British contract, *New York Times*, Jan. 22, 25, 1917; JD to trade editors, May 26, 1917, *ibid.*; JD to WW, June 18, 1917, Daniels Papers.

21. JD to FDR, Sept. 12, 1940, copy in Jonathan Daniels Papers, SHC; JD to his son Jonathan, Mar. 19, 1941, *ibid.*

22. Swanson's compromise, J. L. Bates, "Josephus Daniels and the Naval Oil Reserves," *U.S. Naval Institute Proceedings*, LXXI (Feb., 1953), p. 174; McNab and Doheny, *Proceedings, C.N.D.*, pp. 212-13; WW to JD, June 18, 1917, in Baker, *Wilson Life and Letters*, VII, 119; JD to WW, June 20, 1917, Daniels Papers.

23. On the C.P.I. see James R. Mock and Cedric Larson, *Words That Won the War* (Princeton, 1939); James R. Mock, *Censorship 1917* (Princeton, 1941); George Creel, *How We Advertised America* (New York, 1920); George Creel, *Rebel at Large* (New York, 1947), pp. 156-208.

24. WW to JD, May 16, 1917, in Baker, *Wilson Life and Letters*, VII, 7; JD to ANPA, "Criticism in Wartime," *Outlook*, May 8, 1918, p. 51; JD and "The Fourth of July Fake," Creel, *How We Advertised America*, pp. 28-44; Oliver Gramling, *AP—The Story of News* (New York, 1940), pp. 265-66; JD, *Wilson Era, Years of War* (Chapel Hill, 1946), pp. 229-30.

25. Pegler to Jonathan Daniels, May (undated) 1954, Jonathan Daniels Papers; Oliver Pilat, *Pegler: Angry Man of the Press* (Boston, 1963), p. 74; Pegler on JD, "As Pegler Sees It," syndicated column in *New York Journal-American*, undated clipping (1948), in files of The News and Observer Publishing Co., Raleigh, N.C.

26. On Burleson, JD, *Wilson Era, Years of War*, p. 224; Connor to JD,

June 18, July 10, July 21, 1917, H. G. Connor Papers, SHC; JD to Connor, July 19, and quotation July 25, 1917, *ibid.*

27. Brisbane episode, Jonathan Daniels, *The End of Innocence*, p. 128; Lowell Thomas, *Old Gimlet Eye* (New York, 1933), pp. 243, 244.

28. WW and partial text of his speech, JD, *Wilson Era, Years of War*, pp. 42-45; David Lawrence, *The True Story of Woodrow Wilson* (New York, 1924), p. 221; Navy League Episode, *New York Times*, Aug. 15-31, 1917, *passim*, and Jan. 9, 1918; Jonathan Daniels, *The End of Innocence*, pp. 239-40.

29. Louis B. Wehle, *Hidden Threads of History* (New York, 1953), pp. 19, 24; JD quoted, *ibid.*, p. 30.

30. Macy appointment, JD to WW, Aug. 24, 1917, Daniels Papers; JD's motion, *Proceedings, C.N.D.*, p. 249; on conscription, *ibid.*, p. 228.

31. JD, *Wilson Era, Years of War*, p. 196; Raymond B. Fosdick, *Chronicle of a Generation* (New York, 1958), pp. 146, 161-63.

32. "Johnny Appleseed of Jazz," New Orleans *Times-Picayune*, reprinted in *News and Observer*, Dec. 31, 1958; Fosdick, *Chronicle of a Generation*, p. 146.

33. JD to Governor R. G. Pleasant, Sept. 24, 1917, Daniels Papers; Behrman to JD, Oct. 1, 1917, *ibid.*; JD to Behrman, Oct. 18, 1917, *ibid.*; JD to Clinical Congress, Oct. 22, 1917, in *Men Must Live Straight If They Would Shoot Straight* (Washington, n.d.), p. 15.

34. JD's exercise, Jonathan Daniels, *The End of Innocence*, pp. 230-31; JD, *Wilson Era, Years of War*, p. 194.

35. On Newport, *New York Times*, June 21, 22, 1917; Mrs. JD, *Recollections of a Cabinet Minister's Wife*, p. 97.

36. On Lehman, Allan Nevins, *Herbert H. Lehman and His Era* (New York, 1963), pp. 57-58; on McGowan, JD to McGowan, Dec. 15, 1920, Samuel McGowan Papers, Duke University Library.

37. Frank Tannenbaum, *Osborne of Sing Sing* (Chapel Hill, 1933), pp. 279-80.

38. Dates of articles: *Outlook*, Mar. 27, 1918; *Public*, June 29, 1918; *Forum*, Sept., 1918; on yeomanettes, JD, *Our Navy at War*, pp. 328-30; JD to Connor, July 5, 1918, Connor Papers.

39. Description of banquet, *Proceedings, C.N.D.*, pp. 216-17; Tardieu quoted in translation from article in *Gringoire*, Paris, by JD in diary-letter, Mar. 19, 1938, Bagley Family Papers.

40. Sunday revivals, Mrs. JD, *Recollections of a Cabinet Minister's Wife*, pp. 18-19; bands for Sunday, W. G. McLoughlin, *Billy Sunday Was His Real Name* (Chicago, 1956), p. 88; on Sousa, JD, "Life Begins at Seventy" MS, Jonathan Daniels Papers.

41. On Sims, WW to JD, Jan. 31, 1918, in Baker, *Wilson Life and Letters*, VII, 514; JD to J. P. Tumulty, Jan. 31, 1918, Daniels Papers.

42. Lodge in the Senate, June 6, 1918, *Cong. Record*, 65th Cong., 2nd Sess., LVI, 7412-14.

43. JD-Baruch correspondence in 1918, especially Baruch to JD, July 22, 1918, Daniels Papers; on Eagle Boats, Norman Beasley, *Knudsen, A Biography* (New York, 1947), pp. 84-85; Allan Nevins and Frank E. Hill, *Ford, Expansion and Challenge, 1915-1933* (New York, 1957), pp. 71 ff.

44. FDR to JD, Apr. 5, 1918, Kilpatrick (ed.), *Roosevelt and Daniels*, pp. 43-44; Howe and New York primaries, Lila Stiles, *The Man Behind Roosevelt* (Cleveland, 1954), p. 64.

45. JD's mother; JD diary, May 18, 19, and July 18, 1918, Daniels Papers; on Garfield, JD, *Wilson Era, Years of War*, p. 243.

46. JD to WW, June 10, 1918, Daniels Papers; WW to JD, June 10, 1918,

ibid.; on White House conference, Howard F. Cline, *The United States and Mexico* (Cambridge, Mass., 1953), p. 187; JD to WW, July 29, 1918, Daniels Papers.

47. JD to Connor, Aug. 5, 1918, Connor Papers; Geddes visit, JD, *Wilson Era, Years of War,* pp. 329-32.

48. JD on false armistice, *ibid.,* pp. 238-43, with Roy Howard's recollection; JD's contemporary rebuke, *New York Times,* Nov. 9, 1918.

49. House to JD, Sept. 11, 1917, Daniels Papers; legislation, JD to WW, Nov. 30, 1917, *ibid.*; JD and Suffrage Amendment, *New York Times,* Jan. 9 and 12, 1918; WW and Texas legislature, WW to Mrs. E. H. Potter, Mar. 8, 1918, copy in Daniels Papers; JD on soldier vote, JD to Newton D. Baker, May 20, 1918, *ibid.*; Weaver's re-election, JD to WW, Oct. 3, WW to JD, Oct. 4, 1918, *ibid.*

50. WW and Ford, Baker, *Wilson Life and Letters,* VIII, 210-11 n.; Ford campaign, Nevins and Hill, *Ford, Expansion and Challenge,* pp. 118-23; JD campaigning, *New York Times,* Oct. 25, 1918.

51. WW's appeal, Oct. 28, 1918, Baker, *Wilson Life and Letters,* VII, 513-14; JD on 1918 election, JD, *Wilson Era, Years of War,* pp. 306-10.

52. JD quoted on G.O.P., Charles Michelson, *The Ghost Talks* (New York, 1944), p. 204; on Newberry, Nevins, and Hill, *Ford, Expansion and Challenge,* pp. 117-23, 300-301; JD on Lodge vs. Wilson, *New York Times,* July 6, 1927, and JD, *Wilson Era, Years of War,* p. 467.

53. Bryan, JD to WW, Nov. 14, and WW to JD, Nov. 16, 1918, Daniels Papers; Thomas A. Bailey, *Woodrow Wilson and the Lost Peace* (New York, 1944), p. 96; JD quoted, *News and Observer,* Apr. 24, 1930.

54. WW to JD, Dec. 7, 1918, Daniels Papers; TR's December meeting with Lodge and Root, Arthur Walworth, *Woodrow Wilson, World Prophet,* p. 209 n.; JD to WW, Mar. 6, 1919, Daniels Papers; WW to JD, Apr. 15, 1919, *ibid.*

Chapter Five

1. JD's speech, "Return to the Promised Land," is in JD, *The Navy and the Nation,* War-Time Addresses (New York, 1919), pp. 257-65; quoted also, with commentary, in JD, *Wilson Era, Years of War* (Chapel Hill, 1946), p. 220; Ukraine pogrom protest, *New York Times,* Nov. 25, 1919.

2. On secret document, see Washington dispatch in *News and Observer,* June 29, 1930. Discussion based on Harold and Margaret Sprout, *Toward a New Order of Sea Power, American Naval Policy and the World Scene, 1918-1922* (Princeton, 1946), pp. 73-85.

3. JD's support of three-year program, *New York Times,* Oct. 23, Nov. 21, Nov. 26, Dec. 31, 1918; JD to WW, Jan. 25, Mar. 4, 1919, Daniels Papers, LC; JD endorses sinking of German warships, *New York Times,* May 4, 1919; withdrawal of three-year program, U.S. House Naval Affairs Comm. *Hearings on Estimates Submitted by Secnav,* 66th Cong., 2nd Sess. (May, 1919), *passim.*

4. JD to Merchant Marine Comm., *New York Times,* Dec. 13, 1918; JD's proposed radio legislation, *ibid.,* July 24, 25, 1919.

5. Ben Dixon MacNeill, "Josephus Daniels," *American Mercury,* XXIX (July 1933), 297-98.

6. *News and Observer,* Feb. 14, 1919.

7. *Ibid.*

8. On JD and UNC presidency, L. R. Wilson, *The University of North Carolina 1900-1930* (Chapel Hill, 1957), pp. 311-12; JD diary, June 14, 1919; J. S. Bassett, *Our War With Germany* (New York, 1919), p. 122.

9. JD to MCD, Mar. 22, 1919, Bagley Family Papers, SHC.

10. JD to his son Frank, Mar. 30, 1919, in possession of Mr. Frank Daniels, Raleigh, N.C.; Robert Gaines in Rhineland, JD diary, LC, Apr. 19, 1919.

11. JD to his son Frank, Apr. 5, 1919, in possession of Mr. Frank Daniels, Raleigh, N.C.

12. Admiral Benson at the opera, JD, *Wilson Era, Years of War*, pp. 393-94, and JD diary, Mar. 26, 1919; Benson and Daniels also were scandalized by a ballet preceding a French presentation of awards to American Aviators, *ibid.*, Apr. 12, 1919; JD to Miss Ethel Bagley, Apr. 13, 1919, Bagley Family Papers.

13. JD diary, Apr. 18-20, 1919; JD to FDR, Apr. 18, 1919, Daniels Papers; JD to Mrs. Bagley, Easter Sunday [Apr. 20, 1919], Bagley Family Papers.

14. Allan Nevins (ed.), *The Journal of Brand Whitlock* (New York, 1936), p. 558; JD to WW, May 9, 1919, Daniels Papers; King Albert's visit to WW, JD diary, Nov. 1, 1919.

15. King George–JD anecdote, Mrs. JD, *Recollections of a Cabinet Minister's Wife* (Raleigh, 1945), p. 189; Lady Astor quote, *ibid.*, p. 186.

16. On Wannamaker, *New York Times*, Feb. 5, 1914.

17. On Towers and Read, JD, *Wilson Era, Years of War*, pp. 568-69; see also Joseph L. Morrison, "The Forgotten First Trans-Atlantic Flight," *News and Observer*, Jan. 10, 1965; JD quoted, *New York Times*, June 21, 1919.

18. JD on San Diego, U.S. House. Naval Affairs Comm. *Hearings on Estimates Submitted by Secnav*, 66th Cong., 2nd Sess. (Jan. 12, 1920), p. 5.

19. On Pearl Harbor drydock, JD, *Wilson Era, Years of War*, p. 576; JD and WW at Seattle, Edith Bolling Wilson, *My Memoir* (Indianapolis, 1938), p. 279.

20. Walter Lippmann, *Public Opinion*, Ch. 1 (New York, 1922), reprinted in Wilbur Schramm (ed.), *Mass Communications* (Urbana, Ill., 1960), p. 479.

21. See George Creel, *Rebel at Large* (New York, 1947), pp. 222-23; JD to Overman, JD diary, Dec. 2, 1919.

22. On Red Scare, see Robert K. Murray, *Red Scare: A Study in National Hysteria, 1919-1920* (Minneapolis, 1955); also appropriate index entries in Stanley Coben, *A. Mitchell Palmer* (New York, 1963); on Palmer's imposing on a sick President, JD, *Wilson Era, Years of War*, p. 547; Jonathan Daniels to Max Lowenthal, May 27, 1950, Jonathan Daniels Papers, SHC.

23. JD's Jackson Day address, Jan. 8, 1919, copy in Carter Glass Papers, University of Virginia Library.

24. For onset of hearings, see JD diary for Dec. 1919, *passim;* Admiral Sims at Harvard, Mrs. Theodore Roosevelt, Jr., *Day Before Yesterday* (Garden City, 1959), p. 123; Sims's testimony, U.S. Senate. Naval Affairs Subcomm. *Hearings, Awarding of Medals in the Naval Service*, 1920, 66th Cong., 2nd Sess., pp. 245-361, hereinafter *Medal Award Hearings*.

25. Sims to Bagley, Dec. 22, 1919, in *ibid.*, p. 287; Bagley's cable of Jan. 8, 1920, cited in *ibid.*, p. 519; Sims's behavior toward H. B. Wilson, *ibid.*, pp. 498-503.

26. JD, *Wilson Era, Years of War*, p. 521; JD unearthed new material on the Jenkins case during his ambassadorship to Mexico (see *ibid.*, pp. 529-32).

27. Leasing bill of Feb., 1920, J. L. Bates, "Josephus Daniels and the Naval Oil Reserves," *U.S. Naval Institute Proceedings*, LXXIX (Feb., 1953), 174-75.

28. Senator Hale's invitation to Sims, *Medal Award Hearings*, p. 304; text of Sims's "Certain Naval Lessons . . . ," *ibid.*, pp. 309 ff.

29. Sims and the leak to Davison, U.S. Senate. Naval Affairs Subcomm.

Naval Investigation Hearings, 1920, 66th Cong., 2nd Sess., I, 276, hereinafter *Naval Investigation.*

30. Elting E. Morison, *Admiral Sims and the Modern American Navy* (Boston, 1942), p. 455; parallel charges of Sims and Penrose, *Naval Investigation,* II, 2470-71.

31. JD praises Sims, U.S. House. Naval Affairs Comm. *Estimates Submitted by Secnav, 1916,* 64th Cong., 1st Sess., III, 3781 (Apr. 3, 1916); JD on Sims's recommendation of Coontz, JD to Sims, Aug. 7, 1916, Daniels Papers; Sims to JD, Jan. 15, 1919, *ibid.*

32. Sims to his wife in Morison, *Admiral Sims and the Modern American Navy,* p. 478; Sims to Pratt, *Naval Investigation,* II, 2784; JD to Sims, July 26, 1919, Daniels Papers; Hendrick memoir, Oral History Project, Columbia University; Sims to JD, July 28, 1919, Daniels Papers; JD refuses to discipline Sims, JD diary, Nov. 3, 1919, *New York Times,* Nov. 5, 1919.

33. Sims quoted, *Naval Investigation,* I, 310.

34. Mitchell quoted in his *History of the Modern American Navy* (New York, 1946), p. 255; JD quoted, *Naval Investigation,* II, 1983. A one-sided account of the issues in the naval investigation, written by a member of Sims's staff and using that title of Sims's accusatory letter, is Tracy B. Kittredge, *Naval Lessons of the Great War* (Garden City, 1921). For a more balanced discussion, see Morison, *Admiral Sims and the Modern American Navy,* pp. 433-62.

35. Jenkins to Jonathan Daniels, July 12, 1954, Jonathan Daniels Papers; statement of Representative James F. Byrnes, *Naval Investigation,* I, 328-29; Sims and Northern Mine Barrage, *ibid.,* II, 2036, 3147; false telegram, *ibid.,* II, 2111-12.

36. Mrs. Dewey quoted, JD diary, May 8, 1920; WW-JD anecdote, JD, *Wilson Era, Years of War,* pp. 623-24.

37. FDR to Mrs. W. S. Sims, Dec. 24, 1919, cited in Frank Freidel, *Franklin D. Roosevelt, The Ordeal* (Boston, 1954), p. 40; FDR's advice to JD, JD diary, Jan. 18, 1920; FDR's speech of Feb. 1, 1920, cited by Freidel in *FDR, The Ordeal,* p. 40; JD diary, Aug. 6, 1920.

38. FDR in March, Freidel, *FDR, The Ordeal,* p. 48.

39. FDR quoted, *ibid.;* FDR to Senator Hale, June 4, 1920, in *Naval Investigation,* II, 3392; FDR in 1940, H. L. Ickes, *The Secret Diary of Harold L. Ickes* (New York, 1954), p. 374.

40. JD diary, April 11, 1920.

41. Van Dyke's "exam," *ibid.,* Dec. 15, 1917; "mourning," Mrs. JD, *Recollections of a Cabinet Minister's Wife,* p. 104.

42. On Osborne probe, Frank Freidel, *FDR, The Ordeal,* pp. 43-46; JD quoted, Frank Tannenbaum, *Osborne of Sing Sing* (Chapel Hill, 1933), pp. 282-83.

43. Edison quoted, Matthew Josephson, *Edison* (New York, 1959), pp. 452 n., 454, the latter quoting the *New York World,* Feb. 23, 1923; on lab's location, JD to Edison, Nov. 5, 1920, Daniels Papers; on radar, JD, *Wilson Era, Years of War,* p. 107. JD generously gives Edison indirect credit for the development of radar, saying that it had its origin in the laboratory set up in 1917 on Edison's recommendation.

44. Thomas A. Bailey, *Wilson and the Peacemakers* (New York, 1947), p. 271. This volume combines in one book the author's *Woodrow Wilson and the Lost Peace* (1944) and *Woodrow Wilson and the Great Betrayal* (1945).

45. H. L. Mencken, *Heathen Days, 1890-1936* (New York, 1943), pp. 177, 182.

46. Senator Lewis, in *Fayetteville* (N.C.) *Observer* clipping in Daniels Papers; Cohen to JD, Sept. 9, 1918, *ibid.*; JD to Cohen, Sept. 18, 1918, *ibid.*

47. Colby's maneuver, JD, *Wilson Era, Years of War*, pp. 555-57; JD's speech, *ibid.*, pp. 554-55; FDR's nomination, Freidel, *FDR, The Ordeal*, pp. 64-69.

48. Leasing bills of 1920, J. L. Bates, *U.S. Naval Institute Proceedings*, LXXIX (Feb., 1953), pp. 174-75; oil men quoted, *ibid.*, p. 175; JD on need for Act of June 4, JD to T. S. Butler, Mar. 5, 1920, in U.S. Senate. Comm. on Public Lands and Surveys. *Hearings, Leases Upon Naval Oil Reserves*, 68th Cong., 1st Sess. (Oct. 22, 1923), p. 213.

49. JD quoted, *New York Times*, July 24, 1920. See also *ibid.*, July 7, 11, 23, 1920.

50. JD to Delaware legislature, *ibid.*, Mar. 20, 1920; JD to Mrs. Catt, Apr. 10, 1920, Daniels Papers.

51. JD diary, Jan. 24, 1920; Mrs. Dewey quoted, Mrs. JD, *Recollections of a Cabinet Minister's Wife*, p. 86.

52. JD to his son Jonathan, Aug. 16, 1920, Jonathan Daniels Papers; JD on foreign vote, "Life Begins at Seventy" MS, *ibid.*; WW's incredulity, JD, *Wilson Era, Years of War*, p. 561; FDR's attitude, Freidel, *FDR, The Ordeal*, pp. 88-91.

53. FDR's going-away gift, JD diary, Aug. 6, 1920; FDR to JD, Aug. 6, 1920; JD to FDR, Aug. 9, 1920, in Carroll Kilpatrick (ed.), *Roosevelt and Daniels* (Chapel Hill, 1953), pp. 67-69; on FDR's being *persona non grata* to the President, see Jonathan Daniels, *The End of Innocence* (Philadelphia, 1954), pp. 295-99. FDR's well-known friendships with British Embassy people may have been an added irritant to Wilson, according to Jonathan Daniels. The President resented the reported slur on Mrs. Wilson by Lord Grey's secretary and had demanded the latter's recall. Unquestionably, Mrs. Wilson was deeply offended. In the writer's opinion, however, FDR's Brooklyn speech was paramount in the *"Persona non grata"* JD diary entry of Feb. 21, 1920, first because the speech was more current than the Embassy matter, and second, because JD, following his diary usage, undoubtedly paraphrased the President in saying, "better let speech pass" (in the interest of party solidarity in an election year).

54. JD diary, Aug. 9, 1920; JD wire to FDR, Aug. 13, 1920, in Kilpatrick (ed.), *Roosevelt and Daniels*, p. 70.

55. JD's reply to Harding, *New York Times*, Sept. 17, 1920.

56. JD quoted, *ibid.*, Oct. 17, 1920. See also, *ibid.*, Oct. 2-21, 1920; also Mitchell, *History of the Modern American Navy*, pp. 185-87.

57. JD on Borah Res., U.S. House. Naval Affairs Comm. *Hearings on Sundry Legislation, 1920-21*, 66th Cong., 3rd Sess., p. 86; JD in Jan., 1921, U.S. House. Naval Affairs Comm. *Hearings on Naval Appropriations Bill for 1922*, 66th Cong., 3rd Sess., p. 936.

58. JD to Baker, May 24, 27, and Nov. 12, 1920, Daniels Papers; on *Indiana* test, Isaac Don Levine, *Mitchell, Pioneer of Air Power* (New York, 1943), pp. 206 ff; JD quoted, Ruth Mitchell, *My Brother Bill* (New York, 1953), p. 231; for JD's reticent account, see his *Wilson Era, Years of War*, pp. 124-25.

59. JD quoted in N.E.A. dispatch, *News and Observer*, Feb. 21, 1921.

60. On Welles, see Richard S. West, Jr., *Gideon Welles, Lincoln's Navy Department* (Indianapolis, 1943).

61. Data from ltr., Admiral Lewis Parks, Chief of Information, to Jonathan Daniels, July 2, 1953, Jonathan Daniels Papers.

62. Fletcher Pratt, *The Compact History of the United States Navy* (New

York, 1957), p. 198. Pratt specifically endorses Daniels' Navy reforms, pp. 196-97.

Chapter Six

1. JD's homecoming quote, *News and Observer*, Mar. 7, 1921; Ochs's offer, JD, "Life Begins at Seventy" MS, Jonathan Daniels Papers, SHC; Denby quoted, *New York Times*, Mar. 20, 1921.

2. JD to Mrs. W. H. Bagley, Mar. 27, 1921, Bagley Family Papers, SHC.

3. JD to FDR, July 16, 1921, Daniels Papers, LC; *New York Times*, July 20, 1921; on the Newport investigation, see Frank Freidel, *Franklin Roosevelt, The Ordeal* (Boston, 1954), pp. 96-97.

4. FDR to JD, Oct. 5, 1921, in Carroll Kilpatrick (ed.), *Roosevelt and Daniels* (Chapel Hill, 1952), p. 75; JD, *Wilson Era, Years of Peace* (Chapel Hill, 1944), p. 131; Jonathan Daniels, *The End of Innocence* (Philadelphia, 1954), p. 29.

5. JD, holograph notes for a speech, undated (summer, 1921), in possession of World Methodist Council, Lake Junaluska, N.C.; JD quoted, James Roosevelt, *Affectionately, F.D.R.* (New York, 1959), pp. 61-62 n.

6. Hearst's offer, Representative Kefauver in the House, Jan. 26, 1948, *Cong. Record*, 80th Cong., 2nd Sess., p. A402; JD to his son Jonathan, Feb. 23, 1923, Jonathan Daniels Papers; interview with L. P. McLendon, Greensboro, N.C., Jan. 12, 1963.

7. JD, "Life Begins at Seventy" MS, Jonathan Daniels Papers.

8. Interview, R. E. Williams, Raleigh, N.C., Dec. 12, 1962; JD to his son Jonathan, Feb. 12, 1923, Jonathan Daniels Papers; JD to his son Worth, Feb. 4, 1923, in possession of Dr. Worth B. Daniels, Washington, D.C. It is understandable that the Bailey Papers at Duke University are silent on this point, but the writer's information—which is confidential—points without question at the Bailey camp as the source of Watts's entrapment.

9. WW to JD, Mar. 11, 1923, Daniels Papers.

10. On MCD, interview with the granddaughter who shared her later years, Mrs. Mary Cleaves Daniels Stenhouse, Goldsboro, N.C., May 1, 1963; JD to his son Worth, Mar. 11, 1923, in possession of Dr. Worth B. Daniels, Washington, D.C.

11. On JD's lecture arrangements, JD to O. B. Stephenson, Emerson Bureau, July 31, 1929, Daniels Papers.

12. Brooks quoted, "Life Begins at Seventy" MS, Jonathan Daniels Papers; JD to Norris, June 16, 1926, quoted in Alfred Leif, *Democracy's Norris* (New York, 1939), p. 295; G. H. Manning, "Tricky Utility Propagandists," *Editor and Publisher*, May 26, 1928, p. 3.

13. "The Education of Buck Duke," *News and Observer*, Oct. 21, 1923; Clark to JD, Oct. 24, 1923, in A. L. Brooks and Hugh T. Lefler (eds.), *The Papers of Walter Clark* (Chapel Hill, 1950), II, 490; on Duke Endowment, see John K. Winkler, *Tobacco Tycoon* (New York, 1942), pp. 294-96, 315-16, 321-23.

14. Derived from J. Leonard Bates, "The Teapot Dome Scandal and the Election of 1924," *American Historical Review*, LX (Jan., 1955), 305. See also the same author's *The Origins of Teapot Dome: Progressives, Parties, and Petroleum, 1909-1921* (Urbana, Ill., 1963), and Burl Noggle, *Teapot Dome* (Baton Rouge, 1962).

15. M. R. Werner and John Starr, *Teapot Dome* (New York, 1959), p. 223; on the alleged precedent set by JD, Samuel H. Adams, *Incredible Era* (Boston, 1939), p. 357.

16. JD, "Life Begins at Seventy" MS, Jonathan Daniels Papers.
17. *Ibid.*
18. Stuart to Thomas J. Walsh, Apr. 9, 1924, in U.S. Congress. Senate. Committee on Public Lands. *Leases Upon Naval Oil Reserves*, 1924, III, 3258-70. See also Noggle, *Teapot Dome*, p. 119, n. 39.
19. On Lane's charges, JD, "Life Begins at Seventy" MS, Jonathan Daniels Papers; JD, "Woodrow Wilson" eulogy, *News and Observer*, Feb. 4, 1924; on JD's "awkward and abashed negotiations," see Jonathan Daniels, *The End of Innocence* (Philadelphia, 1954), p. 292.
20. JD to his son Worth, [Sept.], 1924, in possession of Dr. Worth B. Daniels, Washington, D.C.; JD's income tax returns furnished by Miss Grace Wilder, auditor, News and Observer Publishing Company, Nov. 28, 1962.
21. Letters of JD to Twenty-First Century Press, C. C. Daniels (as attorney), and Adolph Ochs are to be found, abundantly in the first two instances, in 1924-26, in the Daniels Papers. Files of the New York Times Company bearing on this dispute were kindly made available to the writer by ltr. of Alan Sweetser, staff attorney of the company, Mar. 19, 1963.
22. Jonathan Daniels to Robert W. LaFollette, Jr., Nov. 8, 1951, Jonathan Daniels Papers; interview, Jonathan Daniels, Raleigh, N.C., Sept. 10, 1959.
23. On the "mess at Washington," see JD's "Thou Shalt Not Steal" Platform, undated [May, 1924], Daniels Papers; on voting results, anti-Klan Resolution, *Official Report of the Proceedings of the Democratic National Convention*, Madison Square Garden, New York City, June 24–July 9, 1924 (Indianapolis, [1924?]), p. 310; JD quoted, Claude Bowers, *My Life* (New York, 1962), p. 121.
24. See Burton K. Wheeler, *Yankee From the West* (Garden City, 1962), p. 242; JD, "Life Begins at Seventy" MS, Jonathan Daniels Papers; JD combats Wheeler's frame-up, Norman Hapgood to JD, Apr. 18, 1925, and JD to Hapgood, Apr. 20, 1925, Daniels Papers; see also J. Leonard Bates, *American Historical Review*, LX (Jan., 1955), 318.
25. For the spirit in which JD supported the Bryan Breakfasts, see JD, *Appreciation of William Jennings Bryan*, delivered at Houston, Texas, June 28, 1928 (n.p., n.d.); on Bryan in Raleigh, Ben Dixon MacNeill, "Josephus Daniels," *American Mercury*, XXIX (July, 1933), 306.
26. JD to FDR, Dec. 15, 1924, in Kilpatrick (ed.), *Roosevelt and Daniels*, p. 84; JD to FDR, Oct. 1, 1926, *ibid.*, p. 85.
27. JD to his son Worth, Mar. 3, 1926, in possession of Dr. Worth B. Daniels, Washington, D.C.
28. *Ibid.*, Dec. 29, 1926.
29. JD to Kent Cooper, AP, May 15, 1925, Daniels Papers; Melville Stone to JD, May 12, 1925, *ibid.*; on Hendrick, see Ben Dixon MacNeill, *American Mercury*, XXIX (July, 1933), 302.
30. H. L. Mencken, "The War in the Confederacy," *Baltimore Evening Sun*, July 30, 1928, reprinted in H. L. Mencken, *A Carnival of Buncombe* (Baltimore, 1956), p. 165.
31. *News and Observer*, June 30, 1928.
32. JD to V. H. Power of *Manufacturer's Record*, Aug. 28, 1928, Daniels Papers.
33. JD to FDR, telegram, Oct. 2, 1928, Daniels Papers; JD to FDR, Nov. 9, 1928, *ibid.*
34. On Cannon see Virginius Dabney, *Dry Messiah, The Life of Bishop Cannon* (New York, 1949), pp. 190-95 for the 1929 Virginia campaign, pp. 195-228 for Cannon's stock dealings; on the anti-Cannon charges, see also Richard L. Watson, Jr., (ed.), *Bishop Cannon's Own Story: Life As I Have*

Seen It, by James Cannon, Jr. (Durham, 1955), pp. xviii-xxvi; Glass to JD, Oct. 7, 1929, Carter Glass Papers, Alderman Library, University of Virginia; JD to Glass, Oct. 12, 1929, *ibid.*

35. JD memo to Virginius Dabney, Dec. 18, 1946, in possession of Mr. Dabney, Richmond, Va.; JD to Dabney, Dec. 30, 1946, Daniels Papers. The bitterness, of which JD spoke and of which he had personal experience, is minutely documented in two articles by Richard L. Watson, Jr. They are "A Political Leader Bolts—F. M. Simmons in the Presidential Election of 1928," *North Carolina Historical Review*, XXXVII (October, 1960), 516-43; and "A Southern Democratic Primary: Simmons vs. Bailey in 1930," *ibid.*, XLII (Winter, 1965), 21-46.

36. JD to his son Jonathan, Apr. 26, 1930, Jonathan Daniels Papers.

37. JD, "Life Begins at Seventy" MS, *ibid.*; on Bailey-Simmons campaign, see E. L. Puryear, *Democratic Party Dissension in North Carolina, 1928-1936*, Vol. 44 of *The James Sprunt Studies in History and Political Science* (Chapel Hill, 1962), pp. 21-46; also Watson, *N.C. Hist. Rev.*, XLII (Winter, 1965), 21-46.

38. JD to FDR, St. Louis, Mo., Jan. 22, 1941, Daniels Papers. This is a holograph memo that JD wrote en route from Washington to Mexico City, but the message does not appear in the FDR Papers. See Richard L. Watson, Jr., "The Defeat of Judge Parker: A Study in Pressure Groups and Politics," *Mississippi Valley Historical Review*, L (Sept., 1963), 213-34: *ABA Journal*, XXXII (Dec., 1946), 847, cited in *ibid.*

39. On JD's near-candidacy, see E. David Cronon, "Josephus Daniels as a Reluctant Candidate," *N.C. Hist. Rev.*, XXXIII (Oct., 1956), 458-65; on JD's auto accident, A.P. dispatch in *News and Observer*, Jan. 14, 1932; JD to Hoover, Jan. 16, 1932, Daniels Papers; on amount of Baruch's loan, Office of Baruch to JD, Apr., 1936, *ibid.*, Baruch to the writer, Sept. 25, 1962.

40. JD to FDR, Feb. 5, 1932, in Kilpatrick (ed.), *Roosevelt and Daniels*, p. 111; JD to Baker, Mar. 10, 1932, Daniels Papers; JD to Dodd, Apr. 16, 1932, *ibid.*, JD to Baruch, June 17, 1932, *ibid.*

41. Quoted from JD, "Life Begins at Seventy" MS, Jonathan Daniels Papers.

42. JD to FDR, Mar. 30, 1932, Daniels Papers; on Shouse, JD to FDR, Mar. 19, 1932, *ibid.*; on Walker, JD to FDR, May 28, 1932, *ibid.*

43. JD to Misses Bagley, Mar. 26, 1932, Bagley Family Papers; JD to O. J. Coffin, June 2, 1932, Daniels Papers; Frank Daniels to his brother Jonathan, Apr. 4, 1932, Jonathan Daniels Papers; on business conditions, interview with Miss Grace Wilder, auditor of News and Observer Publishing Company, Raleigh, N.C., Nov. 28, 1962.

44. On state convention fight, A. L. Brooks to FDR, June 16, 1932, in A. L. Brooks, *A Southern Lawyer* (Chapel Hill, 1950), p. 141; FDR to JD, June 16, 1932, in Kilpatrick (ed.), *Roosevelt and Daniels*, p. 117; JD to his son Worth, June 17, 1932, Daniels Papers; JD at Chicago, A.P. story in *News and Observer*, June 24, 1932.

45. JD, "Life Begins at Seventy" MS, Jonathan Daniels Papers; JD addresses Convention, A.P. story in *News and Observer*, July 1, 1932.

46. JD to FDR, July 7, 1932, Daniels Papers; JD to Howe, July 9, 1932, *ibid.*; JD to *News and Observer* staff, July 27, 1932 and undated, *ibid.*; JD to Graham, Nov. 7, 1932, U.N.C. Archives, SHC.

47. Hurley and JD at Legion Convention, A.P. dispatch, *News and Observer*, Sept. 13, 1932; JD's editorial on Bonus Army, *ibid.*, July 30, 1932; JD on "Martha Washington," in his *Wilson Era, Years of Peace*, p. 410; on McAdoo, JD, "Life Begins at Seventy" MS, Jonathan Daniels Papers.

48. JD to FDR, Sept. 26, 1932, Daniels Papers; JD to Howe, Sept. 26,

1932, *ibid.*; JD to FDR, "My dear Chief," Nov. 9, 1932, in Kilpatrick (ed.), *Roosevelt and Daniels*, p. 122; FDR to JD, Nov. 17, 1932, *ibid.*, p. 124.

Chapter Seven

1. R. G. Tugwell, *The Democratic Roosevelt* (Garden City, 1957), p. 105, and Tugwell to Jonathan Daniels, Sept. 27, 1954, Jonathan Daniels Papers, SHC; electoral college dinner, *New York Times*, Mar. 4, 1933; JD, *Shirt-Sleeve Diplomat* (Chapel Hill, 1947), p. 16.

2. On Kitchin matter, JD to Garner, Nov. 28, 29, 1932, Daniels Papers, LC; Moley quoted in his *After Seven Years* (New York, 1939), p. 118 (the *Saturday Evening Post*, in the summer of 1939 published the Moley articles of which this book was an expanded version); for contrast with Moley's version, see JD, *Shirt-Sleeve Diplomat*, pp. 18-21; also JD to FDR, July 18, 1939, Daniels Papers.

3. First eyewitness account, Edwin C. Hill broadcast of Mar. 6, 1933, transcript in FDR Papers, Hyde Park, N.Y., quoted in A. S. Schlesinger, Jr., *The Crisis of the Old Order* (Boston, 1957), p. 6; second account, *New York Times*, Mar. 5, 1933; FDR quoted, Cordell Hull, *The Memoirs of Cordell Hull* (New York, 1948), I, 162; Rhamkatte Roaster, *News and Observer*, Mar. 7, 1933; JD at Wilson's tomb, *ibid.*, Mar. 6, 1933.

4. On Mar. 3, 1933, JD had already drafted a tactful refusal of FDR's appointment as commissioner of a Transportation Agency, draft in Daniels Papers; JD quoted, *New York Times*, May 20, 1945.

5. Mrs. JD recalls Veracruz to JD and to FDR, in JD, *Shirt-Sleeve Diplomat*, pp. 2, 4.

6. JD's speech, *New York Times*, Mar. 31, 1933; interview with Herschel Johnson, Charlotte, N.C., Feb. 5, 1964; Press Conf. No. 9, White House Executive Offices, Apr. 5, 1933, I, 116, FDR Papers.

7. On Eugene Bagwell, clipping from unidentified newspaper, Apr. 26, 1933, Jonathan Daniels Papers; trip to Mexico, JD, *Shirt-Sleeve Diplomat*, pp. 12-14; J. Alvarez del Vayo, *The Last Optimist* (New York, 1950), p. 236; W. L. Lander to the writer, Nov. 23, 1962; JD to FDR, Mar. 18, 1933, Daniels Papers.

8. Arthur Constantine, "Uncle Joe Doing Nicely in Mexico," *The State* (Raleigh, N.C.), June 10, 1933, pp. 3-4.

9. On Navy, Arthur Bliss Lane to J. Reuben Clark, May 9, 1933, Lane Papers, LC, cited in E. David Cronon, *Josephus Daniels in Mexico* (Madison, Wis., 1960), p. 26; JD, *Shirt-Sleeve Diplomat*, pp. 25-28; JD to FDR, Apr. 26, 1933, Daniels Papers.

10. On Brinkley, Gerald Carson, *The Roguish World of Doctor Brinkley* (New York, 1960) pp. 199-200; JD, diary-letter, July 20, 1933. JD's diary-letters were sent in multiple copies to the Danielses and the Bagleys. Copies are in their personal papers as well as in the Daniels Papers, LC, and the Jonathan Daniels and Bagley Family Papers, SHC.

11. JD quoted, Hugh T. Lefler and A. R. Newsome, *North Carolina: The History of a Southern State* (rev. ed.; Chapel Hill, 1963), p. 578.

12. Interview, Jonathan Daniels, Raleigh, N.C., Sept. 10, 1959.

13. JD to Graham, June 2, 1933, U.N.C. Archives, U.N.C. Library, Chapel Hill, N.C.

14. JD to Graham, Sept. 18, 1933, *ibid.* The receivership analogy of 1933 is also credited to Raleigh lawyer James Pou in Clarence Poe, *My First 80 Years* (Chapel Hill, 1963), p. 229.

15. E. David Cronon, "A Southern Progressive Looks at the New Deal,"

Journal of Southern History, XXIV (May, 1958), 151-76; "too conservative" anecdote, Drew Pearson's column, July 24, 1943; same sentiment, JD to George Gordon Battle, Mar. 16, 1938, Daniels Papers.

16. JD to FDR, Mar. 30, 1933, in Donald Day (ed.), *Franklin D. Roosevelt's Own Story* (Boston, 1951), p. 165; JD to FDR, July 31, 1933, FDR Papers.

17. JD quoted, J. Fred Rippy to writer, July 11, 1962; Mrs. FDR at Raleigh and Durham, *ibid.,* and *News and Observer,* June 12, 1934.

18. JD to his grandson, Worth Bagley Daniels, Jr., May 21, 1933, in possession of Dr. W. B. Daniels, Washington, D.C.; JD to the Misses Bagley, Oct. 17, 1934, Bagley Family Papers.

19. On Mexico after 1910, see Daniel James, *Mexico and the Americans* (New York, 1963); Frank Tannenbaum, *Mexico: The Struggle for Peace and Bread* (New York, 1950); Howard F. Cline, *The United States and Mexico* (rev. ed., Cambridge, 1963); Ramón Beteta, *The Mexican Revolution, A Defense* (Mexico, D.F., 1937), a collection of Beteta's lectures in the United States, 1930-35.

20. JD to FDR, telegram, Dec. 29, 1933, Daniels Papers. For the voluminous exchange between JD and the State Department, see pertinent annual volumes of U.S. State Department, *Foreign Relations of the United States* (Washington).

21. Herschel Johnson agreed with JD on the special claims (see Johnson to JD, Feb. 16, 1934, Daniels Papers); JD to Hull, Apr. 19, 1934, *ibid.*

22. JD to Hull, Sept. 9, 1933, quoted in Hull, *The Memoirs of Cordell Hull,* I, 316; JD to FDR, Oct. 5, 1933, FDR Papers.

23. JD to FDR, Sept. 9, 1933, and Jan. 29, 1934, Daniels Papers.

24. On McAdoo and Glass, JD to FDR, Oct. 11, 1934, Daniels Papers; on Breckenridge, JD to FDR, Sept. 28, 1934, *ibid.;* on Colby, JD to Moley, Sept. 26, 1934, *ibid.*

25. Calles quoted in JD, *Universal Education,* address of July 26, 1934, n.p., n.d., p. 5. For details of JD's difficulties over his "Universal Education" speech, see Ch. IV, "A Nearly Fatal Speech," in Cronon, *Josephus Daniels in Mexico,* pp. 82-111.

26. *News and Observer* parties, E. Clifton Daniel to the writer, Nov. 8, 1962; Methodist Orphanage parties, R. T. Clay book review of Jonathan Daniels' *The End of Innocence,* in *Durham Herald,* June 20, 1954; Lucy Daniels, "Christmas with Grandfather," *News and Observer,* Dec. 20, 1959; interview with Mrs. Adelaide Daniels Key, Chapel Hill, N.C., Dec. 3, 1962.

27. Williams' report from Washington, Jonathan Daniels to JD, Feb. 8, 1935, Jonathan Daniels Papers.

28. Stephen E. Aguirre to the writer, May 12, 1963.

29. JD, diary-letter, Jan. 15, 1935, also quoted in JD, *Shirt-Sleeve Diplomat,* pp. 302-3.

30. JD to his son Jonathan, Aug. 17, Sept. 30, 1935, Aug. 27, 1936, July 28, 1938, Jonathan Daniels Papers.

31. JD, *Shirt-Sleeve Diplomat,* pp. 91-92.

32. "Under the Dome," *News and Observer,* Apr. 27, 1935; JD quoted on Mrs. FDR, *ibid.,* June 12, 1935; JD, *Freedom in the University,* address of June 10, 1935, n.p., n.d., p. 16.

33. JD to Graham, Feb. 7, 1936, U.N.C. Archives.

34. JD to Graham, Mar. 4, 1936, *ibid.;* Trustee Minutes, May 30, 1936, *ibid.;* JD to Winston, Aug. 7, 1936, R. W. Winston Papers, SHC.

35. Tugwell to Jonathan Daniels, Sept. 27, 1954, Jonathan Daniels Papers; JD, *Shirt-Sleeve Diplomat,* p. 415.

36. *Ibid.*, p. 396; JD to FDR, Apr. 1, 1935, Daniels Papers.

37. Uruapan anecdote, W. H. Lander to the writer, Nov. 25, 1962; on JD's Mexican travels, JD, *Shirt-Sleeve Diplomat*, pp. 485-94.

38. JD to his son Jonathan, Feb. 18, 1935, Jonathan Daniels Papers; JD to John H. Finley, June 28, 1935, Finley Papers, New York Public Library; JD to FDR, Apr. 7, 1936, Daniels Papers.

39. On Archbishop Díaz, JD, *Shirt-Sleeve Diplomat*, pp. 148-50; the souvenir album is Pompa y Pompa (ed.), *Album Del IV Centenario Guadalupano* (Mexico, D.F., 1938), presentation copy in U.N.C. Library, Chapel Hill, N.C.

40. JD to Baker, Feb. 3, 1936, Daniels Papers; JD to his son Jonathan, May 9, 1936, Jonathan Daniels Papers.

41. JD to Martin, Feb. 3, 1936, Santford Martin Papers, Duke University Library; Navy Secretaryship, JD to Roper, Feb. 18, 1936, Daniels Papers, and JD to his son Jonathan, Feb. 29, undated [Mar., 1936], Apr. 8, 1936, Jonathan Daniels Papers.

42. JD to Bowers, May 9, 1936, copy in *ibid.*; JD to FDR, Apr. 30, 1936, Daniels Papers; JD's help with FDR's 1936 acceptance speech, JD "Life Begins at Seventy" MS, Jonathan Daniels Papers; shoelace story quoted from unnamed Philadelphia paper, in *News and Observer*, June 24, 1936; Smith quoted, JD, "Fifty Years Attending National Conventions," *ibid.*, July 19, 1944.

43. H. W. Bagley obituary, *News and Observer*, Oct. 27, 1936; on Bagley's last days, JD to Miss Ethel Bagley, Oct. 10, 1936, Bagley Family Papers, and JD to his children, Oct. 26, 1936, Jonathan Daniels Papers; on J. R. Daniels, JD to his son Jonathan, Aug. 3, 1936, *ibid.*; JD quoted, interview with Mrs. Mary Cleaves Daniels Stenhouse, Goldsboro, N.C., May 1, 1963.

44. Embassy picture, Frank L. Kluckhohn to the writer, Nov. 15, 1962; interview, Chapel Hill, N.C., Oct. 15, 1959, with Earl Slocum, a U.S. visitor in Mexico City; JD, *Shirt-Sleeve Diplomat*, pp. 29-33; JD to his son Jonathan, June 21, 1935, Jonathan Daniels Papers.

45. Kiss anecdote, memo of Mrs. Marie H. Ralph, Oct. 12, 1962, in possession of the writer.

46. American colony, JD, *Shirt-Sleeve Diplomat*, pp. 379-89; Beals to the writer, Feb. 5, 1963.

47. JD to FDR, telegram, Feb. 5, 1937, Carroll Kilpatrick (ed.), *Roosevelt and Daniels* (Chapel Hill, 1953), p. 170.

48. On Quezon, JD, *Shirt-Sleeve Diplomat*, pp. 287-99; on MacArthur, JD to FDR, Oct. 8, 1934, Daniels Papers. MacArthur was not reappointed Chief of Staff but was given a one-year extension on the urging of war Secretary Dern, and then made Field Marshal of the Philippine Commonwealth; Waldo Frank to the writer, Nov. 7, 1962.

49. On Trotsky, JD to the Misses Bagley, Feb. 6, 1937, Bagley Family Papers; JD quoted, Beals to the writer, Feb. 5, 1963.

50. JD, *Address by Ambassador Josephus Daniels*, Brest, France, Aug. 12, 1937, n.p., n.d., p. 18; on the Battle Monuments trip, see JD, *Shirt-Sleeve Diplomat*, pp. 469-79.

51. JD, diary-letter, July 16, 1937, Bagley Family Papers; on C. C. Daniels, see Theodore Gaster, "Elders of Zion, Protocols of," *Universal Jewish Encyclopedia* (New York, 1941), IV, 96; on Ford's involvement with anti-Semitism, Allan Nevins and Frank E. Hill, *Ford, Expansion and Challenge, 1915-1933* (New York, 1957), pp. 311-22.

52. Memo by JD aboard ship, July 14, 1937, Bagley Family Papers; *ibid.*, July 18, 1937; on Hugo Black and Lister Hill, JD, *Shirt-Sleeve Diplomat*, pp. 476-77.

53. JD, *Shirt-Sleeve Diplomat*, p. 478.

54. JD, diary-letter, May 21, 1937, Bagley Family Papers; Aguirre to Jonathan Daniels, Nov. 7, 1951, Jonathan Daniels Papers.

Chapter Eight

1. Frank Tannenbaum to the writer, Dec. 11, 1962; Frank Tannenbaum, *Mexico: The Struggle for Peace and Bread* (New York, 1950), pp. 250-51.

2. Kluckhohn to the writer, Nov. 15, 1962.

3. *Ibid.*

4. JD's paraphrase, U.S. State Department, *Foreign Relations of the United States, 1936* (Washington, 1937), V, 711. For the voluminous exchange between JD and State Department, see appropriate annual volumes of *Foreign Relations*.

5. On the oil crisis, see Harlow S. Person, *Mexican Oil, Symbol of Recent Trends in International Relations* (New York, 1942); on significance of Cárdenas administration, Tannenbaum, *Mexico: The Struggle for Peace and Bread*, also Daniel James, *Mexico and the Americans* (New York, 1963), also Howard F. Cline, *The United States and Mexico* (rev. ed.; Cambridge, 1963), and, for a Mexican view, Ramón Beteta, *The Mexican Revolution, A Defense* (Mexico, D.F., 1937), a collection of Beteta's lectures in the U.S., 1930-35.

6. JD to FDR, Sept. 14, 1937, Daniels Papers, LC.

7. Cárdenas quoted, Boal to E. David Cronon, quoted in the latter's *Josephus Daniels in Mexico* (Madison, Wis., 1960), p. 184.

8. JD quoted, Aguirre to the writer, May 12, 1963.

9. JD to FDR on silver, Mar. 29, 1938, Daniels Papers; JD to FDR on oil impasse, Mar. 24, 1938, FDR Papers; JD to his son Jonathan, Mar. 23, 1938, Jonathan Daniels Papers, SHC; JD to FDR, Apr. 6, 1938, FDR Papers.

10. *El Nacional* article translation in JD diary-letter, Apr. 9, 1938, Daniels Papers.

11. JD to his son Jonathan, Mar. 28, 1938, Jonathan Daniels Papers; interview, Frank Daniels, Raleigh, N.C., Nov. 28, 1962.

12. JD to Black, Sept. 10, 1937, Daniels Papers; Shaw University speech, *News and Observer*, June 2, 1937; on Roland Hayes, JD, diary-letter, Jan. 31, 1938, Bagley Family Papers, SHC.

13. Hotel Raleigh anecdote, *Hoy* (Mexico City), July 9, 1938, translation in Jonathan Daniels Papers; JD, diary-letter, May 21, 1937, Daniels Papers; JD to his son Jonathan, Apr. 6 and undated [April], 1938, Jonathan Daniels Papers.

14. *News and Observer*, May 3, 1938.

15. *Ibid.*; interview, Mrs. Lucy Daniels Inman, Raleigh, N.C., Nov. 28, 1962; interview with Spurgeon Fields, Raleigh, N.C., Nov. 28, 1962.

16. July 8, 1938, translation in Jonathan Daniels Papers.

17. JD reports talk of revolution, diary-letter, Apr. 16, 1938, Daniels Papers; on Cedillo revolt, JD, *Shirt-Sleeve Diplomat* (Chapel Hill, 1947), pp. 259-60; JD quoted, *Hoy* (Mexico City), July 9, 1938, translation in Jonathan Daniels Papers.

18. JD to his son Jonathan, July 25, Sept. 13, 1938, *ibid.*; JD to FDR, Aug. 31, 1938, Daniels Papers.

19. Allan S. Everest, *Morganthau, The New Deal and Silver: A Story of Pressure Politics* (New York, 1950), p. 92.

20. JD, *Shirt-Sleeve Diplomat*, p. 317.

21. *Ibid.* For elaboration on this theme, see J. L. Morrison, "Josephus Daniels—Simpatico," *Journal of Inter-American Studies*, V (April, 1963), 277-89.

22. JD to Mrs. JD, Oct. 29 and Nov. 3, 1939, Jonathan Daniels Papers; JD at requiem, Aguirre to the writer, Nov., 1962; JD paraphrased, W. T. Couch to the writer, Dec. 11, 1962.

23. JD to his son Jonathan, Nov. 8, 1943, Jonathan Daniels Papers.

24. JD, diary-letter, Sept. 21, 1940, Daniels Papers.

25. JD, *Shirt-Sleeve Diplomat*, pp. 328-33.

26. JD to FDR, Mar. 14, 1934, Daniels Papers; JD to his son Jonathan, June 15, 1938, Jonathan Daniels Papers; on aviation, JD to FDR, Feb. 23, 1938, Daniels Papers; on fleet maneuvers, JD to FDR, Feb. 24, 1939, FDR Papers; JD to Ethel Bagley, Oct. [Sept.] 5, 1939, Bagley Family Papers; JD to FDR, Dec. 16, 1939, FDR Papers.

27. Harry S. Truman to the writer, Nov. 13, 1962, Chan Gurney to the writer, Feb. 3, 1964, and *New York Times*, Nov. 24, 1939.

28. JD to FDR, Nov. 2, 1937, Daniels Papers; JD to Maverick, July 28, 1939, *ibid.*; JD to FDR, Sept. 3, 1938, FDR Papers; JD to his son Jonathan, Aug. 8, Sept. 19, 1938, Jonathan Daniels Papers.

29. JD to FDR, Apr. 30, 1940, Daniels Papers; JD, "Diary at Home," May 16-June 16, 1940, *ibid.*

30. On Farley, JD, *Shirt-Sleeve Diplomat*, p. 461; JD, "Life Begins at Seventy" MS, Jonathan Daniels Papers; JD to FDR, Feb. 9, 1939, Daniels Papers; JD, "Life Begins at Seventy" MS, Jonathan Daniels Papers; JD, diary-letter, July 20, 1940, Daniels Papers.

31. Cárdenas quoted, Anita Brenner, *The Wind That Swept Mexico* (New York, 1943), p. 95; on Avila Camacho's visiting the United States, JD, diary-letter, Nov. 12, 1940, Daniels Papers; JD to Bowers; Oct. 8, 1940, copy in Jonathan Daniels Papers.

32. JD to FDR, Nov. 9, 1940, FDR Papers; Maverick anecdote, Betty Kirk to the writer, Apr. 11, 1963; JD to his son Frank, Sept. 17, 1940, in possession of Mr. Frank A. Daniels, Raleigh, N.C.

33. JD to FDR, Sept. 20, 1940, Daniels Papers; on inauguration riots of 1940, see Betty Kirk, *Covering the Mexican Front* (Norman, Okla., 1942), pp 233-63; FDR's advice to Wallace, Sumner Welles to FDR, Dec. 16, 1940, FDR Papers, cited in Cronon, *Josephus Daniels in Mexico*, p. 258; JD to FDR, Dec. 11 1940, FDR Papers; Henry A. Wallace to the writer, Dec. 20, 1962.

34. JD, "Editors See Military Bases," editorial correspondence, June 30, 1947, in *News and Observer*, July 3, 1947.

35. D. E. Lilienthal, *The Journals of David E. Lilienthal* (New York, 1964), I, 247, 248.

36. FDR to JD, Feb. 14, 1941, Daniels Papers; text of JD's Electoral College speech, *News and Observer*, Jan 20, 1941; JD to FDR, June 29, 1941, FDR Papers.

37. JD to Hull, Nov. 17, 1939, copy in Jonathan Daniels Papers; JD to his son Jonathan, Mar. 10, June 19, 1941, *ibid.*

38. JD to Winston, June 18, 1941; Winston Papers, SHC.

39. JD to Winston, Nov. 22, 1939, Winston Journal, Vol. II, *ibid.*; JD to Winston, July 15, 1941, Winston Papers.

40. JD to FDR, July 18, 1941, Daniels Papers; JD to his son Frank, Aug. 15, 1941, in possession of Mr. Frank A. Daniels, Raleigh, N.C.; Morrow's limousine, JD, *Shirt-Sleeve Diplomat*, p. 430.

41. Text of JD-FDR letters on resignation, *ibid.*, pp. 515, 511; FDR quoted, Press Conference 780, Washington, Oct. 31, 1941, XVIII, 267, FDR Papers, also *New York Times*, Nov. 1, 1941.

42. JD at Raleigh, *News and Observer*, Nov. 1, 1941; JD on Outer Banks, *ibid.*, Nov. 2, 1941.

43. Jonathan Daniels, "Patrick Suarez" MS (1955), Jonathan Daniels Papers.

44. JD, *Shirt-Sleeve Diplomat,* pp. 511-13; Ambassador William O'Dwyer to Jonathan Daniels, July 18, 1951, Jonathan Daniels Papers.

45. JD's leavetaking, *El Universal Gráfico* (Mexico City), quoted in Cronon, *Josephus Daniels in Mexico,* p. 283; Arias Bernal caricature, cover of *Hoy* (Mexico City), Nov. 15, 1941; leave-taking photographs, and interview, *ibid.,* pp. 18-21.

46. Hearst column, Mar. 1941, typescript copy in Jonathan Daniels Papers.

Chapter Nine

1. Raleigh Chamber of Commerce, *Welcome Home Celebration . . . Honoring Hon. Josephus Daniels and Mrs. Daniels,* Sunday, Nov. 16, 1941, Raleigh, N.C. (n.p., n.d.).

2. "Mexico" at Wakestone is described in an article by W. H. Lander, *News and Observer,* May 3, 1942; visit of Mexican labor leaders, *ibid.,* Mar. 24, 1942; JD to Wallace, May 18, 1942, Daniels Papers, LC.

3. W. F. St. John, "Josephus Daniels—Fighting Editor," *Atlanta Journal Magazine,* Nov. 9, 1947; Lucy Daniels, "Christmas with Grandfather," *News and Observer,* Dec. 20, 1959; JD, "Life Begins at Seventy" MS, Jonathan Daniels Papers, SHC; interview with Spurgeon Fields, Raleigh, N.C., Nov. 28, 1962.

4. JD dines with Wallace, JD to his son Jonathan, Dec. 13, 1941, Jonathan Daniels Papers.

5. JD, "Life Begins at Seventy," MS, *ibid.*

6. Nine-month school term, see *ibid.;* interview with John W. Umstead, Chapel Hill, N.C., Dec. 7, 1962.

7. Anon., "How Does He Do It?" *The State Magazine* (Raleigh, N.C.), Oct. 3, 1942, pp. 5, 18-19; JD to his son Jonathan, May 9, 1942, Jonathan Daniels Papers; Cedric Foster to the writer, Nov. 26, 1962.

8. Interview, Frank P. Graham, Chapel Hill, N.C., Apr. 7, 1963; commissioning exercises, *News and Observer,* May 23, 1942; decommissioning, *ibid.,* Sept. 28, 1945; JD to his son Jonathan, July 18, 1942, Jonathan Daniels Papers; D. E. Lilienthal, *The Journals of David E. Lilienthal* (New York, 1964), I, 505.

9. JD to Gardner, Nov. 1, 1944, Daniels Papers; interviews with Clarence Poe and Edwin Gill, Raleigh, N.C., the former on Oct. 20, 1959, the latter on Mar. 20, 1963; U.N.C. Trustee Minutes, Executive Comm., Jan. 22, 1945, U.N.C. Archives, U.N.C. Library, Chapel Hill, N.C.

10. JD to Berryhill, Mar. 10, 1945, Daniels Papers; interview, W. R. Berryhill, Chapel Hill, N.C., Nov. 9, 1962.

11. "Treat All Alike" editorial, *News and Observer,* Apr. 19, 1942; interview, L. P. McLendon of the U.N.C. Board of Trustees, Greensboro, N.C., Jan. 12, 1963; Raleigh Typographical Union No. 54, *Proceedings of Special Meeting . . . Presentation Forty-Year Button to Hon. Josephus Daniels,* Raleigh, Jan. 31, 1943 (n.p., n.d.).

12. *News and Observer,* Feb. 15, 1943; Miss Addie's "sixth sense," JD to FDR, Jan. 28, 1943, in Carroll Kilpatrick (ed.), *Roosevelt and Daniels* (Chapel Hill, 1953), pp. 210-11; FDR's Admiral Fiske anecdote, *ibid.,* p. 212; JD's wire to the two Presidents, Apr. 20, 1943, *ibid.,* p. 213; Jonathan Daniels to his mother, Feb. 15, 1943, Jonathan Daniels Papers.

13. The jibe at Bailey, Jonathan Daniels, *Tar Heels* (New York, 1941), p. 323; FDR memo to Marvin McIntyre, Mar. 18, 1943, typescript copy in

Jonathan Daniels Papers; JD to his son Jonathan, Mar. 18, 25, 1943, *ibid.*; *Novedades* (Mexico City), Mar. 29, 1943, clipping in *ibid.*

14. Naval oil reserves matter, 1943-44, J. Leonard Bates, "Josephus Daniels and the Naval Oil Reserves," *U.S. Naval Institute Proceedings*, LXXIX (Feb., 1953), 171-79; text of Littell's memorandum, with his commentary, Independent Petroleum and Consumers Assn.,—*and Now Elk Hills* (Los Angeles, Aug., 1943); Littell quoted, *ibid.*, pp. 61, 63.

15. On Littell's appeal, JD to his son Jonathan, July 6, 1943, Jonathan Daniels Papers; FDR to JD, July 10, 1943, in Kilpatrick (ed.), *Roosevelt and Daniels*, p. 214; JD to his son Jonathan, July 12, 1943, Jonathan Daniels Papers; Jonathan Daniels to his father, July 16, 1943, *ibid.*; JD to Stuart, July 19, 1943, copy in *ibid.*; JD to FDR, Jan. 28, Feb. 14, Apr. 17, June 2, and (quoted) June 17, 1944, Daniels Papers.

16. Daniels to Ethridge, Aug. 6, 1943, Daniels Papers; JD to Baruch, May 3, 1943, *ibid.*; on Baruch, JD to his son Jonathan, Sept. 13, 1943; on Creel, Nov. 8, 1943; on Bowers, July 24, 1943, Jonathan Daniels Papers.

17. On Norris, *News and Observer*, Nov. 6, 1942; *ibid.*, Sept. 4, 1944; Stettinius to JD, Oct. 22, 1943, with JD's holograph PS., Jonathan Daniels Papers; Jonathan Daniels to his father, Oct. 2, 1943, and JD to his son Jonathan, Oct. 4, 1943, *ibid.*; JD to Stettinius, Nov. 2, 1943, *ibid.*; JD to his son Jonathan, Aug. 24, 1943, *ibid.*

18. On Rockefeller, Jonathan Daniels to his father, Dec. 4, 1943, and JD to his son Jonathan, Sept. 15, 1944, *ibid.*; *News and Observer*, Mar. 3, 1946.

19. University Day, JD to his son Jonathan, Oct. 13, 1943, Jonathan Daniels Papers; JD to Scott, Mar. 3, 1942, Daniels Papers.

20. JD to Foster, quoting Royster, May 29, 1943, *ibid.*; Miss Addie described, JD to his son Jonathan, Aug. 4, 1943, Jonathan Daniels Papers; JD to his son Jonathan, Aug. 31, 1943, *ibid.*; Jonathan Daniels to his mother, Sept. 14, 1943, *ibid.*

21. JD to his son Jonathan, Oct. 1, 1943; Mrs. JD to her son Jonathan, Oct. 18, 1943; JD to his son Jonathan, Dec. 13, 1943, *ibid.*; JD to FDR, Dec. 18, 1943, FDR Papers; interview with Spurgeon Fields, Raleigh, N.C., Nov. 28, 1962; Robert G. McGregor to his family, Dec. 22, 1943, in possession of Mr. McGregor, Sarasota, Fla.

22. On Claude Kitchin, JD to Thurman Kitchin, Dec. 23, 1943, quoted by latter to Jonathan Daniels, May 12, 1954, Jonathan Daniels Papers; FDR to JD, telegram, Dec. 20, 1943, in Kilpatrick (ed.), *Roosevelt and Daniels*, p. 215; Jonathan Daniels to his father, Dec. 23, 1943, Jonathan Daniels Papers; Mrs. FDR quoted, JD, *Wilson Era, Years of Peace, 1910-1917* (Chapel Hill, 1944), p. 133; JD to David W. Bagley, copy of telegram, Jan. 5, 1943 [1944], Bagley Family Papers, SHC; JD to his son Frank, Jan. 10, 1944, in possession of Mr. Frank A. Daniels, Raleigh, N.C.

23. JD to his son Jonathan, Mar. 26, May 2, 1944, Jonathan Daniels Papers; JD to his son Worth, Sept. 30, 1944, copy in possession of Mr. Frank A. Daniels, Raleigh, N.C.

24. JD to Mrs. Frank A. Daniels, May 8, 1945, *ibid.*; JD to Lady Astor, Mar. 16, 1946, Daniels Papers; JD quoted, Cedric Foster to the writer, Nov. 26, 1962.

25. Panama Canal dossier, JD to R. G. McGregor, Nov. 16, 1943, and McGregor to JD, Nov. 24, 1943, in possession of Mr. McGregor, Sarasota, Fla.; *Problems of Journalism*, Proceedings of the A.S.N.E., Apr. 18-20, 1946 (Washington, 1946), p. 203.

26. Interview with Harry Golden, Chapel Hill, N.C., Aug. 28, 1962; *News*

and Observer, Sept. 20, 1958; on the Cannon-Goldhurst story, Virginius Dabney, *Dry Messiah: The Life of Bishop Cannon* (New York, 1949), pp. 197 ff.

27. JD to Farley, Jan. 25, 1944, Daniels Papers; JD's role in 1944 convention, "Life Begins at Seventy" MS, Jonathan Daniels Papers; Wallace in N.C., *News and Observer*, Dec. 12, 1943.

28. JD to his son Frank, July 14, 1944, in possession of Mr. Frank A. Daniels, Raleigh, N.C.; freedom of the press plank, Kent Cooper to the writer, Nov. 14, 1962, and *News and Observer*, July 21, 1944; Two-thirds rule, *New York Times*, July 16, 1944; JD's press conference, *News and Observer*, July 16, 1944.

29. JD's speech, *ibid.*, Aug. 19, 1944; FDR's majority, JD to Santford Martin, Sept. 2, 1944, Martin Papers, Duke University Library; JD's regrets at anti-Negro excesses in his *Editor in Politics* (Chapel Hill, 1939), pp. 145, 253, 623; Sumner Welles in N.C., *News and Observer*, June 2, 1943.

30. JD quoted in former Raleighite's letter to Harry Golden, May 12, 1963, and furnished to the writer by Mr. Golden; Cedric Foster to the writer, Nov. 26, 1962.

31. On the "Wilson" film, JD to his son Jonathan, Sept. 15, 1944, Jonathan Daniels Papers; text of JD's statement before House Judiciary Comm., Dec. 2, 1944, *News and Observer*, Dec. 3, 1944; JD's wire of protest to Truman, *New York Times*, May 8, 1945.

32. U.S. House. Select Comm. on Postwar Military Policy, *Universal Military Training Hearings*, 79th Cong., 1st Sess., June 11, 1945 (Washington, 1945), pp. 296-97; Churchill editorial, *News and Observer*, Mar. 6, 1946; JD to Barden, Nov. 9, 1945, Daniels Papers.

33. JD's journalistic slogan in JD, "Reflections at Seventy-Five," May 18, 1937, mimeographed, in possession of the writer; JD's working habits, interviews with R. E. (Fleet) Williams, Dec. 12, 1962, Herbert O'Keef, Nov. 21, 1962, Raleigh, N.C., and Jonathan Daniels to the writer, June 8, 1960.

34. Holmes's sentiment and "elderly" story, interview, Sam Ragan, Raleigh, N.C., Nov. 14, 1962.

35. FDR to JD, Dec. 13, 1944, in Kilpatrick (ed.), *Roosevelt and Daniels*, pp. 215-16; Frank A. Daniels to his brother Jonathan, Jan. 8, 1945, Jonathan Daniels Papers; JD to FDR, Mar. 10, 1945, FDR Papers.

36. JD to FDR, Mar. 30, 1945, original in Jonathan Daniels Papers marked "File"; FDR to JD, Apr. 3, 1945, Kilpatrick (ed.), *Roosevelt and Daniels*, p. 217, original in Jonathan Daniels Papers; John Gunther, *A Fragment of Autobiography* (New York, 1962), p. 113, and also his *Roosevelt in Retrospect* (New York, 1950), p. 371 n.

37. Sherwood to Jonathan Daniels, Nov. 20, 1951, Jonathan Daniels Papers; Francis Biddle, *In Brief Authority* (Garden City, 1962), p. 364; Kluckhohn to the writer, Nov. 15, 1962.

38. Woodrow Wilson Foundation, *Annual Report, 1944-1945* (New York, 1945); JD commiserates with Forrestal, in Charles C. Gidney, Jr., to Jonathan Daniels, Sept. 6, 1952, Jonathan Daniels Papers; Walter Millis (ed.), *The Forrestal Diaries* (New York, 1951), p. 59.

39. Interview, Spurgeon Fields, Raleigh, N.C., Nov. 28, 1962.

Chapter Ten

1. Interviews in Raleigh, N.C., with Mr. and Mrs. Jonathan Daniels, Oct. 10, 1963, Frank A. Daniels, Nov. 21, 1962, Mrs. Lucy Daniels Inman, Nov. 28, 1962, Spurgeon Fields, Nov. 28, 1962, and with Mrs. Adelaide Daniels Key, Chapel Hill, N.C., Dec. 3, 1962.

2. JD to his son Jonathan, Nov. 21, 1946, Jonathan Daniels Papers, SHC.

3. JD to Avila Camacho and Cárdenas, Jan. 1, 1947, Daniels Papers, LC; JD to Mrs. Mary Owen Graham, Dec. 16, 1946, *ibid.*; Mayflower Cup, interview with Sturgis E. Leavitt, Chapel Hill, N.C., Nov. 11, 1961.

4. JD, "Mexico After Five Years," Mexico City, Dec. 5, 1946, in *News and Observer*, Dec. 15, 1946; JD, "Ambassador to Utopia," Mexico City, Dec. 6, 1946, *ibid.*, Dec. 16, 1946.

5. JD, "Life Begins at Seventy" MS, Jonathan Daniels Papers.

6. JD to Wagner, Pepper, Clark, identical letters, Apr. 11, 1947, Jonathan Daniels Papers; JD to Thad Eure, N.C. Secretary of State, Apr. 14, 1947, *ibid.*; JD to David C. Mearns, director of MS Division, LC, Apr. 24, 1947, *ibid.*; JD to his son Jonathan, Feb. 7, 1947, *ibid.*

7. American school, JD to Raymond B. Fosdick, Jan. 20, 1947, Daniels Papers; Strode book review, *News and Observer*, Nov. 16, 1947. The review of the Morley book appeared on June 29, of the Toor volume on July 20.

8. Truman editorial, *ibid.*, Mar. 8, 1947; Daniels received from the *Washington Star* the photo he planned to publish in "Life Begins at Seventy," JD to B. M. McKelway, May 12, 1947, to secretary of Eugene Meyer, May 21, 1947, Jonathan Daniels Papers; Emma de Encinas, as told to David Hellyer, "Why Mexicans Don't Like You," *Saturday Evening Post*, May 31, 1947, pp. 26-27 ff.; W. H. Lander to *S.E.P.* Editor Ben Hibbs, May 30, 1947, in possession of Mr. Lander, Mexico City.

9. JD quoted, Alexander Heard to Jonathan Daniels, Feb. 10, 1953, Jonathan Daniels Papers; interviews with W. R. Berryhill, Chapel Hill, N.C., Nov. 9, 1962, and Kay Kyser, Chapel Hill, N.C., Mar. 27, 1963.

10. Interview, Josephus Daniels, Jr., Raleigh, N.C., Nov. 28, 1962. The Old Man stayed in Raleigh, but he broadcast his own tribute to Edison on radio station WPTF and published the text of that tribute in the *News and Observer*, Feb. 12, 1947.

11. Trustee Minutes, meeting in Raleigh, N.C., Feb. 10, 1947, U.N.C. Archives, U.N.C. Library; *News and Observer*, Feb. 11, 1947, adds the Eugene Talmadge quotation.

12. Editorial quoted, *ibid.*, Feb. 23, 1947; JD testifies, *ibid.*, Feb. 20, 1947.

13. *Ibid.*, Mar. 9, 1947.

14. *Ibid.*, Mar. 4, 1947.

15. Editorial, *ibid.*, Feb. 16, 1947; JD to Lister Hill, Feb. 21, 1947, Daniels Papers.

16. On Lilienthal, JD to Hoey, Feb. 27, 1947, *ibid.*; JD to Mrs. Morris Llewelyn Cooke, Mar. 20, 1947, *ibid.*

17. JD to Kerr, Mar. 6, 1947, *ibid.*, JD to Doughton, Jan. 31, Feb. 3, Mar. 1, 1947, *ibid.*

18. JD to Elkus, Feb. 19, 1947, *ibid.*; on Gardner, JD's editorial eulogy, "Like Niobe, All Tears," *News and Observer*, Feb. 7, 1947; on Alford, *ibid.*, Aug. 2, 1947; JD to Mrs. Morris Llewelyn Cooke, Mar. 14, 1947, Daniels Papers.

19. On European reconstruction, *ibid.*; JD to LaGuardia, Mar. 20, 1947, *ibid.*; the book reviews appeared in *News and Observer*, Jan. 19, 26, and Feb. 16, 1947, respectively; JD, "Life Begins at Seventy" MS, Jonathan Daniels Papers.

20. JD to Gerard, Apr. 15, 1947, Daniels Papers.

21. *News and Observer*, Apr. 7, 1947.

22. *Problems of Journalism*, Proceedings of A.S.N.E., Apr. 17-19, 1947 (Washington, 1947), p. 135; JD at White House, *Savannah Evening Press*,

Jan. 16, 1948; JD, "Health and Education," Washington, May 3, 1947, in *News and Observer*, May 4, 1947.

23. Herschel V. Johnson to the writer, Jan. 10, 1963. JD's editorial correspondence from Lake Success appeared in *News and Observer*, May 11, 1947; on Wilson, JD, editorial correspondence, New York City, May 10, 1947, in *ibid.*, May 12, 1947.

24. Drew Pearson, "Washington Merry-Go-Round," May 18, 1947; JD quoted in A.P. interview by Billy Anderson, *News and Observer*, May 18, 1947, and in U.P. interview by Warren Duffee, *ibid.*

25. JD to Mrs. Cotten, Apr. 29, 1947, Mrs. Lyman A. Cotten Papers, SHC.

26. JD at Lake Junaluska, *News and Observer*, June 2, 1947; Mrs. Douglas quoted, *ibid.*, June 4, 1947.

27. JD's review of *The Wallaces of Iowa*, *ibid.*, Mar. 30, 1947; comparing Wallace and Churchill, *ibid.*, Apr. 20, 1947.

28. Wallace's press conference in Raleigh, *ibid.*, June 6, 1947; "An Iowa 'Idee'" editorial, *ibid.*; Wallace on JD, *New Republic*, July 14, 1947, p. 14.

29. JD's anti-A.B.C. speech, *ibid.*, June 9, 1947; editorial, *ibid.*, June 14, 1947.

30. Interview with Herschel V. Johnson, Charlotte, N.C., Feb. 5, 1964; editorial, *News and Observer*, June 9, 1947.

31. Ralph McGill, book review of *Josephus Daniels Says . . .* , in *ibid.*, Dec. 9, 1962.

32. "The Good Neighbor," Warm Springs, Ga., June 25, 1947, in *ibid.*, June 27, 1947.

33. The text of JD's address is in *ibid.*, June 26, 1947.

34. JD, "Editor on the Sea Shore," Atlantic Beach, N.C., June 28, 1947, in *ibid.*, July 1, 1947.

35. JD, "The Flying Marines," Atlantic Beach, N.C., July 1, 1947, in *ibid.*, July 8, 1947.

36. Anti-U.M.T. statement of July 6, 1947, *ibid.*, July 7, 1947; JD's statement of July 7, 1947, to House Armed Services Comm., *ibid.*, July 9, 1947.

37. Charles W. Armstrong to JD, July 26, 1947, copy in Jonathan Daniels Papers.

38. Interview, Mrs. Adelaide Daniels Key, Chapel Hill, N.C., Dec. 3, 1962; JD, "It's a Peach—the Sandhills," Aberdeen, N.C., July 31, 1947, in *News and Observer*, Aug. 3, 1947.

39. JD's speech at New Bern, *Editor and Publisher*, Aug. 30, 1947, p. 46.

40. JD at *The Lost Colony*, JD, editorial correspondence, Manteo, N.C., Aug. 21, 1947, in *News and Observer*, Aug. 23, 1947; Jonathan's speech, *ibid.*

41. Eisenhower as college president, JD in *News and Observer*, Aug. 1, 1947; JD on Eisenhower's visit, *ibid.*, Aug. 31, 1947; JD wire to Legion, *ibid.*, Aug. 29, 1947; JD to Phillips Russell, Sept. 8, 1947, Charles Phillips Papers, SHC.

42. Labor Day Editorial, *News and Observer*, Sept. 1, 1947; JD quoted on amended Taft-Hartley Bill, *ibid.*, June 25, 1947.

43. JD, "A Grandson Returns to Harvest Celebration," Mattamuskeet, N.C., Sept. 1, 1947, in *ibid.*, Sept. 6, 1947.

44. Jonathan Daniels to W. B. MacNider, Sept. 9, 1947, Jonathan Daniels Papers; JD on LaGuardia's death, *News and Observer*, Sept. 28, 1947; *ibid.*, Oct. 7, 1947 carries the news story from Goldsboro and the text of Daniels' speech there.

45. *Ibid.*, Nov. 2, 1947.

46. JD quoted, *ibid.*; JD to Edward P. Moses, Apr. 21, 1947, Daniels Papers.

47. *News and Observer*, Nov. 4, 1947. The other Aycock editorials appeared on the two preceding days; JD to Hoey, Dec. [Nov.] 5, 1947, Clyde R. Hoey Papers, Duke University Library.

48. JD, "Peace and Youth Dominate at Methodist Conference," Elizabeth City, N.C., Nov. 8, 1947, in *News and Observer*, Nov. 9, 1947; JD described, E. H. Davis, *Franklin Times,* Louisburg, N.C., Jan. 23, 1948; JD's speech, *News and Observer,* Nov. 7, 1947; interview with Robert B. House, Chapel Hill, N.C., Nov. 14, 1962; JD named a delegate, *News and Observer,* Nov. 8, 1947.

49. The book was by Lili Rethie and Frederick L. Roth, and was reviewed in *ibid.,* Oct. 19, 1947; Eleanor Roosevelt, "My Day," syndicated column of Jan. 17, 1948.

50. Gossip linking Mrs. Wilson and JD, interview with Jonathan Daniels, Raleigh, N.C., Nov. 14, 1962; JD described, Ray Erwin to writer, Feb. 21, 1963. Erwin attended the function as reporter for the New York *Sun.*

51. The text of JD's address is in *News and Observer,* Nov. 11, 1947; JD's baggage-less return from New York, Jonathan Daniels, *The End of Innocence* (Philadelphia, 1954), p. 338.

52. Interview with Mr. and Mrs. Jonathan Daniels, Raleigh, N.C., Oct. 10, 1963.

53. JD on Freedom Train, *News and Observer,* Dec. 6, 1947; JD to Mrs. Cotten, Nov. 21, 1947, Mrs. Lyman L. Cotten Papers.

54. Julian P. Boyd to the writer, Nov. 6, 1962; JD's approval of Boyd's speech, *News and Observer,* Dec. 8, 1947. Nell Battle Lewis' hostile column appeared in the issue of Dec. 14, 1947.

55. JD in Richmond, *Richmond Times-Dispatch* quoted in *ibid.,* Jan. 17, 1948; JD's motion, Trustee Minutes, Executive Comm., meeting at Raleigh, N.C., Dec. 10, 1947, U.N.C. Archives; JD in the synagogue, *News and Observer,* Dec. 13, 1947, and Mrs. T. J. Lassiter, Sr., in *Smithfield* (N.C.) *Herald,* Jan. 23, 1948.

56. JD at White House, AP dispatch, Washington, D.C., Dec. 18, 1947, in *News and Observer,* Dec. 19, 1947; JD, "Democratic Reminiscences," extract of address to National Women's Democratic Club, Washington, Dec. 18, in *ibid.,* Dec. 20, 1947; also complete text in Extension of Remarks, Harold D. Cooley, "The Last Speech," *Congressional Record—Appendix,* 80th Cong., 2nd Sess., Jan. 20, 1948, p. A299.

57. *Congressional Record, Senate.* 80th Cong., 2nd Sess., Jan. 16, 1948, p. 231; Lister Hill to the writer, Mar. 9, 1963; Mrs. Wilson's car, JD and the baggage cart, interview with Mrs. Jonathan Daniels, Raleigh, N.C., Oct. 10, 1963.

58. JD's review of Byrnes's book, *News and Observer,* Nov. 16, 1947; Wallace editorial, *ibid.,* Dec. 30, 1947.

Index

305

Joyner, James Yadkin, 265-66
Justice, E. J., 56

K

Kaltenborn, H. V., 229
Kefauver, Estes, 144
Kennedy, Edward, 242
Kent, Frank, 189
Kerr, John H., 255, 266
Kilgo, John C., 32, 39, 272
Kitchin, Claude, 59, 81, 169, 237
Kitchin, Thurman D., 224, 237
Kitchin, William W., 45
Kluckhohn, Frank L., 198, 211, 245
Knight, Austin M., 69
Knox, Frank, 129, 160, 218, 231-32
Knudsen, William S., 213
Ku Klux Klan, controversy at 1924
  Democratic National Convention,
  152-53; in N.C. during the twen-
  ties, 155-56; mentioned, 244
Kyser, Kay, 252

L

LaFollette, Robert M., 37, 149, 152
LaGuardia, Fiorello H., 175, 256, 268
Lamp, The, 206
Lander, William H., 194, 251
Landon, Alfred M., 190, 192
Lane, Franklin K., 76, 86, 123, 134,
  148, 150
Lansing, Robert S., 89, 122, 216
Lash, Joseph, 270
Lawrence, David, 92, 189
Leak, R. H. W., 26
Lehman, Herbert H., 96-97, 213
Lejeune, John A., 114, 136, 264
Leviathan, S.S., 112
Lewis, Hamilton J., 132
Lewis, Nell Battle, 272
Liberty League, The American, 180,
  189, 195
Life Magazine, 71
"Life Begins at Seventy" (JD's un-
  published memoir), viii, 250, 257,
  260
Lilienthal, David E., 216, 229, 255
"Lily White" Republican party, N.C.,
  39
Lippmann, Walter, 118, 258
Littell, Norman M., 231-32
Livingstone, John, 174
Lodge, Henry Cabot, 69, 73, 75, 100-
  1, 105-6, 116-18

Lombardo Toledano, Vicente, 199-
  200, 225
London Naval Conference, 1930, 107,
  109
Lost Colony, The, 221, 266
Louisiana Lottery, 10
Lowell, James Russell, 16
Lusitania crisis, 70

M

McAdoo, Eleanor Wilson, 50, 271
McAdoo, William G., 48, 81, 86, 148,
  152-54, 165-66, 180, 271
MacArthur, Douglas, 193
McCombs, William F., 47-48
McCormick, Vance C., 76-77
McGill, Ralph, 263
McGowan, Samuel, 67, 97
McGrath, J. Howard, 273
McGregor, Robert, 236
McIntyre, Marvin, 89, 231
McIver, Charles D., 13, 19, 27, 32,
  38, 111, 160
McKean, Josiah S., 127
McKinley, William, 31, 36
McLean, Angus W., 164
McLean, Edward ("Ned"), 148
McLean, Ridley, 128
McNab, Gavin, 88
MacNeill, Ben Dixon, 110, 155
McNinch, Fred R., 206
Machado, Gerardo, 178
Mack, Mrs. Norman, 206
Macy, V. Everit, 93
Madero, Francisco I., 62
Mahan, Alfred Thayer, 51, 67
Maine, U.S.S., 33
Manhattan, S.S., 194
Malinche biographical novel project,
  183-84
Mann, James R., 110
Manning, John, 11
Manufacturer's Record, 157
Mare Island, Calif., 58, 92
Marsh, Addie, 15-16
Marshall, George C., 257, 262, 266
Marshall, Thomas R., 146
Marshall Plan, 262
Martin, Franklin H., 86
Martin, Santford, 190
Martínez, Archbishop Luis María, 189
Mason, Alpheus T., 257
Maverick, Maury, 213, 215-16